Routledge Revivals

Great Britain and the German Navy

D1808471

Great Britain and the German Navy

E. L . Woodward

Routledge
Taylor & Francis Group

First published in 1935 by Frank Cass and Company Limited
by arrangement with Oxford University Press

This edition first published in 2018 by Routledge
2 Park Square, Milton Park, Abingdon, Oxon, OX14 4RN
and by Routledge
52 Vanderbilt Avenue, New York, NY 10017, USA

Routledge is an imprint of the Taylor & Francis Group, an informa business

© 1935 Taylor & Francis

Publisher's Note
The publisher has gone to great lengths to ensure the quality of this reprint but
points out that some imperfections in the original copies may be apparent.

Disclaimer
The publisher has made every effort to trace copyright holders and welcomes
correspondence from those they have been unable to contact.
A Library of Congress record exists under ISBN:

ISBN 13: 978-1-138-39276-2 (hbk)
ISBN 13: 978-1-138-39281-6 (pbk)
ISBN 13: 978-0-429-40204-3 (ebk)

GREAT BRITAIN
AND THE
GERMAN NAVY

GREAT BRITAIN
AND THE
GERMAN NAVY

BY

E. L. WOODWARD

FRANK CASS AND CO. LTD.
1964

First published by the Oxford University Press
in 1935 and now reprinted
by arrangement with them

This edition published by
Frank Cass and Co. Ltd., 10 Woburn Walk
London, W.C. 1

First edition   1935
New impression   1964

Printed by Thomas Nelson (Printers) Ltd.
London and Edinburgh

'*Is not the time come when the powerful countries of Europe should reduce the armaments which they have so sedulously raised? Is not the time come when they should be prepared to declare that there is no use in such overgrown establishments? What is the advantage of one Power greatly increasing its Army and Navy? Does it not see that other Powers will follow its example? The consequence of this must be that no increase of relative strength will accrue to any one Power, but there must be a uniform consumption of the resources of every country in military preparations. The true interest of Europe is to come to some common accord, so as to enable every country to reduce those military armaments, which belong to a state of war rather than of peace.*'   SIR ROBERT PEEL, 1841.*

'*Let us terminate this disastrous system of rival expenditure and mutually agree, with no hypocrisy but in a manner and under circumstances which can admit of no doubt—by a reduction of armaments that peace is really our policy.*'   MR. DISRAELI, 1859.*

'*Take it all in all, a Ship of the Line is the most honourable thing that man, as a gregarious animal, has ever produced. By himself, unhelped, he can do better things than ships of the line ; he can make poems and pictures. . . . But as a being living in flocks, and hammering out, with alternate strokes and mutual agreement, what is necessary for him, in those flocks, to get or produce, the ship of the line is his first work. Into that he has put as much of his human patience, common sense, forethought, experimental philosophy, self-control, habits of order and obedience, thoroughly wrought handwork, defiance of brute elements, careless courage, careful patriotism, and calm expectation of the judgement of God, as can well be put into a space of 300 feet long by 80 broad. And I am thankful to have lived in an age when I could see this thing so done.*'   JOHN RUSKIN, 1856.*

PREFACE

I SHOULD like to thank H. M. Foreign Office and the Lords Commissioners of the Admiralty for allowing me access to all British documents which I found it necessary to examine, and for permission to print the documents contained in Appendix VI. I also wish to thank the Principal of Hertford College, Oxford, for reading the manuscript of my book. I would add that I take full responsibility for all statements and personal opinions contained in the text.

Every student of Anglo-German relations in the period between 1898 and 1914 is under a great debt to the editors of the British and German collections of diplomatic documents. I may be allowed to say that independent work on the material used by the editors of the *British Documents* has confirmed my judgement of the completeness and impartiality of the editors' selection. I have found it necessary to criticize a good many of the editorial notes and comments in the volumes of the German collection, and I do not think that sufficient documents are included, even from German sources, in this collection to justify the comprehensive title of *Die grosse Politik der europäischen Kabinette*. At the same time I do not want my criticisms to be taken as an attempt to belittle either the value of this German publication or the labours of those who have produced it. In this context it is enough for me to say that, without the German documents, one half of my book could not have been written.

1934

ABBREVIATIONS

The following abbreviations are used in the footnotes throughout the book.

B.D.D. = *British Documents on the Origins of the War, 1898–1914*, ed. G. P. Gooch and Harold Temperley.

D.G.P. = *Die grosse Politik der europäischen Kabinette, 1871–1914*. Sammlung der diplomatischen Akten des Auswärtigen Amtes, ed. J. Lepsius, A. Mendelssohn Bartholdy, F. Thimme.

D.D.F. = *Documents Diplomatiques Français, 1871–1914*. (Commission de publication des documents relatifs aux origines de la guerre de 1914).

O.A.P. = *Österreich-Ungarns Aussenpolitik von der bosnischen Krise, 1908, bis zum Kriegsausbruch, 1914*. Diplomatische Aktenstücke des Österreichisch-ungarischen Ministeriums des Äussern, ed. L. Bittner, A. F. Pribram, H. Srbik, and H. Uebersberger.

Hansard = *The Parliamentary Debates*. Official Report.

CONTENTS

CONTENTS

INTRODUCTION

Every book dealing with the causes of the Great War, or with the history of international relations between 1900 and 1914, mentions the growth of the German navy and the effect of naval competition upon Anglo-German relations. The subject cannot be ignored ; yet, curiously enough, no English, French, or American writer has made a special study of this important question. Until the last few years a scientific treatment of the negotiations between Great Britain and Germany was impossible because the relevant documents on the British side were not published. The *British Documents on the Origins of the War* are now accessible up to the year 1913. After the year 1913 the naval question continued to affect decisions of policy in Great Britain and Germany, but the long period of negotiations over a naval agreement had come to an end. The two Powers had not reached an agreement. They continued to discuss other matters. They settled the difficult problem of the control of the eastern end of the Baghdad railway. Grey hoped that that Anglo-German collaboration during the Balkan wars would be followed by a general improvement of Anglo-German relations. He believed that the worst period of tension was over. The German Emperor, the Chancellor and the German Foreign Office, German generals and admirals were less hopeful. Most of them thought that there was no escape from a European war. These German observers of European events and rivalries welcomed the change for the better in the official relations of their country with Great Britain. They did not share Grey's view that the two groups of European Powers need not find themselves in 'opposing diplomatic camps'. They were faced, according to their own calculation, with the prospect of a war on two fronts: a war against Russia, and France in alliance with Russia, for the preservation of Austria-Hungary as a Great Power. They wanted to detach Great Britain

4192   B

from her commitments—moral, if not written, commitments—to France and Russia. They were not prepared to reduce, or rather to forgo any chance of increasing, their navy unless they could be sure of British neutrality in the war which seemed to them inevitable. On the British side a promise of absolute neutrality might very well mean acquiescence in the continental hegemony of Germany. For these reasons, the two Powers had given up the discussion of any general agreement of a political kind since the failure of the negotiations begun by Haldane in February 1912.

The diplomatic history of Anglo-German naval rivalry therefore closes in the spring of 1912, or, at all events, in the early summer of 1913, when the German Government explained that they could not accept Mr. Churchill's plan of a 'naval holiday'.

On the other hand, the diplomatic history of the subject does not begin until the year 1906. The first stages of the development of the German navy did not cause great anxiety in Great Britain. The facts were observed. They were unpleasant facts. They required a certain readjustment of British naval strength and the construction of a new naval base. The propaganda of the naval party in Germany was unfriendly to England; but this unfriendliness was based partly upon fears of an English attack. In any case it was not new. The attitude of public opinion in Germany and the language of the German press during the Boer War were violently anti-English, and went far beyond mere unfriendliness. These outbursts of feeling had more effect and caused more disquiet in Great Britain than the first or second Navy Laws—the laws of 1898 and 1900.

Official relations were undisturbed. The Emperor had risked unpopularity in his own country by dissociating himself from the general chorus of dislike; but the Emperor's moods were changeable, and British opinion had not forgotten the Kruger telegram. Political and military co-operation with Germany in the Far East and elsewhere was not happy. German methods differed from British methods; German officers and civilians did not appear to take account of British interests. In China these interests were openly disregarded in order to obtain Russian goodwill.

In spite of the growing estrangement between the two nations—on Bülow's own admission in November 1899 German feeling was more anti-English than English feeling was anti-German—Chamberlain had proposed an alliance between the two countries. The proposal was not accepted by Germany; it was renewed from the German side (or so it was thought in Great Britain), but neither party believed that the terms offered by the other party were worth the risks. The negotiations broke down. The Germans were afraid that Great Britain might bring Germany into a war with Russia; the English were afraid that Germany might bring them into a war with France. Bülow thought that time was on the German side, and that Great Britain would be compelled to accept German terms because she needed help against France and Russia.

The 'diplomatic revolution' which affected the grouping of the European Powers was unforeseen by Germany. This 'revolution' began outside Europe. Great Britain gave up her 'splendid isolation' not for a European but for a Far Eastern alliance; but the Anglo-Japanese alliance at once affected the relations between Great Britain and France. If France had joined Russia in a war against Japan, Great Britain, according to the terms of the Anglo-Japanese alliance, was bound to declare war upon France. From this point of view the Anglo-French agreement was a form of reinsurance. Great Britain could be sure that France would restrain the plans of Russia.

The Anglo-French agreement was concerned with extra-European questions. The foreign policy of Germany was one of the causes of the agreement; the German navy had as yet little to do with the matter. The German Foreign Office, against the judgement of the Emperor, used the Moroccan question to test, and, if possible, to break, the Anglo-French entente. From the British point of view Germany spoilt a good case—as far as Morocco was concerned—by roughness of treatment. The 'shock tactics' of German diplomacy, the determination to go beyond the protection of German economic interests in Morocco and to score a long-desired success in general policy, forced upon the British Government a decision which it had no wish to take. The British Ministers had to choose between isolation in Europe and thorough-going support of France against Germany. There was no escape from this choice. If Great Britain refused to support France after Germany had made the Moroccan question into a question of prestige, an affair of *Machtpolitik*, the entente would have collapsed.

Wisely or unwisely, the Germans had attempted to separate Great Britain from France. The failure of this attempt could not but affect Anglo-German relations. Germans would feel more sharply the need for a strong fleet; Englishmen would consider the use to which Germany might put this fleet. Meanwhile, every year, the German fleet was becoming larger and more powerful.

At this time the British Admiralty decided to build the Dreadnought. The introduction of a new and more powerful—and therefore more expensive—type of ship may have been a mistake. It may have been a clever move which turned a difficult situation to the advantage of Great Britain. Apart from the technical arguments for or against Fisher's policy, there is a certain irony in the fact that the increase in naval expenditure—a progressive increase, since the 'goodwill' of pre-Dreadnought superiority would soon be lost—coincided with the return to office of a Liberal Government. The Liberals wanted a limitation of armaments, because they believed that a great body of European opinion was ready for a far-reaching measure of this kind. They also wanted to reduce expenditure upon armaments because they had a large and expensive programme of social reform. These motives were not inconsistent. The Prime Minister and his colleagues did not attempt to hide their wish to save money on battleships and to spend money on social measures.

The meeting of the second Hague Conference in 1907 gave the Liberal Ministers their opportunity. They announced that they would raise the question of a general reduction of armies and navies. What would Germans think of this proposal? They would notice that even whole-hearted English supporters of disarmament took for granted the naval supremacy of Great Britain. They would point out that the Liberals were asking other Powers to fix a ratio of naval strength at the very moment when, owing to the British lead in the building of Dreadnoughts, the British navy was overwhelmingly superior to the German navy. They would say that Great Britain was taking an unfair advantage in bringing forward proposals for a limitation of armaments which, in effect, asked Germany to accept for good and all a position of inferiority. If Germany refused to accept these proposals, then the German Government would appear before the German people and the civilized world as the enemy of peace.

The German arguments could be answered. Grey might well say that the British navy was the first and only defence of Great Britain, while, even without a fleet, Germany was the strongest military power in the world. These answers were unlikely to affect public opinion in Germany. Distrust of Great Britain was too great, and the desire for naval power too strong. The second Hague Conference therefore merely aggravated the position. German motives were misunderstood in Great Britain; British motives were misunderstood in Germany.

After the Hague Conference all hope of a European move to reduce armaments disappeared. There remained the possibility of direct negotiations between Great Britain and Germany. The British Government decided to try this difficult and unpromising path. At first the Emperor refused any discussion. After some time the insistence of British Ministers was taken as a sign of weakness. It was thought that Great Britain would be unable to stand the financial strain of increased naval expenditure. Bülow accepted the notion—suggested by one of his subordinates —that Germany might use English 'embarrassments', and bargain for concessions in return for the recognition of British naval supremacy. The concession wanted by Germany was a promise of British neutrality in a continental war.

Bülow had resigned, and Bethmann-Hollweg had taken his place, before this 'bargain' was suggested to Great Britain. A few months before Bülow's resignation British opinion had been alarmed by a number of facts pointing to an acceleration in German shipbuilding. If Germany built her ships in advance of her published time-table, she might overtake Great Britain in ships of the Dreadnought class. Tirpitz gave a belated and incomplete explanation of the facts which had caused alarm. The British Government brought forward a programme of eight Dreadnoughts; there could be no doubt that Great Britain was determined to keep her supremacy at sea.

The naval question was now the main factor in Anglo-German relations. The German Ambassador in London sent report after report to his Government that there could be no improvement in these relations while Germany was adding to the burden of the British naval estimates. The Emperor was unwilling to give up his naval plans. He tried to explain that the German navy was not a menace to Great Britain. His explanations— made in a clumsy and tactless way—were not likely to reassure British opinion. The facts were too clear. Bethmann-Hollweg was ready to make concessions of a kind. His offers never went very far; he could not persuade the Emperor and his naval advisers to accept any reduction in the existing naval programme. In 1912 he failed to prevent an extension of this programme.

In any case Bethmann-Hollweg, largely under the

influence of Kiderlen-Waechter, was himself convinced that Germany could only agree to any reduction in her shipbuilding programme if she were assured of British neutrality in a continental war. The Anglo-Russian agreement of 1907 was more than disconcerting to Germany. Attempts to detach Russia from Great Britain and France had been no more successful than attempts to break the Anglo-French entente. The withdrawal of Russia from her Far Eastern schemes had the effect of reopening the Near Eastern question, and of ending the unquiet truce between Russia and Austria in the Balkans. The Turkish Revolution added to the seriousness of the problem. Austria annexed Bosnia and Herzegovina in 1908. Russia was forced to recognize this annexation, because she was not prepared to fight a European war. The Russian surrender was made unwillingly. In a few years' time Russia would be stronger. Austria in a few years' time would certainly not be stronger; a serious internal crisis might follow the death of Francis Joseph. Bethmann-Hollweg was not responsible for the policy which, fifty years after the battle of Königgratz, had left the German people no less subject to Austrian necessities than in the age of Metternich. Yet after 1908 there was no escape from this subjection without a complete change in the methods and aims of the rulers of Germany. Bethmann-Hollweg was not the man to bring about this change. The Emperor would never have made him Chancellor if he had not been content to drift, as the Emperor was drifting, from one expedient to another. There was no attempt to face the situation. Bethmann-Hollweg tried to settle the problem by leaving it to others. He could not bring about any real change in German policy. He suggested a change in English policy, and not merely a minor adjustment or adaptation, but another diplomatic revolution. If Great Britain had promised to remain neutral in a continental war, she would have given Germany a free hand in Europe, and left France and Russia to make such terms as they could obtain.

Bethmann-Hollweg persisted in his demand. Even if his political terms had not been so high, he could offer no equivalent naval concession. In any case Great Britain could hardly accept the German political terms. Lord Morley, who was no chauvinist, told the German Ambassador in 1912 that the British Ministers would be 'idiots' to sign a political agreement on the lines suggested by the German Foreign Office. The British Government sent Lord Haldane to Berlin on a mission which was hopeless from the outset. In the summer of 1912 the last word had been said on the subject of Haldane's mission.

The negotiations between Great Britain and Germany can be read at length in the British and German documents. As far as possible I have let the actors tell their own story. At first sight this diplomatic business may seem little more than a prolonged wrangle of clever men over drafts, formulae, reservations, minute verbal differences. One thinks of the dissection of dogmatic terms at ecclesiastical councils.

This impression is entirely wrong. Upon these formulae hung the fate of millions of men. The diplomatists and statesmen who scrutinized with care, month after month, the proposals and counter-proposals knew very well that they were not playing with words. The issues were not simple—we know that the results of failure have not been simple. These men were trying to solve a complicated equation, and we in our time have learned too well the significance of their x and y. The historian must describe these complications; otherwise he will not give a true account of the facts. *Aut sint ut sunt, aut non sint.* The story must be told as it is told, or it must be left untold.

The diplomatic negotiations begun by the British Government only cover certain years and certain aspects of the problem of Anglo-German naval competition. For all their importance, these discussions between statesmen and ambassadors leave many things unsaid and unrecorded. One knows that certain decisions were taken, and that they were taken for reasons which might not be wholly wise but were not often wholly foolish; but the questions were not merely discussed behind closed doors, or between Foreign Office and Foreign Office. The main facts, though not the details, of these negotiations were known to the public. What did Germans and Englishmen think about the naval rivalry? Here one reaches a most difficult task. The study of public opinion is so very elusive that most writers content themselves with general terms: 'England', 'Germany', 'France', 'Russia'. It is pedantic not to use these terms in the description of national policy; every one knows, or should know, that they do not mean all Englishmen, all Germans, all Frenchmen. If one is trying to obtain an idea of public opinion, one must assume that there is no single, unanimous judgement passed by a whole nation; on the other hand, it is not unfair to speak of the opinion of a dominant majority as an effective public opinion. The trouble does not end here. Even in the 'dominant majority', the spokesmen are few, the listeners are many. It is hard to discover the views of the silent listeners. The history of the average man can only be told in averages.

No one has yet attempted a detailed and scientific study of public opinion in Germany and Great Britain. This study might take the form of regional surveys. It would provide valuable information; its results would be not a little surprising. Until this study has been made the historian must content himself with rough generalizations. He must read the most 'representative' newspapers and the writings and speeches of public men. He must examine the methods of propaganda official and unofficial, and the effects of this propaganda. He will remember that he is dealing with a subject upon which a great many rash statements have been made. *Hic liber est in quo quaerit sua dogmata quisque. Et reperit pariter dogmata quisque sua.*

With these reservations, one may attempt to give an answer, in general terms, to the question: What did Germans think about the growth of the German navy?

One may say that the German people as a whole believed that they should possess a strong navy. The figures showing the growth of the German Navy League tell their own story. The matter was not one of right, but of expediency. No one, outside Germany, ever questioned the right of Germans to build as many ships as they cared to build or could afford to build. The problem which Germans had to answer was a different problem. The building of the German navy would affect the attitude of other naval Powers towards Germany. Would the reaction of these naval Powers, and particularly the reaction of Great Britain, defeat the purpose of the German navy? Was the navy of any real advantage to German security, or a practical instrument for the advancement of German aims? This question must be answered in the historical setting of the world of the early twentieth century. One must take for granted the belief in national sovereignty and in the nation state as an independent, politically self-sufficing unit, the view that a disarmed nation would be at the mercy of other Powers who would at once take advantage of their superior force. This belief was held by the majority of reasonable men in every European country. It was held by almost every member of the governing classes. It was not effectively disputed by the Socialist minority in any European country.

It is difficult to avoid the conclusion, absurd though it may seem, that the German people did not give very serious thought to the question whether a navy really added to their security. A bitter German critic of the Emperor William II has said that his naval policy was based merely upon *Eitelkeit*, a frivolous vanity or love of display. The criticism is unfair, though it has an element of truth. A statement made by Bethmann-Hollweg in 1912 to a member of the British Embassy in Berlin is nearer the mark. Bethmann-Hollweg said that Germany wanted a navy not merely for the protection of her sea coasts and her commerce, but for the 'general purposes of her greatness'. It is probable that this vague answer would have been given by most patriotic Germans. They would have added that in any case their navy was particularly necessary as a means of defence against England. With a strong fleet they were safe from attack. Without a strong fleet they were at the mercy of a grasping and unscrupulous nation which, in the course of history, had taken opportunity after opportunity to destroy the trade of its commercial rivals. In any case, the German public paid more attention to internal 'party bargaining' on the naval question than to any repercussions of the new policy outside Germany.

If Germany could put a sufficient number of ships into the line of battle, England would not risk an attack even with her superior fleet because she would lose so many ships in destroying the German navy that the British navy would then be at the mercy of other naval Powers. An important school of thought in Germany went beyond this view, and interpreted the 'general purposes of German greatness' in a wider and more aggressive sense. They believed that their country was destined to world domination—not world conquest, but world domination. It is easy to show that this school of thought, with its extravagant and bellicose plans of expansion, was not supported by the majority of peaceful citizens in Germany. It is less easy to say that the pan-Germans and the militarists did not play a disproportionate part in the determination of German policy. It is even more difficult to discover how far the German middle classes allowed themselves to be affected by the aggressive mood of pan-Germanism.

Public opinion in Great Britain was less submissive to authority and less ready to listen to official propaganda than public opinion in Germany; there was also less interest in foreign politics. On one question the political parties were united: the maintenance of naval superiority was known to be a matter of life and death to an island Power, dependent upon imported foodstuffs. The British Empire no less than Great Britain would have been at the mercy of any state which defeated the British navy. At the beginning of the twentieth century Englishmen were accustomed to take as their measure of naval superiority the 'two-Power standard'. The British navy must be as strong or stronger than the combined fleets of the two naval Powers nearest in strength. These naval Powers were France and Russia. The growth of the German navy, the change in the relationship of the Powers, made the 'two-Power standard' an unsuitable measure. The development of the navy of the United States added to the difficulties of maintaining a 'two-Power standard'. A war with the United States was regarded as out of the question. The United States were the greatest trade rivals of England; American imperialism was no less aggressive than other forms of imperialism. Large sections of American opinion were not inclined to friendly collaboration. Yet on the British side there was always a belief, strengthened by the conclusion of an arbitration treaty, that no divergencies of interest could be serious enough to cause an Anglo-American war. The navies of France and Russia were not likely to join an anti-English combination. The navy of Italy could be set against the navy of Austria, in spite of the Triple Alliance.

There remained only the German navy. The programmes of naval construction in Germany determined the programmes of Great Britain. Germany was forcing the pace. A reduction in German naval expenditure would benefit the taxpayers of Great Britain as well as the taxpayers of Germany. The 'shock tactics' of German diplomacy, the attitude of the German press towards England, the activities of the Navy League and the pan-German societies caused increasing disquiet. Englishmen were told that Germany must have a navy to protect her commerce and her colonies. No responsible Englishman wanted to attack the German colonies or German commerce. The fleet intended for the defence of these distant possessions and widespread trade consisted largely of battleships, with little coal-carrying capacity, concentrated in the North Sea. The German people had been told by their responsible leaders that the possession of a fleet would give them freedom of action in their relations with England. They would no longer be forced to submit to English dictation. Englishmen might well interpret this language in another way. They might think that the German fleet was intended to limit British freedom of action. They might distinguish between their own and the German navies. A defeat of the German navy would not necessarily open Germany to an invader. The defeat of the British navy meant the starvation of Great Britain. Upon this point there were no doubts in England. Parliamentary speakers in favour of a reduction of British naval estimates did not attempt to deny that the naval supremacy of Great Britain was a matter of national safety. The refusal of Germany to accept any reduction of naval expenditure on terms which allowed Great Britain a safe margin of superiority was not merely exasperating to a people fully determined that they would maintain this superiority at all costs. There was a sinister aspect about this persistent German attempt to 'beggar my neighbour'. In 1909 the belief that Germany had been accelerating the construction of her ships and that Great Britain might have fewer Dreadnoughts than Germany in the spring of 1912 led to something like a panic. These sudden outbursts of excitement must not be exaggerated. On the whole there was more annoyance than fear; irritation at the waste of money, and at the continual disturbance of the comity of Europe by German unrest and German demands for this or that concession.

The Liberal Government made large claims upon the taxpayers; their financial measures were almost revolutionary; but the Cabinet could be sure of public support for any increase in naval armaments after Germany had led the way. The Government also knew that the country supported their foreign policy. The Anglo-French entente was popular. The Anglo-Russian entente was far less popular, especially among the Liberals; but few of the critics of the reactionary internal policy of the Russian Government wanted to denounce the Anglo-Russian agreement. The most outspoken criticism was concerned not with the effect of the agreement upon British relations with Germany but with the fate of Persia. It is difficult to say more without going beyond the limits of ascertained knowledge. One might perhaps notice two important facts. In the first place there was no wish in Great Britain for a preventive war to destroy the German fleet. A few isolated threats in obscure newspapers, a few *obiter dicta* of expansive admirals, count for nothing against the great mass of pacific opinion and the attitude of responsible statesmen. There was no desire for a war to destroy German trade. Germany was a commercial rival; she was also an excellent customer. The trade of Great Britain was increasing; even on the lowest grounds of expediency there were no arguments in favour of a mercantilist war. If evidence is wanted to show that the world of finance, industry, and commerce in Great Britain did not believe that war for economic ends was a profitable business, this evidence may be found in the reports sent by the German Ambassador in London to his own Government.

Even the most cautious survey of public opinion in Great Britain and Germany permits another generalization. Englishmen failed to notice the questions which were of greatest significance to Germany; Germans failed to notice the questions which really troubled public opinion in England. Few Englishmen understood the European importance of the internal problems of Austria-Hungary, or the extent to which German policy was affected by the mortal illness of the 'second sick man in Europe'. It is indeed doubtful whether any peaceful solution of these problems could have been found. Those who knew the facts were unable to suggest a remedy; but there are a good many features in German policy—for example the insistence upon a British guarantee of neutrality—which bear a less aggressive interpretation if they are considered in the light of Austro-German relations.

On the other side, there was little comprehension in Germany of the meaning of sea-power to an island state and a scattered empire. When Mr. Churchill described the British fleet as a necessity and the German fleet as a 'luxury', there was a storm of abuse in Germany. The terms were ill-chosen; but they were not entirely out of place. Germany was the most powerful of the military states of the Continent before the first Navy Bill was debated in the Reichstag. Without a navy Great Britain was a disarmed state. For this reason British opinion could not consider the growth of the German navy merely as an affair which concerned Germans. The language used by the large body of naval enthusiasts in Germany, the wording of the introduction to the Navy Law of 1900, the debates in the Reichstag contradicted the view that the German navy was not a menace to Great Britain. In public discussions and in official negotiations the German people and their rulers took little account of English susceptibilities and fears. They were inclined to complain of exaggerated suspicions and unreasonable anxiety. They did not pay enough attention to the fair and logical deductions which might be made not merely from their words but from the steady increase in the number of their ships.

Many harsh judgements have been passed upon the diplomacy of the years before 1914, and upon the attitude of public opinion in the great states towards questions of war and peace. It has been said that the acquisition of wealth, the exploitation of the weak, the use of force and the fear of force were the ruling factors in the western world. Nation stood to nation as 'persons of sovereign authority, . . . in continual jealousies and in the state and posture of gladiators, having their weapons pointed, and their eyes fixed on one another, that is their forts, garrisons, and guns upon the frontiers of their kingdoms, and continual spies upon their neighbours; which is a posture of war'. This posture of war was evident. A good deal of the writings of patriotic citizens about the evil intentions of their neighbours might be summed up in the words 'cet animal est très méchant; quand on l'attaque, il se défend', while many measures of so-called defence were concealed, and barely concealed, preparations for attack. The failure of every attempt to escape from the international anarchy, the resigned and almost complacent pessimism of statesmen, make an ironical background to this picture. There was foreknowledge of danger, but the time and thought given to the gravest questions of European importance were as nothing compared with the hours spent in idleness, enjoyment, or lesser disputes over the plunder of the world.

Moritur et ridet. On this view the calamities which came upon Europe in 1914 were inseparable from the 'robber economy' of the time, and the generation which suffered the first and most terrible wave of calamity deserved no better fate. They might have avoided these evils if they had been less bound in covetousness, fear, and pride.

There is not much novelty in the view that man is full of fears; that all men have fallen short of the grace of true knowledge and a perfect intention of the will, and that civil society is vain, for ever at war with itself, and always subject to corruption. It is perhaps wiser and more profitable to remember that every age carries the burden of past history. One may notice certain dominant motives, or patterns of behaviour, or standards of excellence proper to this or that time. These motives have superseded other motives, these patterns of behaviour have taken the place of other patterns and modes of social organization. Are they better or worse? What is the test to be applied to them? How can we measure their improvement or regression? The age immediately preceding our own was conditioned in all its actions by a vast period extending back into the centuries before any written records. Are we to condemn every generation except our own? Or are we to give the benefit of 'extenuating circumstances' to every age except the age into which our fathers and grand-fathers were born? Edmund Burke once said that he did not know how to draw up an indictment against a whole nation. It is even more absurd to pass an absolute judgement upon the manifold activities and purposes of five or six nations. I do not mean that one can forgive everything which one can explain. I mean that no movements in history, no forms of human organization have escaped perversion by evil-minded men. Well-minded men are not always wise men, and wise men cannot always set to rights the confusion which they inherit. Moreover, in the perpetual ebb and flow of things, those who are occupied in the difficult and thankless work of government tend to look for stability, and to take a certain poise and balance as a test of the good health of the body politic. They may even notice that most so-called revolutions are attempts to reach stability, and most revolutions fail because their leaders are attempting to control forces which are both fitful and elusive in their nature. It is true to say that through indolence or habit of possession the rulers of states often resist the advance of change or neglect obvious warnings of danger; but for the most part they are engaged in dealing with the incessant changes and transformations of everyday things. The limits of human capacity are obvious enough; yet they are too often ignored by those who possess after-knowledge of events. The force of circumstance is noticed in tragedy, and is a general theme of play-acting; yet it is forgotten or underestimated in the popular verdict upon the actors in public affairs. We, who do not know to-morrow, assume that the men of yesterday knew to-day and that every sower can foresee every harvest.

In the last analysis, therefore, one may be more merciful than fate or the gods themselves, and admit that, in spite of the general will of a society, rulers and subjects alike may be surprised and overwhelmed by a sudden turn of events which they can no more prevent than their ancestors long ago could have prevented the spreading of the icecap.

A century or more hence, when recrimination is useless and passion out of place, the historian may look upon the turn of events in 1914 as one of those affairs of circumstance, when the accumulation of past errors was let loose upon the present, and the measure of retribution in every case far outweighed the measure of guilt.

It is also possible that this historian, when he passes our tombstones close to those of our fathers, may see less of a moral and intellectual gap between the first and third decades of the twentieth century than we are inclined to see. He may remember that only twenty years were added to the experience of the human race, and the sum of human wisdom, between the year 1914 and the year 1934.

I

THE GERMAN NAVY LAWS OF 1898 AND 1900

IN the month of June 1894 the Oberkommando[1] of the German Navy issued a memorandum on the importance of sea power. This memorandum, which was written mainly by Captain Alfred von Tirpitz, contained a statement of the case for a powerful German fleet, a fleet strong enough to meet an enemy at sea and not merely to harass merchant shipping by cruiser raids. Tirpitz summed up his argument in three long sentences:

'A state which has oceanic, or—an equivalent term—world interests must be able to uphold them and make its power felt beyond its own territorial waters. National world commerce, world industry, and to a certain extent fishing on the high seas, world intercourse and colonies are impossible without a fleet capable of taking the offensive. The conflicts of interests between nations, the lack of confidence felt by capital and the business world will either destroy these expressions of the vitality of a state, or prevent them from taking form, if they are not supported by national power on the seas, and therefore beyond our own waters. Herein lies by far the most important purpose of the fleet.'

Tirpitz was neither a profound political philosopher nor a profound student of history. He never attempted to analyse the political terms which he borrowed from current literature; his historical illustrations give one the impression of facts learnt, carefully but uncritically, from lectures and text-books at military colleges. The importance of his views is to be found not in their scientific value but in the fact that they were shared by the Emperor William II. Until 1894, indeed, William II, though he was most anxious to strengthen the German

---

[1] In 1889 the German Admiralty was divided into an Oberkommando der Marine, or executive command, and a Reichsmarineamt or administrative section. A Naval Cabinet was established for the Emperor. Tirpitz suppressed the Oberkommando when he set up a Naval General Staff.

navy, had not thought out a naval policy. The Emperor liked tall ships as an earlier Hohenzollern had liked tall soldiers.[1] He was impressed by the power of England; jealous of the impregnable position held by the British fleet. There was more than an undercurrent of rivalry in his desire to see Germany strong at sea as on land; yet the Emperor had not considered the measure of strength which would be sufficient, and refused to think of England as an enemy. The Emperor's imagination was turbulent, overcharged with emotions of a second-rate order, over-filled with military sentimentality, overawed by the traditions of his military ancestors and the influence of his military entourage. The constitution of the German Empire placed enormous responsibilities upon the Emperor. No man could undertake these responsibilities with hope of success unless he were a good judge of other men, and knew how to choose wise advisers and work with them. William II was not a good judge of character; few men, from first to last, could work with him. Bismarck had been dismissed. Bismarck's successors were subordinates. The Emperor realized their limitations, but could find no better men, partly because he looked for the wrong qualities in his servants, partly because the political life of Germany in the years before the Emperor came to the throne had not been propitious for the training of good men. Bismarck had created a void around his own immense personality.

In these circumstances the discovery of Tirpitz was of the greatest significance. Tirpitz was considerably older than the Emperor; he had joined the navy as a cadet in 1865. He was fully equipped in the technical side of the naval service, particularly in the torpedo branch, but he was never wholly absorbed in details. He had thought

---

[1] It is said that the great naval review of 1889, and earlier visits to the Isle of Wight, influenced the policy of the Emperor. Other factors affecting the Emperor's opinion between 1890 and 1900 were (1) the publication of Mahan's *The Influence of Sea Power upon History* (1890), (2) the Spanish-American War, (3) the 'surrender' of France at Fashoda. Even as Crown Prince the Emperor tried his hand at designing battleships.

out a consistent plan for the development of the German navy; he was far more skilled than the ordinary naval officer in explaining his ideas and in justifying them by an appeal to principle. As a junior officer he had watched the confusion of policy which was hampering the growth of the navy. Bismarck had obtained colonies for Germany by methods which contradicted Tirpitz's theory that without a navy German overseas expansion must depend entirely upon the goodwill of the naval Powers. This fact carried little weight with the naval enthusiasts: here as in other spheres of policy Bismarck was, in Delbrück's words, 'everything else, but not an educator of his people'. Bismarck was not very much interested in the navy, or, for that matter, in the German colonies. He had won the colonies because the Germans wanted colonies, and because he could secure these colonies by methods which did not interfere with his general continental plans, and did not require a navy. Throughout the Bismarckian age the navy had been left in a half-developed state. During the Schleswig-Holstein war the small Prussian fleet could do no more than prevent Denmark from carrying out an effective blockade of the north German coast. In 1865 the Prussian Parliament had considered a proposal that Prussia should begin a ten-years' programme of construction which would make her into a second-class naval Power: the plan was rejected owing to opposition from the Liberals. Two years later, after the North German Confederation had given to Prussia the control of the naval forces of the Confederation, a ten-years' programme was accepted. Sixteen large and small armoured ships were to be built. It is significant that only one of these ships was built in Germany. The Franco-German war broke out before this programme had run its course. There was but a single naval action in the war—a fight between a small German gunboat and a French dispatch-boat off the island of Cuba.

For a number of years the success of the land forces turned attention from the navy to the army. In 1872

Lieut.-General von Stosch, Chief of the Imperial Admiralty, again brought forward a ten-years' plan. The plan was accepted after a second report had been laid before the Reichstag in 1873. Ten years later—in 1883— von Stosch composed a memorandum upon the execution of his programme. The plan had not been ambitious. Its aim had been the defence of German interests in distant waters. In the case of war with any of the great naval Powers of Europe only raids were contemplated. Even so, the programme of 1873 had not been fully carried out. No substitute had been provided for an armed frigate lost in a collision in the English Channel. Stosch also drew up a second memorandum. The new plan covered three or four years only, but still kept to the thesis that Germany could not attempt to fight a sea battle against any of the great naval Powers.

In 1883 another general, Count Caprivi, was appointed Chief of the Admiralty. Caprivi was still inclined to limit the offensive plans of the German fleet to cruiser warfare against enemy commerce, and to concentrate upon a large fleet of torpedo-boats, though he recognized the need of a 'high seas fleet' to support the cruisers on foreign service and began the construction of the Kiel Canal. On the other hand, he could not easily get money from the Reichstag, and was too much influenced by the general belief that the coming of the torpedo meant the end of the era of large battleships. Caprivi left the Admiralty in 1888, and, after various changes, Admiral Hollmann became Secretary of the Reichsmarineamt in 1890. Hollmann remained in office until 1897. He was not a good speaker. He could not persuade the Reichstag to spend money on ships; he was unable to settle the dispute in naval circles about the strategic purpose of the navy. Tirpitz made up his mind upon this subject as early as 1891, while he was chief of staff to the Admiral in command of the Baltic squadron; he drew up a memorandum on the importance of developing a battle fleet and a system of tactics suitable for naval warfare on the open sea. In 1892 Tirpitz was called to the Oberkommando in Berlin. Here he composed the document which converted the Emperor to the plan of building a battle-fleet.[1]

It was impossible to build this fleet at once. The German people were not convinced of the dangers threatening their commerce and colonies owing to the lack of a German High Seas Fleet in the North Sea. There were, indeed, at this time relatively few battleships in the North Sea. The strongest units of the British and French fleets were in the Mediterranean. British naval defence was concerned with France, and secondarily with Russia. The Emperor's plan of asking for a large loan for naval purposes was hopeless from a parliamentary point of view. Assistance came from a most unlikely quarter. In the summer and autumn of 1895 the relations between the Boers and the Uitlanders in the Transvaal had almost reached breaking-point. The German Emperor, with the support of German opinion, wanted to take the side of the Boers. In October 1895 the British Ambassador in Berlin warned the German Secretary of State for Foreign Affairs that serious results might follow from German encouragement of the Boers. The Emperor's comment was: 'We must make capital out of this affair for our demands for the fleet which is to protect our increasing commerce.'[2] The Jameson raid provided more capital. On 3 January 1896 the Emperor sent a telegram to President Kruger congratulating him upon the suppression of the raiders. From the point of view of Anglo-German relations the telegram was a political blunder. Germany could do nothing to help the Boers. She had already provoked English feeling by objecting to English pressure upon President Kruger to secure the enfranchisement of the Uitlanders after five years' residence. The Jameson raid was disavowed at once by the British

---

[1] For the history of the first Navy Law, and the memoranda drawn up by Tirpitz, see H. Hallmann, *Krugerdepesche und Flottenfrage*, and B. Michalik, *Probleme des deutschen Flottenbaues*.   [2] D.G.P. xi. 5–7, and 12.

Government; it had shocked and humiliated public opinion in Great Britain. The Emperor's telegram gave some colour to the statements of those who planned the raid that Germany was encouraging the Boers to attack British interests. Yet from the point of view of the naval enthusiasts in Germany the telegram had useful consequences. The powerlessness of Germany to interfere in South Africa was an object-lesson in the importance of sea-power.[1] The mobilization of a British flying-squadron brought the lesson home.

In June 1897 Tirpitz was appointed Secretary of the Reichsmarineamt. The Emperor now thought the parliamentary situation more favourable. The idea of a battle-fleet was accepted as a matter of course after Tirpitz's appointment. Even before the Jameson raid Tirpitz had been asked once again to state his views. He had drawn up another memorandum containing the first suggestion of the 'risk' theory which played so important a part in the development of the German navy. The German fleet must be powerful enough to inflict serious damage upon the fleet of the strongest naval Power. The strongest naval Power would not venture to attack a powerful German fleet, since its own fleet would be so much weakened in the process of destroying the German navy that it would be at the mercy of other naval Powers.

From the time of the Jameson raid to the publication of the first Navy Law the Emperor had been pushing his plans. He was almost obsessed with the idea of British naval superiority, and the failure of his schemes for a

---

[1] Sir C. Spring-Rice took a different view of the German reaction to the outburst of feeling in Great Britain. 'It has been a lesson (to Germany). They have been kicking us for years, on the assumption that they were kicking a dead ass. It is a great surprise to see starting up a live lion. The effect is curious. The press articles are almost friendly.' (*Letters and Friendships of Sir C. Spring-Rice*, S. Gwynn, i. 189.) Metternich pointed out, in 1902, that before 1895–6 'the general view was that if only you trampled on an Englishman heavily enough he would give way to you'. This view did not survive the events of 1895–6. D.G.P. xvii. 13.

continental league against English aggression outside Europe only strengthened his belief that Germany was in danger of attack. He pointed out to his Chancellor in October 1896 that 'once again we can see how wrong-headed we have been to begin a colonial policy ten years ago without a fleet, and to develop this policy without keeping pace with it in naval construction. Now we are burdened with great colonial possessions which are the Achilles' heel for a Germany hitherto out of England's reach.'[1] Count Hatzfeldt, the German Ambassador in London, answered with good sense that England had no intention of attacking the German colonies, and thereby driving Germany into the arms of Russia.[2] Nevertheless the Emperor was still anxious. In July 1897 the British Government decided not to renew the Anglo-Belgian and Anglo-German commercial treaties of 1862 and 1865, which prevented the colonies from giving preference to Great Britain, but to secure a new treaty on the terms of the 'most-favoured nation'. William II at once saw prospective ruin for German trade, and concluded that Germany must build a strong fleet without delay. 'Caeterum censeo naves esse aedificandas.'[3]

The first Navy Law gave Tirpitz what he wanted, or rather the programme for which he thought it safe to ask. The German fleet would consist of nineteen battleships, twelve large and thirty small cruisers, eight armoured coast-defence ships. The life of a battleship was calculated at twenty-five years, the life of a large cruiser at twenty years. A programme of construction was designed to cover the years from 1898 to 1903; the total non-recurrent expenditure would be over £20,000,000.[4]

---

[1] D.G.P. xiii. 4: William II to Hohenlohe, 25 October 1896.

[2] D.G.P. xiii. 5–7: Hatzfeldt to Holstein, 28 October 1896.

[3] D.G.P. xiii. 34: 31 July 1897.

[4] The law authorized the construction of seven battleships and two large cruisers in addition to ships already under construction. The German battleships built immediately before 1898 were smaller than those of Great Britain. The German ships were under 10,000 tons, with a coal-carrying capacity of 680 tons. The British ships of the *Majestic* class were 15,000 tons, and carried 1,850 tons of coal.

The scheme was announced to the German public in November 1897. Statistics showing the strength of the world's fleets had been circulated among members of the Reichstag and important civic functionaries. At the same time Germany seized Kiao-Chau for occupation as a naval base in the Far East.[1] The coincidence of this occupation with the announcement of a naval programme was significant. The programme under the Navy Law extended to the financial year 1903–4. It was clearly only the first stage of a larger plan. Otherwise the acquisition of a Far Eastern port was merely offering another hostage to fortune and another potential prize to the British navy.

The Navy Law was passed by 212 votes to 139 at the end of March 1898. Tirpitz at once began an intensive propaganda among the German people. His work was done with thoroughness and energy.

'We organized meetings and lectures, and made special efforts to get in touch with the Press on a large scale. We instituted tours to the waterside and exhibited the ships and the wharves; we turned our attention to the schools and we called upon authors to write for us; stacks of novels and pamphlets were the result. Prizes were to be given by the Ministry of Education to the schools.'[2]

Tirpitz lamented that 'the spirit of Treitschke had disappeared from the teaching of German history',[3] though he did his utmost, and with success, to overcome the 'aloofness' of many of the 'savants'. The chief instrument of propaganda was the Navy League. The League was founded in 1898 with funds largely provided by the firm of Krupp; within three years of its foundation it had obtained 240,000 private members.[4] It was under imperial patronage; practically all state officials found it advisable

---

[1] For the seizure of Kiao-Chau see D.G.P. xiv, pt. i. c. 90 and B.D.D. i. c. i.

[2] Tirpitz, *My Memoirs* (Eng. trans.), i. 112–13.

[3] *Ib.* 111. Treitschke had regarded an Anglo-German war as inevitable.

[4] A number of societies of a patriotic kind were affiliated to the League. The membership had risen to 600,000 in March 1900. For the later history of the Navy League, see below, *passim*.

to support a cause highly favoured by the holders of place and power.

It was impossible to carry on a sudden and intensive propaganda of this kind without reference to Great Britain and the British navy. Bülow, who had been appointed to the foreign secretaryship in 1897 largely because the Emperor relied on his help to get a naval law through the Reichstag, wrote from Windsor in November 1899 that German feeling was far more anti-English than English feeling was anti-German.[1] This anti-English feeling was deliberately fostered by those who directed the propaganda in favour of the navy. The outbreak of the Boer War gave an opportunity too good to be lost. Public opinion in Germany was wholly on the side of the Boers. It was almost too easy for the advocates of a strong navy to point out how different would have been the policy of Germany if she had possessed a strong fleet. The Emperor himself made no secret of the fact. He told the British Ambassador in May 1899—before the outbreak of the war—that 'he knew that England was powerful at sea and Germany weak, and therefore the former could act with impunity, but the time would come when even England would have to consider the German fleet as an important factor, and he only hoped . . . that Germany would not by that time have formed other combinations which would certainly not be agreeable to England'.[2] To Bülow the Emperor was more plain-spoken. He wrote at the beginning of the Boer War: 'I am not in a position to go beyond the strictest neutrality, and I must first get for myself a fleet. In twenty years' time, when the fleet is ready, I can use another language.'[3] Even so, the

---

[1] D.G.P. xv. 413–20.   [2] B.D.D. i. 118; cf. D.G.P. xiv, pt. ii. 592.

[3] D.G.P. xv. 408: 29 October 1899. The Emperor emphasized the point by one of his coarser allusions. Five months later the Emperor drew the same conclusion, though in more delicate language than he had used in writing to Bülow. He told the Queen of the Netherlands in March 1900 that preparation at sea was essential, in case the Lord should decide to use Germany or Holland as the instrument of His vengeance. Silence and work were necessary until the ships were ready (D.G.P. xv. 539).

Emperor, with Bülow's approval, used the whole force of diplomatic action to obtain minor concessions in Samoa. In Bülow's words, 'we should be blamed for lack of diplomatic skill, if we did not obtain a satisfactory settlement of several of the questions outstanding between us and England—especially that of Samoa'.[1]

On 24 October a notice appeared in the German press that a new naval law would shortly be introduced. There had been rumours of this law for some time past, in spite of denials by Tirpitz. The new proposals were laid before the Reichstag in January 1900. Their publication almost coincided with the detention by British warships of German ships alleged to be taking contraband and volunteers to Delagoa Bay. Once again the naval party could not wish for better arguments to prove the helplessness of Germany on the high seas. Tirpitz, in introducing the first Navy Law, had stated that the German fleet was not being laid down against England; he found it necessary, in introducing the second law, to say openly that the fleet must be equal to its 'most difficult task', in other words, to a 'naval battle in the North Sea against England'.[2] Bülow also connected the new plans with the changes in the world situation. He made it clear that the fleet was a necessity for Germany in her dealings with

---

[1] D.G.P. xv. 396 n. The pressure exercised at a moment of British embarrassment to secure an immediate settlement of a minor matter affecting a group of islands with 30,000 native and 500 white inhabitants, and an annual trade of less than £200,000, caused irritation in Great Britain. Salisbury, who proposed at one moment that the disposition of the islands should be settled by lot, wrote to the British Ambassador at Berlin that the German Ambassador had 'urged this transaction upon me with extraordinary vehemence, intimating in no obscure language that the future friendship of Germany could only be obtained at this price. What measures he meant to indicate as constituting an exhibition of the friendship of Germany, or what policy of an opposite kind he referred to as resulting from a failure to obtain this advantage, I am not myself able to judge. I have not however held out to him any hope that I can consider these proposals from such a point of view. . . . I do not think that (a Samoan agreement) is at this moment pressing, or that the danger in Samoa of deferring it for a short time can be looked upon as serious' (Salisbury to Lascelles, 6 October 1899: B.D.D. i. 125–6).

[2] Tirpitz, *op. cit.*, i. 122–3.

England. The construction of this fleet might lead to uneasiness and mistrust in England, but Germany must fulfil her destiny; 'Our fleet must be built with our eyes on English policy.'[1]

The new Navy Law provided for the construction of a much larger fleet than that planned under the law of 1898. Under the new plan the battle-fleet in 1920 would be made up of two flagships, four squadrons of eight battleships, eight large and twenty-four small cruisers. Four battleships, three large cruisers, and three small cruisers would form a fleet reserve. There would also be a foreign service fleet of three large and ten small cruisers. During the discussion of the law in the Reichstag the Government was forced by the Centre party to drop five large and five small cruisers, and to reduce the cruiser reserve by one large and two small cruisers.[2]

The law of 1900 marks a decision of very great importance, and must be recognized as a deliberate act of policy. The plan was very costly. The new law doubled the number of battleships. The first of the new ships were larger than the ships laid down under the law of 1898; the ships laid down under the law of 1898 were larger than their predecessors. The upkeep of the fleet would become progressively more expensive. The new construction was not the only 'non-recurrent burden'; as a burden it could hardly be called 'non-recurrent'. In addition to the new ships required to provide the battle-squadrons, seven large armoured ships reached the end of their years

---

[1] For Bülow's attitude on the naval question, see W. Becker, *Fürst Bülow und England, Front wider Bülow* (ed. F. Thimme), and Michalik, *op. cit.*

[2] For the history of these cruisers, see below, p. 97. On 7 February 1900 the Social Democrats held nineteen large meetings in different parts of Berlin to protest against the Navy Law. These meetings were also addressed by speakers (mostly professors) in favour of the law, but in every case resolutions were passed against the naval proposals. During the first stages of the debate on the Navy Law in the Reichstag Bebel put forward the view, which he repeated year after year, that the naval party wanted a fleet for use in an offensive war against England. Bebel thought that other naval Powers would increase their armaments, and that Germany could not meet the cost of competition.

of life within two years of the introduction of the law of 1900; three more were due for replacement between 1902 and 1913, and a larger number between 1914 and 1917. It was, therefore, necessary to lay down a time-table of construction, with an average of three ships a year for the next sixteen years. The shipbuilding industry in Germany could lay down plant to provide for this great scheme of construction only if there were no doubt that the yards would receive a steady stream of orders. Tirpitz pointed out that a decision once taken must be regarded as irrevocable. He did not hide the difficulties. He wanted to spend £80,000,000 on ships, and £13,000,000 on dockyards and harbours. He proposed to raise £38,500,000 in loans, and hoped that between 1900 and 1916 an increasing revenue would supply the remaining £54,500,000. These figures were reduced by the Reichstag; but they might be taken as a low estimate. The size and armament of battleships were increasing, and the whole scale of naval preparations tended to become more costly.

For these and other reasons, such as the need for making provision on a sufficient scale for harbours and other works, the scheme must be given statutory form. 'Only a firm will, expressed in legal form, will ensure success.' It is important to notice these facts. They were pointed out at the time of the passing of the law; they were recognized by the German people, as far as any legal act of this kind is recognized by the whole of a nation. They were accepted, with all their financial consequences, as necessary for the security of Germany. The law of 1900 was regarded as immutable in the sense that, although it might be transcended, it could never be abrogated. Acceptance of the law became an article almost of spiritual faith in Germany. If German opinion was curiously blind to the political consequences of the law, or to the firm hold upon Englishmen of the 'two-Power standard',[1] British opinion did not realize the 'moral' significance of the building of the fleet and the funda-

[1] For the text of the law of 1900, see *Brassey's Naval Annual*, 1900, pp. 429-33.

mental character of the law of 1900. The British public in the twentieth century was unfamiliar with any long-range plan of naval construction. The Naval Defence Act of 1889 was almost forgotten. Great Britain was determined to remain supreme at sea, but this naval supremacy was maintained by observing the programmes of other Powers, and by shaping British plans in accordance with these foreign programmes. Germans, looking at the obligations which they had laid upon themselves, did not consider the effect of the growth of their fleet upon British opinion. They were merely fulfilling a legal duty. Englishmen, determined to uphold a supremacy which was a matter of life and death, could not understand why German naval programmes were less flexible than those of Great Britain. Moreover, Tirpitz and his collaborators did not consider the effect of their propaganda. This propaganda was something new. From time to time in the last quarter of the nineteenth century other Powers, long familiar with sea-power, had reviewed their naval position, and added to their forces. Great Britain had replied to increases in the naval programmes of France and Russia; but these developments had never been accompanied by a campaign of strident publicity. The French nation already possessed a long and honourable tradition of naval strength; the Russian people were not consulted by the Russian Government. The rulers of Germany could not ignore public opinion, and were unable to appeal to the past history of German naval enterprise or to any firmly established view that German safety depended on predominance, absolute or relative, at sea. These facts were not realized in Great Britain, though they explained a good deal of the extravagance of language used in Germany on behalf of the navy. The Germans themselves seemed to be unconscious that, apart from the deliberate and dangerous stimulation of anti-English feeling, phrases intended to arouse in inland Germany enthusiasm for ships might have an aggressive tone and a sinister meaning in other countries where no such language was necessary because the need of a strong fleet was already understood.

A plan extending over a period of twenty years, and adding an enormous financial burden to a country which was increasing in wealth but still short of capital, was unlikely to be accepted without some theoretical justification. It was not enough to show why Germany must have a fleet; as far as national pride was concerned, recent events seemed to have provided sufficient argument. It was also necessary to show that Germany could secure her interests at sea without possessing a fleet as large as the fleet of Great Britain. Here again Tirpitz gave a lucid and plausible explanation of his aims, though he could not take the German people into his confidence without at the same time making it clear to Great Britain what purpose the German fleet was intended to serve.

Tirpitz explained his case in a memorandum attached to the Navy Law. The memorandum may be summed up very shortly. The German Empire, for the security of its economic development and world trade, needed peace, on land and sea; not indeed 'peace at any price, but peace with honour, satisfying the just requirements of Germany'. A naval war for economic interests, particularly for commercial interests, would cost Germany's opponents very little if the German coasts could be blockaded. The enemy would cover his war expenditure by the improvement in his own trade. Hence the only effective means of protecting German overseas trade and colonies lay in the construction of a battle-fleet. This fleet must be of sufficient strength that even the strongest naval Power could not attack it without endangering its own position in the world. For this purpose it was not absolutely necessary for the German battle-fleet to be as strong as that of the greatest naval Power. This latter Power would not, as a rule, be able to concentrate all its forces against Germany. In any case, the defeat of the German fleet would so weaken the enemy that, in spite of his victory, his own naval position in the world would be insecure; that is to say, the German navy would have damaged the victorious fleet to such an extent that it could no longer meet a coalition of other naval Powers. This 'risk theory', as it was described in Germany and elsewhere, had already been outlined by Tirpitz in 1896.[1] The statement of the theory contained no mention of Great Britain. Yet the theory could only apply to Great Britain. Great Britain was the strongest naval Power. The British fleet was dispersed throughout the world. Its most recent units were in the Mediterranean. It was impossible to conceal the fact that the 'risk' theory was a direct challenge to the 'two-Power standard' adopted by Great Britain. Germany intended to build a navy which even in the hour of German defeat could sink enough British ships to reduce the British navy below the numerical level required by the 'two-Power standard'. The German navy might have disappeared, but Great Britain would be powerless before the combined fleets of France and Russia. Hence Great Britain would not dare to attack Germany. Germany could therefore use her fleet as a diplomatic instrument to exert pressure upon Great Britain. Moreover, the German fleet would be in the hands of men who regarded war for economic and commercial ends not merely as justifiable but as practicable. What then would Englishmen think about the development of this instrument of coercion? Tirpitz had considered the point. He realized that there was a danger zone to be passed before the German fleet could cause sufficient 'risk' to an attacking Power. To German military experts this danger zone was very real. The idea of a preventive war was not considered either morally wrong or politically impracticable by those who prided themselves upon the realism of their politics. The record of Great Britain appeared to show that the doctrine of preventive war had been practised with success by Englishmen. The history of the seizure of the Danish fleet in the Napoleonic wars was taken from its context and

[1] See above, p. 24.

mentioned again and again in public discussions about the German navy. The naval party argued that it was not creating the 'danger zone'. Upon Tirpitz's view, which was limited to considerations of sea-power, the helplessness of Germany before the British navy was a fact. The only way of escape lay through a danger zone which already existed. Moreover, the hazards were not too great; the 'risk' was not enormously increased by the policy of the Navy Law. Tirpitz thought it unlikely that British public opinion would accept the idea of a preventive war until the most favourable moment had passed. Meanwhile the risk must be taken. The additional element of danger must be accepted, because it could not be eluded.

Tirpitz's views were broadcast throughout Germany. Some of his supporters went beyond the limits of the 'risk theory'. One may take an example of these many variations on a single theme. In March 1900 Freiherr von der Goltz wrote an article in the *Deutsche Rundschau* on 'Seemacht und Landkrieg'. Von der Goltz was one of the most prominent men in Germany; the *Deutsche Rundschau* was a journal of high standing and wide circulation among the professional and upper classes in Germany. The article opened with certain general considerations about sea power, with special reference to English plans of world conquest, and the reasons why Germany needed a strong fleet. Von der Goltz gave statistics of the increase of German trade, the growth of the population of Germany, and, as a corollary of the growth, the large imports of corn. He pointed out that modern wars might be long wars, and that Germany must be prepared to resist and break a blockade. From a military point of view the control of the Baltic against the fleets of France and Russia was essential in the case of a war on two fronts. A few paragraphs sufficed for the problem of a Franco-German and a Franco-Russian war. The main argument was devoted to the question of war with England.

'In the first place we must contradict the widespread view that such a war is beyond the range of possibility. . . . The experience of the small and peaceful South African Republics should teach us a lesson once and for all. We must not overlook the fact that the opinion of large sections of the British public is favourable to a war of annihilation [*Vernichtungskampf*] against Germany. The anti-English feeling among all the continental nations—and not least in Germany—has strengthened this opinion in Great Britain. . . . German independence is regarded as in the nature of an unjustifiable revolt against British predominance.'

Von der Goltz followed Tirpitz in attributing English hostility, in the last resort, to jealousy of German trade and fear that the growth of Germany meant the collapse of Great Britain.

'We can be sure that an English Government—the present Government, and probably future Governments, will try to resist the strong current of national feeling, and will prefer peaceful competition to the decision of war; but we must ask—will those Governments succeed? In the last resort we must admit that the use of force is the good right [*ein gutes Recht*] of nations which are beginning to fear for their existence.'

Von der Goltz thought that the interference with German steamers on the African routes was a sign of British commercial jealousy, and that the reason for this interference was an attempt to destroy confidence in the security of German steamship lines. This interference was 'one of those light shocks which are usually the prelude to earthquakes, and it would be foolish to assume that a war with England is an impossibility'.

Could Germany arm against the chances of a war with England? The view that England could always defeat any German attempt to resist her at sea was weak and suicidal. In the first place the continental position of Germany gave her 'a certain influence on the relations of other Powers with England'. Furthermore, 'if we compare the forces on either side, even without reckoning upon the assistance of others, the chances in the future

of resisting England are not hopeless; on the contrary
the hope of success will increase from day to day'. Then
followed a reference to the dispersion of the British fleet.
Some of the overseas squadrons could be brought home,
but not all the foreign stations could be left, and in any
case the return journey would take time. England might
be engaged in war in some distant part of the world; a
bold enemy would doubtless make use of this moment of
weakness.[1] India, Canada, Australia, once lost would be
lost for ever; England could not therefore afford to concentrate her forces. The protection of the British mercantile marine would increase English difficulties. Von
der Goltz then calculated the strength of the fleet which
Great Britain could keep in home waters. Even if this
fleet were increased in numbers (and the question of man-
power set limits to the growth of the British fleet) 'it will
not be an insuperable enemy for our future navy. . . .
Careful preparation and quick mobilization can give a
weaker enemy actual superiority for a considerable time.[2]
. . . There are places enough where England's greatness
is mortal.' . . .

One may notice certain flaws in Tirpitz's reasoning,
and in the bolder conclusions of writers such as von der
Goltz. These arguments were drawn from the political
situation in the last decade of the nineteenth century.
This situation might change. It would indeed be changed
by the appearance of a powerful German navy as a new
factor in international politics. It might also be changed
by decisions taken in France or Russia or Great Britain—
decisions over which Germany had no control. During
the last decade of the nineteenth century when Tirpitz

---

[1] This phrase should be noticed ('ein kühner Gegner würde unzweifelhaft
solch' einen Moment der Schwäche zum Handeln benutzen'). Unconsciously
von der Goltz took the attitude not of defence against British attack, but
of using the occasion of British embarrassment for an attack on Great
Britain.

[2] It is interesting to notice the anger in Germany five years later when
Mr. Lee spoke of the possible results of British measures to secure the advantage of quick mobilization. See below, pp. 94–6.

was elaborating the 'risk' theory, Great Britain was, politically, on bad terms with France and Russia; she could not allow her navy to fall below the requirements of a 'two-Power standard'. If Great Britain ceased to be on bad terms with France and Russia, there would be no reason to suppose that these Powers would use the opportunity of the temporary weakening of the British fleet after a naval war with Germany to destroy the world position of Great Britain. It was far more likely that France would take the chance of recovering Alsace-Lorraine from Germany, and that Russia would affirm her position in the Near East not at the expense of Great Britain but at the expense of Austria. If there were no 'risk' in a naval war with Germany, the German fleet would be of little value as a diplomatic instrument unless it could reasonably expect to defeat the British fleet.

Furthermore, if Great Britain were on good terms with France and Russia, it would be unnecessary for her to keep the strongest units of her fleet far away from the North Sea. The concentration of the fleet of the strongest naval Power would diminish the relative fighting value of the German fleet.[1] Tirpitz's policy increased the chances of a friendly agreement between Great Britain, France, and Russia. Hitherto Great Britain had not been willing to make any great concessions to France or Russia. The existence of a German fleet might provide the motive for these concessions. French diplomacy would be quick to seize a splendid opportunity. The surrender of France upon the Fashoda question had shown that France dared not risk war with England because the 'risk' theory would apply on land and sea. Even in the unlikely case of a French victory, France would be crippled for years to come in relation to Germany. If France could not oppose England, it was clearly in

---

[1] As late as July 1904 Tirpitz still maintained that in 1912 the German fleet would not merely be stronger than the French fleet, but would be relatively superior to the British fleet, 'that is to say, it would be numerically stronger than the Channel Fleet and its reserves'. D.D.F. 2nd ser. v. 338.

French interests to come to an agreement which would at least secure the benefits of English support. Russian interests were more difficult to harmonize with those of England in the Near, Middle, and Far East. Yet Germany had already begun schemes of economic and political penetration in Asia Minor which would bring her into conflict with Russia, and Austro-Russian relations in the Balkans, though temporarily quiet, might not remain quiet for ever.

A calculation of possibilities hardly justified the adoption of the 'risk' theory by German naval strategists. One might add a number of technical considerations. It was not at all certain that a naval war between a stronger and a weaker naval Power would result in any serious weakening of the forces of the stronger Power. Decisions at sea are generally more absolute than decisions on land; a more powerful fleet can inflict heavy damage upon a less powerful enemy with little loss to itself.[1] The only hope even of temporary German success lay in the dispersion of the British navy; but a closer study of naval history might have shown that, even if the political assumptions made by Tirpitz were correct, it was unsafe to suppose that Great Britain would be taken unawares, or that her admirals would allow their squadrons to be caught one at a time by a German battle fleet. On the German side preparations on a scale necessary for modern naval warfare could not be concealed, and even if the general and normal disposition of the British fleet remained unchanged, ships could be brought from the western Mediterranean in time for the business of defence and attack, whenever any danger threatened from Germany. If Great Britain were the aggressor, she would choose her own day and hour. It was unlikely that any other Power would make use of a temporary weakening of British sea power in the Mediterranean. The danger of reprisals from a victorious and relatively undamaged British fleet, after the German navy had met its fate, would have been too

[1] See below, p. 106.

serious. The possession of a numerically inferior high seas fleet was not therefore any safe insurance for Germany against the chances of overwhelming defeat by Great Britain.

Was there any likelihood of a British attack? The memorandum appended to the Navy Law assumed that a war for 'economic interests, particularly for commercial interests', might be profitable to a naval Power which could blockade the coasts of Germany. This view implied that Great Britain, jealous of the increasing trade of Germany, and anxious for her own trade interests and a commercial supremacy which was being won from her by Germany, would go to war for the destruction of German trade.

From a political point of view, the chances of a mercantilist war could hardly seem serious at a time when Great Britain was making overtures to Germany. In March 1898 Chamberlain had suggested, informally, but seriously, that England might make an alliance with Germany. The policy of splendid isolation could not be maintained. Russia had refused an agreement upon Far Eastern questions, and the time had come for Great Britain to take 'far-reaching decisions'.[1] The offer was refused. Bülow thought that time was on Germany's side. 'England cannot in the long run avoid fighting for her existence, and other allies and better friends than Germany she will not find.'[2] Meanwhile Chamberlain's offer seemed dangerous. England was not to be trusted. An Anglo-German treaty would only bind the British Government in power at the time when the treaty was made.

'If therefore the enemies of the Anglo-German group wished . . . to fight their rivals singly, and fell first upon Germany, I

---

[1] D.G.P. xiv, pt. i. 196–7; 29 March 1898. For the history of Chamberlain's offers, see Garvin, *Life of Joseph Chamberlain*, vol. iii, books xiii–xv; Eckardstein, *Lebenserinnerungen und politische Denkwürdigkeiten*, Oncken, *Das Deutsche Reich und die Vorgeschichte des Weltkrieges*, vol. ii, and W. Becker, *op. cit.*

[2] D.G.P. xiv, pt. i. 207.

must certainly say that at present I do not think that the English party to the treaty would . . . come to our assistance with all possible force. It would be more in the spirit of British policy . . . for the Government which had engaged itself to us by treaty simply to go out of power and to be followed by one which, remembering the warning received, would obey public opinion and confine itself to the traditional role of spectator.'[1]

In the light of later events, Bülow's view of British perfidy makes curious reading. It is still more curious to notice that the British Foreign Office took precisely the opposite view. Bertie wrote in 1901 that 'in considering offers of alliance from Germany it is necessary to remember the history of Prussia as regards alliances and the conduct of the Bismarck Government in making a treaty with Russia concerning and behind the back of Austria the ally of Germany'.[2] Bertie was never friendly to German advances. Sir Thomas Sanderson, Permanent Under-Secretary of State for Foreign Affairs from 1894 to 1906, was more balanced in his judgement; he also pointed out in 1901 that 'there must be a certain amount of qualifying words' limiting the scope of any Anglo-German alliance. 'These qualifications are likely to be the cause of serious dispute—and the Germans will be much less scrupulous in making use of them to throw us over than we can be in leaving them in the lurch. Our public opinion would not allow it—theirs would.'[3]

The German view of British policy might be right or wrong. It did not give much support to the idea that, in the near or even distant future, Great Britain might attack Germany for commercial reasons. Upon a question of this kind one turns to the evidence of fact.[4] How

[1] D.G.P. xiv, pt. i. 199–200. Bülow to Hatzfeldt, 30 March 1898.
[2] B.D.D. ii. 73–4: 9 November 1901.
[3] B.D.D. ii. 66: 27 May 1901.
[4] A full survey of the relation between public opinion and economic rivalry in England and Germany has yet to be made, and must depend for its accuracy upon preliminary 'regional surveys'. R. J. S. Hoffmann's *Great Britain and the German Trade Rivalry, 1875–1914* (1933) is interesting as a general account of the development of German competition and the reaction of Great Britain to this competition. The book is written from a

far was British resentment at German economic competition a serious factor in determining the political relations between the two countries? Were British merchants, industrialists, and bankers seriously alarmed at the menace of this competition? If they were alarmed, did they make any attempt to influence public opinion in favour of a war on mercantilist principles? It is only possible to answer these questions in general terms; but the answer shows that, at the time of the first and second naval laws, and throughout the years between 1900 and 1914, German competition was not undermining British prosperity. British trade in the chief markets of the world was taking a full share of the general increase in world trade. The commercial classes in Great Britain, so far from looking to war as a means of destroying German commerce, were most anxious for an improvement of Anglo-German relations. German economic rivalry only affected the diplomatic course of events at points where Germany was seeking political power, and not merely an open door for trade. *The Times* wrote on 11 January 1906, at the height of the Moroccan controversy, that the British people 'smiled' at the suggestion of their 'deadly envy' of German commercial success. No such envy was felt of the United States, though American competition was more severe than German.

During the last two decades of the nineteenth century there had been misgivings in England at the sudden development of German trade. At times of economic depression these misgivings resulted in a current of pessimism about the economic future of Great Britain, and a growing irritation at the pertinacity and, at times, the unscrupulousness of German methods, such as the fraudulent

point of view more sympathetic to Germany than to Great Britain, and is rather superficial in its treatment of British public opinion. Mr. Hoffmann does not give sufficient consideration to the question whether German methods rather than German competition irritated English traders and manufacturers. For the views of German observers in England upon the question of economic rivalry, see below, p. 46. For a German banker's view in 1907, see P. Swabach, *Aus meinen Akten*, pp. 120–1.

use of trade-marks. It must also be remembered that a free-trade country regarded as unfair, and even as dishonest, the practice of selling goods cheaply abroad at the expense of a protected home market, and the habit of using diplomatic pressure to secure special treatment for German merchants in foreign countries. The two periods in which this irritation was expressed most clearly in the British press coincided with periods of hard diplomatic bargaining on the part of Germany. In the years after 1880, and particularly in 1884 and 1885, Bismarck was making sharp—from the British standpoint unreasonably sharp—demands for colonial concessions as the price of German support against France and Russia. The second period of disquiet occurred about the time of the Kruger telegram. An article in the *Saturday Review* of 11 September 1897 may be taken as an extreme statement of this irritation. The *Saturday Review* at this time was losing its circulation; an anonymous article (apparently written by an American!) describing the inevitability of a German trade war was little more than a journalistic coup to attract attention. No responsible English newspaper supported the thesis of a trade war; there was no reason for attention to be paid to a single alarmist cry. The fact that attention was paid in Germany to this particular article, which could be matched by scores of similar outbursts in German journals, is better evidence for the state of feeling in Germany than in Great Britain.[1]

The trade figures for the last two decades of the nineteenth century show that Germany was making great progress, and that this economic progress, as far as overseas and continental trade were concerned, was made largely at the expense of Great Britain. It could indeed hardly be made at the expense of any other Power. One

[1] This article in the *Saturday Review* was brought into prominence again by Tirpitz eleven years after its publication! Metternich told Bülow that the writer could not be taken seriously. Bülow annotated Metternich's view: 'Certainly not' (D.G.P. xxviii. 45–9). H. Kantorowicz (*Geist der englischen Politik*, pp. 346–7) points out that the article is quoted in Bülow's *Imperial Germany* as evidence of the perils from which Bülow saved Germany!

may doubt whether, on a general balance, the expansion of German trade was ever detrimental to British interests. Within certain fields, however, this expansion resulted in a loss of markets, and the encroachment upon British trade was particularly irritating to British merchants in areas opened up by British enterprise and hitherto providing for Great Britain almost a monopoly of trade. The important fact from the point of view of the development of German naval power is that this commercial and industrial progress at British expense was less noticeable after 1900. The growth of the export trade of Great Britain in the decade before the war was scarcely less than the growth of German export trade. On the continent of Europe Great Britain had lost her monopoly before the rise of German competition. In any case Germany possessed obvious geographical advantages in central and eastern European markets. Certain British markets were invaded by German manufactured goods, but British textiles, machinery, iron and steel goods still found a good sale in Germany. As late as 1913, one half of the British exports to Germany consisted of manufactured goods. In 1911 the British export trade with Germany was slightly more valuable than the export trade with the United States, and only a little below the value of the export trade with India. The loss of the British export trade with Germany would have been as serious as the total exclusion of British goods from Canada and Australia. In the Far East German competition, which had caused great resentment at the end of the nineteenth century, was less severe than the competition of the United States and, on a lesser scale, the competition of Japan. Between 1905 and 1913 British trade with China was about four times as great as German trade, and it is clear from the trade statistics that Great Britain and Germany were not seriously impeding each other's activities at any point in the Far East.

In South and Central America, where the competition of the United States was also more severe than that of

Germany, there was no important displacement of British trade. Within the British Empire British predominance was overwhelming. Here was a rapidly increasing market in which Great Britain already had the advantage, if advantage there were, of a measure of imperial preference. In the shipping and shipbuilding industries, which were of vital importance to Great Britain as a reserve for the navy, there was again little reason for complaint or pessimism.

Finally it should be noticed that the German colonial enterprises which had been started in the Bismarckian age were disappointing from the commercial point of view. In 1911 the budgets of all the German colonies except Samoa and Togoland were subsidized from the Imperial Exchequer. The male German population of the colonies, excluding soldiers, officials, missionaries, and children, was only 8,679 in 1911.[1] Less than half of the total imports (£9,900,000) into the German colonies came from Germany, although these imports included a large quantity of government stores. Less than half of the exports—mainly raw materials—from the colonies went to Germany. Ballin noted on a visit to the East the contrast between the commercial character of Hong Kong and the military character of Kiao-Chau. If Great Britain felt the keenness of German economic competition, she could at least assure herself that she still led the way in the art of developing colonies. Germany might envy Great Britain the extent and riches of the British Empire; but Great Britain could have no desire to go to war to acquire any of the German colonies.

Moreover, the trade statistics are in themselves a little misleading. It is not surprising to find that Germany, whose industrial development in 1870 had been far behind that of Great Britain, showed a far more spectacular pic-

---

[1] The figure is slightly less than 8,679; since this total includes officials, women, and children at Kiao-Chau. At the end of 1903 the number of Germans, including women and children, in the German African and Pacific colonies was 5,125, including 1,567 officials and members of the colonial forces.

ture of expanding trade in the last quarter of the nineteenth century. In this earlier period of expansion a great many English firms were working too easily under monopolistic conditions; they were unprepared to meet and unable to resist young and energetic competitors. The German criticisms of English 'decadence', though expressed in supercilious terms, contained a great deal of truth. Great Britain in the last quarter of the nineteenth century suffered from the ease of wealth. The builders of the great commercial houses were dead; too many enterprises were in the hands of rich men's sons. Too many firms were content to follow a routine which had brought large profits in the past. Germany was a poor country. Her business men had to win a place for themselves. They were forced to develop a high technique of production and an equally high technique of selling goods. They were bound to study markets as well as the processes of manufacture. They had to establish a careful system of industrial education and commercial training. They were not burdened with expensive and out-of-date machinery and equipment.

In the twentieth century Germany lost many of these initial advantages; Germans were beginning to enjoy this dangerous ease of wealth. The standard of life, or rather the standard of expensive living, had risen. The sudden increase in wealth had upset the balance of German life. An English observer once noticed that champagne, or its German equivalent, was the most-advertised product in Germany. At the other end of the social scale the German working class was demanding a greater share in the new wealth. These demands, backed by strikes, could not always be resisted. They brought shorter hours, higher wages, and a greater expenditure on the luxuries desired by the lower middle classes. The task of the German manufacturer anxious to undersell his rivals was not made easier. On the other hand the sharp lesson of German competition had taught British manufacturers and business men that they must change their methods.

Great Britain still had the benefit of the high reputation of her goods and her merchants. She possessed ample resources for the re-equipment of her older industries and the foundation of new manufactures. She had a greater number of skilled artisans than Germany. Her geographical position was more favourable for the development of overseas trade. She was learning German methods. Her diplomatic and consular services were slowly giving up the old *laisser-faire* traditions. Her educational system was being remodelled and extended to provide technical training.

Whatever the reasons for the decreasing severity of German competition, or, from another point of view, the increasing power of British industry and commerce to meet this competition, British manufacturers and business men were fully convinced that there was room enough for Germany and England in the world, and that a war between the two countries, so far from benefiting British commerce, would impoverish Great Britain and ruin one of her best customers. The desire for peaceful relations may be seen in the trades journals, and not least in the journals of those industries most affected by German competition.[1] The German ambassadors in England never reported a feeling in favour of a mercantilist war.[2] As for the nation at large, the electorate returned in 1906 and again in 1910 a free-trade majority. The issues were

[1] Hoffmann, *op. cit.*, p. 278, quotes an article in the *Chemical Trades Journal* of 21 March 1908.

[2] For Hatzfeldt's views, see above, p. 25; for Metternich's views in 1900 see below, p. 65. Metternich's opinion on this point was unchanged twelve years later, see pp. 198 and 364. For Stumm's views, see below, p. 171. Eckardstein, Bernstorff, and Kühlmann were at different times chargés d'affaires at the London Embassy. None of them believed that trade rivalry would lead Great Britain to attack Germany. It is curious that in 1907 the Emperor himself agreed that commercial jealousy was not the cause of English mistrust of Germany. Metternich reported a conversation in which he had agreed with Balfour that English commercial classes wanted peace and stability, and that Great Britain was in alliance with one of her most important trade competitors—Japan—and on excellent terms with her greatest competitor—the United States. The Emperor's comment was 'Quite right' (D.G.P. xxi, pt. ii. 470-5).

no clearer than usual at these elections; the fiscal argument was beyond the comprehension of most of the electors, but even the doubtful acceptance of a protectionist programme wrecked the electoral chances of the Conservative party. The adoption of protective tariffs by Great Britain, and the formation of an imperial customs union might have had a serious effect upon German trade; a protectionist Germany could hardly have described these measures as acts of war. One might indeed counter the view that Great Britain, driven to desperation by German commercial competition, would declare war on Germany. It might be said that many Germans envisaged a 'trade' war in German interests. At the close of the nineteenth century Germany imported large quantities of raw material and foodstuffs. Nearly a quarter of her increasing population was living on imported corn. A number of German economists feared the exclusion of German trade from the 'closed areas' of the Great Powers. These writers were thinking not merely of the possibility of a British Zollverein but of areas more important from the point of view of food supplies, i.e. Russia and the United States. They envisaged a new mercantilist age, and found a way of escape only in the creation of a large central European Zollverein comparable in size and bargaining power with these other important units, together with the acquisition of richer and more fertile colonies.[1] These facts might justify the building of the German fleet; but in this case the argument in favour of a powerful fleet was not based upon defence against British attack, and still less upon the prospective ruin of British commerce and industry through German competition. The fleet would be necessary to give effective force to German demands, not to resist British aggression.

The economic arguments of a mercantilist kind by which the German people were warned of the danger

[1] See, *passim, Handels- und Machtpolitik*, 2 vols. 1900, by a number of university professors and others.

of an attack on their trade did not have a genuine ring about them in English ears. On the other hand, the widely advertised purpose of the German fleet as a means of pressure upon England could not escape notice. The announcement of the German naval programme and the passing of the Navy Law in 1900 were unlikely to have any sudden effect upon public opinion in England. The wave of anti-English feeling which swept over Germany at the time of the Boer War was of greater immediate importance thàn either of the Navy Laws in its effect upon Anglo-German relations. A Power which had long understood the importance of protecting sea-borne commerce found nothing aggressive in the German desire for a fleet. This fleet was pointed against England: its construction was based upon a theory which indirectly envisaged a check to British naval supremacy; but these facts demanded, at first, nothing more than an attitude of cautious expectation. In October 1899 *The Times* commented in a leading article that 'it would be ridiculous as well as futile to object' to the German naval plans. On the other hand, 'we can hardly be expected to welcome a policy on the part of Germany which, whenever we see it brought into action, may make a considerable addition to our naval estimates a necessity'.[1] A few weeks later, after Bülow's speech in the Reichstag on the need for a strong German navy, *The Times* again made a comment showing that the 'danger zone' through which Germany had to pass might be indefinitely prolonged. 'Whatever our position may be at a given moment, we must be ready to make it still stronger, if other Sea Powers build more ships.'[2]

The passing of the Navy Law in 1900 brought similar comments. 'We not unnaturally regard the growing naval ambition of Germany with a certain feeling of genuine sympathy, which is, nevertheless, not unalloyed with concern. . . . Programmes are not always performances', but the Navy Law might have an important effect upon the

---

[1] *The Times*, 30 October 1899.   [2] *The Times*, 12 December 1899.

development of the British navy.[1] Three days after the passing of the law of 1900 the Emperor sent a telegram of congratulation to the North German Lloyd Company: 'Forward with the work. . . . Then we shall be able to impose [*gebieten*] peace on the water as on the land.' The English press took little notice of this flamboyant threat. *The Times* remarked that it was 'unnecessary to attach extraordinary importance to an exchange of telegrams couched in the peculiar patriotic idiom of (Germany)'.[2]

During the next sixteen months there was little mention of German shipbuilding in *The Times*. No reference was made to the Emperor's speech at the Elbe regatta in June 1901 that the future of Germany lay on the water.[3] In September 1901, and again in November, Lord Brassey wrote long letters to *The Times* on the comparative naval strength of the maritime Powers. The German navy was not mentioned in these letters, though another correspondent wrote to point out the omission of 'the German fleet which is being built in rivalry of' England.[4]

At the end of October 1901 an article in *The Times* discussing the possibility of a change in British foreign policy contained an indirect reference to the development of German sea-power. The discussion arose out of an article in the *National Review*. The *National Review*, which represented the strongest anti-German currents in British journalism, thought that an Anglo-German understanding was impossible owing to the strength of feeling hostile to England among the upper and middle classes in Germany. Germany had come forward as a naval Power. 'The question inevitably presents itself whether . . . it is not wiser (for Great Britain) to look in other quarters for an arrangement on a common basis of

---

[1] *The Times*, 13 June 1900. See also Appendix II.

[2] *The Times*, 16 June 1900.

[3] 'Although we do not yet possess the navy we ought to possess, we have nevertheless fought for our place in the sun and won it. Our future is on the water. . . . As soon as the German has accustomed his eyes to a distant outlook he will lose that pettiness which is now and then apt to cling to him in his daily life.'   [4] *The Times*, 3 October 1901.

interest.' It is curious that Russia, and not France, was still the Power with which this 'arrangement' was contemplated. 'The naval predominance of Germany would not necessarily be to the advantage of any other European Power—perhaps, least of all, to that of Russia. The raw material for an Anglo-Russian agreement abounds.' *The Times* thought that an agreement with Russia 'would not hinder, to say the least, the revival of a better understanding between the French and ourselves'.[1]

There was no immediate sequel to this suggestion. Events in the East reversed the order of procedure. An Anglo-French understanding, undertaken by Great Britain partly as a form of reinsurance against the possible consequences of the Anglo-Japanese alliance preceded an Anglo-Russian understanding. It is important to notice that already the validity of the 'risk theory' was being undermined.

The German navy was, however, still in the background, as far as British public opinion was concerned. *The Times*'s review of the events of the year 1901 did not mention German naval construction or the German navy. At the end of January 1902 a certain note of alarm appeared. It was no longer prudent to think that the programme of the Navy Law might not be carried out. The Socialist paper *Vorwärts* had caused excitement by printing a confidential document from the German Admiralty foreshadowing an extension of the naval programme in 1904–5. There was some indignation in Germany that the Reichstag had been deceived in 1900 by the naval experts in their promises of finality. *The Times* thought that the charge of deceiving the Reichstag was unfair. No 'finality' was possible in naval programmes. Yet 'the recent and prospective expansion of the German navy' was 'a matter of very serious concern to this country.

---

[1] *The Times*, 29 October 1901. The suggestion was coldly received by the Russian press, but in January 1902 the *Novoe Vremya* pointed out that if Russia had to choose between Germany and England, the chances were greater that she would choose the friendship of England.

We cannot prevent it, if we would; we have no right even to resent it.' It was unnecessary, in spite of the views of the Pan-Germans, to assume that the German fleet was being built for use against England.[1] A few days later *The Times* spoke of the 'new aspects' of the question of British naval defence.[2] The German navy was mentioned in the House of Commons during the debate on the naval estimates. The First Lord said that the Admiralty was watching other countries, but that 'promises were not always performed'.[3] Ministers and the responsible sections of the Press were therefore tending to reassure public opinion in England, and at the same time to supply a slight undercurrent of warning about the future. There was no further reference to the steady growth of the German navy until August 1902. The warning was then a little sharper. 'Some of our rivals have worked with feverish activity . . . and they are steadily increasing their efforts. We cannot allow them to gain upon us without imperilling our all.'[4] No doubt remained about the change in the naval situation. 'Programmes' were becoming 'performances'; Germany was building her fleet with a 'characteristic continuity of purpose'.[5]

Moreover, in spite of Bülow's caution, the direct connexion between British and German naval construction was openly discussed at important meetings in Germany. At a congress of the National Liberal Party held at Eisenach in October 1902, Herr Bassermann, one of the prominent members of the party, used significant language about Anglo-German relations. 'We must keep cool, and until we have a strong fleet it would be a mistake to let ourselves be driven into a hostile policy towards England.' Early in 1902 the Emperor had presented to the Reichstag a table, drawn up by himself,

---

[1] *The Times*, 3 February 1902.   [3] Hansard, 4th ser. ciii. 974.

[2] *The Times*, 8 February 1902. On 21 February *The Times* mentioned the annual meeting of the German Navy League. The membership of the League had increased from 600,000 to 626,000; 3,300,000 copies of *Die Flotte*, the journal of the League, had been distributed during the year.

[4] *The Times*, 16 August 1902.   [5] *The Times*, 28 January 1903.

showing the comparative strength of the British and German navies. The table was intended for display in the central lobby of the Reichstag building.

One of the first results of the realization of the German programme was a change in the general disposition of the British fleet and the construction of a new naval base on the North Sea coast. The official announcement of the choice of Rosyth was made in March 1903. The decision to construct a new naval base was not wholly due to the growth of the German navy. The British fleet was outgrowing its establishments before the passing of the first and second German Navy Laws. Goschen set up a committee in 1900 to consider 'present and prospective accommodation for ships in H.M.'s Dockyards and the use of harbours and other anchorages and waters'. This committee reported in 1902 that a new naval base was necessary because the existing ports would soon be unable to accommodate the ships of the fleet. The Firth of Forth was chosen as the most suitable site for the new base.[1] Whatever the reasons for the decision, the significance of the step was realized in Germany. If there were a concentration of the British battle-fleet in the North Sea the 'risk theory' would cease to apply, or at all events, would lose a good deal of its importance. The *Grenzbote*, of Leipzig, had already made the curious comment that the German fleet could not be a menace to England, while the creation of a British North Sea squadron would be a serious menace 'not to Germany alone', and would 'compel other Powers to think of a coalition'.[2] Within a fortnight of this singular forecast, M. Cambon had made a friendly speech upon Anglo-French relations and the correspondent of *The Times* in Paris had pointed to the first stages of a 'striking evolution of public feeling towards England', coincident with a similar movement in England towards France. 'With a little goodwill on the part of diplomacy and the Press of the two countries

[1] Hansard, 4th ser. cxviii. 1551–2; 5 March 1903.
[2] *The Times*, 24 February 1903.

we shall, perhaps, not have so long to wait for an Anglo-French entente . . . as a few incorrigible sceptics may be inclined to think.'[1]

Towards the end of September 1903 the first of the two home fleets laid down under the Navy Law of 1900 was constituted on a 'permanently active' basis, and concentrated in home waters for immediate action. On 28 September *The Times* published a leading article on the growth of the German navy. The German plan need not be regarded as a fixed resolve to challenge British naval supremacy, but as an attempt to play the part of the Irish party in the House of Commons. It was, however, doubtful whether Germany could afford to be equally strong on land and on sea. In any case 'a great many things may happen' before pan-German ambitions could be satisfied; but Great Britain 'must recognize that the balance of naval power is changing, and it is not changing to our advantage'. One of the results of this change would be to deprive the 'two-Power standard', adopted primarily in relation to the fleets of France and Russia, of its usefulness as a suitable measure of British naval requirements.[2] The true measure of security would be found only in a fleet strong enough to meet 'all reasonably probable contingencies of international conflict'. This formula was 'more scientific and elastic' than the two-Power standard, and more acceptable 'because it enabled Great Britain to take due account of the mutual friendship now so happily re-established between this country and France'.[3]

[1] *The Times*, 6 March 1903. On 11 March a leading article in *The Times* mentioned the 'hope of a real rapprochement' with France.
[2] For the history of the two-Power standard, see Appendix II.
[3] *The Times*, 25 November 1903.

II

GERMANY AS A NEIGHBOUR, 1898–1903

IF one observes the attitude of public opinion in Great
Britain towards the German navy in the months immediately before the announcement of the Anglo-French
Agreement, it is difficult to avoid a conclusion which
seems a little illogical and inconsistent. On the one hand
there was a certain anxiety about the development of the
German navy. This anxiety was not as yet very serious. It
was tempered by the fact that, in spite of the declaration
made in 1900 about the ultimate purpose of the German
fleet, a good many years must pass before this fleet
could be regarded as a dangerous challenge to British
sea-power. The existence of a German battle-fleet in the
North Sea had already produced a change in English
naval policy and was soon to cause an important redistribution of British squadrons,[1] but the Admiralty appeared
to be acting in a slow and leisurely way. It was not
thought necessary to press forward with the development
of Rosyth. The taxpayers' pockets were hardly affected
by the German programme, and German construction
was scarcely ever mentioned in parliamentary debates
upon the British naval estimates or upon the comparative
strength of the naval powers. *The Times*[2] expressed the
general feeling in England that the German fleet was
certainly an inconvenience, and might become a danger,
but that Great Britain had not the least right to object
to the growth of this fleet. German overseas commerce
had grown; it was not unreasonable that Germany should
wish to protect this commerce in the usual way. The
existence of a battle-fleet to support German cruisers and
other commerce-destroying craft was taken as natural
and inevitable by a great sea Power. The idea of a preventive war to sink the German fleet before it should

---

[1] See below, pp. 84–5.   [2] See above, *passim*.

become too powerful was not seriously considered in Great Britain. There was even less desire to go to war in order to destroy German commerce and sink the German mercantile marine.

On the other hand, there was a deep and widespread distrust of German aims in England, and a growing belief that Germany would be at least a *tertius gaudens* if Great Britain and the British Empire should meet with disaster. It was also thought that Germany was an extremely difficult neighbour, and that any attempt at friendly collaboration in matters of common interest was difficult, if not impossible. This distrust played an important part in determining the attitude of British opinion towards the German navy in the years following the Anglo-French agreement. Upon what grounds was it based? By what events was it fostered?

The violence of Anglophobe sentiment in Germany at the time of the Boer War surprised English opinion, although the outburst of feeling at the time of the Jameson raid had shown that German sympathies would certainly not be on the English side. It is impossible in this context to discuss the rightness or wrongness of the judgement of continental Europe upon the political morality, if such a term may be used, of British action in South Africa. It is clear, and was clear at the time, that no one of the continental Powers had reason, in view of its own past history, to take up a position of moral superiority or to claim that its own actions in Africa or Asia were ruled by loftier motives. There was indeed a distinction drawn between attacks on nations of European ancestry and attacks upon decadent Oriental kingdoms, or semi-organized native races; but these subtler refinements of imperialist morality were not very logical. In any case criticism of the fact that Great Britain was attempting to suppress by force the liberties of two small republics was a different thing from criticism, based upon false or distorted news, of the manner in which the war was being fought. This type of criticism again was different from mere abuse of the

British army and the Sovereign of Great Britain. The German newspapers were extremely bitter in their judgement of the issue between Great Britain and the Boers. No effort was made to understand the British standpoint.[1] In February 1902, when the tone of the German press was changing as a result of British victories, Conan Doyle wrote to *The Times* that no German publishing firm would bring out under its own name even a moderate statement of the British case, although all the expenses of publication were guaranteed.[2] From first to last the attitude of the German press towards the British army was insulting. The terms 'mercenaries' and 'hirelings' were in daily use. These terms, with an additional variant, 'the scum of society', were employed at a meeting in Berlin at which the well-known scholar Gierke was present. Six hundred and eighty Lutheran clergy signed a protest in which it was stated that the British army put Boer women and children in front of the firing line.[3] The German comic papers printed obscene cartoons attacking Queen Victoria and the British Royal Family. A work published by a reputable firm, and containing contributions from well-known German writers, included a picture of Queen Victoria, with the Princess of Wales, and other Princesses of the Royal Family, presenting the Victoria Cross to a young soldier of thirteen because he had outraged eight Boer women.[4] These filthy slanders were deeply resented in England. Similar indecencies were, for a time, on

[1] Early in January 1902 a deputy was called to order in the Reichstag for describing Chamberlain as 'the most accursed scoundrel (*der verruchteste Bube*) on God's earth', and the British army as 'in great part a pack of thieves and brigands'. A few days later this deputy had received 311 telegrams approving his language (*The Times*, 11 and 15 January 1902).

[2] *The Times*, 4 February 1902.

[3] The *Kölnische Zeitung* protested against this action of the Lutheran clergy, though this journal spoke of the contrast between 'English mercenaries who serve for money, and the German nation in arms'.

[4] *Der Burenkrieg*, p. 24 (Albert Langen, *Verlag für Litteratur und Kunst*, Munich). This work also contained a cartoon of the Prince of Wales in a drunken sleep (p. 30). A collection of specimens of Anglophobe literature was made in 1902 by The Athenaeum.

public sale in France; but it was well known in England
that the German press was far more under official control than the French press. Any libel on the German
army or the German Imperial family would have been
suppressed at once, with severe punishment for its authors.
Yet the most offensive attacks upon Queen Victoria and
the British army were on sale at the bookstalls of the German state railways. Bülow indeed gave instructions that
the newspapers should not be too triumphant over English
reverses. 'Too obvious a display of satisfaction would turn
English feeling against us, and Germany cannot yet meet
England at sea.'[1] These mild precautionary suggestions
had little effect.

Within a short time, however, the German press began
to take alarm at the effects of its own violence. As early
as March 1900 the *Post* acknowledged that in attacks upon
England 'the German press is an easy first in point of
brutality, while it must no doubt leave the palm to the
French for diabolical malice'. In July 1902 the *Kölnische
Zeitung* wrote that 'looking at back numbers of the comic,
journals we are shocked at their coarseness'.[2] Two months
earlier the *Nationale Zeitung* had printed a favourable review
of Conan Doyle's book,[3] and admitted the humanity of
British methods. About the same time, Baron Richthofen, the Secretary of State for Foreign Affairs,[4] had

---

[1] D.G.P. xv. 414 n.: 31 October 1899.

[2] At the outbreak of the Herero rebellion in 1904 the *Kölnische Zeitung* was
afraid that 'England would pay the Germans back in the coin of the overwhelming malice with which they had passed their verdicts upon British
mistakes'. The payment was not made, but *The Times* called attention to
the fact that General von Trotha set a 'regular tariff' on the heads of rebels,
'a proceeding which Germans, we trust, will repudiate with the shame and
indignation that would be felt by other civilised nations, did their soldiers
stoop to such methods of barbarism' (*The Times*, 22 May 1905). Trotha's
proclamation was condemned in Germany and withdrawn. *The Times* also
noticed that the mortality among Herero prisoners in German concentration camps during the months of February, March, and April 1905 was at
the rate of 750 per 1,000 per annum (*The Times*, 22 August 1905).

[3] *The War in South Africa; its cause and conduct.*

[4] Richthofen succeeded Bülow as Foreign Secretary when Bülow took
Hohenlohe's place as Chancellor in 1900.

acknowledged the excellence of the treatment given by the British to their prisoners. Yet the apologies were at times scarcely less offensive than the attacks. The *Kreuz-Zeitung*, for example, in making some apology for criticisms exceeding the bounds of 'prudent hostility', explained that these criticisms were due to reasons of which Germans need not be ashamed. The journal went on to balance the items of profit which had accrued to Germany from her neutrality. *The Times* thought that the balance sheet came near to 'a confession of blackmailing'.[1]

Moreover, this change of tone followed the turn in the fortunes of war. A similar change of attitude and language had been noticed in the German press at the time of the Spanish-American War. British observers thought that the German Government allowed the attacks in order to stimulate enthusiasm for the fleet. In any case the outburst of hostility had shown that not merely the Junkers but also the industrial and commercial classes, and even the lower middle classes and the Social Democrats were strongly Anglophobe. This hostility, combined with a carefully directed zeal for the navy, was a factor with which British statesmen would henceforward have to reckon. Even the *Kölnische Zeitung*, which, in spite of its remarks about English 'mercenaries, serving for money', had never followed the scurrility of less responsible papers, had advised the 'German Michael to clench his fist in his pocket, go on building ships, and trust in the German God'.[2]

At the end of the war *The Times* summed up the 'average' English view in two sentences. 'The task of

[1] *The Times*, 5 June 1902. Before the surrender of Cronje at Paardeburg the *Kölnische Zeitung* had remarked that Germany was 'keeping her hands free' in case 'the Boers, by protracting the war, cause England serious difficulties in international politics'. At a meeting of the Seniors of the Berlin merchants, it was said that contracts and orders amounting to thousands of millions of marks in Great Britain and the British Empire were among the 'losses' caused by the attitude of the German press (*The Times*, 9 May 1902).

[2] The *Kölnische Zeitung* was frequently used by the German Foreign Office to express the views of the Government. Bismarck once said that this newspaper was 'worth an army corps on the Rhine'.

dealing with the attitude of German national feeling towards England will often occupy the pen of historians in years to come, nor is the practical significance of the subject by any means exhausted. And there are strong grounds for believing that British statesmen will now remain alive, as they have never been before, to the meaning of this factor.'[1]

Englishmen were not unreasonable in looking for some connexion between the German naval programme, the anti-English press campaign, and the pan-German movement.[2] The pan-Germans were so extreme in their views and demands that public opinion in England did not take them too seriously. At the same time the pan-Germans were never whole-heartedly disavowed. Their propaganda was useful, and the more useful because it made Germans, and foreigners, familiar with plans which might seem less preposterous if they were insisted upon year in year out. Moreover, the demands of the German Government would seem moderate by the side of pan-German extravagance. Halle's *Volks- und Seewirthschaft* may be taken as an example of the difficulty of distinguishing between the real aims of German policy and these unofficial extravagances.[3] Halle had suggested that Germany should absorb the Dutch colonies and put economic pressure upon Holland to accept a military and naval convention binding the Dutch to join Germany in case of war, and to include their country in the German defence scheme. Halle was a professor at the University of Berlin; his book was dedicated to Tirpitz and published by the official publishing house of the German General Staff and the War and Naval departments. The theme

---

[1] *The Times*, 3 June 1902. See also Swabach, *op. cit.*, p. 61.

[2] For the literature of pan-Germanism, see *German Ambitions as they affect Britain and the United States*, 'Vigilans sed Aequus', 1903. (The author of this work was W. T. Arnold.) O. Nippold, *Der deutsche Chauvinismus*, 1913; M. S. Wertheimer, *The Pan-German League, 1890–1914.*

[3] E. von Halle, *Volks- und Seewirthschaft*, 2 vols, 1902. Halle suggested that the South African question would have borne a different aspect if Holland had joined the German Zollverein two generations earlier.

of a close alliance with Holland, enforced by a threat to divert German trade from the Rhine to the Ems, was familiar to all readers of pan-German literature. The Rhine was not merely important for commercial reasons, but as a 'sally-port' (*Ausfallsthür*) against England. The *Norddeutsche Allgemeine Zeitung* once printed a reference to the plan which had appeared in an obscure paper; the quotation was noticed in *The Times* with the comment that Bismarck had often tested public opinion by quoting articles from obscure newspapers.[1] The German penetration of Rotterdam and, for that matter, Antwerp, was proceeding quietly and systematically. According to an investigation undertaken by the staff of the *Phare de la Loire* in 1905, one-fifth of the members of the Chamber of Commerce of Antwerp were Germans. The President was German, the Vice-President a naturalized German. Eight of the committees had German chairmen; three others had German vice-chairmen. The President, Vice-President, and four out of fourteen administrators of the Central Bank were Germans. The Germans were gradually securing a foothold in all large industrial and commercial concerns, and preparing for the absorption of the Belgian Congo. Similar facts were alleged about German control in Rotterdam. It was said in 1902 that in Switzerland, where the pan-Germans were particularly active, one-third of the inhabitants of Bâle and one-quarter of the inhabitants of Zurich were German, and that the press in the German-speaking districts of Switzerland was almost entirely under German control.

During the Boer War the attitude of the German Government was correct, if a little frigid and persistent in pressing German claims. The German Emperor was criticized in his own country for his long stay in England

---

[1] *The Times*, 16 February 1900. Bismarck's successors also used this method. The fact was generally known, and is mentioned, for example, in the article on the German press in vol. xxxi of the tenth edition (1902), and in vol. xix of the eleventh edition (1910) of the *Encyclopaedia Britannica*. For a short note on the most important German newspapers, see O. J. Hale, *Germany and the Diplomatic Revolution*.

at the time of the death of Queen Victoria.[1] It might have been possible to distinguish between the official policy of Germany and the outburst of anger among a people without much training in political tact. Yet before the formation of the Anglo-French agreement two attempts to secure a political agreement with Germany had failed. The suggestions made by Chamberlain had not been accepted by Germany;[2] the revival of the subject came from Germany, but the attitude of German opinion, the disillusionment of Chamberlain, and the caution of Salisbury now made it unlikely that Great Britain would bind herself to defend German continental interests. The Emperor, rightly or wrongly, would be content with nothing less than a formal, parliamentary treaty of adhesion to the Triple Alliance. The German Government believed that, sooner or later, Great Britain would be forced to accept these terms.[3] This view took little account of the circumstances. It might be true that England would only find allies at a price, but events were to show that the friendship of other Powers could be obtained on easier conditions. England had much to offer, and English support was worth obtaining. If Great Britain and Germany did not draw together, events would tend to separate them, and ultimately to separate

---

[1] A curious piece of doggerel verse written by one J. Rhoades, and printed in *The Times* of 6 February 1901, shows the effect of this visit upon English opinion, as far as the Emperor's own popularity was concerned.

'Farewell, Sir, mists between us may have been,
But this salt mist that doth the eyelids wet,
Your English tears for love of England's Queen,
England will not forget.'

[2] See above, pp. 39 and 40. Holstein, in particular, held this view.

[3] It is interesting once more to notice that, while Bülow and Holstein thought that time was on Germany's side, the British Foreign Office was taking a different view. In the memorandum quoted above (p. 40) Bertie wrote that the position of Germany in Europe was 'dangerous'. She was 'surrounded by Governments who distrust her and peoples who dislike or at all events do not like her'. An Anglo-French understanding would make the German position 'critical'. Bertie was merely stating his own opinion, but his statement shows that Germany was losing her 'bargaining power' at the time when Bülow supposed that this 'bargaining power' was increasing.

them for good and all. There was, however, a chance that co-operation in matters where English and German interests appeared to be in harmony might lead to closer general agreement. This co-operation actually occurred in two different spheres. In each case the result was unhappy, and the friction between the two countries increased rather than diminished.

The first of these two occasions for joint action was the Boxer rebellion in China. This rebellion moved the Emperor to use language which the German Foreign Office tried, too late, to keep from publication, and gave him the chance to secure the appointment of a German commander-in-chief for the land forces employed in the joint expedition of the Powers. Count von Waldersee was still in Germany when the legations in Pekin were relieved, and on his late arrival in China the situation needed a lighter hand. British officers disliked Waldersee's unnecessary punitive expeditions, and thought that the methods of 'German militarism' were out of place in the treatment of an Oriental people. The enormous demands for money (including £165,000 for German cables and £220,000 for strengthening the defences of Kiao-Chau which had not even been threatened by the rebels), and Waldersee's deliberate neglect of the British and French officers under his command, made a bad impression in England. The refusal of the Germans to treat British railway interests with proper consideration, especially in relation to Russian claims, led to open complaints. *The Times* commented most unfavourably upon Waldersee's 'vindictive punishment of innocent Chinese who had submitted to terms which our own and other commanders judged sufficient to ensure the safety of their troops', and upon the confiscation of the magnificent bronze astronomical instruments belonging to the Imperial Observatory at Pekin.[1] 'Under no circumstances whatever, where our

---

[1] The removal of fifty-six cases of these instruments, and foreign comment upon the fact, caused strong feeling in Germany. The French troops had also taken away some instruments, but had returned them. The German

interests and those of Russia come into conflict, can we expect the slightest real support from the "honest brokers" in Berlin. This is a conclusion which might have been reached long ago by observant Englishmen. Our Chinese experiences merely confirm it.'[1]

Towards the end of the year 1902 Great Britain co-operated with Germany in putting pressure upon the Government of Venezuela. The question was relatively unimportant; it concerned the common troubles of small American states—the denial of justice to foreign merchants and the payment of outstanding debts to foreign creditors. The German admiral with whom the British ships were collaborating went far beyond the instructions given to the British commander, and came within danger of involving his country in war with the United States. The mere fact of common action with Germany caused disquiet in England; public opinion had not forgotten the flood of abuse in the early days of the Boer War. *The Times* published a poem by Kipling in which joint action with Germany was described as an insult to our own dead after German 'mocking'. Kipling used the terms 'the Goth and the shameless Hun', and called Germany the 'open, foe' of England. *The Times* protested against the words 'open foe', but said that English public opinion disliked taking steps which brought Great Britain into disagreement with the United States, and 'in alliance with the government of a people who for years past have made no pretence of friendliness towards us'.[2] On 26 January 1903 *The Times* strongly disapproved of the German bombardment of Venezuelan forts while negotiations were in

Government announced that it had offered to give back the fifty-six cases, but that the Chinese government had refused the offer owing to the 'inconvenience and difficulty' which the return of the instruments would have caused. Bülow stated in March 1902 that the Empress would be 'distinctly offended if the instruments were returned to her, and that they must be put in the category of presents from government to government long customary in China!' Bülow added that the return would have had a serious effect upon German prestige in China.

[1] *The Times*, 1 and 17 May, 26 August, 31 October, 4 November 1901, and *passim* during this period.   [2] *The Times*, 22 December 1902.

progress in Washington. During the debate upon the Venezuelan question in Parliament in March 1903, *The Times* pointed out that Lansdowne did not see the real objection to co-operation with Germany. This objection was based upon something more than resentment at German abuse of Great Britain during the Boer War. The 'universal abuse' of the German press had perhaps been a good thing because it had opened English eyes to the general trend of German policy, and had shown Englishmen that Germans regarded the British Empire as 'an obstacle to be got rid of, or at least reduced, by whatever means may offer'.[1]

The Times was, as a rule, less direct and outspoken in its judgement of German aims. There was a certain feeling that in acting with Germany on the Venezuelan question, Great Britain was playing into German hands, and furthering German schemes for the colonization of large areas in South America. The Hanseatic Colonial Society had already published an ethnographical map marking a part of Brazil as German. The general attitude taken up towards Germany was more clearly expressed in an article dealing with the proposed visit of the German Emperor to England in November 1902.[2] *The Times* wrote that the Emperor was personally welcome in England, but that

'no complaisance can describe the attitude of Germany towards this country as friendly. . . . We shall hope to live on good terms with Germany, and shall try to bear in mind that the brusquerie of her diplomatic methods is experienced by others as well as by ourselves. But the easy-going, indolent, confidence into which we are too ready to lapse must be held out of place in dealing with a Power whose readiness to wound has been so clearly shewn, and whose patient watchfulness to seize upon every advantage, great or small, will not be relaxed in return for any amount of complaisance on our part.'[3]

---

[1] *The Times*, 3 March 1903.

[2] The *Zeit*, of Vienna, wrote that the Emperor would risk his popularity in Germany if he paid another long visit to England.

[3] *The Times*, 8 November 1902.

It may be noticed that there is no mention of any fundamental subject of disagreement, no hint at any danger of war, no reference to the German naval programme. The complaints of *The Times* were little more—though they were something more—than complaints at the exuberance of a people inclined to make great efforts to snatch small profits, and not specially gifted with tact or grace of expression. The *Frankfurter Zeitung* put the case three months later with a directness more common to south German liberals than to north German nationalist journals. 'Thirty years after Sedan we are still looked upon as a parvenu with the characteristics of an intruder. Wherever anything is going on in the world, we want to be "in it". If two millstones are grinding against each other, we should like to have our fingers between them. Whenever a sunbeam falls, we want to be there in order to warm ourselves.'[1]

Two other statements of opinion by Germans show a certain uneasiness at the methods employed by the German Government in dealing with England. Metternich,[2] who succeeded Hatzfeldt as Ambassador in London in 1901, and was chargé d'affaires for some time during Hatzfeldt's illness, wrote two long letters to Bülow from London in 1900. He stated as his considered judgement that an Anglo-French or an Anglo-Russian understanding were improbable, but that England had no aggressive plans against Germany, and no desire to destroy the German navy or German commerce. 'English capital is too strongly interested in Germany to want any diminution of German prosperity, and England would not think it worth while to take upon herself the undying enmity of Germany. . . . I cannot see why the English should think it any advantage for themselves if Europe were in flames. They do very well with things as they are.' Metternich also pointed out the danger of treating English demands

---

[1] Quoted in *The Times* of 28 January 1903.
[2] Count Paul von Wolff-Metternich (b. 1853, d. 1934) had served as Second and First Secretary at the German Embassy in London before 1896.

and interests with less consideration than the interests or wishes of Russia. 'A good deal of ill-humour would have been avoided in the last ten years if we had asked ourselves more often the question: would you treat Russia as you are now treating England?'[1]

Two years later Lichnowsky[2] again pointed out the danger of treating England with roughness. 'It is a mistake to embark upon irritated polemics with (Great Britain); one always strengthens the party one desires to weaken, and the only result is to produce a feeling of very strong dislike which is not without influence upon the attitude of the Foreign Office.'[3]

[1] D.G.P. xvii. 3–14. Metternich pointed out that as far as the two peoples were concerned, there was 'very much more good will in England towards Germany than in Germany towards England'.

[2] Prince Carl Max von Lichnowsky, who was German Ambassador in London from 1912 to 1914, was at this time an official in the German Foreign Office.

[3] D.G.P. xvii. 205: 17 February 1902.

III

THE 'DIPLOMATIC REVOLUTION', 1904

EARLY in the year 1902, and only two months after the break-down of the negotiations between England and Germany on the question of a political understanding of a far-reaching kind, Great Britain and Japan signed a public treaty for the protection of their common and mutual interests in the Far East and the maintenance of the integrity of China and Korea.[1] If either party were attacked by a third Power, the other party would maintain a benevolent neutrality. If this third Power were joined by an ally, then the other party would pass from neutrality to war. The treaty was drawn up in general terms; it was likely that the third Power would be Russia, and that the ally of the third Power would therefore be France. A Franco-Russian communiqué also announced in general terms, that the Dual Alliance extended to eastern Asia; this announcement left no doubt that Great Britain was now pledged in certain circumstances to fight France.

This step had been taken by Great Britain and Japan after each Power had tried and failed to come to an agreement with Russia. In 1900, after separate negotiations with Russia had failed, Great Britain had concluded an agreement with Germany, at German suggestion, whereby the two Powers guaranteed the principle of the 'open door' in China, and the maintenance of the territorial integrity of the Chinese Empire. When Great Britain asked for German co-operation in preventing the advance of Russia in Manchuria, Bülow replied that the agreement did not

[1] Japan had been considering the possibility of an agreement with Russia on the basis of a free hand for Russia in Manchuria, and for Japan in Korea. The British offer was more desirable from the Japanese point of view. The treaty was renewed in 1905. The *casus foederis* was then extended to cover an attack by a single Power on either of the allies. The scope of the treaty was also extended to cover India, and the two Powers agreed to maintain the independence and territorial integrity of China, and the principle of the 'open door' in questions of foreign trade with China.

apply to Manchuria, and that Germany had not the slightest interest in the future of the country. Holstein admitted that the exception was made 'out of sheer goodwill for Russia'.[1] For this reason Great Britain turned to Japan. The abandonment of the policy of isolation was the result not of European but of Far Eastern complications. The German navy was not the determining factor in the change in policy, and Great Britain had obtained not a continental but a Far Eastern ally.

The Anglo-Japanese alliance made it desirable for Great Britain to come to a friendly understanding with France. One notices a curious repetition of the diplomatic situation with which Bismarck had been faced after 1879. Bismarck had been interested in coming to terms with Russia after he had undertaken obligations towards Austria in 1879 and later years. The Anglo-French understanding of 1904 is in some ways parallel to the conclusion of the League of the Three Emperors in 1881 or the Reinsurance Treaty of 1887. If Great Britain was on friendly terms with France, France would exercise control over Russia, and Russia would be less likely to disturb the *status quo* in the Far East, or at all events, less likely to obtain help from France in a policy directed against British or Japanese interests. The *casus foederis* of the Anglo-Japanese treaty would not come into being; the Russian danger would be met without a war.

There were other and obvious reasons for the conclusion of an Anglo-French agreement. The ground had been prepared by proposals, strongly favoured by the British Government, for a treaty of arbitration between the two countries. Lord Cromer, whose influence upon the British Cabinet was considerable, wanted to secure the British position in Egypt. Cromer looked at an agreement with France from this point of view, as Morley was later to consider the Anglo-Russian agreement from the point of view of the settlement of outstanding differences with Russia in the Middle East.

[1] D.G.P. xix, pt. i. 6: 12 July 1902.

Dislike and distrust of German policy also played its part. Here, in a settlement of differences with France, was a means of escape from the ever-recurring German demands, and the methods which made every small affair into a test of Anglo-German friendship on major issues. Here, again, was a settlement which saved Great Britain from the pressure which might be exercised by the German navy, if this navy were used as its designers proposed to use it. It would no longer be necessary for Great Britain to reckon the French navy among potentially hostile fleets.[1] The 'risk' theory had already begun to lose its validity.

It is impossible, in this context, to discuss the opportuneness of the Anglo-Japanese alliance and the Anglo-French agreement.[2] It may be said that the French

---

[1] For a reference by Mr. Balfour to the 'risk' theory, see Appendix II, p. 460.

[2] The Anglo-French agreement consisted of 'open' and 'secret' articles. In the 'open' clauses France promised 'not to obstruct the action of Great Britain in Egypt' by asking that a limit of time should be fixed for the British occupation of the country or by taking other steps contrary to the wishes of Great Britain, while Great Britain declared that she 'had no intention of altering the political status of Egypt'. A secret article provided that, if the British Government proposed to abolish the Capitulations in Egypt, the French Government would not object, on condition that France might make similar changes in Morocco. The open agreement stated that 'it appertains to France...as a Power whose dominions are conterminous for a great distance with those of Morocco, to preserve order in that country, and to provide assistance for the purpose of all administrative, economic, financial, and military reforms which it may require'. Great Britain would not obstruct action taken by France for this purpose, and France declared that she had no intention of altering the political status of Morocco. Neither in Egypt nor in Morocco would there be any inequality of customs dues, other taxes, or railway transport charges. A secret clause allowed a certain portion of Morocco to come within the influence of Spain if the Sultan should cease to exercise authority in this region. This clause implied that France, with the consent of Great Britain, might take the rest of Morocco. The clause was made public in 1911; it may have been known to Germany at an earlier date. Open clauses in the agreement settled the question of the Newfoundland fisheries, frontier demarcation in W. Africa, and minor questions in Siam, Madagascar, and the New Hebrides. The agreement contained no reference to European questions, no promise of mutual aid in case of war, and no military or naval conventions. The text of the agreement and the negotiations on the British side are printed in B.D.D. ii, c. xv, and on the French side in D.D.F. 2nd Ser. iv.

concessions to England in Egypt were worth far less than the British concessions to France in Morocco. Cromer wrote to Lansdowne on 21 January 1904 that 'the French concessions to us in Egypt are in reality far more valuable than those we are making to them in Morocco, and moreover they can hamper us greatly here, whereas if they choose they can carry out their Morocco policy without our help'.[1] Events were to show that this forecast was wrong. In the winter of 1903–4 neither Cromer nor the British Cabinet realized that the Moroccan agreement would lead to greater difficulties with Germany than any of the questions hitherto in dispute between the two countries.

It is a remarkable fact that none of the English critics of the agreement with France anticipated that the terms of this agreement would have a serious effect upon Anglo-German relations. The Foreign Office expected that Great Britain would be more able to resist German pressure in minor questions. No one suggested that the result would be an increase in the seriousness of naval competition. Lord Rosebery was one of the most outspoken critics of the agreement; he feared that Great Britain would find herself involved in difficulties with France. Rosebery did not anticipate, or at all events gave no sign that he anticipated, any dangerous results from the German side.[2] Rosebery came forward to defend Salisbury's policy of isolation. He objected to any kind of agreement binding Great Britain.

'These agreements have all had one special characteristic. They have all been extremely one-sided against Great Britain. There was the agreement about Samoa with Germany. There was the agreement about China with Germany. There was the agreement about Venezuela with Germany. I defy any advocate of the Government to say that these were not wholly one-

---

[1] B.D.D. ii. 340.

[2] On 1 March 1904 Grey had suggested that the negotiations with France might lead to a reduction of armaments. Grey did not mention the German navy. Hansard, 4th Ser. cxxx. 1404–8. The remark attributed to Rosebery in Mr. Lloyd George's *War Memoirs* i. 1, is not supported by contemporary written evidence.

sided agreements against this country. . . . I do not know that a friendly feeling has been produced in Germany by the considerable number of agreements that we have been able to conclude with her. . . . As to the last agreement with France, I am not less glad than you are that an agreement has been brought about with France, but no more one-sided agreement was ever concluded between two Powers at peace with each other. I hope and trust that the Power which holds Gibraltar may never have cause to regret having handed over Morocco to a great military Power.'[1]

The signature of the Anglo-French agreement was a turning-point in the diplomatic history of modern Europe. Its importance cannot be exaggerated. It was bound to affect the question of Anglo-German naval rivalry. What was the attitude of Germany towards the agreement? A few years earlier the German Foreign Office did not think that there was much chance of an Anglo-French rapprochement. There had indeed been warning notes. As early as June 1900, Hatzfeldt had written to Hohenlohe that France and England might come to an arrangement over Morocco. The German fleet could not interfere, and Germany would have to be content with such compensation as she could get.[2] Bülow did not take this suggestion seriously. He mentioned it to Russia, mainly to frighten the Russian Government with the idea that the French might come to terms with England.[3] Eighteen months later Metternich telegraphed to the German Foreign Office that Chamberlain was discussing with the French ambassador the possibility of a general agreement

[1] Speech at a Liberal League meeting in Queen's Hall, 10 June 1904. The audience interrupted Rosebery's reference to the Anglo-French agreement with loud cheers. In a speech in the City on 9 March 1905 Rosebery again welcomed the agreement as good in itself, but regretted its terms. On 22 August 1904 *The Times* published a protest from Rosebery against the 'dangerous and needless concession' made to France. 'This unhappy agreement' was more likely 'to promote than to prevent' unfriendliness between the two nations. Rosebery dated his letter: Bicentenary of the occupation of Gibraltar. The Anglo-French agreement contained a clause that no fortifications were to be erected on the African coast in the neighbourhood of the Straits of Gibraltar.

[2] D.G.P. xvii. 315–16: 1 June 1900.   [3] D.G.P. xvii. 318–20.

on colonial questions.[1] Lansdowne himself mentioned the discussion to Metternich two or three days later but denied that any general settlement of colonial questions had been reached. The German Foreign Office was suspicious, but nearly eight months went by before Richthofen again mentioned to Eckardstein that Anglo-French negotiations appeared to be taking place on the Moroccan question; Eckardstein thought that British public opinion would not tolerate any arrangement over Morocco which endangered the security of Gibraltar.[2] Rumours of a Moroccan agreement appeared in the English press in February 1903, but were described by Lansdowne as 'apocryphal'.[3] Frequent reports of Franco-Spanish negotiations were reaching the German Foreign Office in September 1903, and on 26 November 1903 Lansdowne told Metternich that France, owing to her long Algerian frontier, must be allowed a 'preponderating influence in Morocco'.[4] After the visit of King Edward VII to Paris in May 1903, Eckardstein, who was acting as chargé d'affaires in London, was far more definite than in the previous autumn. He reported that, in his opinion, Anglo-French negotiations were again taking place for a general settlement of outstanding questions. An agreement extending to Russia was desired by French financiers; England would then share the burden of financing Russian loans.[5] Eckardstein's view was also held by Betzhold, an agent of the Rothschilds, but not by Bülow, Holstein, Metternich, or the German Ambassador at St. Petersburg.[6] Bülow summed up his views to the Emperor on 20 May 1903. He thought that the problem

[1] D.G.P. xvii. 342–3: 30 January 1902.

[2] D.G.P. xvii. 345–6: 25 September and 4 October 1902.

[3] D.G.P. xvii. 348–9.   [4] D.G.P. xvii. 362–3.

[5] D.G.P. xvii. 567–70: 10 May 1903. Bernstorff thought that British opinion would favour an 'English-French-American combination. There would be an atmosphere of "liberty" about this which would be extraordinarily pleasing to the English Philistine'. D.G.P. xvii. 576.

[6] D.G.P. xvii. 585–7: 18 May 1903. Holstein described an Anglo-French alliance as *Zukunftsmusik*: an impossibility until the idea of 'revanche' had been abandoned (D.G.P. xvii. 573: 30 March 1903).

of Tangier would be in the way of an Anglo-French understanding, and·that there were even greater obstacles in the way of an understanding with Russia. At the same time care must be taken not to alarm English sentiment on the question of the German navy.[1]

The completeness of the diplomatic revolution is even more striking if it is considered in connexion with the negotiations for the renewal of the Triple Alliance.[2] The third treaty of the Triple Alliance was renewed, without change, in 1897. Italy had wished for a reinsertion of the protocol that the alliance was not directed against England. This statement had appeared in the first treaty of the alliance (1882); it was left out of the second treaty (1887) because Great Britain had concluded the Mediterranean agreement with Italy and Austria.[3] In the third treaty the allies had made provision for the inclusion of Great Britain in the alliance. Germany would not agree to the reinsertion of the protocol in 1897 because the treaty would then be pointed against France and Russia, but Italy made an open declaration that 'friendship with England formed the indispensable complement to the Triple Alliance'.

The alliance was renewed before the announcement of the Anglo-French agreement; but Franco-Italian relations had already begun to improve. The long tariff war with France was closed by a commercial treaty in 1898. In 1899 France and Great Britain assured Italy that they recognized her predominant interests in Tripoli. In 1900 France and Italy settled the delimitation of their Red Sea possessions. Victor Emmanuel III, who succeeded Humbert in July 1900, was less friendly to Germany. The

---

[1] D.G.P. xvii. 588–60.

[2] The third treaty of the Triple Alliance was signed in 1891. Article xiv laid down that the treaty should be in force for six years, and that if it were not denounced a year before this term had been reached, it should remain in force for another six years. For the history of the Triple Alliance, see Pribram, *Secret Treaties of Austro-Hungary* (Eng. trans.), vol. ii, and (for text of the treaties), vol. i and J. V. Fuller, *Bismarck's Diplomacy at its Zenith*.

[3] For the Mediterranean agreements, see Pribram, *op. cit.*

Prime Minister, Zanardelli,[1] was an enemy of Austria, while the French Ambassador in Rome, M. Barère, did his utmost, if not to prevent any renewal of the Triple Alliance, at least to make its terms valueless to Germany. The Italians asked that a statement should appear in the preamble to the new treaty to the effect that Italy had agreed to nothing which might threaten France. The demand was refused on the ground that the alliance was purely defensive, and that any further statement to this effect was unnecessary, but the Italian Foreign Minister told the French Ambassador that France had nothing to fear from the Triple Alliance. The Italian Government even exchanged notes with the French Ambassador to the effect that either country would remain neutral if the other were attacked, or forced by direct provocation to declare war.[2]

The negotiations with Italy showed to Germany that Italian help might not be forthcoming in the event of war with France or England. The bearing of this fact upon the naval question was obvious. The naval position in the Mediterranean would be entirely changed if the Italian fleet would not fight France. The Anglo-French agreement made the position of Germany and Austria still weaker in relation to Italy. It was increasingly likely that Great Britain would be on the French side in case of war. If the 'strategic centre' of the British fleet ceased to be in the Mediterranean, 'the strongest sea power' could concentrate its fleet in the North Sea. This concentration destroyed one of the main supports of Tirpitz's 'risk theory'.

---

[1] Zanardelli became Prime Minister early in 1901. As a young man he had fought as a volunteer against Austria in 1848. He resigned in November 1903 and died in the following month.

[2] The naval agreement of 1913 between Italy, Austria, and Germany is hardly consistent with the terms of the notes to France. In May 1902 the Italians asked that the signature of the treaty might be postponed until the end of June in order that attack from the Opposition in the Chamber might be met by an assertion that the renewal of the treaty had not taken place. Germany and Austria agreed to this demand.

Finally, the Russo-Japanese War also affected the international position of Germany. Russian anger had been directed at first against Great Britain. It was felt that, without an English alliance, Japan would never have dared to go to war with Russia. England was opposed to Russia in the Near East, in China, and on the Indian frontier. In 1903 England reasserted her claim to maritime supremacy in the Persian Gulf.[1] The Russian public received most of its English news through Berlin, and therefore never heard the English side of any disputed question.[2] The result of this deliberate misrepresentation was 'a general and systematic boycott' of the British Embassy at the time of the outbreak of the war. On the night of 21–2 October 1904, the Russian Baltic fleet fired on British fishing trawlers in the North Sea. This 'Dogger Bank incident' nearly led to war between the two countries.[3] Even during this critical period Russian official policy was less hostile than Russian social opinion. The Dogger Bank affair was referred to an international commission which met in Paris. The Russians never believed in their own case. Baron Taube, one of the Russian representatives at the inquiry, has revealed the fact that his chief, Martens, refused to act as senior Russian legal representative because he did not wish to ruin his great reputation as an international lawyer.[4] While the commission was sitting, the chief of the Russian secret police outside Russia came to Taube to explain that the Russian defence was a fraud. Taube admits the fraud, and points out that the real question which interested the Russian Foreign Office throughout

[1] See below, p. 148.

[2] 'Speeches and answers in the House only arrive here in the form of telegraphic abstracts mangled in Berlin. The text is never printed. The Government . . . never inserts formal contradictions.' (Spring-Rice, *op. cit.* i. 403: March 1904.)

[3] The coaling of the Baltic fleet by Hamburg-Amerika liners also caused friction. Ballin had consulted the German Foreign Office on the question (Huldermann, *Ballin*, pp. 145–9). The coal came from South Wales. In British opinion France had also strained the meaning of neutrality.

[4] Taube, *La Politique russe d'avant guerre*, Paris, 1928, pp. 9–11.

the proceedings was Delcassé's wish to include Russia in the Anglo-French entente.[1]

Moreover, the Russian Government knew where it stood with regard to Great Britain. The position in relation to Germany was different. Russian official circles could remember that Germany had encouraged a forward policy by Russia in the Far East. It was not difficult to guess German motives; the humiliation brought by the failure of this Far Eastern policy caused Russian opinion to turn against Germany. Russian diplomatists naturally used different language to English and German listeners. They abused England to Germans; but they made no secret, in talking to Englishmen, of their resentment against Germany. Witte, who had opposed the Far Eastern schemes at least in Korea, told Spring-Rice in June 1905 that

'a continuance of the war meant the general paralysis of Russia as a civilized European Power. It meant also a free hand to Germany in western Europe. Without losing a man or spending a sou Germany had gained more in the last year than by all the sacrifices and victims of 1870. Russia had been forced to surrender to Germany's commercial demands. . . . He could not help believing that the whole policy of Germany for the last ten years had been directed towards the object of creating between Russia and Japan the same relations of permanent hostility as existed between France and Germany.'[2]

The German Emperor had done much to strengthen this resentment. He had used his personal influence to persuade the Tsar to carry out a crusade against the yellow races. He carried on a correspondence by letter and telegram with the Tsar which even Nicholas found embarrassing. The German Foreign Office had protested against this correspondence and yet found it a useful means of putting their views before the Russian Government.[3] The

---

[1] Taube, op. cit. pp. 29–30.

[2] B.D.D. iv. 77: 7 May 1905.

[3] D.G.P. xix, pt. i. 303 n. The letter in which the German Emperor wrote to the Tsar as the 'Admiral of the Atlantic to the Admiral of the Pacific' appears in this correspondence. See The Kaiser's Letters to the Tsar, ed. I. D. Levine, tr. N. F. Grant.

correspondence was not kept as secret as the German Emperor believed. Spring-Rice told Metternich in December 1904 that the German Foreign Office did not realize how indiscreet the Russians were about them in St. Petersburg. 'Every moment one hears that the German Emperor has given this or that piece of information or advice.'[1]

The German Government attempted to use the Dogger Bank affair to bring about a joint Russo-German action against England in which France would be invited to co-operate. The Russian Government had no wish to offend either France or Germany. The Russian Foreign Minister, Count Lamsdorff, took refuge in non-committal phrases. 'D'un côté, il faut avouer . . . mais, d'un autre, on ne peut ne pas reconnaître.'[2] The plan therefore came to nothing. The German Emperor had to resign himself to 'the first failure' which he had experienced.[3]

The Emperor made a second attempt. He met Nicholas at Björkö in July 1905, and brought with him the draft of the rejected Russo-German treaty. The Tsar was away from his Ministers.[4] He was easily persuaded by the Emperor to sign a treaty of mutual aid in case of attack upon Germany or Russia in Europe by a European Power. William II sent an exuberant account of the good work which, under God, he had been able to accomplish. Bülow and Holstein were less satisfied. Holstein remarked that 'with the Tsar in such a mood, surely something more might have been got from him'.[5] The limitation of the *casus foederis* to Europe seemed to destroy its value. Russia could be of no help to Germany in Europe. The Emperor explained that without the limitation Germany might find herself compelled to go to war with England

---

[1] D.G.P. xix, pt. ii. 371.
[2] Taube, *op. cit.* 47.   [3] D.G.P. xix, pt. i. 347.
[4] It should be noticed that the Emperor, Bülow, and Holstein deliberately aimed at committing the Tsar to an agreement at a time when he could not consult his Ministers. Holstein thought that the agreement would bring Russia no direct military advantage. D.G.P. xix, p. ii. 437.
[5] D.G.P. xix, pt. ii. 474.

over Afghanistan.[1] It is possible that Bülow merely intended to make a demonstration against the 'personal' policy of the Emperor. In any case the discussion was academic because the Russian Ministers realized at once the implications of the treaty. The Tsar's promise would have wrecked the Franco-Russian alliance, and therefore left Russia at the mercy of Germany. Nicholas was compelled to write to the German Emperor that his Ministers insisted upon adding to the treaty a declaration that its terms would not come into force in the case of a war with France. The whole fabric collapsed. The German Emperor, who now showed more foresight than his Ministers, pointed out that this safeguarding clause meant that Russia had decided to join France and Great Britain. If Germany were at war with Great Britain, France would seize the opportunity of attacking Germany. In order to anticipate a French attack Germany would have to declare war on France. The German strategical plans depended upon rapid action. Russia would then join France. 'The Coalition is *de facto* in existence.'[2]

Finally, the defeat of Russia in the Far East was likely to have one important result which would affect Ger-

---

[1] William II was clear-sighted enough to see that Russia could give no real help to Germany by a diversion on the Indian frontier in an Anglo-German war. 'As far as "pressure upon India" is concerned, this favourite catchword of diplomatic conversation and stock article in the diplomatic dispensaries for using compulsion against England is a complete illusion. . . . It is as good as impossible for a large army to undertake the invasion of India without enormous and year-long preparation and expense. . . . England would have ample time to have her countermeasures ready. . . . Even so, it is questionable whether the invading army would reach the frontier in a condition fit to attack.' (D.G.P. xix, pt. ii. 477.) Another point in the discussion is of interest. The Emperor assumed that, in the event of a British attack on Germany, the German army would invade Belgium. France would be offered territorial compensation, at Belgian expense, as a substitute for Alsace-Lorraine. Upon this plan Bülow commented: 'Your Majesty's remarks about Belgium hit the nail on the head. Only the Belgians must know nothing about it . . . or they will spend their great wealth on fortifications or give the French a hint in order that they make their plans for such an eventuality' (D.G.P. xix, pt. ii. 480).

[2] D.G.P. xix, pt. ii. 524–5: 26 November 1905, German Emperor to Bülow.

many. Russia was still a great Power. If she were diverted from the Far East she would return to a policy more in harmony with Russian traditions and Russian public opinion. In other words, Russia, driven from the Far East, would reopen the Near Eastern question. She would be less willing to allow an increase of Austrian influence in the Balkan peninsula. Germany was the ally of Austria-Hungary. Therefore Russian interests in the Near East would lead her to look for support against Germany and Austria-Hungary.

The full effect of the Russo-Japanese War was not understood at the time of the announcement of the Anglo-French agreement. The German Government had still to realize the measure of Russian estrangement. For the moment, however, the German Foreign Office was able to concentrate upon the new situation brought about by the Anglo-French entente. The open clauses of the agreement were shown to Germany before their publication. There had been no question of asking German consent. Obviously Germany would have withheld her consent. Germany did not want an Anglo-French understanding, and would have done everything in her power to prevent the conclusion of such an understanding. She would have put forward claims in Morocco which would have blocked an Anglo-French agreement on the question, and therefore prevented the settlement of other matters in which France was making concessions to Great Britain. If the Anglo-French agreement were worth making, it could only be made by secret consultation between the parties concerned. Germany herself had made, and was trying to make, similar agreements without consulting other Powers. German agreements also contained secret clauses. There might be reason for disquiet in Germany; there was no place for moral indignation.

The reception of the agreement in the German press was not hostile. The *Post* said that Germany did not intend to disturb Anglo-French negotiations over Egypt and Morocco; the *Berliner Neueste Nachrichten* mentioned that Germany was not opposed to French expansion in Africa.[1] The *Norddeutsche Allgemeine Zeitung*[2] did not think that German commercial interests would be endangered in Morocco; German as well as French trade would benefit from French action in securing stability and quiet in the country. Bülow announced in the Reichstag on 13 April 1904 that there was no reason to assume that the Anglo-French colonial agreement was directed against any other Power.... 'We have no cause to think that our interests in Morocco may be disregarded or injured by any Power.' A Pan-German Congress at the end of May demanded the acquisition of the Atlantic seaboard of Morocco by Germany, and described the Anglo-French agreement as a 'humiliation for Germany', but the demand was not supported in the press. The Emperor on a tour through the Rhineland, opened a new bridge at Mainz on 1 May 1904 with a reference to the usefulness of the bridge in time of war, and spoke at Carlsruhe of the possibility that Germany might have to intervene once more in *Weltpolitik*; but the Emperor's language had been discounted for years past. In November 1904, at the launching of a battleship, and in December, during a debate in the Reichstag, Bülow made speeches emphasizing the defensive character of the German navy, and pointing out that no nation had anything to gain by 'overthrowing its rivals'. Bülow had little credit left in England, and, as the Austrian press explained with some candour, his speeches were 'marred by overplausibility and a kind of *fausse bonhomie*'. *The Times* put the case more bluntly:

'It will need something more than his [Bülow's] honied assurances to remove or even to weaken the impression made in this

---

[1] These two journals always supported the naval plans of the Government and a 'strong' foreign policy.

[2] This newspaper, originally founded in order to 'place a blank sheet of paper in front of Prince Bismarck', was, in the Bülow era, less closely connected with the Government, but generally took the official view on matters of foreign policy.

country by the acts as well as the words of German statesmen and publicists throughout a long series of years. Only very simple folk forget that timely "anti-Machiavels", to use the Chancellor's historical phrase, form a recognized part of the Machiavellian system of *Realpolitik* which has been the ideal system of Prussia and of "Prussia-Germany" since Frederick II.'[1]

The distrust of Bülow's 'overplausibility' was well founded. The public speeches of the Chancellor gave little indication of the real views which he held and the policy which he was trying to carry out. The German Government had been quick to realize that the Anglo-French agreement might have serious consequences for the future of Morocco. Holstein summed up the position on 3 June 1904.

'Foreign commerce and foreign industry will be driven out of Morocco as out of all French colonies and protectorates. . . . In Morocco, as elsewhere, consideration will be given only to French subjects in railway and mining concessions and in all official business. Morocco is to-day one of the few countries in which Germany has a free field for her economic activities.'[2]

If the question had been kept within these limits, and if Germany had made a friendly approach to Great Britain about the economic future of Morocco, there is little doubt that attention would have been paid to her complaints. British commercial interests in Morocco were far greater than those of Germany, and the policy of the 'open door' was as important to Great Britain as to Germany. It was stated by the British Government that between 1899 and 1901 Great Britain provided 44·7 per cent., France 22·1 per cent., and Germany 11·6 per cent. of the annual imports into Morocco.[3] Great Britain had no interest in assisting France to shut out foreign

---

[1] *The Times*, 7 December 1904.

[2] D.G.P. xx, pt. i. 207.

[3] B.D.D. ii. 312. Owing to the difficulty of obtaining accurate statistics these figures must be taken with a certain caution, but there is no reason to doubt that they represent, roughly, the distribution of the Moroccan import trade.

enterprise from the development of a large and potentially rich country.[1]

From the first, however, the matter was not considered merely on its economic aspects by the German Foreign Office. It was regarded from the point of view of prestige. One may be permitted to ask whether this point of view was not mistaken. If the question were transferred from the solid ground of economic interest, where Great Britain and Germany could make common cause, to the dangerous and indefinite region of national honour, Germany was not in a strong position. If Germany directly attacked the Anglo-French agreement, then France and Great Britain would also consider the question from the point of view of general policy. France and Great Britain would resist any German attempt to destroy their entente. German action would be a justification of the entente. It would strengthen this entente, and transform it from an agreement upon outstanding questions made without consulting Germany but without any real threat to German interests into an alinement of two Powers against a third Power.

Germany was ready to take this risk. The moment seemed favourable for putting pressure upon France. Russia could be of no help, and France could hardly resist Germany on land without Russian help. In April 1904 Count Schlieffen, the Chief of the German General Staff from 1890 to 1905, had pointed out that 'if the necessity of a war with France should arise for us, the present moment would doubtless be favourable'.[2] A year later, in the summer of 1905, Schlieffen told his doctor, General Rochs, of the Army Medical Service, that he could only see one solution—'immediate war with France'. England had been weakened by the Boer War, Russia was at war with Japan, and had taken large numbers of troops from her western frontier. 'We could now deal with France, and we should be entirely justified in so

---

[1] This fact was realized by the German Foreign Office. D.G.P. xx, pt. i. 219.   [2] D.G.P. xix, pt. i. 175.

doing. If France were in our position, she would not hesitate one moment about falling on us.'[1]

It is asserted by some, and denied by other authorities, that Schlieffen influenced Holstein. Holstein used language in 1909 which might have been an elaboration of Schlieffen's argument. He admitted that he had been mistaken in thinking that England would never join France and Russia; he added: 'When this danger was clear before my eyes, I became convinced that, before the ring of the Great Powers enclosed us, we ought to try with all our might to break through the ring, and we must not shrink from the most extreme measures.' England was suffering from the effects of the Boer War, France was weakened by the consequences of the Dreyfus case—which had 'split' the army and the nation, and by the dispute with the Church on the question of the denunciation of the Concordat. The French army was not in a good condition, and France would be 'an easy prey'.

Whatever Holstein's views may have been after the event, the sudden weakness of Russia certainly influenced German statesmen as well as German soldiers. There was little danger in provoking France, and every chance that diplomatic pressure would compel the French Government to make concessions to Germany. The Anglo-French entente could hardly survive a public humiliation of France before Germany.

As early as April 1904 Lichnowsky had supported the suggestion that Germany should send a ship or ships to Morocco, and occupy Agadir or some other point before France had overrun the country. 'We need a success in our foreign policy because the Anglo-French understanding and the Italo-French rapprochement will be taken

---

[1] W. Kloster, *Der deutsche Generalstab und der Präventivkriegsgedanke*, pp. 40–2. There are very few documents of a military-political character of the Schlieffen period in D.G.P. The 'Schlieffen' plan of campaign which was used in 1914 was first drawn up between 1894 and 1899. It thus belongs to the same period as Tirpitz's 'risk' theory, although, in the form in which Schlieffen left it to the younger Moltke in 1905, it was adapted on the military side to meet the changed diplomatic situation.

generally as a defeat for us.'[1] Holstein also thought the question of prestige more serious than the risk to German commerce. 'If we let others trample on our feet in Morocco without a protest, we are encouraging a repetition of the act elsewhere.'[2] Even so, nothing was done until the end of the year. The dispatch of a French envoy to Fez, with a list of reforms demanded from the Sultan, at last brought German action. The action was still indirect. The Sultan was told that the French nationalist party did not want war with Morocco owing to the risk of taking troops from the eastern frontier of France, and that Germany had a political interest in Morocco which could not be measured by the amount of German trade. German and French interests were not identical. France had given no official notice to Germany about the reorganization in Morocco; therefore Germany had no reason to recognize French action. The Sultan became less subservient to France, but Germany took no further steps in his support.

One reason for delay was a sudden anxiety over the naval position. In June 1904 King Edward VII visited Kiel; the German Emperor, somewhat naïvely, paraded the German fleet for his inspection. The impression was deep and lasting; but ocular demonstration was not necessary to convince expert opinion in Great Britain that the programme of the Navy Law was being carried into effect. The Admiralty was already considering a redistribution and co-ordination of the fleet, the withdrawal of obsolete ships and the strengthening of the reserve. The new measures were announced in a memorandum published on 12 December 1904.[3] These measures were an answer

---

[1] D.G.P. xx, pt. i. 202–3: 5 and 13 April 1904.

[2] D.G.P. xx, pt. i. 207–9: 3 June 1904.

[3] Cd. 2335: Navy, Distribution and Mobilization of the Fleet. The paper is generally known as the Selborne memorandum. It was followed in March 1905 by a more detailed account of the reorganization of the fleet (Cd. 2430: Navy, Arrangements consequent on the redistribution of the fleet). The Dogger Bank incident had also shown the need for reorganization. The Channel fleet was at Gibraltar when this incident occurred. It was desirable, from a diplomatic point of view, to avoid any sudden and

to the new situation created by the growth of German sea-power. They increased the number of ships in Home waters. The old Home fleet had been merged in the Channel fleet in 1902. A new Channel fleet was formed of twelve battleships and a number of cruisers in full commission. Hitherto the ships in Home waters were always losing a percentage of their crews and taking on board young and untrained seamen. The Channel fleet would keep its crews intact throughout a period of two years' commission. An emergency squadron could now be provided without dislocating the schools or the nucleus crews or ordering a general mobilization. An Atlantic fleet would be stationed at Gibraltar, and a number of ships brought home from distant stations. The memorandum mentioned the 'changes in the strategical position all over the world arising out of the development of foreign navies'. The German navy was described as 'a navy of the most efficient type and . . . so fortunately circumstanced that it is able to concentrate almost the whole of its fleet at its home ports'.

The concern felt in Germany at the redistribution of the British fleet was increased by a vote in the French Chamber in favour of a large naval programme. Before the publication of the memorandum of December 1904 Captain Coerper, German naval attaché in London, had forwarded to his Government an article from *Vanity Fair* suggesting a preventive war against Germany.[1] Holstein told Bülow that he believed there was serious danger of attack.[2] On 13 December the German Ambassador in London was summoned to Berlin with other members of the embassy. The chances of a preventive war were discussed. The Ambassador and his civilian staff did not think that there was any likelihood of attack, though they explained that British opinion was becoming nervous novel concentration of ships at moments of international tension, when the concentration might appear as a threat of war.

[1] D.G.P. xix, pt. ii. 353–6. An article discussing a preventive war had also appeared in the *Army and Navy Gazette* of November 1904.

[2] D.G.P. xix, pt. ii. 358–9.

about the German fleet. Bernstorff, as chargé d'affaires, had written from London in April 1904 that in his opinion the building of the fleet and not the economic competition of Germany was the main cause of English ill feeling. American economic competition was equally severe, but was not producing anxiety.[1] Bülow summed up the situation in these words: 'Our whole relationship with England depends upon our getting through the next few years with patience and adroitness (Geduld und Spucke),[2] provoking no incidents and not giving the slightest ground for offence. Our position is like that of the Athenians when they had to build the Long Walls at the Piraeus without being hindered by the overmighty Spartans from completing their defences.' The Emperor commented: 'How often, my dear Bülow, have I used this example in the last ten years.'[3]

[1] D.G.P. xx, pt. i. 18: 16 April 1904.
[2] Bülow was probably thinking of the German proverb, 'Mit Geduld und Spucke fängt man manche Mucke'.
[3] D.G.P. xix, pt. ii. 373: December 1904. Swabach wrote to Rothschild that the talk about a preventive war was not taken seriously (besonders tragisch) by his (Swabach's) friends. Swabach, op. cit., p. 56.

IV

THE MOROCCAN QUESTION, 1905-6

As an example of 'patience and adroitness' the action taken by Bülow after his decision not to offend the 'overmighty Spartans' is difficult to understand. This action was the reverse of a policy 'provoking no incidents and not giving the slightest ground for offence'. It can only be explained by one of two hypotheses. Either it was mistaken, the result of confusion in the highest quarters in Germany, or it was based upon a confidence —which also proved to be mistaken—that the Anglo-French entente could be broken by resolute action. It is interesting to notice that the Emperor, although he allowed his hand to be forced, was doubtful about the expediency of the Chancellor's Moroccan policy.

The campaign was opened in March 1905 by an announcement that the Emperor intended to visit Tangier. The Emperor had not wished to visit Tangier, but it was pointed out to him that, once the announcement had appeared, any change of plan would look like a success for France.[1] On 31 March 1905 William II landed at Tangier, and made a speech in which he ignored French claims to a predominant position in Morocco, and announced that Germany would deal directly with the Sultan.

The Tangier visit had not explained German intentions. No one knew what Germany really wanted; so far from enlightening the Powers, Bülow warned the German Foreign Office that 'if the diplomats ask about Tangier and Morocco, please do not answer them, but keep a serious and impassive face. Our attitude on the question

---

[1] Nowak (*Das Dritte Kaiserreich*, ii. 293-5) states that Kühlmann, at this time German Minister at Tangier, drew up the announcement for the press. The publication was forbidden in the German newspapers, but Kühlmann had already approached *The Times* and the *Agence Havas*. Nowak gives no authority for his statement. Hale, *op. cit.*, p. 101, quotes Wolff's view (in *Das Vorspiel*) that the first suggestion came from the Tangier correspondent of the *Kölnische Zeitung*.

should be that of the sphinx, which, though surrounded by curious tourists, betrays nothing'.[1] The 'tourists' had reason to be curious. The Emperor had announced at Vigo, and again at Tangier, the disinterestedness of Germany. Germany asked for no Moroccan territory. This declaration tied Bülow's hands when France offered 'compensation', but did not make German motives any clearer. If Germany only wanted to safeguard her economic interests in Morocco, why this elaborate display? Why had no sign been given in the spring or summer of 1904 that Germany would not accept the Moroccan clauses of the Anglo-French agreement? Why should the German Foreign Office refuse to give any explanation of the Emperor's visit to Tangier? The most likely answer to these questions appeared to be that Germany wished to test, and to break, the Anglo-French entente. A statement of Bülow shows that this answer was not very wide of the mark and that the arguments which had affected Holstein also affected the Chancellor. Hammann, the Director of the Press Bureau of the Foreign Office, asked Bülow on 8 April 1905 for full instructions for guiding the German press. He mentioned the possibility of a German success in destroying the Anglo-French agreement over Morocco. Bülow answered: 'We do not want this, or at least we must not show any sign of such intention.'[2] If war came in sight, Germany must display neither anxiety nor timidity. Holstein still thought that the French would come to realize that English friendship was only 'platonic'. The political situation in England was unstable. Every one expected the fall of the Conservative Government. There was another important factor on the German side. Holstein had always believed that Great Britain would break any agreement rather than fight in a continental war. He had assumed that, if a crisis arose bringing with

[1] D.G.P. xx, pt. i. 271. The diplomats carried out their instructions. Cambon described the attitude of the German officials as 'most extraordinary. They were reticent and 'wooden-faced' ('font visage de bois') whenever they were spoken to about Morocco (B.D.D. iii. 76: 17 May 1905). Cf. D.G.P. xx, pt. ii. 297.   [2] D.G.P. xx, pt. ii. 312-13.

it the chance of war, the party responsible for the agreement would go out of office and allow their successors to
repudiate promises which had been made. A strong
German move would convince the French Government
that the friendship of England was not enough to secure
German consent to the occupation of Morocco.[1]
Yet the situation was likely to develop in a manner not
anticipated by Bülow or Holstein. Holstein's belief in
English perfidy was wrong. If Germany wished to show
that England was only a 'platonic' friend, and that
English support would not be given to France, then it
was clearly to the interest of England to be extremely
forthcoming. If the entente had been worth making, it
was worth keeping. Lansdowne had not anticipated that
the agreement would lead to immediate conflict with
Germany. The situation had arisen; it could only be met
in one way. Great Britain would give full support to
France within the terms of the agreement, while trying
at the same time to find means of satisfying Germany;
but Germany seemed to want nothing more and nothing
less than the destruction of the entente. Metternich
reported to the German Foreign Office from London
on 28 March, and again on 6 April 1905 that the English
press was wholly in sympathy with France, and that German policy was regarded not as a defence of legitimate
economic interests, but as an attack upon the entente.[2]
A similar belief was held in France.[3] On 9 June 1905,
Metternich wrote to Bülow that Balfour had assured him
that 'no sane person in England wishes to have a quarrel
or a war with Germany'.[4] This assurance did not prevent
Bülow from telegraphing to Washington on the following
day that England wanted to destroy the German fleet
for reasons affecting Far Eastern policy. If the German
fleet were out of the way, America could do nothing to
oppose a partition of China.[5]

[1] D.G.P. xxi, pt. i. 207–8: 22 February 1906.
[2] D.G.P. xx, pt. ii. 601–2 and 604.   [3] B.D.D. iii. 75.
[4] D.G.P. xx, pt. ii. 626.   [5] D.G.P. xx, pt. ii. 627–8.

The later history of the Moroccan crisis did not change the view held in Great Britain and France that Germany was more interested in the disruption of the entente than in the economic future of Morocco. It is unnecessary here to enter into the details of the complicated negotiations which took place in the summer and autumn of 1905. The dismissal of Delcassé, mainly as a result of German pressure, the tedious wrangle over the questions to be discussed at a conference, the German suggestion—refused by France—that the two countries should consider a general settlement of outstanding differences, the protracted debates at Algeciras, only strengthened the belief that Germany was aiming at the destruction of the Anglo-French entente, and that the methods adopted were the counterpart of those taken to separate Russia from France.[1]

The Moroccan crisis did not destroy the entente. On the other hand it did not transform the entente into an alliance; but it had one important consequence which was bound to affect the future relations of Great Britain and Germany. The crisis had brought the possibility of a European war into the foreground. If France had been forced into war by Germany, she would have expected British help. Would this help have been given? The most critical moment came during the early days of the conference at Algeciras. The Conservative Ministry had resigned, and the Liberals were fighting a general election. Grey had to take decisions of the greatest importance at a moment when his own colleagues, and public opinion, were distracted by internal affairs. Grey had not been responsible for the conclusion of the Anglo-French agreement, though he had approved of it. The

---

[1] See above, pp. 97–8. The only element of humour in this serious and disagreeable situation was provided by the Sultan of Morocco. When the Sultan heard that his German friends had come to an agreement with France over the programme of the conference 'His Majesty's ill-humour (became) so violent that his minister for foreign affairs was compelled to feign illness for two days in order to avoid approaching His Majesty' (B.D.D. iii. 145: 24 October 1905).

French Ambassador asked for a statement of British intentions in the event of a break-down of the conference followed by war. Grey answered:

'A promise in advance committing this country to take part in a Continental war is very serious . . . it is very difficult for any British Government to give an engagement of that kind. It changes the entente into an alliance and alliances, especially continental alliances, are not in accordance with our traditions. My opinion is that if France is let in for a war with Germany arising out of our agreement with her about Morocco, we cannot stand aside, but must take part with France. But a deliberate engagement pledging this country in advance before the actual cause of the war is known or apparent, given in cold blood goes far beyond anything that the late Government said, or as far as I know contemplated.'[1]

Grey had already taken care to speak to the German Ambassador in stronger terms than he used to Cambon. He had warned Metternich that 'in the event of an attack upon France by Germany, arising out of our Morocco Agreement, public feeling in England would be so strong that no British Government could remain neutral.[2] He felt that if he were wrong in this view, Germany would have no reason to complain.' In other words, language which, if used to France, might be an encouragement, would be a warning to Germany that a war with France might mean a war with England.

Grey went farther in his efforts to keep the peace. It

[1] B.D.D. iii. 177-8: Grey to Bertie, 15 January 1906.

[2] Cambon repeated his question to Grey on 31 January. Grey pointed out that a promise of armed support ought to be more than a verbal engagement. A written promise would change the entente into a defensive alliance, and the British Government could not keep the fact of a defensive alliance secret from Parliament. Sanderson told Cambon that if, without the consent of Parliament, the Cabinet gave France an assurance which involved the country in war, 'the case would be one which would justify impeachment . . . and might even result in that course'. B.D.D. iii. 180-5: Grey to Bertie, 31 January 1906, and Memoranda by Cambon and Lord Sanderson. Grey warned Metternich again on 18 February that, in the event of war between France and Germany, 'public feeling in England would be so strong that the British Government would be involved in it'. B.D.D. iii. 263: Grey to Lascelles, 19 February 1906.

would seem that he asked Rothschild to tell the German banker Swabach that England wanted to see good relations between herself and Germany, and between Germany and France, and that France would welcome an improvement in Anglo-German relations if her own susceptibilities and interests were regarded.[1]

Grey explained his motives in a memorandum drawn up on 19 February 1906, the day after his interview with Metternich. He asked himself what would happen if Great Britain left France to fight Germany single-handed. France would never forgive the desertion.

'The United States would despise us, Russia would not think it worth while to make a friendly arrangement with us about Asia, Japan would prepare to reinsure herself elsewhere, we should be left without a friend and without the power of making a friend, and Germany would take some pleasure, after what has passed, in exploiting the whole situation to our disadvantage, very likely by stirring up trouble through the Sultan of Turkey in Egypt. . . . On the other hand the prospect of a European war, and of our being involved in it is horrible.'

Grey decided to suggest, after the conference, that France should make 'a great effort and if need be some sacrifice . . . to avoid war'. He also considered another point.

'The door is being kept open by us for a *rapprochement* with Russia; there is at least a prospect that when Russia is reestablished we shall find ourselves on good terms with her. An *entente* between Russia, France, and ourselves would be absolutely secure. If it is necessary to check Germany, it could then be done. The present is the most unfavourable moment for attempting to check her. Is it not a grave mistake, if there must be a quarrel with Germany, for France and ourselves to let Germany choose the moment, which best suits her?'[2]

---

[1] D.G.P. xxi, pt. i. 62–3: Bülow to Metternich, 9 January 1906.

[2] B.D.D. iii. 266–7: 20 February 1906. It is interesting to compare this memorandum with a marginal note made by the German Emperor, about the same time, to a statement of the German Ambassador in Rome that the Anglo-French entente was 'not merely a passing incident, but an affair of a generation'. The Emperor wrote: 'For my generation (good) relations with France can no longer be hoped for. . . . England and France have been

There was a further consequence involved in the prospect of war. If there were any likelihood of a war in which Great Britain and France would fight as allies, it was necessary to discuss possible methods of collaboration. Grey, with the consent of the Prime Minister, allowed informal conversations to take place between the British, French, and Belgian military staffs and the British and French naval authorities. These conversations were entirely non-committal and non-binding.[1] They were known in Germany, and their importance was exaggerated there.

The Moroccan crisis was bound to affect the question of Anglo-German naval rivalry. The distrust of Germany was now no longer a general distrust of German aims, heightened by a continual irritation at German methods. Germany appeared to be taking steps to isolate Great Britain. It was not difficult for any one who remembered the preamble to the Navy Law of 1900 to see that an Anglo-French *rapprochement* would destroy the argument—the risk theory—by which the building of the navy had been justified to the German people. The German navy was growing in strength. Public opinion in England had begun to realize this important fact. During the last few years of the Conservative Government the German naval attaché in London had been surprised at the lack of interest in naval questions shown by members of Parliament. The attendance at debates on the estimates was always small; the discussions were

insulted together by the German press, and now they have come together and France is under English influence. . . . Italy joins them—Crimean coalition—and we have let it happen.' D.G.P. xxi, pt. i. 246–8: 3 March 1906.

[1] For the naval and military conversations, see B.D.D. iii and vi, and Grey, *Twenty Five Years*. The German failure to understand the relations between the civilian ministers and the naval and military staffs in Great Britain may have been due in some measure to the very different relationship between the General Staff and the Foreign Office in Germany. The dominance of military control and military considerations in Germany may be seen in the adoption of the Schieffen plan, which involved the violation of Belgian neutrality, in spite of the fact that the political and diplomatic disadvantages would have been obvious to the civilians of the Foreign Office.

jejune and without sensational speeches. Even the increasing cost of the navy was taken as a matter of routine. After the summer of 1906 there was a change. The change was due partly to the desire of the newly elected Liberal members to cut down the high estimates, partly to the exuberant and provocative character of Sir John Fisher who had taken office as First Sea Lord of the Admiralty in October 1904; but the main cause of the change was a sudden growth of anxiety about the intentions of Germany. The events of 1905 and the Algeciras conference did much to produce this anxiety. Moreover, the Moroccan crisis coincided with a further increase in the German navy.

The Emperor had been disturbed by the Selborne memorandum. He wanted public opinion to accept an increase in the German programme of construction as an answer to the concentration of the British fleet.[1] In January 1905 he sent a message to Prince Otto zu Salm, the President of the Navy League: 'may your desires for the strengthening of our naval forces ripen to fulfilment, and may your laudable endeavours and those of the Navy League be crowned with success.'[2] The Navy League was agitating for a programme considerably larger than that of the Navy Law, and Tirpitz found it necessary to explain to the Reichstag that the Emperor's telegram did not mean an approval of the whole programme of the League, but only an approval of the general policy of enlightening the public upon the naval needs of Germany. Meanwhile a speech of Mr. Arthur Lee, a Civil Lord of the Admiralty, on 4 February 1905, made a deep impression in Germany. The place and the occasion of Mr. Lee's speech were unimportant; he was replying to a toast at a dinner held in his constituency. His words were neither well chosen, nor accurately reported. He never expected

---

[1] It is also possible that in the early summer of 1905 the German naval authorities knew of the British plans to build 'all big gun' ships of 18,000 tons. In any case the announcement, in December 1904, of a special committee on designs must have indicated to German experts that a change in type was under consideration in Great Britain; see below, p. 113.

that all Germany would read what he had said. He spoke of the results of the redistribution of the fleet. All the effective reserve ships were now in commission, and ready to go to sea at a few hours' notice. These ships were organized in squadrons, and could be taken into action at once if war were declared suddenly. 'If war should unhappily be declared, under existing conditions, the British Navy would get its blow in first, before the other side had time even to read in the papers that war had been declared. . . .'

These words meant no more than that the fleet was ready and would be in a position to deliver an immediate attack. Count Reventlow, in the *Berliner Tageblatt*, pointed out that there was nothing in the speech which was not already known, and that no element of hostility had been introduced. On the other hand, the speech had been made by a member of the Government. It could not fairly be described as 'a threat of war in a time of peace'—the first comment of the *Berliner Tageblatt*; on the other hand it was open to misinterpretation if it were not read in its full context. In 1904 the Japanese had attacked the Russian fleet in Port Arthur before a formal declaration of war had been made. Did Mr. Lee mean that Great Britain would choose her own time for an ultimatum, and that the British fleet would appear off German harbours before the time-limit of the ultimatum had expired? Naval officers could hardly have taken this fear very seriously, since the preparations necessary for a naval war could not have escaped the notice of German observers. Tirpitz himself merely described Mr. Lee as a 'civilian'; but any reminder of British sea-power emphasized the fact that Germany had certainly not passed through the 'danger zone', and gave the impression that the idea of a 'preventive war' was not confined to irresponsible sections of British opinion.

This speech moved the Emperor to violent language.[1]

---

[1] In a letter to Tirpitz the Emperor described the speech as an 'open threat of war', and explained that he had summoned Lascelles and told him

He did not hide the fact that he was 'building the Long Walls' with all possible speed. After Tirpitz had foreshadowed the introduction of a supplementary naval law in the autumn of 1905, William II entertained a party of six hundred guests, including the Chancellor and Ministers of State and the foreign ambassadors to a Navy League film of *Life in the German Navy.*

There were indeed attacks on the extravagant demands made by the Navy League from the Centre party as well as from the Social Democrats. One speaker of the Centre called the League 'a public danger'. The *Vossische Zeitung*, which supported the foreign policy of the Government but was not chauvinistic in tone, pointed out in May 1905 that the activities of the League and the hints about a possible war with England might result in increased foreign armaments. 'The more shouting there is in Germany, the more ships will England build.' There was a good deal of 'shouting' at the National Liberal Congress held at Dresden in May 1905. Bassermann, in a speech which was continually applauded, said that England was inciting the continental states against one another. England would be the country to profit from a Franco-German war. The principal motive of English policy was hatred of German commercial and industrial competition. It was natural that sympathy for England in Germany, in so far as this sympathy existed, was declining. Germany must be well armed, and Germans should be grateful to the Navy League.

A few days later the Emperor received in audience the President of the League, and telegraphed to the Berlin section his thanks for the 'cheerful promise to co-operate in achieving the aims placed before the League'. In other words, as *The Times* pointed out, the agitation of the League must be regarded as official, or at least as semi-

plainly that unless this 'corsair' were immediately disavowed by his Government, there would be a storm of protest in the German press, followed by a 'colossal' programme of construction. Tirpitz, *Aufbau der deutschen Weltmacht*, i. 14.

official.[1] As for the 'aims placed before the League', Colonel Gädke, one of the leading German press critics on military and naval subjects, explained in the *Berliner Tageblatt* that 'a government must frequently cut its coat according to its cloth, and will seldom be in a position frankly to reveal its ultimate aims'.

The events of the summer and autumn of 1905 were unlikely to lessen public anxiety in Germany or to depress enthusiasm for an immediate increase in the naval programme. A supplementary law was announced in November 1905. The law provided for a large increase in the tonnage and cost of the battleships still to be built under the law of 1900. Six large cruisers and forty-eight destroyers were to be laid down in addition to those provided in the law of 1900, and an annual appropriation of £250,000 was made for submarine experiments. Tirpitz had decided to ask for the cruisers which were refused in 1900, and to come forward again in a few years' time with another supplementary law.

Within three weeks of the announcement of the German supplementary law the British Government published a memorandum on Admiralty policy.[2] The publication of this memorandum was due partly to domestic reasons. The Conservative Ministers, on the eve of an election, wanted to justify their plans of reorganization and to show that they had done everything possible to reduce the cost of the navy. The greater part of the memorandum was concerned with points of detail, but there was a lucid account of the new system of Fleet

---

[1] *The Times*, 27 May 1905. The *Frankfurter Zeitung*, which supported the naval policy of the Government, but disapproved of the methods of the Navy League, wrote that there were disadvantages in allowing the League to act as a private organ of the Government and an organization partly under Imperial control. In February 1905 Bebel had attacked the League in the Reichstag, on the ground that it was asking for armaments with the object of fighting Great Britain. The League at this time went through an internal crisis which had little or no effect upon its schedule of demands.

[2] A Statement of Admiralty Policy (Navy, Cd. 2791, 1905). This statement is generally known as the Cawdor memorandum. Lord Cawdor succeeded Lord Selborne as First Lord of the Admiralty in March 1905.

Reserve intended to secure that the ships in reserve 'should always be instantly ready for action'. It was also explained that 'the kaleidoscopic nature of international relations, as well as variations or new developments in Sea-power, not only forbids any permanent allocation of numbers, but in fact points the necessity for periodic redistribution of ships between our fleets to meet the political requirements of the moment'. The British naval requirements for the next few years were also discussed. It was assumed that Great Britain could still build ships more quickly than other Powers.

'However formidable foreign shipbuilding programmes may appear on paper, we can always overtake them in consequence of our resources and our power of rapid construction. At the present time strategic requirements necessitate an output of four large armoured ships annually, and unless unforeseen contingencies arise, the number will not be exceeded. . . . The Board have come to the conclusion that the right policy is to make out their programme of shipbuilding for the next year only, and while they anticipate at present that the output of four large armoured ships a year should suffice to meet our requirements, there would be no difficulty whatever in increasing this output to whatever may be necessary in consequence of any increase of Naval Power abroad.'

In other words, British programmes would depend upon German programmes.

The matter, however, did not rest here. The Selborne memorandum of December 1904 had announced the intention of the Board of Admiralty to

'review the principles on which the different classes of modern war-ships are constructed and the features embodied in them. In order temporarily to assist the Board and the Director of Naval Construction in the elucidation of the problems involved it has been decided to appoint a special Committee on Designs which will be composed of naval officers and scientific and professional experts and will begin work early next year, the Board of Admiralty first laying down as a basis what they consider to be the fighting requisites of the desired types of war vessels and the governing features of each types to which the other features shall be subservient.'[1]

Eleven months after this announcement, the Lords of the Admiralty paid an official visit to Portsmouth where a battleship was being built with the greatest possible speed. This ship was the Dreadnought. There was always a curious mixture of advertisement and secrecy about the methods of Sir John Fisher. No details of the Dreadnought were revealed, but every one knew that she would be original in design and more powerful than any battleship afloat.

The beginning of a new era of naval competition coincided with the renewal of mutual distrust in England and Germany, and with an attempt by a Liberal Government in Great Britain to bring proposals for naval disarmament into the foreground of international politics. The coincidence of these different facts was neither to the immediate nor to the ultimate advantage of the civilized world.

[1] See above, p. 84.

V

THE COMING OF THE 'ALL-BIG GUN' SHIP, 1905–1906

THE fall of the Conservative Government in England at the end of 1905 made little immediate difference to British foreign policy. The general election was fought on other issues; few references were made to European questions in election speeches or manifestoes. The Anglo-French entente was popular in the country. The tradition of the Liberal party was more Francophil than the tradition of the Conservatives. The Conservative Ministers had failed to come to any agreement with Germany; after this failure they had turned to France and accepted the conditions of an Anglo-French entente. The 'shock' diplomacy of the Moroccan crisis was not likely to bring about any change of view. The new Foreign Secretary, Sir Edward Grey, was a supporter of an agreement with France. The Foreign Office felt relief at the greater freedom which Great Britain had obtained. The country was no longer driven from small concession to small concession in an effort to satisfy Germany and retain her friendship. Germany had raised the Moroccan question to a major issue with the intention of breaking the Anglo-French entente. The policy of Bülow and Holstein only strengthened the view that collaboration with Germany was difficult; German aims were dangerous in their vagueness as well as in their threat to European peace.

Before the Liberals came into office Grey had shown that there would be no break in British policy. The opportunity for making a statement to this effect was given by a violent attack upon Lansdowne in the *Neue Freie Presse*, a Viennese paper known to be in close relations with Bülow.[1] The *Neue Freie Presse* blamed Lans-

---

[1] The correspondent of *The Times* in Vienna thought that Bülow was not responsible for the attack, but that the articles (there were several of them)

downe for the Moroccan crisis and assumed that England was encouraging France even at the risk of war. 'No more than Macbeth will Lansdowne be able to purge from his raiment the stain. . . .' A summary of the attack in the *Neue Freie Presse* appeared in *The Times* of 19 October 1905. Two days later Grey described the foreign policy which would be followed by a Liberal Government. He pointed out that 'the last thing which is likely to change British foreign policy is an attack upon the personal character of a British foreign minister of either party'. A Liberal Government would uphold the alliance with Japan, the entente with France, and friendship with the United States. It would aim at an improvement of relations with Russia, and a similar improvement of Anglo-German relations, on condition that this improvement did not take place at the expense of British relations with France. *The Times* commented on Grey's speech: 'Our official relations with the German government are perfectly friendly. Towards the German people we bear not the slightest feeling of animosity. . . . What has hitherto prevented any marked improvement in Anglo-German relations has been a distrust founded on observation of the policy pursued by the German government.' Morley also spoke in favour of the agreement with France. He looked upon the agreement 'with more satisfaction than he could express, and he had a right to do so because he had always advocated it'.[1]

These and other expressions of opinion reassured France that the Liberal Government would not, as the German press hinted, bring about a change of policy. The discussions with Cambon in January 1906, the military conversations, and the attitude of Great Britain at Algeciras left no doubt of British loyalty to the Anglo-French agreement. There was no intention of giving up the policy of

were the 'unintentional results of a long course of bad semi-official education'. (*The Times*, 25 October 1905.)

[1] Speech at Arbroath, 23 October 1905. Morley thought that the Anglo-Japanese alliance 'would at all events facilitate an understanding with Russia'.

the Anglo-French agreement, but rather a wish to extend this agreement by an understanding of a similar kind with Russia.

Liberal Ministers were none the less anxious to improve British relations with Germany. Grey had put forward this view in his memorandum of 20 February 1906.[1] On the other hand, a permanent improvement of Anglo-German relations was unlikely if the competition in naval armaments continued to affect public opinion in the two countries. This competition in armaments was already beginning to dominate other issues between Great Britain and Germany. There were few outstanding points of difference on colonial questions, or rather, few points upon which Great Britain was not being asked or expected to make concessions to Germany; attention would be concentrated, at least on the British side, on the question of sea-power and rivalry in naval armaments. Public opinion in Great Britain, rightly or wrongly, would not accept an agreement with Germany in which diplomatic, colonial, or economic concessions were made without securing any relief from the burden of naval expenditure. The Liberals, as a party, wanted to bring forward a measure of general disarmament. The Prime Minister, Sir Henry Campbell-Bannerman, believed that a proposal made by Great Britain would be welcomed by public opinion in other countries. Apart from the question of principle, the development of a large and expensive social policy would force the Liberals to cut down expenditure upon armaments. The new Government was pledged to a programme of social reform. The cost of these reforms was not yet realized; the additional burden upon the taxpayer would be heavy.

From the German point of view the intentions of the Liberal Government would appear less disinterested and altruistic. The Navy Law was accepted in Germany as a permanent fact of national policy. Its scope had recently been enlarged, but a strong party in Germany was asking

---

[1] See above, p. 92.

for another extension. The programme of 1900 had been carefully planned not merely to meet the needs of German naval defence, as interpreted by the naval experts, but also to suit the conditions and requirements of German shipyards. Years of skilful propaganda had made the German people familiar with these needs, and accustomed them to an increasing rate of expenditure upon naval armaments. They did not think this expenditure a crushing burden; they considered that the fleet was as much a matter of life and death to their own prosperity as the British fleet was a matter of life and death to Great Britain. The support given to France on the Moroccan question seemed to justify German anxiety and certainly aroused German feeling. An attempt by a foreign Power to interfere with the legislative fulfilment of the naval programme was regarded as a subtle and dangerous threat to the safety of Germany. The attitude of Liberal opinion in England was peculiarly exasperating. The Liberal Ministers wanted a limitation of armaments, but they had no thought of giving up the British claim to supremacy at sea. They were trying to keep this supremacy without cost to themselves; they were interfering or attempting to interfere with the right of Germany to settle for herself the measure of naval strength necessary for the protection of German interests. It is possible that the Liberal hopes for disarmament might have been of more practical effect if opinion, official and unofficial, in Great Britain had accepted the naval law of 1900 and the supplementary law of 1906. On the other hand, from the British point of view, this acceptance would have meant postponing for years to come any measure of disarmament. The British taxpayer would have had no relief from the burden of increasing naval expenditure.

The situation was more difficult because the Emperor continued to think that every new German warship was a pledge of peace. He was so deeply committed to the policy of a strong navy that he could not easily propose any modification of the naval programme. It mattered little that the 'risk theory', upon which he had justified his naval policy in 1900, had now been undermined by the Anglo-French agreement. The decision had been taken. There comes a time in the history of every state when it is practically impossible, whatever the logical possibilities, to make a sudden and violent change in foreign policy without a revolutionary change in the governing body of the state. This revolutionary change was outside the range of possibilities in the German Empire. Without a change of system, a change of personnel, events would follow the course which had been laid down for them. The policy of building up a strong navy would be continued. If this policy did not bring the desired results, if the measures taken by Great Britain, either within the sphere of naval construction or naval concentration, or in the larger field of diplomatic relationships, affected the position of Germany, then the German naval programme would be increased. The alternative policy involved a recognition of British naval supremacy, and —as Germans had been taught to believe—German helplessness before an unscrupulous enemy. Every year of this naval competition would increase the tension between England and Germany. Ultimately the affair would become a trial of will between the two states. It was already recognized as such in Germany.

The situation was serious from the point of view of European peace. Improvement was unlikely; at any moment a crisis on the scale of the Moroccan controversy might make matters worse. A new complication was indeed introduced owing to the sudden technical change in the design of large warships. The Dreadnought was launched on 10 February 1906, and began her sea trials on 3 October 1906—a year and four days after the laying of the first plate of the keel in Portsmouth Dockyard. No great warship had ever been built in so short a time.

The Liberal Government was faced with a problem which added very greatly to the difficulties of disarma-

ment; a Liberal Prime Minister who had put the limitation of armaments in the foreground of his political
programme was compelled to meet the charge that England had begun a new and more expensive form of competition in large ships of war.

Why was the Dreadnought built?[1] Mr. Lloyd George,
in a speech of 28 July 1908, put the matter very simply.
'We said, let there be Dreadnoughts. What for? We did
not require them. Nobody was building them, and if
any one had started building them, we, with our greater
shipbuilding resources, could have built them faster than
any other country in the world.' Every one of these
statements would have been denied by those responsible
for the building of the first Dreadnought, except the
claim that Great Britain could build ships more quickly
than other countries, and even this statement was misleading. The Dreadnought type of ship represented a
more complete adaptation of the battleship to the purposes which it was intended to serve. 'The Dreadnought
policy embodied the views of naval officers, giving them
the kind of ship they wanted for the tactics they thought
most desirable.'[2] A battleship is a floating battery of guns
intended for the destruction of similar ships. Upon the
assumption of equal skill in gunnery on each side, equality
in torpedo craft between two fleets, the fleet armed with
the largest number of guns firing the heaviest shells at the
longest range and with the widest arcs of fire, and possessing the greatest freedom of tactical movement—i.e.
speed—will destroy its opponents without heavy loss to
itself. This destruction will be absolute on an open sea
where the enemy cannot run for protection to a fortified
harbour, or escape behind a minefield. There is no
natural cover at sea other than mist, cloud, or darkness.
A ship which can fight an action out of range of the

[1] The main features of the new type of 'all-big gun' ship, with the reasons
for their adoption were explained in a short memorandum issued by the
Admiralty in 1906. (Memorandum explanatory of the programme of new
construction for 1905-6, with details not included in the Navy Estimates for
1906-7: Navy, Cd. 3048.)   [2] *The Times*, 22 October 1913.

heavier guns of her opponents is fighting an unarmed enemy. During the Great War a British squadron under Admiral Sturdee sank four out of five ships of Admiral von Spee's squadron with the loss of seven men.[1] The Dreadnought was a ship intended to outrange in the heaviest armament, and to outpace in speed and manœuvre, any other type of battleship. Her main armament consisted of the heaviest guns, ten 12-in. guns, each capable of throwing, at high muzzle velocity, a projectile of 850 lb. over a distance of 18,500 yards. The guns were mounted in pairs in hooded turrets. Six guns could fire ahead, eight on either broadside. Hitherto no battleship had been armed with more than four 12-in. guns, of which only two could fire ahead. A line of ten Dreadnoughts was therefore equal to a line of twenty pre-Dreadnought battleships at long range, and one Dreadnought firing ahead was equal to three pre-Dreadnought battleships. The Dreadnought had no secondary armament; that is to say, no guns of intermediate calibre suitable for engagement at a 'medium' range.[2] The great guns would have done their work at about 10,000 yards before an enemy ship had come within effective range of guns of lesser power. Only small artillery was necessary to ward off the attacks of destroyers.

This 'all-big gun' armament had important advantages from the point of view of fire-control. An enemy ship moving at high speed is no easy target at a range of 10,000 yards or more.[3] Observations of fire and exact range-finding are more difficult on sea than on land. In any case observation is easier if the observer is dealing

---

[1] *Gneisenau, Scharnhorst, Leipzig, Nürnberg.* The cruiser *Dresden* escaped, but was caught three months later. Admiral von Spee had sunk two British cruisers with still smaller loss to his own fleet two months before the arrival of Admiral Sturdee's squadron.

[2] The secondary armament was restored in later ships of the Dreadnought type.

[3] The maximum range of British 13·5 in. guns in 1914 was 24,000 yards, though 16,000 yards was regarded by Admiral Beatty as the most effective range for observation and control of fire. Weather conditions in the North Sea tended to lower the average 'effective' range.

only with guns of one calibre, and if he can watch the effect of salvoes at slightly different ranges. Furthermore the higher the velocity of the projectile, the flatter the trajectory at long range, and therefore the greater the chance of hitting the target. From the point of view of fire control the Dreadnought was a return to a simpler type of battleship. The size of the ship was determined by the number and position of the great guns. It was necessary to place these guns in positions where they would obtain the widest arcs of fire without interference from blast. The displacement required for this purpose gave a margin which could be used for more armour, more coal, or a higher speed. The Admiralty chose higher speed (21 knots), and made every use of this by-product, by the employment of turbines.[1] The use of turbines meant a saving of £100,000 in cost, and 1,000 tons in displacement.

The Dreadnought was not very much larger or more expensive than her immediate predecessors, the battleships laid down in 1903 or 1904. The *Lord Nelson*, the last of the pre-Dreadnought battleships, was only 65 feet shorter, 1,500 tons less in displacement, and £181,000 less in cost. The difference was not 'revolutionary', if it be considered in relation to earlier increases. The real change lay in the provision of a ship far more suited than her predecessors for destroying an enemy ship under conditions which would hold in modern war.

This 'new type of floating gun-carriage' was built after consultation with officers of the fleet and leading naval architects. The design of the ship was the logical conclusion to be drawn from the gunnery experiments made by Sir Percy Scott.[2] The design was approved by a special

[1] Turbines had already been tried by the Admiralty experimentally on two ships. An additional advantage of their employment was that the engines were lower in the ship, and could be given more protection. The battle-cruisers of the *Invincible* type were given a higher speed than the Dreadnought. These cruisers were intended, among other purposes, to protect large liners such as the *Mauretania* which might be bringing foodstuffs to Great Britain in time of war.

[2] Similar experiments were being tried in the U.S. navy by Admiral Sims, a close friend of Sir Percy Scott.

committee of inquiry to which were submitted instructions drawn up by Sir J. Fisher after consultation with officers such as Sir A. Wilson and Lord Charles Beresford. Among civilians Lord Kelvin, Sir John Isaac Thornycroft, and Sir John Biles served on the committee. The committee had the benefit of secret, and early, reports of the naval engagements in the Russo-Japanese war. The main decisions were reached before the battle of Tsushima, though certain modifications were made in the design after the details of this battle were known.[1]

Was the technical advance made in the building of the Dreadnought more than offset by certain inevitable changes in the balance of naval power? The Dreadnought was so much more powerful than other battleships that all pre-Dreadnought battleships at once deteriorated in fighting value. The initial gain from this depression fell to Great Britain. Until other Powers built Dreadnoughts for themselves, British naval superiority was very much increased. On the other hand, Great Britain had the largest fleet of pre-Dreadnought ships. She was now leading the way in a new type; by this very act she was lowering the value of her older battleships. As other Powers, notably Germany, built Dreadnoughts, and the striking power of fleets came to be measured by this new standard, the pre-Dreadnought battleships of Great Britain would cease to count as ships of the first line. The 'goodwill' of British naval superiority would be lost, and other Powers would start the construction of Dreadnoughts almost on level terms. Was there any need to make this sacrifice? The British fleet was far stronger than its rivals when the Dreadnought was laid down. If any other Power began to build these 'all-big gun' ships, Great Britain, with her facilities for rapid construction, could soon overtake them. The policy of watching the programmes of other Powers had been followed with success for many years. It was unlikely that Germany would be

[1] The committee considered six variations of design.

the first Power to make this new experiment; the Kiel Canal was too small for battleships of 18,000 tons.

If there were no urgent reasons for a policy which was wasting the superiority in capital ships[1] built up at great cost over many years, there was good cause for hesitating before a step which would certainly increase the naval estimates. Few docks in Great Britain could berth a Dreadnought. The cost of providing these docks and their machinery would be heavy. Moreover, if the Dreadnought cost only £181,000 more than the *Lord Nelson*, there was no reason to suppose that the Dreadnought type would not itself be enlarged and become more expensive. It was indeed suggested that the prospect of a new and more expensive form of naval competition might lead other Powers, particularly Germany, to ask whether anything was to be gained from continuing the challenge to British sea-power. *The Times* put this point with some caution: 'The Dreadnought is assuredly calculated to advance nearly every existing battleship a long way on the road to premature obsolescence. . . . It may seem paradoxical to suggest that an opportunity is thus offered for a reconsideration by all the Powers of the established measure of their respective naval preparations.'[2] It was most unlikely that Germany would agree to the stabilization of naval power on a basis which would ensure an immense British predominance at the very moment when the deadweight of British pre-Dreadnought superiority appeared to be lifting. Germany, as well as England, would feel the burden of larger and more expensive ships; but Germany would gain more by the sacrifice of her smaller and less powerful fleet of pre-Dreadnought ships. For every ship Germany took out of the line, Great Britain would take out two ships.

Sir William White, who had preceded Sir Philip Watts as Director of Naval Construction, thought that, from almost every point of view, the Dreadnought policy

---

[1] For the use of the term 'capital ship', see Appendix III.
[2] *The Times*, 16 February 1906.

was a mistake.[1] Mr. Balfour pointed out in July 1906 the general effect of this policy:

'While at first sight you might be inclined to say that the fact that we were the first to design and build vessels (of the Dreadnought type) gives us an advantage in one sense, I am afraid it may entail upon us an expenditure which otherwise you might have avoided. And for this reason. If the new type carries out the full expectations of its designers, a squadron of four of these battle-ships is almost invulnerable to any existing naval combination. Therefore, if we are really to keep pace as regards battleships, we shall have to build this new type at a rate equal to any two Powers.'[2]

To these arguments the supporters of the 'all-big gun' ship answered that the construction of such ships was inevitable. If they were not built by Great Britain they would be built by other Powers. The fact that they would depress the value of all existing battleships was the greatest incentive to the rivals of Great Britain to take a step which would reduce the fighting value of the British fleet. The question therefore was not whether the 'all-big gun' ship would be built, but whether Great Britain would make the best of an unpleasant position, and establish a lead in these ships. It was not altogether safe to assume that Great Britain, in Sir William White's words, could 'watch the trend of foreign construction and take the necessary steps to have ready for service our replies to foreign designs before they were represented by actual ships'. There were no precedents for this policy of 'watching and waiting' in so vital a question as the design of a ship which would be more than a match for any battleship afloat. The margin of time for preparing the 'replies to foreign designs' might be dangerously short. The First Lord of the Admiralty had stated in 1902 that 'the consideration of new designs, or the improvement of existing designs, is a long and anxious task; and when a decision has been arrived at it takes months before the sketch designs can be worked out in every detail so that

[1] Manning, *Life of Sir W. White*, c. 28.   [2] Hansard, 4th Ser. clxii. 111–12.

the dockyards or contractors can build to them'.[1] The shipbuilding capacities of foreign Powers, and of Germany in particular, were increasing. If Germany wished to take Great Britain by surprise, it would not be very difficult for her to prepare designs in secret, and to order the guns and armour well in advance of laying down the ships.[2] The fact of the orders might be kept secret for some time. In any case their purpose would not be known. The completion of the Dreadnought within a record period of twelve months was due to careful preparation of this kind, and, incidentally, to the use of turrets made for another ship. The 'trend of foreign construction' was too vague and indefinite a term to express the situation which the British Admiralty might have to meet. Three or four ships might have been laid down in foreign yards. The material for the construction of these ships might have been accumulated, but the British 'replies to foreign designs' would not exist even in the form of paper drawings. The building of the Dreadnought, in spite of the unwise advertisement given to it by Sir J. Fisher, upset the plans of German constructors to such an extent that no battleship was laid down in any German yard for a whole year. After this delay the first two German Dreadnoughts, *Nassau* and *Westfalen*, were not wholly satisfactory ships; it was rumoured that Germany had tried to sell them to Turkey![3]

The advantages of taking the initiative, after full and deliberate consideration of the new designs, could be seen at the end of 1906. It was then calculated that Great Britain would have nine 'all-big gun' ships—six battleships (Dreadnoughts) and three large cruisers (Invincibles)[4]—before the end of the year 1909. Germany had not yet laid down one of these ships; unless she could

---

[1] Memorandum accompanying the naval estimates of 1902–3.

[2] For the problems raised by the question of the accumulation of material, see below, c. x. [3] Similar rumours were current about the cruiser *Blücher*.

[4] Much confusion was and is caused in the discussion of the 'all-big gun' ship by the use of the term 'Dreadnought' to cover battleships and battle-cruisers. See Appendix III.

accelerate her rate of construction, she would only have completed three before the year 1910. If the new ships were inevitable, these figures showed that the Admiralty had been right in facing the facts—the increase in cost, and the 'premature obsolescence' of the pre-Dreadnought battleships and large cruisers. Once a commanding lead had been obtained, it would be almost impossible for Germany to approach parity in ships of the new type against the efforts of Great Britain. Moreover the expense of widening the Kiel Canal and improving the German harbours would limit for years to come the amount of money which Germany could spend on new construction.

The question still remains to be answered: Were the new ships 'inevitable'? This question could only be answered, if at all, by a full examination of the plans under discussion in foreign Admiralties at the time of the building of the Dreadnought. Even if an examination of this kind were possible, it would not be conclusive. One cannot say, for example, whether in the years 1905, 1906, or later, Germany would have or would not have decided to build these ships. The German Admiralty might have come to the conclusion that the only way to make the German navy into an effective instrument was the expensive but sure method of adopting a new type of ship. The 'risk theory' was breaking down. The 'danger zone' was being indefinitely prolonged. The only solution lay in reducing the value of the immense numerical superiority of the British fleet. The fact that the British Admiralty anticipated other Powers shows that no decision had been reached. The delay in German construction after the main features of the Dreadnought were known shows that Germany had not already decided to build ships of 18,000 tons. On the other hand, the question of building ships of a larger tonnage had actually been under consideration in Germany early in 1905. Müller, who subsequently became Chief of the Naval Cabinet of the Emperor, wrote to Tirpitz on 8 February 1905:

'It is clear that, as far as we are concerned, the most important factors are ships of the line and destroyers. It is equally clear that, if there were no natural obstacle, we should be bound to choose the very large ship of the line as the type of the future, and also that we should do well to counter the newest types built by our opponents with a certain acceleration of our own construction. But we are faced with a natural obstacle—the Kiel canal. One might indeed say that the concentration of power in a 17,000 or 18,000 ton ship is so very important that we must do without the canal rather than the big ships. But I do not value the big ships as highly as this. I prefer the possibility of strategical combination by means of the canal to the tactical concentration in the 'large type', and only after the domestic situation has allowed us to enlarge the canal would I build the big ships.'[1]

It is impossible to say whether the German naval experts had begun to consider this sudden change in the size of battleships before they knew any facts about the Dreadnought. Sir John Fisher had announced the formation of the special committee on design in December 1904. The German Admiralty must have understood that the questions under consideration were an increase in the armament and tonnage of battleships. In the beginning of December 1904 the German naval attaché in London reported that Vickers had produced plans of a battleship armed with ten or twelve 12-in. guns.[2] The Emperor annotated the dispatch: 'In my opinion this is the armament of the future.' Three months later the German Admiralty decided to increase the number of heavy guns in the battleships of the 1906 programme, but the decision to build ships of 18,000 tons does not appear to have been taken until September 1905.[3] By this time, in spite of the

---

[1] Tirpitz, *op. cit.*, i. 15. After the defeat of the Russian fleet the question of the Kiel canal became of less immediate importance. Until Russia had rebuilt her fleet, there was less need for Germany to concentrate her largest battleships in the Baltic.

[2] F. Uplegger, *Die englische Flottenpolitik vor dem Weltkriege*, p. 39. Uplegger gives the date of this dispatch as 8 December 1904.

[3] It has been asserted that this decision was reached in 1904, and that Germany was actually preparing a 'surprise', and that she had designed ships of the same tonnage as the *Lord Nelson* (16,500) tons, but more heavily armed. See article by H. C. Bywater in the *Navy League Annual*, 1910–11, pp. 188–90.

parade of secrecy, it is more than likely that the general plan and dimensions of the Dreadnought were known in Germany.[1]

In any case the question of the 'all-big gun' ship was under discussion in other countries. Before the Dreadnought was laid down, the Italian naval constructor, Captain Cuniberti, had designed an 'ideal British battleship' of 17,000 tons, with an armament of twelve 12-in. guns.[2] An Austrian designer, Sigfrido Popper, had also designed an 'all-big gun' ship. The Japanese Admiralty laid down a ship of greater displacement than the Dreadnought, though not of the same type, five months before the Dreadnought was begun. Lieutenant Poundstone, of the United States Navy, is said to have shown the plans of an 'all-big gun' ship to the United States Design Bureau as early as 1903.[3] It was not therefore fantastic or absurd for Sir J. Fisher, or any one else, to think in 1904 or 1905 that some other Power, and particularly Germany, might anticipate the Dreadnought. The policy of building ships, of accumulating squadrons 'of less fighting worth than existing knowledge made possible' was very dangerous.[4] The lessons of Tsushima reinforced the arguments in favour of the Dreadnought type of ship. The 'risk', if one may so put it from the British point of view, existed, and the Admiralty had to make their decision upon a calculation of probabilities. Whether their decision was right or wrong is a question to which it is impossible to give an answer.

If the Admiralty were right, no less than if they were wrong, from a technical point of view in taking the initiative in the construction of an 'all-big gun' ship, their

[1] It has been said that the German Admiralty obtained possession of the plans of one of the British cruisers of the *Invincible* class. Mr. McKenna admitted in the House of Commons in 1909 that certain drawings of the *Indomitable* had disappeared (Hansard, 5th Ser. xii. 1168 and 1203).

[2] See *Jane's Fighting Ships*, 1903, pp. 408-9.

[3] See article on 'The Evolution of the Capital Ship', by M. Prendergast, in the *Navy League Annual*, 1911-12, pp. 210-28.

[4] This point of view is taken by Captain B. Acworth in *The Navy and the Next War*, p. 232.

action added very considerably to the task of a Liberal Government, anxious to economize on armaments and to spend money on social reform. This action also intensified naval competition between England and Germany. British naval supremacy was secured overwhelmingly, for a few years, and might be secured for years to come, though at an increasing cost.

From the German point of view the position was very different. For the next few years, while Great Britain alone possessed a fleet of Dreadnoughts, the outlook appeared extremely dangerous. The idea of an English attack was taken far more seriously in Germany than in England; a large and influential section of opinion in Germany looked upon a 'preventive war' as a legitimate means of defence, a grave act of policy which might be forced upon a nation. A preventive war might be a gross political blunder; it was not necessarily a crime, or an offence against civilization. German opinion was still obsessed with the history of the taking of the Danish fleet, and with a belief that Great Britain was finding the strain of economic competition too strong to bear. If Great Britain had chosen to begin a naval war against Germany in 1907, 1908, 1909, or 1910, the 'risk theory' would not have acted as a deterrent. The superiority of the British navy in the newest type of ship, as well as in older types, was overwhelming. On the other hand, there was now a chance that if the new 'danger zone' were passed, the coming of the 'all-big gun' ship would favour Germany more than England. Within ten years the pre-Dreadnought ships would have sunk low in the scale of fighting values. The British lead in Dreadnoughts would diminish relatively, with the launching of every German battleship. The international situation might not always favour the concentration of the British fleet. The United States and Japan were possible rivals to Great Britain in regions far away from the North Sea. The victory of the Liberals in the general election of 1906 was an advantage to Germany. Tirpitz hoped that the Liberal party would work for a reduction in the British naval estimates in spite of the German programmes. The Liberals were unlikely to fight a 'preventive' war. They would spend a good deal of time in trying to persuade other countries to accept their disarmament proposals. During this time they could hardly make very large additions to their own navy. If Germany maintained or increased her rate of building, and Great Britain allowed her to make headway, the initial advantage of introducing the Dreadnought would be lost.

Such were the views of the Emperor and his naval advisers. They were supported by the Chancellor and by the public opinion which they had done so much to create. There are no words proper to the vocabulary of historians by which this policy can be praised or blamed. If the German Government and the German people thought that they saw an opportunity to challenge British sea-power, and to find safety in the very moment of danger, the only judgement which a foreign, and particularly an English, observer is entitled to pass is a judgement upon the accuracy of the German calculations.

If the calculations were wrong, what would be the consequences of the mistake? The political situation at the end of 1905 had convinced the German Emperor that he must reckon upon a possible coalition of France, Russia, and Great Britain. The 'risk theory' no longer applied to the relations between Great Britain and the French or Russian fleets. For some time to come a temporary weakening of the British fleet would not endanger British interests in the Far East or in American waters. Neither Japan nor the United States could afford to see the disappearance of Great Britain as a sea Power.

There remained only the possibility of overtaking Great Britain in shipbuilding and of meeting her on approximately equal terms as far as great ships of the line were concerned. Yet there was very little chance that the Liberal Government would give up a 'safe' margin of supremacy. British public opinion was not much interested in the details of continental politics; on the question of naval supremacy there was no division of opinion. German observers themselves were peculiarly exasperated to find that most British supporters of a limitation of armaments assumed that the British navy must always be stronger than the navies of other Powers. Moreover, the history of the last twenty years had shown that British public opinion could be excited very easily on the naval question. Already in the year 1906 there were signs of uneasiness; a serious challenge to British naval supremacy would cause an outburst of feeling which no ministry could resist.

The campaign carried on by Lord Roberts in favour of compulsory military service was likely to make Englishmen feel anxious. The question of compulsory military service could be raised only in direct connexion with the possibility of a defeat of the British navy followed by a German invasion. The prestige of Lord Roberts gave the agitation more publicity than it would otherwise have received. Few British naval or military authorities accepted Lord Roberts's view of the technical chances of a German landing in England; but the sensational press quickly realized and exploited the dramatic value of the subject. Lord Roberts made the mistake of associating himself with some of the worst of these exploitations. On 13 March 1906 there appeared in *The Times* a full-page advertisement of a novel by William Le Queux on the invasion of England by Germany in 1910. The novel was to appear in serial form in the *Daily Mail*. The advertisement consisted of a large map of Great Britain with suitable captions—'London invested, bombarded, and sacked', 'Parliament finally meets at Manchester'. The Prime Minister, in answer to a question in the House, pointed out that the Government could take no action to prevent mischievous publications of this kind, but that the matter might well be left to be judged by the good sense and good taste of the British people.[1] The figures

[1] Hansard, 4th Ser. cliii. 1120.

of naval power for the year 1910 did not leave much room for anxiety about the 'invasion of England' in that year. The subject might give a pleasant thrill; it would certainly have a repercussion in Germany, where it would be taken as an example of the unscrupulous methods used to persuade the English people to increase their armaments. Yet there was one safe inference open to a dispassionate observer. For good reasons or bad, the British nation, having no wish for compulsory military service, would take every care to maintain a fleet superior in strength to the fleets of any rivals.

This inference was not drawn by those responsible for the control of German policy; but, once again, it is dangerous to assume that a high-spirited people will be content to decide its policy on calculations of numerical strength or a mechanical disposition of forces. The history of England would have been very different if Great Britain had made a calculation of this kind in relation to the naval power and world position of Spain in the sixteenth century. The history of Prussia would have been different if Frederick II had done no more than add up the numbers of the troops of Austria and France, and compare the totals with the army of Prussia. The history of France would have been different if the Girondins and Jacobins had not been ready to challenge the whole of Europe, in the belief that audacity and will power counted more than numbers.

At the end of 1905 the German Admiralty presented the Reichstag with a statement on the development of German maritime interests. The moment was well chosen. The time had come for another act of will, another declaration that the events of the last two years had neither forced the German people into surrender nor persuaded them that their plans for a strong navy had been defeated by the reaction of England and the changes in the international situation. The memorandum was of considerable length. It covered some 280 quarto pages. Its theme was summarized in these sentences.

'The examination made in 1897 of the maritime interests of the Empire served even then to establish the general conviction that the creation of a strong navy was indispensable,, and that the necessary expenditure was, from an economic point of view, no more than a reasonable premium of insurance which the German people could and must pay. Further developments in all directions during the succeeding eight years have only tended to confirm and strengthen this conviction. The duty of feeding and employing a steadily increasing population in such a manner as to raise the standard of living as far as possible throughout the community, and thereby to maintain and promote a healthy social development, can only be fulfilled by affording a properly extended protection to those important branches of economic activity which enable German capital and German labour to find profitable employment abroad, and especially in countries beyond the seas. The amount of money to be devoted to this protection must increase with the increasing value of the objects protected as well as with the increasing expenditure of other naval Powers.'[1]

The cost was not too heavy, and did not restrict expenditure on other national objects.

The memorandum appeared almost immediately after the acceptance of the supplementary law by the Reichstag.[2] The comments of *The Times* on the statement of policy were not unfriendly. The figures were not wholly accurate, and had been manipulated, by the inclusion of obsolete British ships, and the exclusion of similar German ships, to exaggerate German inferiority. But the case for an increase in the fleet was not unreasonable. 'Not much exception could be taken to the principle (i.e. the "risk" theory) of the bill of 1900, though it might have been less provocatively expressed.' On the other hand, the arguments in the German memorandum applied with equal force to Great Britain. 'We can see no substantial ground for alarm in the proposed increase of the German navy, though it will react in the usual manner

---

[1] *Die Entwickelung der deutschen Seeinteressen im letzten Jahrzehnt.*

[2] See above, p. 97. For the discussions among the naval authorities in connexion with the law, see Tirpitz, *op. cit.*, i. 16-30.

on our own defensive policy, and though the necessity is to be regretted, it is nevertheless inexorable, nor is it of our seeking.' Great Britain had already offered to reduce armaments if other Powers would do the same.[1] The offer still held. *The Times* thought that, on the whole, the German statement was reassuring to

'those people in this country who are wont to see in the growth of the German navy a threat to the naval supremacy of Great Britain. . . . Elements in Germany lend countenance to this view, but the figures of German trade shew conclusively that if we are to discern in the growth of the German navy a deliberate menace to the naval supremacy of this country, not only must we overlook the deep-seated and far-reaching causes which go far [*sic*] to explain, even if they do not wholly justify, the expansion of the German navy, but we must also attribute to Germany a singular lack of intelligence and perspicacity in adapting the means to the ends.'[2]

In other words, any German attempt to overtake the naval superiority of Great Britain was certain to fail, and the Germans therefore were too intelligent to make the attempt. A further inference to be drawn from the memorandum, according to *The Times*, was that in case of war German commerce would be at the mercy of Great Britain.

The reference in *The Times* to the possibility of a reduction of armaments was due not to any belief that the suggestion would be accepted in Germany—*The Times* was always sceptical on this point—but to the fact that the matter was now under discussion in Europe and America. In April 1906 Russia had invited the Powers to a conference at The Hague.

---

[1] See below, Appendix IV. [2] *The Times*, 23 April 1906.

VI

THE SECOND HAGUE CONFERENCE, 1907

THE Russian invitation to the second Hague Conference had followed tentative proposals from the United States; these proposals in their turn had arisen out of preliminary discussions at a meeting of the Inter-Parliamentary Union held at St. Louis in 1904. The Russian invitation was welcomed by those English Liberals and Radicals who favoured disarmament. The Prime Minister was known to have set great hopes upon the success of the Conference, though Grey, who was in closer touch with the realities of European politics, was never very optimistic. There were debates in May 1906 in the Houses of Parliament on the subject of disarmament.[1] The form of resolution proposed in the House of Commons declared that the large and increasing expenditure on armaments restricted national and commercial credit, added to the problem of unemployment, diminished the resources available for social reforms, and was a particularly heavy burden on the working classes. These conclusions were in direct conflict with the statement given to the German people by the German Admiralty in the previous month. The argument used by Mr. Balfour that the British fleet was purely defensive, while the fleets of other Powers were offensive instruments, was not likely to carry much conviction in Germany. On the other hand, Grey said that he thought the debate was valuable as evidence of the strength of feeling in England in favour of a limitation of armaments. This evidence might possibly affect other countries. 'I do not believe that at any time has the conscious public opinion in the various countries of Europe set more strongly in the direction of peace than at the present time, and yet the burden of military and naval expenditure goes on increasing. We are all waiting on each other.' Grey hoped that the House of

[1] Hansard, 4th Ser. clvi. 1383–1416, and (H. of L.), clvii. 1517–48.

Commons would take some positive step in favour of disarmament.

In the House of Lords Lord Fitzmaurice pointed out the difficulty of finding a 'unit' of disarmament, and a tribunal which should decide the manner in which a measure or standard could be applied. *The Times* described the debate in the Lords as 'a very practical discussion of what is in the nature of the case a rather academic subject'. Goschen's invitation made at the time of the first Hague Conference had 'fallen on deaf ears'.[1] Grey had now renewed the suggestion, but his proposal had been coldly received in Germany. The correspondent of *The Times* in Berlin thought that some of the German Liberals and Radicals, as well as the Social Democrats, sympathized with the idea, and felt that the 'isolation' of Germany was due to her own restless policy. On the other hand, the German people as a whole were accepting the view that Great Britain thought Germany at the end of her financial resources, and was laying a trap for her. Disarmament was associated with Social Democracy as something unpatriotic and 'un-German'. A section of Conservative opinion held it advisable to accept a temporary limitation of armaments, in order that the money saved on shipbuilding could be spent on other naval purposes. The Kiel Canal must be widened, and the Elbe and Weser connected by a canal with the waters of the Jade. The view of the Government was indicated in an article in the *Kölnische Zeitung* explaining that German armaments could not be measured by the same standards as those of Great Britain and France, since the German fleet was at an earlier stage of development. The only solution was that other Powers should allow Germany to bring her naval armaments up to their level. From the first there was a fear in Germany that Great Britain intended to use the opportunity of The Hague Conference to compel Germany to keep within her existing naval programme.[2]

[1] See Appendix IV.
[2] The annual meeting of the German Navy League was held at Hamburg

The Times thought that the agitation begun by pacifists in Great Britain was dangerous and useless. It was useless to claim that the burden of armaments was excessive when other countries did not hold this view. At the first Hague Conference Colonel Gross von Schwartzhoff had denied that Germany was 'crushed by militarism'. The French view was even stronger. 'Les pacifistes sont les complices des conquérants, parce qu'ils sollicitent leurs cupidités en énervant les résistances.'[1] *The Times* did not wonder that other nations felt 'a very natural reluctance to commit themselves to proposals, however admirable, which might jeopardise all the national ideals and interests that they hold dear'.[2]

The British Government went beyond a mere gesture. An announcement was made in July that the British ship-building programme was being cut down from four to three large ships, and that the construction of one of these three ships would be held over until after The Hague Conference in the hope that some agreement might be reached. This decision had followed a good deal of discussion. On 21 June a deputation of a hundred and twenty Liberals asked the Prime Minister to reduce the programme of construction. The Prime Minister told King Edward VII on 10 July that the Admiralty insisted upon three ships at least; the Cawdor memorandum had assumed that an output of four ships a year was necessary. On this same day Lord Haldane proposed the compromise that the third ship should not be laid down at once, and might be cancelled if The Hague Conference accepted a reduction of armaments.

The reception of this 'gesture' was not encouraging. Mr. Balfour pointed out that the Government could not claim that Great Britain had set a good example to other Powers, and at the same time assure the nation that

in May 1906. A special naval detachment was sent to Hamburg at the time of the meeting. The membership of the League was just under a million.

[1] E. Denis, quoted in *The Times* of 20 July 1906.
[2] *The Times*, 22 June 1906.

British naval supremacy was not in danger.[1] Lord Tweed-mouth, in the House of Lords, gave a different reason for the reduction in the number of ships to be laid down. He said that owing to the delay in the execution of the naval programmes of other Powers Great Britain need not build more than three large ships, and that the reduction in the number of smaller ships was due to experiments on a new type.[2] *The Times* at once commented that Tweedmouth's explanation was inconsistent with the statements made in the House of Commons, and that the action of the Government would not deceive any foreign Power.[3] The French press had already said that Great Britain was not running any real risk, and that France was in arrears with her shipbuilding and could not be expected to follow the British example.[4] The Belgian view was that Great Britain was simply looking for a cheap way of maintaining her naval supremacy.

[1] Hansard, 4th Ser. clxii. 106–113 and (7 March 1907) clxx. 681. In the latter speech Mr. Balfour outlined the answer which foreign statesmen might give to the British 'gesture'.

' "Your claim to the British people is that while you effect economy, you are increasing your military and naval strength, and you come to us and you ask us foreign nations not to diminish our expenditure but to diminish our forces: so that at the very moment that you are increasing . . . your own strength you are asking us to reduce ours." . . . It is a fundamental error of some politicians to think that the mere expression—the mere covering of any policy with a phrase expressing good intention is quite sufficient; that you need never look below the surface for the reality of the thing; and you should never be explicit but should allow the reality to float about in this charming manner in this agreeable atmosphere of benevolent platitudes. Benevolent platitudes have no effect upon foreign diplomatists, and if we can do no more than to put up benevolent platitudes before them, then the great object of the right hon. Gentleman . . . is not the object he is likely to accomplish. It is quite impossible . . . to ride two horses at the same time. It is quite impossible to successfully explain to your own country that you are increasing the strength both of your Army and of your Navy, and to persuade other people that you are making great sacrifices in the interest of international disarmament. The two arguments cannot cling together . . . and I venture to suggest that the right hon. Gentleman does not do a service to the cause of international peace when he uses arguments which can be at once exposed, and will be at once exposed, if indeed they can even for a moment persuade or mould the opinion or move the intellect of anybody who listens to them.'

[2] Hansard, 4th Ser. clxii. 302–3.   [3] *The Times*, 31 July 1906.
[4] e.g. *Le Temps*, 30 July 1906.

Grey was doing his best to clear the ground for a discussion. He explained to Cambon on 24 July 1906 that 'Great Britain had sometimes been held up to other Parliaments as the nation which was forcing the pace and necessitating expenditure. Now we were anxious to make it clear that we were not forcing the pace, and to get this recognized, in the hope that public opinion abroad would discourage increased expenditure by other Governments.'[1] Grey thought that Germany held the key of the situation; though, at a time when the Dreadnought was nearing completion the German Government might well have replied that Great Britain was forcing the pace.[2]

On the day after his interview with Cambon, Grey told the American Ambassador that Great Britain would 'like to see discussed at The Hague the question of the reduction or limitation of expenditure on armaments. We ourselves would be able to announce, next year, some reductions in the Army and Navy. At the Conference, we should be prepared to propose still further reductions on the Navy in future years, provided the other Powers would do something of the same kind.'[3] Lord Haldane had already given to Stumm, the German chargé d'affaires in London, the answer which Grey had given to Cambon.[4]

Within three weeks the German Emperor brought a certain chilliness into the atmosphere. During a visit to Germany King Edward VII had spoken to the Emperor in terms which his Ministers would certainly have repudiated. According to the Emperor's version, King Edward VII described the discussions about The Hague Conference as 'humbug'.[5] The Emperor did not remember that the policy of the British Government was determined not by the King but by his Ministers; he hoped

[1] B.D.D. viii. 191.
[2] The fact that the Liberal Government had no responsibility for the decision taken to build the Dreadnought was likely to carry less weight in Germany than in Great Britain.
[3] B.D.D. viii. 191.   [4] D.G.P. xxiii, pt. i. 30–1: 8 June 1906.
[5] For King Edward VII's view of the Prime Minister's article in *The Nation* (see below, p. 130), see Lee, *King Edward VII*, ii. 467.

that Germany and Great Britain would act together, and that common action would improve the relations of the two countries.[1] The Emperor fully agreed with King Edward's views on disarmament. He had refused to follow the advice of the Chancellor and the Foreign Office, and to accept the suggestion made at a meeting of the Inter-Parliamentary union in London that the next meeting should take place in Berlin. He soon withdrew his refusal, on condition that the German army and navy were not discussed.[2] His mood at this time can be seen from a speech which he made at Fraulein Bertha Krupp's wedding. 'To you, my dear Bertha, God has ordained a magnificent sphere of influence.' After his conversation with King Edward, he told the British Ambassador and Sir Charles Hardinge that he still hoped that the Conference would not take place.

'There was however one point upon which he had definitely made up his mind. . . . If the question of disarmament were to be brought before the Conference, he should decline to be represented at it. Each State must decide for itself the amount of military force which is considered necessary for the protection of its interests and the maintenance of its position, and no State could brook the interference of another in this respect.'[3]

The Emperor used almost the same language to Haldane in September when Haldane tried to argue in favour of a plan for slowing down the rate of expenditure on armaments.[4]

Grey commented on the Emperor's remarks to the British Ambassador. He pointed out that 'disarmament' would not be discussed at The Hague Conference. On the other hand, the United States Government had an-

---

[1] D.G.P. xxi, pt. ii. 456–7 n., and xxiii, pt. i. 84–6.

[2] D.G.P. xxiii, pt. i. 78–82.

[3] B.D.D. viii. 192: 16 August 1906. For the Emperor's conversation with Hardinge, see B.D.D. iii. 366–70. Hardinge said that there would be no question of British and German co-operation to prevent the meeting of the Conference.

[4] B.D.D. iii. 380–1. Haldane, *Before the War*, p. 45; D.G.P. xxiii, pt. i. 86–7.

nounced to Russia that they reserved the right to raise the question of the reduction of armaments. 'We have said to Russia that we are favourably disposed to the discussion of the question. . . . The Emperor must take his own course; he can render the whole discussion abortive, but it is a grave responsibility to take. He is entitled to claim a free hand in expenditure as a matter of right; the question is not one of right but of expediency.' Grey also pointed out the difference between the British and German views of the 'force required for defensive purposes', and the British claim to possess for defensive purposes a predominant navy.

'To defend the United Kingdom we must be able to take the offensive outside our own territory at sea and drive the enemy off the sea. If we are placed on the defensive, we are ruined. We must therefore have a naval force superior to our enemy or enemies. A military Power on the other hand by acting on the defensive, can put even a superior enemy in the inferior position by obliging him to fight in a hostile country prepared for defence.'[1]

The argument was strong and, from the British side, unanswerable. Yet the German navy was also regarded in Germany as a means of defence. The development of this navy had been proceeding according to legislative enactment for nearly ten years. Circumstances had compelled the German Admiralty to enlarge their programme of construction. The action of the British Admiralty in building the Dreadnought had added greatly to the burden of shipbuilding. Yet the British Government was now suggesting that Germany should recognize for good and all British predominance at sea, and leave the German navy powerless before the fleets of its rivals. Great Britain was putting the odium of a refusal upon Germany, and forcing Germany to appear before the world as the Power opposed to any limitation of armaments. Finally, the British proposals were made in general terms, and offered no practical basis of negotiation.

[1] B.D.D. viii. 193.

The views of the Liberal Government were clearly expressed in a letter written by Grey in November 1906 to Lord Knollys for the benefit of King Edward VII:

'We could not resist the Conference without a sharp difference with the United States, and feeling in the House of Commons is strongly in favour of the Conference. I share that feeling personally, but even if I did not, I do not think it would be possible for the Government to oppose the Conference. . . . If (the German Emperor) wishes to bring the Conference to nothing, he can probably do so, but it must be made clear that the responsibility for this is upon him and not upon us. He can, if the Reichstag votes the money, oblige us to add another ten or twenty millions a year to the Navy Estimates in the next few years, but if this is done, I want people here and in Germany, who will have to vote the money, to realize that it is he, who has forced our hand in spite of our wish to limit expenditure.'

The Prime Minister approved of the letter. 'The Conference . . . must be kept alive whether an individual attempt at general understanding fails or not, and we are bound to be as helpful to it as we may, not only by our public promises but by our honest opinions.'[1]

Early in 1907 Kühlmann explained to Sir Fairfax Cartwright, the British Minister at Munich, the plan by which Germany hoped to meet a proposal for disarmament. He said that Germany was fully aware that if the question of general disarmament were brought forward for discussion at the Conference, it would be the work of her enemies and a plan to put her in an awkward position.[2] On 9 February 1907 the banker Paul von Swabach wrote to Crowe, probably at Bülow's suggestion, that English action in advocating disarmament might be taken as an anti-German move.[3] Bülow himself told Metternich that the point of Grey's statement was directed against Germany.[4] Grey would not agree that the discussion of the

---

[1] B.D.D. viii. 198-9.   [2] B.D.D. viii. 201-2: 29 January 1907.
[3] Swabach, op. cit., pp. 118-19.
[4] D.G.P. xxiii, pt. i. 116: 10 February 1907. On 23 February 1907 Bülow wrote to Marschall, at this time Ambassador at Constantinople, that he (Marschall) had been chosen as first German plenipotentiary owing to

limitation of armaments—a term which he was careful to use instead of the wider term 'disarmament'—was merely a plot to isolate and discredit Germany. He explained to President Roosevelt on 12 February 1907 that the question of the limitation of naval armaments depended upon England and Germany.

'If we two were to agree to stop new construction for a few years, or to agree to limit it, the whole of the rest of Europe, and perhaps the world, would feel the relief. I believe they would all stop building, except of course Russia, who must repair the losses of the war. But if Germany insists upon the high line that Naval expenditure concerns only herself, and won't discuss it with us, we are bound to go on building to keep ahead of her, and the whole world will feel the strain of increasing navies. . . . It will be a poor lame Conference if the Powers all meet there and shirk the question.'[1]

Once again, a German critic might have answered that Germany was not in a very different position from Russia. The Russian navy had been destroyed; the German navy had not yet reached the strength which Germany thought necessary for her safety. If Russia were allowed to rebuild her navy, why should not Germany continue plans which had been laid down at an earlier date? The additional expense to the British taxpayer could hardly be used as an argument to convince the German people. The assertion that Great Britain would outbuild Germany, whatever the cost, might be included among those 'paper programmes' of which the English press had talked so much in earlier years.

A month later—on 8 March 1907—Grey told Metternich that he wanted to discuss the best method of raising the question of expenditure on armaments without causing friction. Great Britain wanted a discussion of the

his great diplomatic experience. Bülow added that 'the representation of our interests at The Hague Conference will offer many difficulties, since we must always reckon that an attempt will be made to isolate us over the disarmament question, which England and America intend to introduce, and to brand us in the eyes of the world as the destroyers of peace'. D.G.P. xxiii, pt. i. 257 n.   [1] B.D.D. viii. 203.

question. Public interest had been aroused. A large amount of naval expenditure was in suspense. If no agreement could be reached, this expenditure could not be avoided.[1] Ten days before this interview the Prime Minister had written an article for the first number of a new Liberal weekly, *The Nation*, on 'The Hague Conference and Disarmament'. The effect of this article had merely been to increase German suspicions. There is little doubt that by this time the British Government, though determined to raise the question, was not hopeful of any agreement. Austria was as unwilling as Germany to accept a discussion. Aehrental held the view that 'every country, and especially every monarchical country', formed its own idea of the policy most suitable for its own interests. 'With that policy no other Powers had anything whatever to do.'[2]

At the beginning of May Grey was more definite about the plan which he intended to bring forward. The plan was not over-ambitious. It was now clear that a general discussion of any proposals for the limitation of armaments would have little positive result. Grey hoped that a less direct method of approach might have more effect upon parliamentary opinion in foreign countries.

'The proposal I had had in my mind,' Grey told the Russian Ambassador, 'was that the different Powers should communicate their Naval programmes to each other before disclosing them to their own Parliaments and being publicly and officially committed to them. This would provide an opportunity for negotiations, and would help the Powers to realize how much in some cases the Naval programme of one Power is dependent upon that of another. At present, Naval programmes were announced publicly, and the Governments were committed to them in such

---

[1] B.D.D. viii. 214–15. The German and Austrian Governments were also putting pressure on Russia. The Tsar told the German Ambassador in January 1907 that he had lost his earlier illusions about disarmament, and did not want to be associated with the English proposal (D.G.P. xxiii, pt. i. 109: 28 January 1907). There is a certain irony in the fact that the favourite metaphor used by German, Austrian, and Russian statesmen in discussing the best way of getting rid of proposals for disarmament was taken from burying the dead.   [2] B.D.D. viii. 218–19: 23 March 1907.

a way that they could not modify them; and when one Government had done this, another was obliged to follow suit.'[1] This plan for an interchange of information became the basis of Grey's negotiations with Germany after the Conference. It is clear from his own words that he regarded the plan as the first step towards a reduction of armaments.[2] The Emperor was opposed to the idea of exchanging information. He thought it nothing more than a piece of Jesuitism suggested by Fisher. England wanted to be forewarned about German intentions.[3]

Bülow told the Reichstag at the end of April 1907, in a speech on foreign affairs, that he did not hope for practical results from a discussion on disarmament. The German Government had not found any formula which would meet the great diversity in the geographical, economic, military, and political factors affecting the countries concerned, and at the same time furnish the basis of an agreement. An attempt to interfere with these conflicting interests might defeat its own purpose. The prospect of a discussion at the Conference would not 'exercise a tranquillizing influence' upon the international situation. Germany would therefore leave this discussion to other Powers. It had been said that the German representatives could safely take part in the discussion because nothing would result from it. Bülow thought it a more correct and dignified course frankly to state that Germany would not enter into a debate which seemed to her to be unpractical even if it did not involve risks.

The French Minister of Foreign Affairs, M. Pichon, also said in June 1907 that France would consider taking part in the discussion, but was not hopeful of the results since no satisfactory formula had been suggested.[4]

Grey was now afraid that the action which the British Government wanted to take might only make matters

[1] B.D.D. viii. 228. For the later history of this proposal see below, cc. xv and xvi.
[2] B.D.D. viii. 231.   [3] D.G.P. xxiii, pt. i. 215–17.
[4] *The Times*, 8 June 1907; cf. also B.D.D. viii. 241.

worse. In a private letter to Nicolson at St. Petersburg he explained the position:

'If discussion is impossible or fruitless, we shall go on with the Naval expenditure which we now have in suspense. We cannot force things at the Conference against the will of the other Powers. Nothing can be done except by good will and agreement. And if these are not forthcoming . . . we shall not make difficulties which will impede the work of the Conference, or produce unpleasantness after it has met.'[1]

Grey asked Mr. Whitelaw Reid, the American Ambassador, his opinion about the proposal for the exchange of information upon naval programmes. The Ambassador did not think Germany would even consider the plan.

'He believed it to be her desire to build a Fleet which should be stronger than ours. I [Grey] said that if she tried to do this we should certainly build so as to keep ahead of her. . . . It was easy to see that, however superior our Fleet was to the German one, we should never be in a position to conquer Germany, while if her Fleet rivalled ours we should be in danger owing to the size of our Army of being conquered by her.'

An increase in German construction would therefore be followed by a British increase. 'This would force the pace for the world in general, and I thought this a great pity.'[2]

The instructions to the British plenipotentaries at The Hague contained a reference to the limitation of armaments. Great Britain wanted the question to be raised, ·but 'after the apparently final declaration of the German Government, that under no circumstances would they take any part in such a discussion', the question must be left untouched if there were danger of friction. Should the matter be discussed, the British plenipotentiaries were to propose

'that the Great Powers should communicate to each other in advance their programmes of new naval construction. If this were done, they might be led to realize how closely in some cases the naval construction of one Power is dependent upon

[1] B.D.D. viii. 228–9: 1 May 1907.   [2] B.D.D. viii. 231: 2 May 1907.

that of another; and an opportunity would be given for negotiations with the object of reducing the programmes, before the Governments of the Great Powers were finally committed to them by announcing them to their respective Parliaments. His Majesty's Government are aware that this would not necessarily lead to any reduction in expenditure, but they are hopeful that the mere fact of communications between the Powers would provide opportunities for negotiations that do not now exist.'[1]

The instructions given to the German plenipotentiaries also mentioned the question of disarmament.

'As is known, we are only willing to take part in any consideration of this question if there is no more than a repetition of the *vœu* of 1899[2] without discussion. The Delegation must keep away from any further negotiations. If the plan suggested in St. Petersburg by ourselves and Austria is not followed, . . .[3] and the President does not suspend the session of the Conference for a short time upon the non-acceptance of the *vœu*, then the first plenipotentiaries of Germany and Austria-Hungary must make the following short declaration: "according to their instructions the delegates can take no part in any further discussion of the question of disarmament, and therefore ask for a suspension of the session, in order to allow their own and other Delegations holding similar instructions an opportunity to withdraw from the proceedings."'[4]

While the Conference was holding its sessions Grey made one more public appeal.

He told the House of Commons that the British Government did not wish to 'turn what is, and ought to be, a friendly Conference into one . . . divided by controversy. But with regard to making an appeal to the other Powers to meet us on the subject of the reduction of armaments, that appeal has been made emphatically and in the most public way by the Prime Minister. I supported it at least on one occasion in this House, and even

---

[1] B.D.D. viii. 243: 12 June 1907.   [2] See Appendix IV.
[3] The German Government had been trying to secure a promise from Russia that the Russian President of the Conference would adopt this method of 'burying the question'. On 14 June the German Ambassador at St. Petersburg reported that Russia had agreed to the German and Austrian suggestion. D.G.P. xxiii, pt. i. 253.   [4] D.G.P. xxiii, pt. i. 259.

if no definite results can be achieved at the Hague Conference, I trust that at any rate, we shall have prevented the subject from dropping out of sight, and that the appeals which have been made to public opinion generally, though they may not have borne any direct result, may, at any rate, indirectly help forward the study of the question. I remain as impressed as I have ever been with what is almost the pathetic helplessness of mankind under the burden of armaments. . . . It is natural that people should feel that if there were only the good will to discuss the matter with each other, it ought to be possible to do something to reduce the burden. Yet they remain as helpless under the burden, apparently, as ever. Of course it is natural, in these circumstances, feeling how much might be done if the nations would only agree, and how little is done, that there should be strong pressure upon one nation to step out in advance and set an example. The difficulty in regard to one nation stepping out in advance of the others is this, that while there is a chance that their courageous action may lead to reform, there is also a chance that it may lead to martyrdom. We must proceed at such a pace as will carry the leading countries of the world with us.'[1]

It is unnecessary, in a history of the effect of naval rivalry upon Anglo-German relations, to follow in detail the deliberations of The Hague Conference.[2] Sir Edward Fry, the senior British plenipotentiary, raised the question of the limitation of armaments in a general resolution.[3] There was some discussion over the terms of the resolution. The British Government proposed:

'La Conférence confirme la résolution adoptée par la Conférence de 1899 à l'égard de la limitation des charges militaires: et vu que les charges militaires se sont considérablement accrues dans presque tous les pays depuis la dite année, la Conférence déclare

---

[1] Hansard, 4th Ser. clxxix. 1315–16: 1 August 1907.

[2] The question of the right of capture at sea affected the position of the maritime Powers. The decisions, however, made little difference to the main issues of naval strength and had little or no effect upon Anglo-German competition in shipbuilding.

[3] Marschall described Fry, who was then in his eighty-third year, as 'entirely unworldly (weltfremd) and quite without experience of modern political life'. D.G.P. xxiii, pt. i. 269.

que la question est plus que jamais urgente et qu'il est désirable de voir les gouvernements reprendre l'étude de cette question.'[1]

The President of the Conference did not think it safe to distribute in advance copies of the resolution. He was afraid of a number of amendments and of a prolonged and perhaps dangerous discussion. Marschall agreed on behalf of Germany to the British form of words with a slight change in the last sentence. He thought it better to conclude with the words: 'La Conférence déclare qu'il est hautement désirable de voir les gouvernements reprendre l'étude sérieuse de cette question.'[2]

Sir Edward Fry brought forward his motion on 17 August; at the same time he offered to exchange information about prospective naval plans, 'with a view to facilitating a restriction of naval armaments from year to year by mutual consent'. Fry's speech was received with applause. The main resolution was seconded in a letter to the President of the Conference from the first American plenipotentiary. It was also supported by M. Bourgeois, on behalf of France, and by the representatives of Argentina and Chile. The President announced that Russia agreed with the proposal, and the resolution was then accepted unanimously amidst general applause. The German delegates did not speak; Marschall, in a report to Bülow after the Conference was over, again used the metaphor of the burial service to describe the whole affair.

The disarmament question, 'a decoction of empty and meaningless phrases', to use another of Marschall's terms, was put aside; the German plans were completely

---

[1] B.D.D. viii. 261–2.
[2] B.D.D. viii. 263: D.G.P. xxiii, pt. ii. 305–9. Marschall was also shown the draft of Fry's speech. He objected to the words: . . . 'la grande masse d'hommes que ces préparatifs de guerre forcent de se livrer à des travaux stériles et ingrats', as directly anti-militarist. 'The passage about "travaux stériles et ingrats" contradicts in an almost offensive way our national view that military service is an indispensable part of national education.' Fry was content to substitute the phrase 'à abandonner leurs travaux'. D.G.P. xxiii, pt. ii. 309–10 and 315.

successful, though Marschall had been afraid until the last moment that the 'comedy' might be spoiled by a full discussion.[1] Marschall's view of the British attitude towards the question was entirely cynical. England was acting, as usual, from selfish motives; she always defended her own interests on grounds of

'freedom, humanity, and civilization. And the world is convinced. These three catchwords are not the common property of all nations. They are the monopoly of England; when they are employed by England, they exercise an irresistible attraction upon large masses of people throughout the whole world. Herein lies one of the elements of English strength. One cannot feel a grudge against Englishmen if they exploit the situation to the best of their ability.'

Marschall went on to describe the methods by which Great Britain, after building up her trade by means of restrictive measures of all kinds, then began to agitate for freedom of markets in the interest of the whole world, 'so that the products of industry needed by the human race could be bought in the cheapest market, that is to say, in the British market'. Great Britain was now taking a similar line of action on the question of armaments. In the twentieth century, after the British fleet had been increased up to and beyond the 'two-Power standard', England was asking for an agreed limitation of armaments. The analogy was striking. In the past England wanted to secure and maintain in perpetuity her commercial and industrial supremacy; she was now trying to secure her supremacy at sea. In the past the proclamation of a dogma (freedom of trade) had been sufficient; a world agreement was now a safer method. All the nations of the world were to bind themselves by a declaration guaranteeing the 'two-Power' supremacy of the British fleet. 'Mankind is groaning under the burden of arma-

---

[1] D.G.P. xxiii, pt. ii. 315. Marschall's account of the session is full of sarcasm and unkindliness. He told Bülow that Fry spoke French with an English accent, and that some French ladies sitting near Lady Fry could scarcely control their laughter . . . &c.

ments. Freedom, humanity, and civilization demand a limitation of armaments, that is to say the perpetuation of a state of things which is to the present advantage of England. It (the debate) was a moving spectacle.' Marschall was sure that Germany and Austria-Hungary alone were responsible for the failure of the British plan.

'Spain and Portugal always voted with England, whatever the matter under discussion. Italy found it difficult, owing to Italian public opinion, to oppose England on "questions of humanity". Neutrals in general, that is to say, non-military states, naturally favoured disarmament. France was entirely on our side, but would never have been strong enough to take an independent line against England if we had not covered her. The treaty between Chili and Argentina shews that talk about disarmament finds a fruitful soil in America.[1] Japan, according to her principles, would have refused to vote. And Russia? No one knows.'[2]

This record of triumph makes strange reading a quarter of a century later. It is doubtful whether Marschall and Bülow were wise in treating English pacifist opinion with such disdain and in ignoring the attempts of the Liberal Ministers to escape from a situation for which they were not wholly responsible. The German attitude at the Conference was not without effect upon British opinion. The comments of the British representatives were as outspoken as those of Marschall himself, and not least outspoken in describing Marschall's own behaviour. Sir Edward Fry, in his official report, included among the reasons for the meagre results of the Conference the number of important subjects under discussion, the number of states taking part in the debates, the 'chaotic' procedure of the commissions and sub-commissions, and 'the evident wish of some of the Great Powers that the results . . . should be as small as possible'.[3] Crowe was more explicit in a

[1] A treaty of mutual naval disarmament was signed between Argentine and Chili in January 1903.
[2] D.G.P. xxiii, pt. i. 282–3: Marschall to Bülow, 28 October 1907.
[3] B.D.D. viii. 295: 16 October 1907.

private letter written to Tyrrell in the second week of October 1907. He spoke of the

'perpetual flurry, and tedious and invariably useless work. . . . Nothing really important depends on what goes on here. The interesting thing is the political grouping. Germany, Austria, and Italy, and their satellites (which, curiously enough, comprise Greece, Roumania, and Belgium) have completely succeeded in wrecking everything in the most open manner. But the most remarkable phenomenon has been the close rapprochement between Germany and Russia on the one hand, and Germany and the United States on the other. The Russians, whenever there was a divergence between France and Germany, have steadily and ostentatiously taken the German side. The French have realized that they have no influence whatever over their Russian colleagues. The Americans have, except in the case of obligatory arbitration, also gone with Germany and against us in every possible way, most markedly in all naval questions, and often obviously in a sense quite opposed to their own interests. The whole Conference practically united against us on every question of naval warfare. . . . Many of the smaller Powers, notably Sweden, Norway, and Denmark, clearly intimated that even where their interests seemed to demand their going with us, they dare not do anything that might expose them to the ill will of Germany. As for Italy, she made reparation for Algeciras by supporting the triple alliance partners through thick and thin. Portugal and Spain steadily held with us all the time, and Japan supported us whenever she could. The dominating influence in the conference clearly has been *fear* of Germany. The latter has followed her traditional course: cajoling and bullying in turn, always actively intriguing. Marschall is the embodiment of this double faced spirit of intrigue. He seems to me cunning and false to a degree, very plausible, very determined, and a most dangerous person, deep in all newspaper intrigue. He has here a regular press bureau installed in his hotel. Even Saunders of *The Times* is not proof against his tricks. He *certainly* works several English newspapers from here. I do hope that we may never have Marschall as German Ambassador in London. He would play the very devil there. It is his ambition.[1]

---

[1] Crowe thought that a hint might be given to Bülow. It was believed in the British Foreign Office that Bülow disliked Marschall. In May 1912,

'If the present position of Germany allows her to take up the domineering attitude she assumes here, what will be her bearing when with the further support of Russia and perhaps with our connivance, she gains a more complete hegemony in Europe and the world? One shudders to think of what would then become of British interests.'[1]

Lord Reay, another of the British delegates, was not much more hopeful, though he looked at the Conference from a different point of view. He thought that France and Italy had been afraid of isolating Germany; the smaller continental Powers had been afraid of offending her. Germany herself had been anxious to conciliate the United States and to prevent the combined action of the United States, France, and England. 'One of the objects of Germany was to reduce to a minimum the positive results as regards additions to or alterations of existing rules of international law . . .' Russia wanted 'to secure a bill of indemnity' for actions contrary to international law in the Russo-Japanese war; she had not dared to risk German displeasure.

'It is safe to draw the conclusion that the result of the attitude of Germany . . . will be to give an impulse to the manufacture of balloons and mines and instead of encouraging disarmament the Conference has certainly increased the existing feeling on the Continent of Europe that no Power can afford to neglect its means of offence and defence. The strongest guarantee of peace is the knowledge that all are prepared for war and that in case of war the issue depends on the relative strength of the armies and navies which are engaged. The Conference has not given any new guarantee for the maintenance of peace and has confirmed the fact that the Powers are constantly preparing for

when there were rumours of Marschall's appointment to the London embassy, Cambon told Nicolson that Marschall employed as 'un homme de main pour toutes les besognes . . . un juif allemand nommé Paul Weitz, correspondant de la *Gazette de Francfort*, vulgaire, mal élevé, bavard, pénétrant partout . . . distribuant secrètement aux journalistes. . . . Il a accompagné le baron Marschall à la Haye'. Nicolson answered that he knew Weitz by reputation and that the Foreign Office would take precautions if Weitz came from Constantinople with Marschall. D.D.F. 3rd Ser., pt. ii. 442–3.

[1] B.D.D. viii. 287–8: 11 October 1907.

war. . . . It has not given a greater sense of security, but rather the reverse.'[1]

Finally, one may quote a simple comment made by Mr. Chien Hsun, Chinese Minister in Holland, and one of the two Chinese representatives at the Conference. Mr. Chien Hsun reported:

'The first Conference was nominally intended to effect the limitation of armaments, and on this occasion (i.e. the second conference) England made this her main suggestion, but on proceeding to discuss it, the members of the Conference could not refrain from smiling, for, when every Power is competing to the uttermost, which of them is likely voluntarily to impose checks upon its own martial ardour?'[2]

[1] B.D.D. viii. 299–300.

[2] *The Times*, 20 February 1908. One curious little fact is worth mention. On 19 October 1907, at the conclusion of the second Hague Conference, *The Times* used the word 'pacificists'—in inverted commas.

VII

THE ANGLO-RUSSIAN AGREEMENT, 1907

THE failure of the second Hague Conference made it unlikely that the naval competition between Germany and Great Britain—a competition intensified by the building of 'all-big gun' ships—would be ended by agreement or compromise. If an agreement were not reached, the competition would become more serious, and its effect upon the relations between the two countries would be more disturbing. The Liberals in England would be forced to spend more money on armaments and ask for larger sums from the taxpayers. This expenditure could be justified only by telling the electorate that the British Government had tried and failed to obtain an agreement with Germany. Public opinion would support an increase of expenditure if it were shown to be necessary. The demonstration would be made by reference to the facts; that is to say, to the growth of the German fleet. The electors would look at the question from this angle, and would consider that Germany was responsible for keeping up a senseless and extravagant competition.

On the German side exasperation at British 'hypocrisy' would spread from the Government to the people. The German Government would also have to persuade the electorate that an ever-increasing naval expenditure was necessary. This explanation would take the form of press campaigns and propaganda through the Navy League and patriotic societies. A campaign of this kind would be noticed in Great Britain; it would add to British suspicions of German designs and German unwillingness to break away from the vicious circle of military preparation and counter-preparation.

Moreover, the policy of Germany in directions other than the expansion of the navy was leading to results which would in their turn disturb German opinion. It would not be difficult to convince those who knew little of the secrets of state that Great Britain was attempting to isolate Germany in Europe. Once again, therefore, it is necessary to turn from the study of naval affairs to other regions of policy.

After the failure of his attempt to detach Russia from France, the German Emperor had assumed that a coalition against Germany existed in the logic of events. The Emperor's calculations took little or no account of one question upon which British and Russian interests were becoming sharply contrasted with those of Germany. A less aggressive policy on the question of the Baghdad railway might have prevented the Anglo-Russian agreement of which the Emperor was afraid. Kühlmann, writing after the event, has pointed out that Germany made the great mistake of following at the same time a naval policy which alarmed Great Britain, and a Middle Eastern policy which alarmed Russia.[1] Kühlmann's views at the time were less clear-sighted; he was one of the strongest supporters of the Moroccan policy which strengthened the British entente with France. Nevertheless, it is difficult to avoid the conclusion that the German attitude upon the Baghdad railway removed the greatest obstacle to an agreement between England and Russia.

The history of a railway project connecting the Mediterranean with the Persian gulf goes back to the period of the Crimean War.[2] A Euphrates Valley Railway Company was formed in 1856. The engineer and representative of the company at Constantinople was General Chesney who, twenty-one years earlier, had commanded the Euphrates Survey Expedition. Lord Stratford de

[1] Kühlmann, *Thoughts on Germany*, p. 19.

[2] There is no authoritative study of the Baghdad Railway question. E. M. Earle, *Turkey, the Great Powers, and the Baghdad Railway* (1923), was published before the appearance of the *British Diplomatic Documents*. The early history of the project is summarized in the *Quarterly Review* of October 1917, by A. Parker, formerly Librarian of the Foreign Office. For the diplomatic negotiations see B.D.D. ii, c. xii, pt. 3 iii and D.G.P. xiv, pt. ii, c. xciv; xvii, c. cxiv; xxv, c. clxxxv; xxvii, pt. ii, cc. ccxvi and ccxvii; xxxi, c. ccxlv; and xxxvii, pts. i and ii, cc. cclxxxiv and cclxxxvi.

Redcliffe obtained a concession for the company in 1857 for the construction of a railway from Suedia, opposite Cyprus, to Basra. Although the Turkish Government offered a 6 per cent. guarantee for the unprofitable section from the Syrian coast to the Euphrates, no British capitalists would undertake the work without official help, and no help was forthcoming from the British Government. The opening of the Suez Canal made the success of a railway scheme even more hazardous. Disraeli took account of the possibilities of the railway when he secured the Cyprus Convention from Turkey in 1878, but the occupation of Egypt soon diverted British attention and British capital elsewhere, and, incidentally, affected the relations between Great Britain and Turkey.

At the time when British influence in Turkey was declining, Germany began to look to Asia Minor as a possible region for German enterprise. Moltke had been one of the first, though not the only German, to point out this fruitful field.[1] In 1888, after Constantinople was joined to western Europe by railway, one M. Kaulla, acting on behalf of the Württembergische Vereinsbank, the Deutsche Bank, and a group of London capitalists, obtained certain valuable railway concessions from Turkey. The Haidar Pasha–Ismidt railway, a short line of some fifty-seven miles, was brought under the administration of the syndicate, and an extension was projected as far as, or beyond, Angora.[2] The British members soon left the syndicate. Turkish finances were insecure, and better opportunities were offered for British capital and British railway contractors in India, Africa, and the New World. German banking enterprise was more skilfully organized, with more direct support from the German Government. On the political side, Great Britain had no wish to exclude Germany from Asia Minor. Sir William White, the British Ambassador at Constantinople, saw an advantage

---

[1] Moltke, 'Deutschland und Palästina', in *Gesammelte Schriften*, ii. 279–88.

[2] The syndicate owed their success partly to their readiness to provide the Sultan with a loan (well secured) of £T1,500,000.

in attracting Germany to a region where Great Britain
had long borne the weight of resisting Russia. 'England
has this day acquired a powerful ally in her agelong guard
against the Russians on the Bosphorus.'

Salisbury agreed with this judgement. Germany was
left alone in the field, although British interests in the
Smyrna–Aidin railway would suffer if a line from Constantinople drew off the rich trade of the Konia district.
In 1890 the first stage of the extension of the Haidar
Pasha–Ismidt line was opened. In the following year the
Sultan asked for German help in prolonging the railway
to Baghdad. A concession was granted in 1893 for an
extension from Angora to Kaiserieh, and ultimately to
Baghdad, with a branch from Angora to Konia. The
British Government protested against the concession,
partly in the interest of the Smyrna–Aidin company,
partly from a certain nervousness about the security of
the routes to India and the long-standing predominance
of Great Britain in the Persian Gulf. The German
Government not only refused to listen to the protest, but
threatened to withdraw their support of British schemes
in Egypt. This pressure was successful; but for the next
five years Turkish finances were not in a position to provide the high kilometric guarantee promised in the convention of 1893.

Germany had taken care not to lose her place at Constantinople by attacking the Sultan over the Armenian
massacres.[1] In the autumn of 1898 William paid a visit

---

[1] In 1912 the French Ambassador at Constantinople summed up German
policy in Turkey in these words: 'La politique de Guillaume II à l'égard
de la Turquie ne se distingue pas par l'originalité, puisqu'elle est renouvelée
de celle inaugurée il y a quatre siècles par François Ier, au scandale de
l'Europe d'alors. . . . Le Congrès de Paris avait bien, il y a un demi-siècle,
fait entrer en principe la Turquie dans la société des nations européennes
et il l'avait théoriquement admise à la jouissance de toutes les prérogatives
qui en découlent, mais dans le fait il s'en était toujours fallu de beaucoup que
l'assimilation fût réelle et la Turquie continuait en réalité à être considérée
par l'Europe comme un État d'un genre particulier contre lequel les Puis-
sances avaient des intérêts communs à défendre. Guillaume II a le premier
rompu avec cette tradition et il l'a fait non sans éclat, ayant choisi, pour

to Abdul Hamid who was then boycotted by the rest of the civilized world. Earlier in the year, Marschall, at this time German ambassador at Constantinople, pointed out that the time was ripe for a further German advance not merely on the question of the Baghdad railway but towards the waterways of the Tigris and the Euphrates.[1] In 1899 Germany asked for a concession for building a commercial harbour at Haidar Pasha. It was decided to secure the larger railway concession before arousing English susceptibilities about competition on the Mesopotamian rivers.

The concession was granted in December 1899.[2] Germany now held the right to build a railway to Basra. The Sultan, for military reasons, wanted the line to run by way of Sivas, but Germany made the engineering difficulties of this route a reason for choosing the southern way through Konia. The German Government was particularly anxious to use this southern route in order to avoid offending Russia. Russia already disliked the Haidar Pasha concession, and was opposed to any railway which added to the prosperity and therefore the military strength of Turkey.[3] Marschall described the position in a dispatch written on 12 April 1899. Turkey could be developed only by foreign capital. Foreign capitalists wanted political stability in a country where their money was invested. An increase in the amount of foreign capital invested in Turkey therefore widened the circle of those interested in the maintenance of the Turkish Empire. Russia did not want the maintenance of this Empire. 'The preponderance of economic interests which is a sign of the present time compels with a certain elementary power those states from which capital is drawn to adopt a conservative

manifester son affranchissement des préjugés européens, le lendemain des massacres arméniens.' D.D.F., 3rd Ser. iv. 35.

[1] D.G.P. xiv, pt. 2. 465. 9 April 1898.

[2] The concession was promised a month earlier.

[3] On the other hand, French financiers were ready to co-operate with Germany. The French Ambassador at Constantinople suggested an 'entente' between France and Germany in Turkey. D.G.P. xiv, pt. ii. 481.

Eastern policy, and therefore to oppose Russia's final aim.' Russian opposition to the Baghdad railway was inevitable. 'The Russian orthodox propaganda with its monasteries, churches, and schools, and the high towers which give far-reaching and visible expression to the Power of Russia, will not turn the scale against the weight of a mighty undertaking decisive for the welfare of a population extending over thousands of square kilometres.'[1] Russian opposition was shown at once in a demand that Turkey should concede to Russia all railway construction in northern Asia Minor. A Russo-Turkish agreement to this effect was signed in April 1900. The agreement with Turkey was confirmed in 1902 and again in 1903. The German agreement of 5 March 1903 constituted a Baghdad Railway Company in which the Anatolian Railway Company, hitherto the principal party in the German negotiations, took shares. The line would run from Konia through Adana, Mosul, and Baghdad to Basra; branch lines would be built to Aleppo, Urfa, Khanikin (on the Persian frontier), and to a point on the Persian Gulf. The concession included a high kilometric guarantee, and allowed the railway company mining rights, harbour facilities, and privileges of inland navigation within the sphere of its operations.

The German financial group wanted to secure British support. After some discussion the British Government came to the conclusion that British participation was possible, if it were clearly understood that the railway was an international concern from sea to sea. The British Ambassador at Constantinople supported the plan of co-operation, but public opinion in Great Britain had begun to fear that co-operation with Germany meant the sacrifice of British interests. Opposition was shown in Parliament and the press. The financiers became alarmed, and the Government gave way. Mr. Balfour stated in Parliament that the terms offered by Germany did not give sufficient security for the international control of the

---

[1] D.G.P. xiv, pt. ii. 480–9.

line.[1] It was thought in England that the financial success of the scheme depended upon the consent of Great Britain to an increase in the Turkish customs dues; without this increase Turkey could not provide the kilometric guarantee.

The objections raised in Great Britain were not unreasonable. Under the proposed scheme eight of the thirty members of the Board of Directors were German, eight French, and eight British; three were nominated by the Boards as a whole, and three by the Austrian and Swiss groups. It would be possible for any two Powers to block the proposals of a third Power. After the Anglo-French entente Great Britain might have been fairly certain that France would not support Germany against British interests, but the entente had not been concluded in March 1903. It is also fair to remember that two years earlier the German chargé d'affaires in Constantinople had used language which showed very clearly that Germany did not intend to allow an equal partnership between herself and Great Britain. The chargé d'affaires was surprised that Sir Nicholas O'Conor, the British Ambassador at Constantinople, 'after his long experience of Turkey has not yet seen that an "economic" partnership (*Ehe*) between Germany and England here is an impossibility. For us this would mean the burial not only of the Baghdad railway but of all our other economic plans.'[2]

The failure of the negotiations between the British and German financial groups left the control of the railway in German hands; but the main political questions remained

[1] Hansard, 4th Ser. cxxi. 222. The arguments against British participation were that the railway scheme would mean offending Russia, risking a large sum of money, and assisting German enterprise to drive Great Britain out of regions where she had opened up trade and established transport services. These arguments were expressed very strongly in a leading article in *The Times* of 22 April 1903. The financial group interested on the British side included names which did not inspire much confidence. Sir E. Cassel was a German who had become a naturalized British subject. Sir Charles Dawkins was connected with the firm of Morgan, and therefore with the unpopular Atlantic shipping combine.

[2] D.G.P. xvii. 405: 15 August 1901, Wangenheim to Bülow.

unsettled. On 5 May 1903 Lansdowne announced in Parliament that Great Britain would resist any attempt by a European Power to establish a naval base or fortified port on the Persian Gulf.[1] It was thus fairly clear that German and British interests would come into conflict at the eastern end of the railway. For a time the question was in suspense. The railway reached Bulgurlu on the west side of the Taurus at the end of 1904; but work was then discontinued for financial reasons until 1908.

Russia shared British anxiety about the Baghdad railway, although Russian and British interests were sharply opposed in Persia. If Russia and Great Britain settled their differences, these two Powers would be in a much stronger position to resist Germany. In other words, Germany, not Great Britain, now threatened to cut across the Russian approach to the Mediterranean and the Persian Gulf, and Germany, not Russia, threatened the long-established hegemony of England in the Gulf. The propagandist literature of the pan-German party only increased the uneasiness of Russian and British opinion.[2]

Russia and Great Britain had begun to discuss a settlement of outstanding differences in the year 1903.[3] The discussions were interrupted by the Russo-Japanese War. There followed the change of Russian sentiment towards Germany resulting from the defeat of Russia in the Far East. Witte—whose language was chosen tactfully to suit German or English listeners—told Spring-Rice in the autumn of 1905 that Germany had been working for ten years to estrange Russia from Japan in order to profit by their quarrel.[4] On the other hand, the loyalty of Great Britain to France on the Moroccan question was an object-lesson to Russia.[5] In October 1905 Count Benckendorff, the Russian Ambassador in London, reopened unofficially

---

[1] Hansard, 4th Ser. cxxi. 1348. Hitherto Russia alone had aroused British fears about the Persian Gulf. See Ronaldshay, *Life of Lord Curzon*, vol. ii, c. 23, and above, p. 75.   [2] See above, p. 59–60.

[3] B.D.D. iv. 183. The history of the Anglo-Russian agreement may be read from the British side in B.D.D. iv.

[4] B.D.D. iv. 77: 7 May 1905.   [5] B.D.D. iv. 199: 6 September 1905.

the question of an understanding. Lansdowne thought it would be a mistake to attempt too much, or to allow it to be understood that the two countries were on the eve of a comprehensive transaction analogous to that which had taken place between France and Great Britain. Lansdowne wanted the two Governments to take up questions of detail and attempt to settle each question as it arose.[1]

This caution was justified. The internal situation in Russia made negotiations difficult. The return of the Liberal Party, known to be in sympathy with constitutional movements in Russia, affected the attitude of the Russian governing and higher social classes.[2] Isvolsky succeeded Lamsdorff on 12 May 1906. He wanted to secure an agreement with Great Britain but was extremely careful to avoid offending Germany. The German Government on their part made it clear that they expected Russia to take account of German interests, and that the future political relations between the two countries would depend upon the consideration given to these interests.[3]

There could be no lasting compromise between a policy which was primarily in German interests and a policy which was directed towards collaboration with Great Britain. The decisive choice was made early in February 1907 at a special meeting of the Russian ministerial council. The main subject of discussion was the Baghdad railway. Russia could not neglect German susceptibilities, and Isvolsky did not wish to meet the fate of Delcassé.[4] Nevertheless the time had come to settle the attitude of Russia towards the railway. Its construction was now assured. The line was so injurious to Russian interests that no 'compensations' could make up for the surrender on the main question. 'We must therefore be content to

---

[1] B.D.D. iv. 204–5: 3 October 1905.

[2] On the other hand, Benckendorff was on excellent terms with Grey. His Russian colleagues nicknamed him 'Grey-m'a-dit' because his dispatches generally opened with these words. Taube, *op. cit.*, p. 160.

[3] For the attitude of Isvolsky, see Nicolson, *Life of Lord Carnock*, c. ix. The German documents on the Anglo-Russian understanding are printed in D.G.P. xxv, pt. 1. cc. 183–4.   [4] See above, p. 90.

limit as far as possible its bad effects.' Separate negotiations might be opened with Germany on the railway question, but without the help of England Russia would not expect to obtain good terms. Therefore concessions must be made to British interests. Russia must give up the plan of bringing the whole of Persia under her influence and building a railway through Persia to a fortified station on the Persian Gulf.[1]

The Anglo-Russian Agreement was signed on 18/31 August 1907.[2] Its terms were published at once. The Agreement contained no secret clauses, and was concerned only with questions outside Europe. Persia was divided into British, Russian, and neutral spheres of influence. The other clauses of the document dealt with Afghanistan and Thibet. There was no threat to Germany in the agreement. Russia could not fight Germany for years to come, and had no wish to be involved in another war. On the British side, Lord Morley, who was no chauvinist, praised the agreement as 'one of the most skilful performances in the records of our British diplomacy'.[3] Nicolson has described the policy and views of the Foreign Office.

'There was no question of "encircling" Germany. Notwithstanding the fact that in dealing both with France and Russia we had honestly no other object than to place our relations on a safer and more secure basis in the general interests of peace, yet the subconscious feeling did exist that thereby we were securing some defensive guarantees against the overbearing domination of one Power. . . . It can be safely postulated and admitted that neither France nor Russia nor Great Britain had the remotest desire to disturb the peace or impair the relations between themselves and Germany, Austria, and Italy. It can be asserted with absolute truth that there was not an aggressive or bellicose feeling or aim existing among members of what came to be called the Triple Entente.[4] . . . Had Germany reci-

[1] B.D.D. iv. 270-1. The document is printed in German in Siebert, *Graf Benckendorffs diplomatischer Schriftwechsel,* i. 1-9.

[2] The agreement was accompanied by Russian and French agreements with Japan.   [3] B.D.D. iv. 587.

[4] In May 1909 the Foreign Office advised Nicolson not to use the term 'triple entente' in official dispatches referring to the joint action of Great

procated this, and had she reciprocated these amicable senti-
ments, and recognized that the creation of the Triple Entente
had nothing minatory in character, there should have been no
reason why these two European groups should not have existed
side by side (and worked for peace). I am by no means over-
stating the case for the Triple Entente when I assert that unless
the Powers composing it were exposed to aggression, or to a
wilful invasion of cherished interests and rights, they were
resolved that peace should be maintained throughout Europe.
It was indeed their hope, though not perhaps their expectation,
that, as time proceeded, a general unity of all the Great Powers
might eventually be attained. Germany, however, was persuaded
that the Triple Entente was established with a jealous intention
of circumscribing her progressive activity, and was misled by
information[1] that secret agreements to that end existed between
France, Russia, and Great Britain; while the rivalry and eventual antagonism between Russia and Austria-Hungary with
regard to Balkan affairs introduced fresh elements of discord
and distrust.'[2]

The repercussions of the Anglo-Russian agreement
belong to the general history of Europe in the seven years
between 1907 and 1914. The effect of the new grouping
of the Powers upon the problem of Anglo-German naval
rivalry was extremely serious. Once more the contrast
between the British and German views of the international
situation had been sharpened. German diplomatists,
politicians, and writers were unable to see in the action
of the Liberal Government at The Hague Conference anything more than a hypocritical attempt to secure British
naval predominance without additional cost to the British
taxpayer. These observers found their views confirmed
by the Anglo-Russian agreement. Moreover, on the
technical side the naval position was less hopeful for
Germany. The 'risk' theory was even more remote from

Britain, France, and Russia. 'This expression is one which is no doubt
convenient, but if it appeared in a parliamentary Blue Book, it would be
assumed to have some special official meaning and might provoke inconvenient comment or enquiry.' Nicolson, *op. cit.*, p. 308.
    [1] Information of an alarmist kind was given to Germany through an
agent in the Russian Embassy in London.   [2] Nicolson, *op. cit.*, pp. 235-7.

the facts. The intention of the Admiralty to concentrate the British navy in the North Sea was now obvious; this concentration would destroy the thesis that the 'strongest naval Power' would be unable to prevent the dispersal of its fleet. The building of the Dreadnought had increased the cost of shipbuilding and also made larger floating docks necessary. At the same time the change in the political situation appeared, in German eyes, to make war more likely; but the German navy had lost a great deal of its value. The squadrons were there; the fleet was efficient. German sailors hoped that, ship for ship, and crew for crew, their navy would be a match for the navy of Great Britain. Every year gave them greater experience of seamanship and gunnery. Yet the immense numerical superiority of the British fleet, supported by the fleet of France, and, in a few years time, by a new Russian fleet, made the chances of victory very remote. A high-spirited nation would not suddenly give up its ambitions. Surrender on the naval question appeared to be surrender of Germany's world position. The temper of the people had been raised to a high degree of excitement. The elections to the Reichstag in January 1907 were fought by Bülow with an appeal to German patriotism. Bülow gave his support to the Imperial Association for combating Social Democracy and addressed a manifesto to the President of the Association. The President was General von Liebert, a well-known Pan-German chauvinist who had declared at the Pan-German Congress in September 1906 that German 'lack of diplomatists must be compensated for by brute force'. The Navy League also took an important part in the elections. Some fifteen millions of its pamphlets were distributed; 124,000 were sent to school teachers.[1] According to the *Leipziger Neueste Nachrichten*, the Emperor

---

[1] The British naval attaché in Berlin reported the effect of this propaganda. 'England has been constantly held up to hatred by Navy League Orators in every village in the Empire.' Captain Dumas also mentioned the result of the efforts made to teach schoolchildren that 'England wished to destroy Germany'. He had spoken to children whose 'teacher had begged them always to remember that England was their enemy'. B.D.D. vi. 122.

congratulated the President of the League on its work during the elections. The League continued this business of agitation in the months between the elections and the meeting of The Hague Conference. The membership now exceeded 900,000. At the general meeting in May 1907 the usual speeches were made about British envy and jealousy of Germany. According to Stresemann[1] a large section of the British press was telling its readers that 'on the day when the German mercantile marine is destroyed, every Englishman will be a pound richer'.

The leaders of the German nation did not attempt to turn back from the path which they had taken. If the naval competition continued, the terms of the Navy Law of 1900 and the supplementary law of 1906 were insufficient. Rumours of a new plan for increasing the striking power of the German fleet appeared in the German press a few days after the close of The Hague Conference. On 3 October 1907 the British naval attaché in Berlin reported that newspapers of various political views were forecasting a new supplementary law. The *Berliner Neueste Nachrichten* suggested that an ultimatum had been sent to the Government by the manufacturers of armour plate.[2] The *Kieler Neueste Nachrichten* had spoken of a reduction in the age of battleships and cruisers. In November the text of a proposal to this effect was published in the *North German Gazette*. The life of a battleship would be shortened from twenty-five to twenty years. The reasons given for the change were that the actual life of a battleship in the German navy was nearer to thirty than to twenty-five years. The period of twenty-five years was calculated from the date of the first instalment of the money for building the ship to a similar date in the case of its successor. The obsolete ship was not struck off the active list until its successor was ready for commission. The argument was not impressive. It ignored the fact that the age of the ship to be replaced had been calculated not from the date of its completion but from the first stage in its construction.

[1] At this time deputy for Dresden.   [2] B.D.D. vi. 60-1.

The ship remained in commission for two years after the construction of its successor had begun; but it had started its own 'life' as an effective ship two or three years before it had been ready for commission.[1] The supplementary law had an important effect upon the strength of the German navy in modern ships. A Dreadnought would take the place of every 'dead' battleship. The text of the supplementary law was accompanied by a table of construction. Three Dreadnought battleships were to be laid down annually in 1908, 1909, and 1910, two in 1911, and one battleship and large cruiser annually from 1912 to 1917 inclusive. This table showed that between 1908 and 1917 three new modern battleships would be added to the German fleet by the reduction in the 'effective' life of older battleships. On the other hand, the replacement of one armoured cruiser was postponed until after 1917. The significance of the proposal lay, however, not merely in the addition of three modern battleships to the German navy over a period of ten years, but in the distribution of the programme of replacement. It was desirable to 'spread' the programme over the ten years 1908–17. There had been no regular, unbroken sequence of construction before the first naval law; hence the number of ships becoming obsolete in any given year was not uniform. Six new ships would be wanted in 1909, and only one in 1910. The 'spread' was not evenly made. A larger amount of new construction was tabled for the earlier part of the ten-year period. If the new construction sanctioned by the naval law were added to the construction necessary

[1] e.g. ship A is laid down in 1890, and its 'life' is counted from the first financial grant for its construction. In 1905 this ship is twenty-five years old, and due for replacement. It is not actually replaced until 1908, when its successor is ready for commission. But ship A did not come into commission until 1893. Its effective life as a commissioned ship would only be twenty-five years if it were finally paid off in 1908. Tirpitz's argument that a long period might elapse between the final decision about the plan of a ship and the first financial instalment for its construction was not supported by the facts of German procedure in shipbuilding. (A German ship, under the naval law of 1900, was paid for in four annual instalments.)

for replacement, the German programme would be as follows:

Year	Battleships	Large cruisers
1908	3	1
1909	3	1
1910	4	0
1911	2	1
1912	1	2
1913–17	1 (annually)	1 (annually)

Between 1908 and 1911 Germany intended to lay down twelve battleships instead of eight—the number prescribed in the programme of the naval law. In 1910 the German fleet would include four Dreadnoughts and one Invincible; in 1911, seven Dreadnoughts and three Invincibles, in 1912, ten Dreadnoughts and four Invincibles.[1] This increase might not mark the limit of the expansion of the German navy. The budget committee of the Reichstag accepted the supplementary law in January 1908. Public opinion was undoubtedly in favour of a measure which strengthened the fleet, and the proposals could not be taken as final. The Navy League was not satisfied and continued to ask for more ships. In December 1907 Colonel Gädke, who opposed the extravagance of the League, wrote in the *Berliner Tageblatt* that after 1912 the necessity of keeping the shipbuilding yards employed might lead to a programme of four new battleships or large cruisers a year.

Within a few months after The Hague Conference the Liberal Cabinet had given up hope of any limitation of armaments by general agreement. The result can be seen in a speech made by Grey at Alnwick on 15 January 1908. Grey no longer expected any diminution in naval expenditure. He made it clear that Great Britain had no right to complain of the measures taken by other states to protect their commerce and keep open their lines of communication overseas. The British fleet, however, protected not only the trade of England, but the very life and

[1] The German proposals were analysed by the British naval attaché in two long reports. B.D.D. vi. 68–76 and 118–21.

independence of the country. The Admiralty must maintain a safe margin of security. There was no need for panic or undue haste because Great Britain could still build more quickly than other Powers. A week later Lord Tweedmouth spoke of the need for 'cautious observation' of the programme of other Powers.

These two speeches were intended to prepare Liberal opinion for an increase in the British naval estimates. The main difficulty of the Liberal Ministers lay indeed in persuading their own supporters to vote for any increase in these estimates. The Liberal press still hoped for an agreement with Germany and a limitation of expenditure on armaments. On 5 February 1908 Mr. J. M. Macdonald proposed an amendment to the Address regretting 'that there was no indication of any intention to reduce expenditure on armaments'.[1] The amendment was withdrawn after the Government had promised a debate on the question later in the session. On 13 February Grey stated in the House that the British offer at the Conference was still open; the British Government was prepared to exchange information with other naval Powers on the number and cost of ships to be laid down under the naval programme of any given year.[2] Metternich reported the offer to the Emperor, but William II merely commented: 'Nonsense, they know it [the German programme] already.'[3]

Before the debate on the limitation of armaments the general committee of the National Liberal Federation passed at their annual meeting a resolution in favour of a reduction of armaments. The discussion in the House did little more than show the dissensions within the Liberal

[1] Hansard, 4th Ser. clxxxiii. 883–4.

[2] Mr. Asquith stated on 9 March 1908 that the offer was 'known to all the Powers'. Hansard, 4th Ser. clxxxv. 1132–3.

[3] D.G.P. xxiv. 31–2. Lascelles reported a statement in the German press giving the views of the German Government on the subject. General information about German naval plans was already accessible, while no Admiralty would be willing to disclose details of construction, &c. An exchange of information about proposed construction would only lead to more acute competition between naval Powers, and would therefore defeat its own ends. B.D.D. vi. 137: 24 February 1908.

party; Mr. Macdonald and his supporters still failed to understand the significance of the German attitude at The Hague Conference, and the suspicion with which German opinion looked upon any attempt to interfere with the legal execution of the German naval programme.

The Government, however, left no doubt that financial reasons would not prevent Great Britain from maintaining a safe margin of superiority. The Prime Minister deplored expenditure on armaments, but claimed that British naval policy was defensive in character, and that an 'unassailable supremacy' must be secured.[1] The terms in which the British naval estimates were framed were equally clear. 'His Majesty's Government have every intention of maintaining the standard of the British Navy which has hitherto been deemed necessary for the safeguarding of our national and imperial interests.' It was proposed to lay down one battleship, one large cruiser, six fast protected cruisers, and a number of destroyers and submarines. 'This programme suffices for 1908–9; whether, and to what extent, it may be necessary to enlarge it next year, or in future years, must depend upon the additions made to their naval force by Foreign Powers.'

An impulsive act by the German Emperor did not improve the position. The Emperor visited England in the autumn of 1907. The usual speeches were made; they were followed by the usual comments. Early in February Metternich reported that the German naval programme was causing considerable anxiety in Great Britain. Tirpitz had told the Reichstag that there was no such anxiety. Metternich thought it necessary to correct this statement, and to say that England intended to maintain her naval superiority. 'It is in the interest of good Anglo-German relations that there should be no illusions on this matter in Germany.'[2] Stumm had also pointed out the dangers latent in the attitude of English opinion. 'Even the strongest supporters of a policy friendly to Germany

---

[1] Hansard, 4th Ser. clxxxv. 376–7. For the debate, see Appendix II.
[2] D.G.P. xxiv. 30–1.

accept the view that two English ships must be built for every German ship.'[1] The Emperor now took the curious step of writing to Lord Tweedmouth to explain that the German fleet was not being built as 'a Challenge to British Naval Supremacy.... If England built 60, 90, or 100 battle-ships, there would be no change in the German plans. It was unpleasant for Germans to notice that in discussions about the British programmes of construction, there was always some reference to the German navy. People would be very thankful over here if . . . Germany were left out of the discussion.'[2] The letter was answered by King Edward VII and by the Foreign Office. King Edward's reply was short. The first paragraph was an acknowledge-ment of a letter from the Emperor saying that he had written to Lord Tweedmouth. A second paragraph described the Emperor's action as a 'new departure'.[3] 'I do not see how he [Tweedmouth] can prevent our press from calling attention to the great increase in the build-ing of German ships of war, which necessitates our in-creasing our navy also.'[4]

The Foreign Office memorandum pointed out that the German press often used the British navy as an illustra-tion of the need for increasing the German navy. It was not unnatural that a section of the British press should make similar use of the German navy. 'It would be futile to pretend that the increase of the German fleet is not one of the factors which has to be taken into account in any calculation of the strength at which the British Navy must be maintained. To prevent the British Press

---

[1] D.G.P. xxiv. 21 n.: 25 November 1907. Stumm was acting as chargé d'affaires in London.

[2] D.G.P. xxiv. 32–5: 16 February 1908. The Chancellor and the German Foreign Office knew nothing of the Emperor's letter until after it had been received in England. On the other hand, the Chief of the Naval Cabinet, Admiral Müller, had made a copy of the letter in his own hand. The letter also contained some offensive remarks about Lord Esher.

[3] The Emperor once complained to Queen Victoria about the policy of Lord Salisbury. The Queen's answer was in much stronger terms than the letter of King Edward. See *The Letters of Queen Victoria*, 3rd Ser. iii. 381–2.

[4] D.G.P. xxiv. 36.

from freely stating and commenting upon so obvious a fact would be neither equitable nor possible.'[1]

Lord Tweedmouth would have been wiser to have kept the Emperor's letter secret. The facts, however, became known to Colonel Repington, the military correspondent of *The Times*. Repington wrote to *The Times* that an attempt had been made, in German interests, to influence the Minister responsible for the British navy estimates. An explanation in general terms was given by Tweedmouth in the House of Lords and the Prime Minister in the House of Commons.[2] Neither the letter nor the memorandum was published.

The ill-timed assurances of the German Emperor carried even less conviction when British public opinion turned to the question of the relative rate of building ships in England and Germany. Lord Tweedmouth had maintained that Great Britain could build her ships, large and small, more quickly than any of her rivals. This view had been accepted for many years as demonstrable by facts. It had been asserted in the House of Commons by Liberals and Conservatives. Mr. Gladstone, in one of his last speeches, had said:

'If I am rightly informed, the difference between the time necessary from the laying down to the completion of a great ship is for England three years and for France four and a half years. . . . Our means of construction are overwhelming compared with foreign countries. If we have superiority of means, what about our methods of construction? Happily, they are already far more rapid. My hope is—and I must say my anticipations are—that we shall further gain in that business of despatch, and if we do it is an element of most vital consideration. . . .'[3]

In 1893 Lord Spencer pointed out in the House of Lords that the *Royal Sovereign* had been completed in three years,

---

[1] B.D.D. vi. 134–7. The memorandum was not a direct answer to the Emperor's letter; it had been drawn up in reply to complaints which the Emperor had made to Lascelles about the attitude of the British press.

[2] Hansard, 4th Ser. clxxxv. 1067–8, 1072, and 1135–6.

[3] Hansard, 4th Ser. xix. 1793: 19 December 1894.

while other countries took five years to build similar ships. 'That illustrates one of the sources of strength of this country—that we are able to build ships much more rapidly than other countries. We are thus enabled to watch carefully what other countries do, and if necessary, we can overtake them in an emergency by laying down ships enough to make up for any possible deficiency, as we build so much more rapidly.'[1] Five years later Mr. Goschen made the same claim: 'The resources of this country, both in shipbuilding and engineering—with our power of manufacturing for ourselves what we require— the rapidity with which we can build ships if we lay them down, as others lay them down, will enable us to keep pace with, if not to outstrip our neighbours.'[2]

The first note of warning was given by a private member, Mr. Kearley, in the debate on the naval estimates on 21 March 1901. He complained of the slowness of British building. 'At the present moment Germany is giving us the go-by, and if we drag along in this way, I am confident that in two or three years time we will find that Germany has gone ahead of us. Germany has ample resources and also the determination to put things through in a practical, business-like manner.'[3] The belief in British superiority was, however, not much questioned before 1906. In this year Mr. Balfour said, during the debate on the shipbuilding vote, that 'if the Germans think it worth their while, I do not think we can count upon building quicker than they can. As soon as they see that it is economical and advantageous to build quickly, I think it will be found that they will build as quickly as we can.'[4] The Prime Minister answered that neither France, nor Germany, nor any other country can equal us in rate or cheapness of building.[5] Finally, in 1907, Mr. Robertson still asserted that British naval programmes

---

[1] Hansard, 4th Ser. xii. 1030: 16 May 1893.
[2] *Id.* lxii. 861: 22 July 1898.
[3] *Id.* xci. 804.   [4] *Id.* clxii. 112.
[5] *Ib.* 117. The order in which France and Germany are placed should be noticed.

could be based upon the view that 'our capacity for output' would enable us to deal with 'unforeseen developments.'[1]

The question of 'capacity for output' was not a simple question. The rate of construction of large warships was not determined merely by the speed at which the hulls could be built. A warship was a floating repository of armaments. It was possible to 'complete' a first-class battleship, or a number of battleships, as far as the work of the shipwrights was concerned, before the guns, armour, gun-mountings, and machinery were ready. Ships and engines were built for commerce as well as for war; armaments were made only as instruments of war. Their construction required elaborate plant. This plant could not be improvised. Hence the potentialities of shipbuilding and marine engineering might outrun, at any given time, the potentialities of armament manufacture. There had been an instance of this difficulty within recent memory. In order to complete the Dreadnought within a record time, two gun-turrets originally ordered for other ships were used because the turrets of the Dreadnought were not ready for mounting.

Sir William White, who belonged to an older generation and a time when the superiority of British shipbuilding resources was beyond question, was compelled to admit this difficulty even when he was arguing against Fisher's Dreadnought policy in 1906. In 1906 he had put the matter in these words:[2]

'Unless the output and capability of establishments devoted to the manufacture of all the items which are requisite for the completion of warships are properly proportioned to the programme of shipbuilding so that the several parts may be ready at the dates required for their ready incorporation into the structure, fittings, or equipment of the ship, delays and increased cost will be inevitable. A modern warship is recognized to be "a box of machinery". . . . Besides the propelling apparatus, with its enormous weight and power, a great number of powerful

---

[1] Hansard, 4th Ser. clxx. 659.   [2] *The Times*, 15 November 1906.

engines have to be introduced into protected positions deep down in the hold; and when all that is possible has been done to minimize dimensions and weights, it still remains true that many cumbrous and heavy parts have to be passed down into places in the structure that are difficult of access, and there erected into complete machines. In many cases the structure has to be left unfinished until these operations are completed. It will be understood therefore, that unless great care is taken to have the details of the designs of all this machinery and equipment settled before the construction of warships begins, and to place the orders for them in good time so as to ensure delivery at dates suitable for the advancement of work on the ships, there must be delays and difficulties of a serious nature. Moreover the scale and rapidity of warship construction will be determined by the number, magnitude, and possible output of the allied manufacturing industries; not by the shipbuilding and marine engineering capabilities of a country. Therein lies one of the greatest sources of the superiority of warship building in this country. . . . It is probably near the truth to say that, whereas we could provide each year from existing resources armour, guns, and gun-mountings for ten or twelve first-class battleships, Germany would not be able to provide for more than four or five similar ships.'

Six weeks later Sir William White elaborated this conclusion in another article.[1] The output of merchant ships in the United Kingdom between 1900 and 1905 had averaged 1,402,300 tons annually; the figures for 1905 were 1,623,200 tons. The average annual output in Germany for the same period was 213,100 tons; the figures for 1905 were 255,400 tons. In 1905 twenty-eight warships of about 130,000 tons in all were launched in Great Britain, and sixteen warships of about 39,000 tons in Germany. The ratio between the number of warships and merchant ships launched in Great Britain between 1903 and 1905 was from 1 : 8 to 1 : 12·5 and in Germany in 1905, 1 : 6·4. From 1903 to 1906 Great Britain had voted £55 millions for new construction and naval armaments, while Germany had allowed only £20 millions. Great

---

[1] *The Times*, 25 December 1906.

Britain had also been able to build on a very considerable scale for foreign countries. She had a very large number of skilled artisans, Germany a 'relative scarcity'. Other countries could overtake Great Britain, but only at heavy cost. Moreover, their efforts would not be unobserved. 'Would our administrators . . . fail to note such action, or leave it unanswered? Unless there was wilful blindness or neglect, this could not happen.' Here then was the most favourable statement of the problem at the end of 1906. Within a short time the British public was asking whether the facts were not much less reassuring. No secret was made of the greatly increased potentialities of German construction. During the year 1906 Count Reventlow had collected[1] statements from the six most important private shipbuilding yards in Germany upon their resources. The firm of Krupp replied that they could complete a battleship or large cruiser in 24–30 months. They had seven slipways, and could lay down two ships a year. Howaldt of Kiel also promised delivery after 24–30 months, and at the rate of one ship a year after the first two years. The Vulkan works at Stettin could lay down two battleships of 18,000 tons, and two large cruisers of 15,000 tons a year, and complete them within 24–30 months, if the guns and armour were delivered in time. When the new Vulkan yards at Hamburg were ready the productive capacity of the firm would be increased by 50–75 per cent. Blohm and Voss could lay down two large ships a year, and build them in 2–2½ years if they were sure of a continuous succession of orders. Schichau could 'comfortably' take four 18,000-ton ships on the stocks simultaneously, and complete the equipment of two or three more. This firm had built a battleship in 30 months, but suggested 30–6 months as an 'average' time. The Weser Shipbuilding Company had built new yards in which it could complete two battleships and two cruisers in 24–30 months.

[1] These statements from Reventlow's *Weltfrieden oder Weltkrieg?* (1907) were summarized for English readers in *The Times*, 30 March 1907.

These figures (which did not include the Government yards) showed that German yards could deal with a sudden stream of orders for ships if the armour and armaments were forthcoming. The British lead in shipbuilding capacity was therefore narrowing down to a lead in the output of guns and armour, although there had also been an acceleration in the rate of British construction. In 1908 two years were allowed for battleships, and a slightly longer period for cruisers of the Invincible type. On the other hand, between 1906 and 1908 the German yards had been improved and extended.

Count Reventlow's figures were not widely known until after the debate on the naval estimates in 1907; but their significance was realized long before the debate in 1908.[1] Mr. E. Robertson, Secretary to the Admiralty, said that the Admiralty estimated that the relative strength of Great Britain and Germany would be twelve and six in ships of the Dreadnought type in the autumn of 1910. Great Britain would have completed nine battleships and three cruisers; Germany would have completed four battleships and two cruisers. This forecast was not made as in previous years, without qualification. 'To be perfectly frank, he should say that there were certain possible accelerations—only possible, but possible, which might affect the result at the end of 1910. Germany might have seven battleships and three cruisers completed.' In other words, there might be an acceleration in the German rate of construction. Mr. Robertson included the *Lord Nelson* and her sister ship *Agamemnon* in his calculation of British Dreadnoughts, but excluded the two ships of the 1908–9 programme. He added that these ships would be ready as soon as, if not sooner than the additional German ships. If they were included in the forecast, the strength of Great Britain in Dreadnoughts would be fourteen in the early part of 1911.

The Opposition refused to accept Mr. Robertson's figures. It was pointed out that the *Lord Nelson* and

[1] Hansard, 4th Ser. clxxxv. 1146–1234, 1335–72.

Agamemnon were not ships of the Dreadnought class, and that Tirpitz had stated that Germany could build ships of the line as quickly as Great Britain. Moreover, the German ships were laid down, as a rule, in June and July of the year in which they were voted by the Reichstag. The British ships were not laid down until the winter, or even until the spring of the following year. The four German ships of the German programme for 1909–10 would therefore be ready for service before the end of 1911, Germany would then have thirteen Dreadnoughts and Invincibles to the twelve completed by Great Britain in the autumn of 1911. Mr. Asquith answered that Germany could have completed thirteen ships only if her programme were carried out 'to the letter', and one of the ships were completed 'within thirty months of its being laid down'.[1] It was doubtful whether Germany would be able to maintain this rate of construction. The assumption that Great Britain would have no more than twelve ships of the Dreadnought class in the last two months of 1911 took no account of any ships which might be laid down in 1909 under the estimates of 1909–10, and completed within two years.

'I will say without the faintest hesitation, that if we find (in the spring of 1909) that there is a probability or a reasonable probability [*sic*] of the German programme being carried out in the way the paper figures suggest, . . . we should provide not only for a sufficient number of ships, but for such a date for laying down those ships that at the end of 1911 the superiority of Germany . . . would not be an actual fact. I hope that is quite explicit. That is the policy of His Majesty's Government. It remains on record, and I think it ought to reassure the House that we do not intend in this matter to be left behind.'

The discussion was renewed in July during the debate on the shipbuilding vote.[2] Moreover, Mr. McKenna had taken Lord Tweedmouth's place as First Lord of the Admiralty. The Opposition now used arguments which looked

[1] The German programme for 1909–10 consisted of three large battleships and one large cruiser.

[2] Hansard, 4th Ser. cxcii. 424–526: 13 July 1908.

beyond the year 1911 to the situation in the year 1912. If the German yards could turn out ships as quickly as the English yards, the German programme of four ships for the year 1910–11 might be ready in the course of 1912. Germany would then have completed seventeen ships of the Dreadnought type. If Great Britain wished to maintain an equality with Germany, she would have to lay down five ships in 1909. Mr. McKenna answered that in the spring of 1911 Great Britain would have twelve, Germany nine Dreadnoughts. It was possible that at the end of 1911 Germany might have completed the four ships of her 1909–10 programme; but the British Admiralty could change their practice of waiting until November or December before laying down the ships voted during the summer. Mr. McKenna agreed that 'something might turn next year upon the date at which the ships were laid down. . . . The Admiralty, being fully conscious of that fact, would have their plans ready in time to enable them to lay down the ships earlier should it appear to be necessary to do so.'

Already therefore in the summer of 1908 the British Government was making a cautious admission that the naval estimates of 1909–10 might include a large increase in the ship-building programme, and already there was an element of uncertainty in the estimates. The ship-building capacities of Germany were increasing rapidly, and no one in Great Britain could forecast the significance of this increase. If the estimate accepted by the Government should prove inadequate, a very large programme would be necessary in 1909. In any case this programme could hardly be less than double the programme of 1908. The question of an Anglo-German agreement for the limitation of naval armaments was even more urgent than in the months before The Hague Conference. Was there any chance of obtaining this agreement?

VIII

THE GERMAN EMPEROR, BÜLOW, AND METTERNICH; MARCH–AUGUST, 1908

IN the spring of 1908 the Liberal Government had been in office for more than two years. The experience of these two years had cleared away a good many illusions about the possibility of disarmament, and brought Ministers face to face with the realities of the European situation. The rank and file of the party blamed the Government for their failure to reach an agreement with Germany; but even these critics accepted the view that Great Britain dared not risk the loss of her supremacy at sea. On the other side of the House the Conservatives attacked the naval programmes not because they were too large but because they were too small, and took insufficient account of the rapid growth of the fleet and shipbuilding resources of Germany.

The policy of the Government was clear and open. They wanted to cut down expenditure on armaments. They would not cut down this expenditure below a margin of safety. The measure of their shipbuilding programme was the shipbuilding programme of Germany. A reduction in the German programme would be followed by a reduction in the British programme. It was impossible to avoid public mention of the German fleet, or to hide the fact that ships were being laid down in Great Britain as an answer to ships laid down in Germany.

At the same time the British Government was unwilling to leave the question of a limitation of armaments entirely outside the range of political discussion and diplomatic negotiations. A general European or world agreement was impracticable. The German Emperor had refused to consider more limited proposals, but the British Ministers were not ready to accept his refusal as final. They knew that the Emperor was the greatest obstacle to any cool and common-sense conversations; they could make no progress while the question of ending or moderating a race in shipbuilding was regarded as an attack upon the Emperor's prerogative. Therefore they chose indirect methods of approach. They tried to reassure the Emperor and his advisers that there was no deep-laid plot behind their suggestions. They explained to Metternich the consequences which would follow any large and continued increase in the German naval estimates; they made it clear that Great Britain was resolved, at all costs, to maintain a safe lead in capital ships.

During the spring and summer of 1908 Metternich reported these conversations with British Ministers, and emphasized the importance of taking notice of British opinion. The dispatches were seen by the Emperor. They did not convince William II, though they finally lost Metternich his post.[1] The Emperor was in a difficult mood. The British answer to the Tweedmouth letter, and the polite but firm refusal to accept the view that Great Britain need not take account of the German fleet, did not have a soothing effect. German foreign policy had not been very successful. The Emperor had failed to win Russia over to the German side, in spite of his dramatic success with Nicholas II. His Moroccan adventure had been disastrous. The British Government would not listen to his persuasion, and continued to make suggestions about a limitation of armaments. The Emperor began to think of these suggestions as an insult to himself as well as an interference with his rights.

Metternich's long letters became a little tedious; the same arguments were repeated again and again, and rejected by the Emperor in the same uncompromising, angry terms. In a long dispatch of 8 March 1908 Metternich wrote:

'No Englishman can agree that the building of the German fleet is a matter of indifference to English interests. Two different views are taken in England about the German fleet.

---

[1] See below, p. 364.

One section of opinion holds that the fleet is being built for the purpose of attacking England; the supporters of this view point to the assertions of the (German) Navy League, and other Anglophobe statements. The other view is that our fleet is not a deliberate threat of aggression, but a possible danger to England. Whether the threat is deliberate or potential, both sections of opinion, and all England, agree that the danger exists. The consciousness of this danger naturally increases with the expansion of our fleet. We are the only Power whose fleet is a source of anxiety to England. In our fleet the English see a possible menace to their security and existence. They pay less attention to a long-period programme than to the annual execution of this programme, expressed in terms of the yearly naval estimates and the laying down of ships. For this reason they think our programme for this year an innovation because the shorter life of the ships means a more rapid increase in numbers (*substitutes !!*)[1] and a quicker "tempo" in our rate of building.

'The English are afraid only of our fleet, because we are their nearest neighbours and we appear to them more efficient than other people. We must pass by their island in order to reach the oceans of the world. They believe the French fleet to be of less value, apart from their political relations with France. (*They could have the same relations with us, then there would be no more trouble.*) The Japanese fleet is at the other end of the earth, and whatever one may think of the Yellow Peril, this danger has less effect upon English nerves (*let Metternich ask English merchants in Eastern Asia. They will tell a different story*) than a concentrated, powerful fleet, supported by the strongest army in the world and built up on the shores of the North Sea. Sir Edward Grey told me confidentially that the British Government never includes the fleet of the United States in a calculation of the "two-Power standard". He described a war between the United States and England as "unthinkable". (*Very superficial. Such a war could quite well come about—or one with Japan*). . . . A defeat in the North Sea means the end of the British world Empire. A lost battle on the Continent is a long way from the end of Germany. . . . Is there any chance of making the potential enemy into a friend and getting his strength on one's own side? England has taken this policy into consideration. She is however afraid of becoming politically dependent upon us, and

---

[1] Annotations by the Emperor are printed in italics.

therefore chooses to support herself elsewhere. Hence her sudden zeal for alliances and ententes. . . . It all comes back to our fleet. (*Nonsense. All English mistakes.*) Hitherto, as I have always maintained, there has been no intention, in responsible quarters, of preventing us by force from building up our fleet. It is possible that in the course of years, with the increase of our fleet, this idea may take stronger hold. For the present it is still hoped that the peoples themselves (*only the German!*) will be wearied of this huge burden of armaments, and that the Governments (*only the German!*) will be compelled to limit their expenditure; though it is always assumed that England will keep the lead she already holds, since supremacy at sea is much more a question of existence for England than it is for other Powers.'

The final comment of the Emperor was that England was making great political mistakes; the 'mad' policy of building Dreadnoughts, and not the German fleet, was responsible for British nervousness. The old superiority in numbers was lost because other Powers were building Dreadnoughts. 'The English must get used to the German fleet. And from time to time we must assure them that the fleet is not built against them.'[1] In June 1908, the Emperor still thought that an Anglo-German alliance or entente provided the simplest solution.[2] Metternich repeated his view that 'nothing and no one will convince the English that a powerful fleet, increasing in strength, and close to the English coasts, is not a danger—the greatest danger which an Englishman can imagine. We are determined to possess a strong fleet, and we must not have any illusion about the consequences.' The Emperor's answer was: 'Very simple. Let them make an entente with us.'

[1] D.G.P. xxiv. 44–6: 8 March 1908. The Emperor was excited at this time about the effect of the Tweedmouth letter; but his comments were of a similar character throughout the year.

[2] D.G.P. xxiv. 87–8. Metternich was reporting a conversation with Sir C. Hardinge. Hardinge explained that the increase in British naval expenditure owing to the growth of the German fleet prevented any improvement of Anglo-German relations. In five years' time the financial burden would be heavier, and the exasperation of the British taxpayer even more serious

Metternich was not alone in his warning that henceforward the naval question would settle the character of Anglo-German relations. Stumm wrote his views for Bülow's information. He thought that English distrust of Germany was due almost entirely to the expansion of the German fleet. Differences in national characteristics or traditions were not the cause of antipathy between the two countries. Economic rivalry only affected particular interests which were damaged or threatened by German competition.[1] English statesmen had been forced to give up the policy of 'splendid isolation'; their aim was now to limit the possible allies of Germany in an Anglo-German war. This policy was defensive in character; most Englishmen wanted a peaceful policy. Yet defence would change to offence whenever English naval supremacy appeared to be threatened even by an 'isolated' Germany. Stumm's views made little impression upon the Emperor. William II felt, as a sovereign, that English suggestions of a mutual restriction of armaments were an attack upon his prerogative. The turning-point in the Emperor's relations with Metternich was reached in the summer of 1908. On 14 July Grey invited Mr. Lloyd George to meet Metternich. Metternich reported the conversation to Bülow. The British Ministers pointed out that Anglo-German relations centred round the problem of naval competition. The German naval programme, with its increased rate of construction, would be answered by Great Britain. Good relations between the two countries were impossible while this competition continued. There was no thought in England of an invasion of Germany. Mr. Lloyd George mentioned Bismarck's comment that if an English force landed on German soil, he would ask the police to arrest them. On the other hand, the existence of England as an independent Power was

---

[1] D.G.P. xxiv. 88–90. Stumm thought that the attitude of *The Times* towards Germany was due originally to the fact that the paper-mills owned by the Walter family had been forced to close down owing to German competition.

bound up with the British navy. Every Englishman would spend his last penny on maintaining British supremacy at sea. Metternich suggested that the real cause of the increased financial burden was the introduction of the Dreadnought type for which Great Britain was responsible. In any case the question of a limitation of armaments could be discussed only after Great Britain had shown that her policy of ententes was not directed against German interests. Mr. Lloyd George thought that a diminution in the *tempo* of the German rate of construction would have more effect than any political action. Metternich told Bülow that in his opinion Great Britain did not intend to force Germany either to give up her naval plans or go to war. The British Government had no wish to threaten Germany, but rather to avoid any danger of war by coming to an agreement.[1]

'I have made it clear to the two Ministers that the fulfilment of their wish depends upon conditions the interpretation of which is in our hands. I should have closed the door to future possibilities and made the position unnecessarily acute if I had given them to understand that we should refuse, at any time and in any circumstances, to come to an agreement upon questions of naval expenditure. It will be a long while before Sir E. Grey is ready to pay the price which I have named for this agreement.'[2]

The Emperor's comments were very violent. He was indignant that Metternich had allowed himself, even unofficially, to listen to the 'shameless suggestion that English friendship depended upon the curtailment of German sea-power'. Metternich must be told that the Emperor did not wish for good relations with England at the expense of the German fleet. 'If England will hold

[1] Sir E. Cassel, whose friendship with King Edward in England and Ballin in Germany made him a useful intermediary, discovered at this time from Ballin that if the Entente Powers asked Germany what limits she intended to put to her armaments the result would be war. Huldermann, *Ballin*, p. 210. (Ballin was Director-General of the Hamburg-Amerika Company, and a friend of the Emperor.) There is no evidence that the Entente Powers ever intended to put this question to Germany.

[2] D.G.P. xxiv. 99–102: 16 July 1908.

out her hand in friendship only on condition that we cut down the numbers of our ships, the suggestion should have been rejected *a limine* as a piece of measureless impertinence and a gross insult to the German people and their Emperor. France and Russia would have the same right to demand a limitation of our land forces.'[1]

A fortnight later Metternich again discussed the naval question with Grey and Mr. Lloyd George. Grey explained once more why the growth of the German fleet disturbed British public opinion.[2] Mr. Lloyd George spoke of the dangers which would follow if no agreement were reached on the subject of naval competition. The numerical relation between the two fleets would not have changed, but British public opinion would have become exasperated. Great Britain might introduce a tariff for revenue purposes, and conscription might be accepted as a necessary protection against the risk of a German invasion. Mr. Lloyd George mentioned his 'favourite idea'—a reduction in the *tempo* of German shipbuilding. He thought that the 'two-Power standard' implied that the British fleet should be as strong as the combined navies of Germany and any one other Power, but not twice as strong as the German fleet. He suggested a permanent ratio of 3 : 2 between the British and German fleets. 'If Germany and Great Britain agreed to cut down their programme of construction by one Dreadnought a year, there would be a complete change in British public opinion.' Metternich repeated his view that some proof of British friendship was necessary before German public opinion would be ready to give up a naval programme which they had already accepted.[3]

---

[1] D.G.P. xxiv. 103–4. The whole dispatch was peppered with violent exclamations. It is interesting that, while the Emperor's attitude became more distrustful and uncompromising, Metternich had begun to feel more confidence in Grey. He reported on 1 August 1908 that he regarded Grey 'as an opponent, but an honourable and peaceful opponent'. D.G.P. xxiv. 110.   [2] D.G.P. xxiv. 109–15: 1 August 1908.

[3] Mr. Lloyd George did not explain whether he meant by a 'reduction in tempo' a temporary reduction, followed by an increase in the number of

Once again the Emperor lost his self-control. 'I must beg him [Metternich] in future to repudiate all expectorations [*Expektorationen*] of this kind.' Metternich had made the mistake of listening to proposals which he should have rejected at once. 'He should tell muddle-headed people [*Schwärmer*] of this type to go to h——. He is too flabby.'[1]

Bülow was less inclined to take the high line of refusing to consider any agreement for the limitation of armaments. He had said indeed on 25 June 1908 that Germany could not discuss the limitation of her fighting strength, and that 'a Power demanding such an agreement must clearly understand that such a demand means war'.[2] Yet Bülow was impressed by Metternich's arguments. These arguments were reinforced by an appeal from Ballin. Ballin was sure that the strained relations with England, and possibly, the danger of war, were due to the German navy, and particularly to the rate at which Germany was building battleships. In Ballin's opinion Germany could not have the largest army and the largest fleet in the world. German resources would not be able to sustain a competition in Dreadnoughts with a richer country. The relations between the two fleets in battleships would be unchanged for a long time to come. Germany would therefore be wise to come to an understanding with England upon the extent and measure of naval expenditure.[3]

ships laid down annually, or a real reduction in the programme set out in the tables appended to the Navy Law of 1900 and later amendments of the law. The Berlin correspondent of the *Frankfurter Zeitung* had a long interview with Mr. Lloyd George during his visit to Berlin in August 1908, and was astonished at Mr. Lloyd George's ignorance not merely of German political conditions, but of the German Navy Law and the tables of construction attached to the law. 'I had to explain the simplest things to Mr. Lloyd George and his companions.' [Mr. Harold Spender and Sir C. S. Henry, M.P.] During this discussion Mr. Lloyd George suggested a 'reduction in tempo' as an alternative to a definite reduction in the number of ships ultimately to be laid down. D.G.P. xxiv. 140–3.

[1] D.G.P. xxiv. 116.
[2] Brandenburg, *From Bismarck to the World War* (Eng. trans.), p. 281.
[3] D.G.P. xxiv. 96–9.

On 5 August 1908, after reading Metternich's long dispatch, Bülow asked whether it would be a good tactical move to explain that the German fleet was being built for defensive purposes, and particularly to meet the possibility of a Franco-German war in which England took the French side. If England would promise to remain neutral in a Franco-German war, Germany would find it easier to introduce a slower *tempo* into her shipbuilding programme.[1] Metternich's answer was not encouraging. Once more he pointed out that the German naval programme was causing great anxiety in England. No one in England thought seriously of a preventive war; no one disputed the German right to build a fleet. On the other hand, English Ministers and the English people believed that their naval superiority would be lost if the German programme were not countered by new construction on a large scale in England. The British Government wanted to avoid making this reply, and spending large sums of money on battleships. Hence their desire for an agreement. The two political parties knew that this expenditure could not be avoided unless there were a reduction in the *tempo* of German construction.

Metternich thought that he could mention in conversation the idea of an English promise of neutrality in the event of a Franco-German war. He must take care not to cause suspicion that Germany was trying to estrange France from England. Every one in England would deny that France had any aggressive intentions. No one would feel morally bound to support France if she were the attacking party. But the definition of the term 'aggressor' would depend upon the circumstances. A promise of neutrality would not easily be obtained because it would mean the destruction of the entente.[2]

Metternich's answer was written on the day before King Edward VII visited the Emperor at Schloss Friedrichshof. Grey had given the King a memorandum explaining that an increase in the British naval estimates

[1] D.G.P. xxiv. 117–19.   [2] D.G.P. xxiv. 132–3: 12 August 1908.

would be the inevitable result of the latest addition to the German programme.

'We have to take into account not only the German Navy, but also the German Army. If the German Navy ever becomes superior to ours, the German Army can conquer this country. There is no corresponding risk of this kind to Germany: for however superior our fleet was, no naval victory would bring us any nearer to Berlin. . . . If the Germans are willing to arrest the increase of their Naval expenditure, we should do the same. There need not even be any formal agreement between the two countries. If we announce in Parliament that, as a matter of fact, German shipbuilding was not proceeding at a rate which required any increased expenditure on our part, the result would be to allay the apprehensions of those numerous persons, both in England and in Germany, who credit the other country with hostile intentions; and feeling generally would improve.'[1]

A second memorandum dealt with the same problem from a different angle. It was explained that there were no diplomatic questions which Germany and England had not been able to discuss in a frank and friendly way. On the other hand, public opinion in each country was uneasy and suspicious. This feeling of anxiety was now centred round the rivalry in naval expenditure. If this expenditure increased, then public anxiety would increase. If there were a decrease in naval expenditure, there would be decrease in anxiety. Grey was careful to avoid irritating the Emperor by any suggestion which might be taken as an infringement of his prerogative.

'The British Government would not think of questioning the right of Germany to build as large a Navy as she thinks necessary for her own purposes nor would they complain of it. But they have to face the fact that at the present rate of construction the German Naval programme will in a very few years place the German Navy in a position of superiority to the British

[1] B.D.D. vi. 779. The date of this memorandum was 31 July 1908. The second memorandum was dated 6 August 1908, and was intended for the King and Sir C. Hardinge. The first memorandum was evidently drawn up for the King's use in private conversation, and contained a guarded reference to the possibility of an agreement between the two monarchs. The second memorandum is printed in B.D.D. vi. 173–4.

as regards the most powerful type of battleship. This will necessitate a new British programme of construction to be begun next year. It will be demanded by public opinion; it must avowedly be accounted for solely by reference to the German programme; for the other nations of Europe are either not adding appreciably to their navies or have no navies of importance; and nations outside Europe are too distant or have not armies sufficient to threaten the independence of Great Britain.
. . . Without therefore attributing any sinister motive to the building of the German fleet it is a paramount necessity to increase British naval expenditure to meet the German programme, though we fear that this may be taken as a sign of increasing rivalry and distrust and though we regret anything which is likely to be a barrier to better feeling.'

King Edward VII found it wise to avoid a thorny subject in his conversations with the Emperor. He mentioned that he had a paper giving the views of the British Government on the naval question; the Emperor did not ask to see the paper, and the King thought it tactful to say no more on the matter.[1] For this reason Sir C. Hardinge decided that he must venture on a direct approach. The discussion was not helpful. According to the Emperor's account Hardinge was reprimanded for impertinence, and went home 'a sadder but a wiser man', convinced that no reduction could be expected in the German naval programme.[2] Hardinge's version of the interview was less highly coloured, but no less final. The Emperor had

'failed to see any reason for nervousness in England, or for any increase in the British fleet on account of the German naval programme. This programme was not a new one; it had been passed by law; and it had become a point of national honour that it should be completed. No discussion with a Foreign Government could be tolerated; such a proposal would be contrary to the national dignity, and would give rise to internal troubles if the Government were to accept it. He would rather go to war than accept such dictation.'

[1] It is clear from the Emperor's comments upon a reference to the interview that he did not want a discussion with King Edward. D.G.P. xxiv. 161.

[2] D.G.P. xxiv. 125–9 and 135.

Sir C. Hardinge also talked over the question with Jenisch, who was attached to the Emperor's suite. Jenisch gave answers similar to those of the Emperor. The German naval programme could not be deferred; 'no changes were possible which could be interpreted as due in any sense to the suggestion of another Power'. Hardinge thought that the 'conversations had been foreseen and a reply prepared'. His impression was that the German Government realized the chauvinistic spirit of their own people and dared not risk the charge of surrender to the dictation of a foreign Power.[1]

Bülow repeated his doubts about the wisdom of an absolute refusal to discuss the possibility of a limitation of armaments or an Anglo-German naval agreement. He approved of the Emperor's refusal to open official negotiations, but thought it undesirable and even dangerous to forbid any private conversation on the subject. An absolute refusal of this kind would only increase English anxiety, and also convince the Government that England must build more ships.[2] Bülow was afraid, in spite of Metternich's reassuring letters, that England might make a 'preventive' attack upon Germany. Yet he still insisted that the situation would improve after Germany had passed through the danger-zone, and he was still ready to use flattering language about the naval policy of the Emperor. He did not attempt to define the limits of the 'danger-zone'.

Within a few weeks after the failure of King Edward VII and Sir C. Hardinge to move the Emperor, a new turn was given to the naval controversy. The German Foreign Office began to think that the British desire for a naval understanding might be used to obtain concessions in other fields. This idea may have been encouraged by the efforts of Mr. Lloyd George to obtain financial relief for his next budget. The suggestion of a bargain was made by Stumm on 8 September 1908:

'I am inclined to think, although I appear to be stating a para-

---

[1] For the British accounts of this interview, see B.D.D. vi. 173–200, and especially, 184–90.   [2] D.G.P. xxiv. 148–51: 26 August 1908.

dox, that the British anxiety about the development of our fleet may facilitate the conclusion of an agreement. The . . . nervousness with which all England watches the growth of our forces at sea, the heavy financial burdens imposed by the attempt to be twice as strong as ourselves, the difficulties . . . in the way of immobilising almost the whole of the British fleet in the North Sea, all these considerations seem to me to show that our naval policy gives us a valuable trump card in relation to England. The enthusiastic reception of the American fleet. . . in Australia must have convinced a good many thoughtful English politicians that the interests of the British Empire would be better served if English battleships could shew by their actual presence the value and extent of the protection afforded by the Mother-Country. . . . I am unable to say how we can persuade the English people that there is no need for them to be afraid of a German challenge to their naval supremacy. If we are able to persuade them, in my humble opinion we ought to secure valuable concessions in return. The kind of agreement wanted by politicians here (i.e. in England) and affecting nothing more than the naval policy of the two countries is, I think, impracticable because it does not take sufficient account of the advantageous position in which we are placed with regard to England. We ought rather to have in mind an eventual agreement on the broadest possible basis in order that we may receive compensation in other spheres for the surrender of the favourable position in which we stand in relation to British naval requirements. The Anglo-Russian agreement about central Asia, which has freed England at least superficially and for a time from her fears of a Russian invasion of India, shews what can be gained by using English embarrassments [*Zwangsvorstellungen*].'

Stumm thought that Germany must walk carefully. He disapproved of the support recently given in Germany to the idea of an agreement on the question of armaments. The bargaining power of Germany would improve if the German people gave solid support to the Emperor's views on the question of defensive forces. The British taxpayer must be convinced of the cost of an unfriendly attitude towards Germany. At the same time there was a danger that the Liberal Government might be defeated on this very question of an Anglo-German agreement. A 'unionist-imperialist-protectionist' Government would come into office. The chances of success would then be less. On the German side 'the bow must not be too loose, but it must not be drawn too tightly'.[1]

Bülow gave his whole-hearted approval to Stumm's suggestions. Herein lay one of the most curious and vital differences between the English and German points of view. The anxiety of Great Britain to reach an understanding with Germany on the naval question was genuine. Yet no one in Great Britain supposed that the advantages of such an understanding were all on the British side, and that Germany would be making a concession. British naval supremacy existed as a fact, whether this fact was or was not 'recognized' by Germany. Hardinge put the matter with his usual conciseness a year later when the German argument was being put forward in all seriousness.

'It is desired that the recognition of the supremacy of the British navy should be regarded as a great concession, meriting counter-concessions on our side. . . . Such a recognition would be of no value unless the British navy were really supreme, and as long as our navy is supreme it does not matter whether it is so recognised in Germany or not. Consequently the concession is dependent entirely on the intentions of His Majesty's Government to maintain a supreme navy, and as there is a consensus of opinion on this point in England it thus becomes a paper concession or no concession at all.'[2]

British naval supremacy existed and would be maintained. An attempt by Germany to overtake Great Britain in shipbuilding would be met by an increased British effort. British statesmen thought that their country could stay the pace more easily than Germany. The competition in armaments appeared the more exasperat-

[1] D.G.P. xxiv. 156–8: 8 September 1908. Bülow made five comments on the dispatch: *Sehr richtig—sehr beachtenswert—richtig—gut—sehr richtig*. For Stumm's view of the general effect of German shipbuilding on British opinion, see also D.G.P. xxiv. 143–7: Stumm to Bülow, 20 August 1908.
[2] B.D.D. vi. 299.

ing and useless because in Great Britain at all events there was no doubt about the result. It was within the power of Germany to prolong the competition. It was not within the power of Germany to win the race. The German Government was merely wasting the money of German and British taxpayers. These were the facts. Germany might ignore them; but a 'recognition' of the facts of British naval supremacy did not constitute a claim to compensation in other fields. Great Britain might put forward similar claims in return for recognizing the numerical superiority of the German army over the British army or for keeping the British market open, without tariff restrictions, to German goods.

The financial relief which would follow a naval understanding would benefit German as well as British taxpayers. Germany, as France and Russia pointed out to Great Britain, would be able to spend more money on her land forces and land defences. Finally, the 'compensation' which Germany expected to receive involved nothing less than the abandonment by Great Britain of her existing ententes, while the concessions made to Great Britain were not to affect the full and regular execution of the naval programme already authorized by law.[1]

[1] D.G.P. xxiv. 162.

IX

THE BOSNIAN CRISIS AND ANGLO-GERMAN RELATIONS, 1908-9

Wᴵᴛʜɪɴ a month of Stumm's remarks about English 'embarrassments' and the advantageous position of Germany, another sharp change in the European situation showed that Germany had already lost her freedom of action, and that Great Britain was unlikely to desert the policy of the ententes with France and Russia. Bülow had never been very definite about the length of the 'danger-zone' through which Germany was passing; but he had assumed, rather loosely, that it was a matter of a few years. This 'danger-zone' concerned the period of development of the German fleet. There was another danger-zone from which Germany would not escape for an unknown number of years. The maintenance of Austria-Hungary was vital to the security of the German Empire. This fact was realized by the German Emperor and Bülow after the rejection of the Björkö treaty and the failure to break the Anglo-French entente. A memorandum drawn up by Bülow at the time of the Emperor's visit to Vienna in the early summer of 1906 put the case without reservation.

'I agree with Tschirschky (1) that our relations with Austria are now more important than ever because Austria is our one sure ally, (2) that we must reveal as little as possible of our relative political isolation to the Austrians. It is only human nature that if I tell a man I need his horse, he puts a very high value on the horse. Therefore we must neither let Vienna observe in us an unduly strong desire for Austrian support nor do anything to give an impression that we feel ourselves at all isolated . . . Hence we must make out that our relations with Russia, Italy, and England are better than they really are, and we must even restrain our legitimate indignation, for example, against Italy.'[1]

[1] D.G.P. xxi, pt. ii. 360-1.

In July 1907 the Triple Alliance was renewed; the renewal took place, according to the terms of the treaty of 1902, without discussion. None of the parties cared to denounce the treaty, although its positive value had disappeared. From the Austrian standpoint the existence of the treaty put some check upon Italian irredentism.[1] Bülow even remarked that it was better to allow long-standing treaties 'to disappear of their own accord, rather than to break them up with éclat, even if they do not entirely suit the changed conditions'.[2] Germany might restrain her 'legitimate indignation' against Italy, in spite of the lack of Italian support during the Moroccan crisis; but she could not hide from herself the weakness of her 'one sure ally'. Austria-Hungary was passing through an internal crisis which, according to many competent observers, was likely to end in the dissolution of the monarchy. Until the internal problems of Austria-Hungary were settled, Germany would be compelled to consider European questions not from her own point of view but from the point of view of the security of her ally. The most important of the problems of Austria-Hungary was the question of the southern Slavs; the seriousness of this problem was increased because it affected the interests of Russia as well as the internal stability of the Austro-Hungarian monarchy.[3] There were nearly five million Southern Slavs within the monarchy, and approximately another million Christian Slavs in Bosnia and Herzegovina. The kingdom of Servia included about two million Slavs. Another three-quarters of a million belonged to Montenegro, and some 500,000 were still within the Turkish Empire. The southern Slavs included in the Empire were dissatisfied with their position, and open to propaganda from the independent Slavs on the borders of Austria-Hungary. In 1906 a palace conspiracy of a

[1] D.G.P. xxi, pt. ii. 386.   [2] D.G.P. xxi, pt. ii. 387–8
[3] For the history of the southern Slav questions see R. W. Seton-Watson, *The Southern Slav Question and the Habsburg Monarchy*. The term 'Servia' and 'Servian' were generally used in Great Britain until the end of 1914.

brutal kind had overthrown the reigning dynasty at Belgrade and brought back the rival Karageorgevitch family. The conspirators and the new reigning family were Russophil, and the Austro-Hungarian Government feared that Russia would use the position to increase Slav disaffection within the monarchy. In 1906 the British Minister at Sofia wrote to Grey that, according to Servian information, during a visit of William II to Vienna there had been talk about Servia as 'a bone in the throat to be got rid of'.[1]

During the period between 1897 and 1906 the Near Eastern question had been less of an anxiety to European statesmen than at any time since the Congress of Vienna. Russia and Austria-Hungary agreed in 1897 upon the maintenance of the *status quo* in the Balkans. If there were any disturbance of the *status quo*, neither Power would make, or allow other Powers to make, conquests. Austria-Hungary reserved the right to annex 'when the moment arrives' the provinces of Bosnia and Herzegovina which had been 'occupied' and 'administered' by her under the terms of the Treaty of Berlin. The Russian Government suggested that when 'the moment'—the collapse of Turkey—arrived, the question of annexation might be discussed in detail. In other words, Russia would require 'compensation'.

For the time Russia was concerned mainly with the Far East. The relative calm in the Balkans was, however, no more than a truce. Neither Germany nor Austria had any illusion about the final aims of Russia. Marschall went to Constantinople as Ambassador in 1897; his reports are full of complaints about Russian policy, or, in Marschall's phrase, 'a wild offshoot of something which is ordinarily called policy'. This mixture was formed

'not out of the knowledge of leading statesmen but out of the religious and national instincts of wide circles of the Russian people, which press impetuously forward towards the realization of certain ideals in the East. . . . The maintenance of peace

---

[1] B.D.D. v. 153–4: Buchanan to Grey, 10 July 1906.

and quiet in the Turkish Empire depends . . . upon the attitude of "official" Russia and the amount of resistance to this pressure. The reserve and tranquillising talk of Russian diplomats cannot conceal the fact that "official" Russia has long identified itself with the Eastern policy of orthodox nationalist tradition and pursues the same ends: that is to say, the freeing of the Christians from the Turkish yoke and the inclusion of further large tracts of Turkey within the Russian sphere of influence. . . . If Austrian statesmen think that (the agreement of 1897) forms a *magna charta* for the consideration of Austrian and Balkan interests by Russia, they will certainly be disillusioned.'[1]

Nearly a year later Marschall wrote that Russian eastern policy was 'always revolutionary'. If Austria-Hungary wanted to maintain the *status quo*, she would be compelled, ultimately, to support her wishes by force. 'Whatever the means, the end of Russian policy remains the same; the disruption of the Turkish Empire in favour of a new arrangement, the details of which may not be clear, but the decisive feature is that Slav nationalities [*Völkerschaften*] under the protection of Holy Russia will take the place of Turkish rule.'[2] In July 1903 Marschall repeated the same thesis. He was able to give Russian authority for his views. Zinovieff, the Russian Ambassador at Constantinople, had complained to him that Russian Eastern policy was mistaken.

'Ninety per cent. of the Russian people would be ready to guarantee Turkey in the possession of her dominions for a hundred years. . . . But all the leading men (in Russia) are affected to some extent by fanatical minorities upon whose banners is inscribed the unfortunate word "Tradition". There is the orthodox tradition, fostered by ambitious priests with the aid of a few prominent old ladies, which aims at St. Sophia and the Holy Places, and there is the Slav propaganda. At the head of the two movements are complete nullities. Unfortunately my Government has not the power to free itself from them.'[3]

[1] D.G.P. xviii, p. i. 117–22: 14 January 1901.
[2] D.G.P. xviii, pt. i. 149–57: 5 November 1901.
[3] D.G.P. xviii, pt. i. 309–10: 15 July 1903.

The distinction of aim between Russia and Austria was summed up by Bülow after an interview with Francis Joseph and Goluchowski, the Austro-Hungarian Foreign Minister, in September 1903. Austria would not divide the Balkans with Russia, and could not tolerate the creation of a greater Servia or a greater Montenegro. She could not allow Constantinople to fall into Russian hands. 'From the moment when Russia occupied Constantinople or a great Slav state came into existence between the Adriatic and the Danube, the Austrian Empire would be at an end. The centrifugal Slav elements would destroy it. Before Austria could allow one or other of these eventualities she would appeal to the sword.'[1]

In the early twentieth century the interest of the Powers was concentrated on the Macedonian question. Marschall described this question as insoluble. 'No formula would be found to secure even relative tranquillity and content among the Turks, Albanians, Bulgarians, Greeks, Servians, Kutso-Vlachs of Macedonia, even if the divergent interests of the Powers allowed them to agree upon a single remedy.'[2] A temporary solution was found in October 1903 and accepted by the Sultan. The scheme provided for a gendarmerie to which Great Britain, France, Austria, Italy, and Russia sent officers. The gendarmerie was unable to suppress the bands of political brigands harassing the country. The Austrian and Russian civil agents attached to the Turkish Inspectorate-General were unable to carry through any real reforms. Austria, Italy, and Russia concentrated their attention on political control and railway schemes which would bring political control. The German Government would not press further reforms upon the Sultan; Germany did not want to lose Turkish support of the Baghdad railway. In 1907 local disturbances again broke out. Grey tried to carry through measures of pacification, but Austria attempted to exclude Great Britain and Italy from any action in

---

[1] D.G.P. xviii, pt. i. 361: 20 September 1903.
[2] D.G.P. xviii, pt. i. 189: 28 November 1902.

Macedonia.[1] Isvolsky, to the annoyance of Aehrenthal, revealed these plans to Great Britain.

A year later the absolute government of Abdul Hamid was overthrown. A secret committee of Union and Progress, the members of which were known as the Young Turks, started a rebellion in July 1908.[2] Abdul Hamid collapsed at once. A meeting between King Edward VII and Nicholas II at Reval in June 1908, had appeared to the Turks to foreshadow an anti-Turkish policy in Macedonia. The Turks decided to strike first. Their success alarmed Austria and Germany. Germany had worked steadily with Abdul Hamid and turned a blind eye to his most hideous acts of tyranny. For the moment Abdul Hamid's friends were unpopular, and England, which had refused to condone Abdul's massacres, suddenly recovered a lost popularity.

The revolution in Turkey affected the future of Bosnia and Herzegovina. The Turks might well appeal to national patriotism by asking for the return of provinces surrendered under the old régime. Austria-Hungary had to consider what policy she would adopt if the revolutionaries summoned deputies from Bosnia and Herzegovina to the new Turkish Parliament, and if the Parliament claimed the right to legislate for the two provinces.

Austria and Russia were already on bad terms over railway concessions. Before the outbreak of the Turkish revolution Aehrenthal had obtained a concession for a railway in the Sanjak of Novi Bazar. The line would meet the railway from Salonika at Mitrovitsa and link up Austria with the Aegean coast.[3] The proposal was disloyal to Russia because it was against the spirit, if not the letter, of the agreement to keep the balance of power in the Balkans; it was disloyal to the Concert of Europe in

[1] D.G.P. xxii. 411-12.
[2] Mr. G. H. Fitzmaurice thought that the victory of Japan over Russia was one of the causes of the Turkish revolution. 'The success of Japan over Russia, the traditional enemy of the Turk, made every fibre of the latter's body tingle.' B.D.D. v. 268: 25 August 1908.
[3] The plan was unsound for commercial, strategic, and engineering reasons.

exacting favourable terms from the Sultan at a time when the Powers were trying to put pressure on him.[1] Russia had attempted to counter the plan by asking for a concession to build a railway connecting Rumania with the Adriatic, and therefore crossing the Sanjak line.

Nevertheless the Turkish revolution had caused anxiety in Russia as well as in Austria. Isvolsky thought that he might make a bargain with Austria. He suggested that Austria should annex Bosnia, Herzegovina, and the Sanjak, and, in return for Russian consent, allow Russia to bring her warships through the Straits.[2] The consent of the signatories to the Treaty of Berlin was also necessary. It may be noticed that the Russian proposal was directly against the known policy of England, with whom Russia had concluded an entente. Aehrenthal appears to have answered on 27 August 1908 that Austria might be compelled by circumstances to annex Bosnia and Herzegovina; in this case she would withdraw from the Sanjak, and agree to a 'confidential and friendly exchange of views in regard to the Straits'. On 15–16 September Aehrenthal and Isvolsky met at the castle of Buchlau in Moravia. It is difficult to reconstruct the conversations between the two men because one cannot trust the word of either of them. It would seem that Isvolsky agreed to the Austrian proposals for annexation, but expected that, before the annexation took place, Russia would have been able to secure the consent of the Powers to the opening of the straits to Russian warships.

The annexation of Bosnia and Herzegovina was announced on 6 October 1908.[3] Isvolsky had not persuaded

[1] Nicolson, *op. cit.*, p. 267. For the history of the Sanjak railway project see J. M. Bernreither, *Fragments of a Political Diary*, ed. J. Redlich, pp. 37–40.

[2] The closing of the Straits had been very troublesome to Russia during the Russo-Japanese War. The Russians were unable to use the Black Sea Fleet, or the port of Odessa. Men and military material from South Russia could not be transported by a sea route. For the history of the closing of the Straits to non-Turkish ships of war see Sir J. Headlam-Morley, *Studies in Diplomatic History*.

[3] For the history of the crisis of 1908–9 see in addition to B.D.D. v, cc. xl–xli; D.G.P. xxvi, pts. i and ii, and O.A.P. i and ii. See also, Bernreither, *op. cit.*, pp. 40–72.

Great Britain and France to agree to the opening of the Straits; he now said—rightly or wrongly—that Austria had taken Russia by surprise. Once more there was danger of a European war. The annexation had caused intense anger in Servia. The Servians might begin a war in which other Powers would be involved against their will. Throughout the winter of 1908–9 the dispute continued. Finally the Russians decided that they were not in a position to go to war. As soon as this decision was known to the German Foreign Office, the Emperor remarked: 'Now we can go ahead.'[1] In the fourth week of March 1909—a significant week from the point of view of Anglo-German naval relations[2]—the German Government asked Russia for an unconditional acceptance of the annexation. Russia had to choose between surrender or war. Nicolson was told by Isvolsky that the Russian council of ministers sat for three hours before they decided to give way. Russia dared not risk war; 'the Austro-German combination was stronger than the Triple Entente'.[3]

The Bosnian crisis was of outstanding political importance for several reasons. In the first place the old rivalry between Bismarck and Gortchakoff repeated itself, in different circumstances, in the rivalry between Aehrenthal and Isvolsky. Aehrenthal died in 1912; Isvolsky lived until 1919. He was Russian Ambassador at Paris from 1910 to 1917. He never forgot the manner in which Austria had overreached him; he never forgot the German ultimatum of March 1909. William II made matters worse in 1909 by speaking, in his *Siegesallee* style, of Germany the loyal ally, standing in shining armour by the side of Austria at a grave moment. The speech was made in Vienna, and offended Francis Joseph. Russian statesmen hardly needed this elaboration of the moral. They had only given way because, on a calculation of

---

[1] D.G.P. xxvi, pt. ii. 683.   [2] See below, pp. 230–8.

[3] B.D.D. v. 732–3. O. H. Wedel, in *Austro-German Diplomatic Relations, 1908–1914*, takes a different view of the German action, but his view of British and German policy in this question does not seem to me convincing.

force, they had decided that the advantage did not lie on their side. The conclusion which they would draw was serious for the future of Europe. They would try to make sure that, at the next crisis, Russia was strong enough to resist Germany. They did not decide to break away from the Triple Entente. It is hardly conceivable that they should have taken such a decision. They had nothing to gain from joining the friends in shining armour. In the Near East and in the Middle East they were faced with the inevitable hostility of Germany.

From the German point of view the situation was disquieting. The ultimatum to Russia had only strengthened the Triple Entente, in spite of Grey's refusal to let Russia have her way on the question of the Straits, and in spite of Russia's acknowledgement that, even with allies, she dared not fight Germany and Austria. Yet Austria had involved Germany in a quarrel from which she could not withdraw and in which she had no direct interest. There was little hope of an improvement in Austro-Servian relations. As early as September 1908 Aehrenthal complained to Schön, with some nervousness and a request for absolute secrecy, that one of the aims of his Balkan policy was the complete destruction of 'the Servian nest of revolutionaries'. He hoped for German support in this work, and suggested that Servia might be handed over to Bulgaria.[1] The Emperor and Bülow were annoyed at the haste shown by Aehrenthal. William II spoke of Aehrenthal's 'fearful stupidity', and the dangerous effect of the annexation upon the relations between Germany and Turkey.[2] Emperor and Chancellor alike agreed that Germany must stand by Austria even in her mistakes.[3]

The effect of the crisis upon the naval problem was no less important. German observers feared that their country might be involved in a land war on two fronts. The attitude of Great Britain would depend on the circumstances leading up to the outbreak of war. The German

[1] D.G.P. xxvi, pt. i. 28: 5 September 1908.
[2] D.G.P. xxvi, pt. i. 112.	[3] D.G.P. xxvi, pt. i. 111.

General Staff knew that if their plan of campaign were to be carried out with success, Germany must mobilize simultaneously in the East and West, and must assume that France would help Russia, and that Russia would help France. On this hypothesis Germany must take the initiative and strike at France before Russia was ready. It might therefore be necessary for Germany to act technically as the aggressor and to declare war upon France even if she were defending herself or Austria-Hungary against hostile action by Russia. British opinion was ill-informed about European affairs. The ignorance of Mr. Lloyd George was shared by some of his own colleagues in the Cabinet. It would be extremely difficult to persuade British opinion that Germany was not the aggressor in a war which might begin with a German ultimatum to France and Russia. Hence the anxiety of German statesmen to obtain from England a promise of neutrality in the case of a Franco-German war. An indefinite promise that Great Britain would take no part in any aggressive combination against Germany was not a sufficient guarantee. In the years following the Balkan crisis of 1908-9 the German Government insisted that a general promise of neutrality was the condition of an agreement upon the naval question. At first, the mistaken belief that use might be made of English 'embarrassments' maintained the illusion that a promise of this kind was not impossible. German public opinion would not accept any reduction of the naval programme except on these terms. The Emperor and the naval party which surrounded him would not accept a reduction of the naval programme on any terms. On the other hand British opinion would have regarded as fantastic a change in foreign policy which did not bring with it any lasting financial relief. In any case, there was no need to pay the price of abandoning the ententes in order to win more cheaply a competition in armaments which Great Britain would not lose. The 'race in naval armaments' meant a futile and exasperating expenditure of public money;

but the acceptance of the German conditions would secure to Germany the political control of Europe. Germany could exact her own terms from France and Russia. France and Russia would be more than angry at British treachery, and Great Britain would ultimately have put herself at the mercy of Germany. There was no reason for throwing away the advantage which the ententes had brought with them. The Foreign Office had no wish to return to a state of affairs in which Germany could drive hard bargains and transform any minor incident into a test case of British friendship.

What judgement can one pass upon the German view of the situation? The concessions offered by Germany were not enough to obtain a promise of neutrality in the 'war on two fronts' which loomed so large in German calculations. Was the policy of 'all or nothing' the only safe policy for Germany? What was the 'risk' in making concessions to Great Britain on the naval question? Was this risk greater than the risk which Germany would run by refusing to consider an agreement except upon terms which Great Britain was unlikely to accept?

The concessions for which Great Britain asked were not very great. A 'reduction in *tempo*' would have satisfied Mr. Lloyd George at least for the time. A promise to exchange information about shipbuilding programmes would have been received by Grey as a friendly act, and might have prevented the recrimination and suspicions of the spring of 1909.[1] A reduction of one capital ship in the shipbuilding programme of 1908–9 would not have affected the relative strength of the German and British navies if it had been accompanied by a reduction of two ships in the British programme. Germany would have had more money available for strengthening her defensive forces on land. In any case the ships laid down in Germany in 1908 would not in normal circumstances join the fleet for two or three years, unless special measures were taken to accelerate their construction; meanwhile they

[1] See below, c. x.

counted for nothing in the balance of naval power. This consideration was important during the Bosnian crisis.

An arrangement with Great Britain which relieved the strain of naval competition would have brought about a great change in the relations between the two countries. The civilian members of the German Embassy in London held this view; Bülow himself agreed with them. If the aggravating factor of naval competition were removed, there were no questions of major interest separating Germany from Great Britain. The problem of the Baghdad railway was not insoluble. This problem was apparently solved a few months before the outbreak of the Great War.

If Germany aimed at security, and not at Continental domination, the improvement of Anglo-German relations offered solid and undeniable advantages. Grey and his colleagues believed that Great Britain might act as a mediating Power between the two continental groups. It was not true to say that Germany would gain nothing from a surrender—to use her own term—on the naval question, unless she could obtain a promise of British neutrality. An Anglo-German agreement would have been of real service to the cause of European peace only if Great Britain remained faithful to her ententes with France and Russia,[1] and if Germany did nothing to make England, France, and Russia suspect her of trying to tamper with these ententes. Within the circle of the Triple Entente Great Britain could do a great deal to serve Germany. British opinion had no wish to follow Russia in a policy of adventure or to see the collapse of Austria-Hungary. Only under the strongest compulsion of necessity would Great Britain allow Russia the control of Constantinople; Austrian and British interests had coincided on this point since the Congress of Vienna. No influential party in England wanted to provoke a

[1] Hitherto Great Britain had held no naval conversations with Russia. These conversations, about which Germany was particularly suspicious, were sanctioned by Grey only in April 1914. If Germany had agreed to any limitation of naval armaments, it is most unlikely that these Anglo-Russian conversations would have taken place. See Grey, *op. cit.* i. 283–300.

European war, or to use the chance of a European war to destroy the German fleet or German commerce. France would not encourage Russian adventures. The French creditors of the Russian Government wished for nothing more than a long period of quiet during which Russian finances might recover from the war with Japan and the troubles of the revolution. If Great Britain and France were sure of the peaceful intentions of Germany, they could be relied upon to put the strongest possible pressure upon Russia and to take into account the fears and wishes and interests of Austria-Hungary.

A foreign observer of the decisions taken by Germany can scarcely avoid the conclusion that, in the last resort, the self-will of the Emperor was mainly responsible for the failure to come to an agreement on the subject of naval competition. The Emperor must take final responsibility; but the Imperial Chancellor was the adviser of the Emperor, and must share this responsibility for the foreign policy of the German Empire. Bülow's German critics have maintained that he supported the naval plans of the Emperor only because his place depended upon this support. He made a *sacrifizio dell'intelletto* in order to keep himself in power. Bülow himself told Eulenburg that 'in matters of this kind (i.e. the largest questions of policy) a sovereign has a particular instinct to which we must give way'.[1] It is difficult to accept this view as a full solution. Bülow's own words show that he did not support the naval policy merely to please the Emperor, even though he may have owed his appointment to his early conversion to the view that the future of Germany lay on the water. Bülow had accepted the 'risk' theory; he had accepted the 'danger-zone theory', the analogy of the building of the Long Walls from Athens to the Piraeus. He believed that as soon as the danger-zone was passed, English friendship would be less necessary, and the German fleet could be used as a means of putting political pressure upon England. He considered that British policy was selfish,

[1] *Front wider Bülow*, p. 12.

deep-laid, and dangerous; but he acted as though British statesmen were unsuspicious and gullible. As late as January 1909 he asked Metternich to explain yet once more that the German fleet was not being built in competition (*Konkurrenz*) with England.[1] At the same time he summed up for himself the task of German statesmanship in the words: 'How can we get through the danger-zone which we have to traverse until we are so strong at sea that in attacking us England would run a risk out of all proportion to any probable result?' Bülow thought that a firm, confident, and consistent foreign policy, 'without rhodomontade or provocation', would be enough to divert the English from the real end of German policy.[2] The readiness with which he had accepted the view that Germany held a 'trump card' in her hand and could drive a hard bargain in return for a naval agreement gives the measure of Bülow's incapacity to see German naval policy as it appeared to British observers.

Bülow had none of the insight of Bismarck, but he was an abler man than the Emperor William II. He realized that Tirpitz's lack of moderation was bringing the whole weight of English opinion and English influence against Germany. He was impressed by Metternich's arguments. He had discussed the naval problem with Metternich in August 1908, and had agreed that some steps must be taken to improve the position. He began to feel a little doubtful about the expediency of pressing forward the construction of battleships.

The declaration by the Prime Minister that Great Britain intended to maintain a superiority of 10 per cent. in capital ships above the fleets of the two naval Powers nearest in strength seemed to throw doubt upon the possibility of wearing out British resistance.[3] Bülow read with interest an article written by Admiral Galster to the effect that Germany ought to concentrate upon coast defences, mines, submarines, and other defensive weapons.[4]

---

[1] D.G.P. xxviii. 66: 17 January 1909.   [2] D.G.P. xxviii. 70.
[3] See Appendix II.   [4] D.G.P. xxiv. 162 n.

He could not but notice the suggestion in the German press that the naval policy had been responsible for the Anglo-French entente. Rathenau, for example, had written in August 1908 that England was determined to maintain the two-Power standard, and that the German policy of battleship construction was ruinous and gave a wrong impression of German aims. Rathenau supported the idea of an understanding with England on the question of capital ships, and the revival of the older view that Germany should rely on coast defences and guerrilla warfare at sea. Maximilian Harden, in the Socialist journal *Die Zukunft*, and Socialist deputies in the Reichstag had also said that the naval policy of Germany was largely responsible for German 'isolation', and that this policy of ship-building would not affect the relative strength of the British and German fleets. The Social Democrats were regarded by Bülow and the bourgeois parties as undemocratic; but even the Conservative *Kreuz-Zeitung*, which opposed the financial measures of the Government, criticized the policy of battleship construction. Germany was bound to maintain a 'two-Power standard' on land, and could raise five army corps for the cost of three battleships.[1]

During the Bosnian crisis Bülow thought it necessary to check Tirpitz and the naval party. For the first time he ventured upon a direct challenge. The attack was dangerous. Bülow's own position was weak; he had accepted Tirpitz's assumptions, and could not easily reject his conclusions. Tirpitz enjoyed the full confidence of the Emperor. Müller, the chief of the naval Cabinet, was at this time a strong supporter of Tirpitz.[2] The Emperor was still in an exalted mood, and unwilling to listen to 'civilians'. At this point William II took one of those impulsive steps with which Europe was all too familiar. He allowed an English friend to publish in the *Daily*

---

[1] *Neue Preussische (Kreuz-) Zeitung*, 4 September 1908.

[2] Müller has described himself as 'one of the most zealous champions of Tirpitz during the whole of my period of Cabinet office until the outbreak of the world war'. *Front wider Bülow*, p. 183.

Telegraph of 28 October 1908 an account of a conversation on Anglo-German relations. The Emperor said that he was a friend of England, but that the German people as a whole were far less friendly and wanted war with England. He explained that, as a friend, he had told the British General Staff how to win the Boer War. Finally, he repeated the view that the German fleet was not a menace to England, and proved his case by hinting at the possible use of the fleet against Japan.[1] *The Times* commented that the chances of a war in the Pacific seemed 'really a surprising reason for the accumulation of a great naval force in the Baltic and North Sea, many units of which notoriously lack coal-capacity to make lengthy cruises of any kind'.[2] The Emperor's belief that the majority of Germans were Anglophobe was already held in Great Britain, while British public opinion had become accustomed to the Emperor's exaggerated statements. The effect of the publication of the interview was greater in Germany than in England. It is still uncertain whether Bülow and the Foreign Office failed to examine the text of the interview before authorizing its publication, or whether the Chancellor deliberately allowed the Emperor to make another mistake in order that he might increase his own influence in matters of high policy.

In any case Bülow took the chance of putting direct questions to Tirpitz. At the end of November he asked whether Germany could meet an English attack with confidence.[3] Tirpitz took nearly three weeks to reply, and then admitted that Germany was still in the danger-zone. Bülow pointed out once more the risk of a 'preventive' war, and inquired whether, in view of the dangers of a blockade, it would not be wiser to spend more money on coast defences and the like, and at the same time calm English opinion by reducing the rate of building large ships.[4] Tirpitz insisted that economic rivalry was behind

---

[1] For the diplomatic history of the *Daily Telegraph* interview, see B.D.D. vi. 201–26 and D.G.P. xxiv. 167–210.   [2] *The Times*, 29 October 1908.
[3] D.G.P. xxviii. 21–3 and 26–30.   [4] D.G.P. xxviii. 36–40.

British ill feeling and anxiety, and that no naval concessions would remove this resentment.

This view was contradicted by Metternich.

'The cardinal point of our relations with England lies in the growth of our fleet. It may not be pleasant for us to hear this, but I see nothing to be gained by concealing the truth.'[1]

'I have been in touch with many representatives of industry and commerce in England and Scotland, and I have never found greater desire for the continuance of good relations and greater anxiety lest these good relations should be harmed. If the relations between the two countries depended merely upon the commercial interests, and all the representatives of these interests, our mutual relations would be excellent. . . . To attribute to (London financial circles) any desire for war would be absurd. They tremble with terror at any kind of political complication. German commerce and industry are no longer in the foreground of British anxieties.'[2]

On 18 December 1908 Metternich discussed the question with Grey. Grey explained that the British programme of construction was dependent upon the German programme, and that any reduction on the German side would be followed at once by a reduction in the number of ships to be laid down in Great Britain. Any relaxation of the strain would have a good moral effect in Europe. 'The whole world was now watching the rivalry between German and English shipbuilding, and if it became apparent that this rivalry was diminishing, this would be taken as real evidence that neither nation cherished hostile intentions against the other.'[3]

[1] D.G.P. xxviii. 18.

[2] D.G.P. xxviii. 47. A year earlier Captain Coerper, German naval attaché in London, had written that 'the continually increasing sea-power of Germany is the greatest hindrance to English political freedom of action. This is the root of all the unsatisfactory relationships between the two nations. All other causes which are frequently alleged—rivalry in commerce, industry, shipping, (our) partizanship in the Boer war, etc., are of a secondary character.' D.G.P. xxiii, pt. i. 48. Bülow told Tirpitz that Metternich's view was supported by other diplomatic representatives of Germany.

[3] B.D.D. vi. 172–3; D.G.P. xxviii. 34–5. The word Dreadnought was misspelt three times in the Foreign Office draft of the dispatch to Goschen giving an account of the interview.

Bülow thought that the time had come to make some positive suggestion, but he could not escape from the idea of a bargain or from the belief that no agreement was worth while which did not provide for a promise of neutrality if Germany were at war. He asked Metternich whether there would be any chance of obtaining concessions from England in return for a promise to slow down the rate of laying down capital ships. The concession required was the promise of neutrality. The concession offered was limited to a reduction in the rate of carrying out the German programme. There would be no reduction in the number of ships ultimately laid down.[1]

Metternich answered that the proposal would be cold comfort to the English, since in the long run England would have to build as many ships. No political concession could be obtained for such an offer.[2] Metternich did not agree with Tirpitz's view that fear would ultimately compel England to come to terms with Germany.

'Only a minority of the leaders of English opinion believe that the German fleet is being built in order to attack England; but every one realizes that this fleet . . . will limit very seriously British freedom of action, confine the British fleet to home waters . . . and remain a permanent threat to British coasts and British sea-power. . . . English statesmen are afraid of being politically dependent on us, should they have differences with other Powers or ourselves. The system of friendships and ententes and the increase of their own forces on sea and land seem to them a safer way to remain independent of German policy. The English people will not "bow to the inevitable". Their fear will have the very different result of setting England in arms against us.'[3]

Bülow contradicted another of Tirpitz's arguments. Tirpitz had assumed that Great Britain could not stand the financial strain of competition. Bülow answered that England was in a better position than Germany to meet the cost of shipbuilding.[4]

Tirpitz argued that the danger of war would be

[1] D.G.P. xxviii. 35–8.   [2] D.G.P. xxviii. 44.
[3] D.G.P. xxviii. 48–9.   [4] D.G.P. xxviii. 76: 27 January 1909.

increased by any surrender on the part of Germany. A reduction of the *tempo* of German construction would be exploited in England as a humiliation for Germany, and would have a discouraging effect upon the German people. Tirpitz still believed in the 'risk' theory, although the theory was based upon political circumstances which had vanished long since to the disadvantage of Germany. 'Every new ship increasing our battle fleet means an increase in the risk for England if she attacks us.'[1] Tirpitz was ready to accept an agreement whereby Great Britain would build not more than four, and Germany not more than three, capital ships annually over a period of ten years.[2] The suggestion was made only after strong pressure from the Chancellor. Bülow thought that there was little chance of persuading England to accept these terms. Tirpitz can hardly have expected any other result.

At the beginning of February 1909 Bülow's exasperation with Tirpitz was at its height. He had failed to move Tirpitz by his arguments. To his complaints that German policy was being countered all over the world by English opposition, and that the growth of anti-German feeling in England was becoming a serious danger, Tirpitz answered: 'Our duty is to arm with all our might.' Tirpitz could not find any value even in a British guarantee of neutrality if Germany were involved in a continental war. If England declared war on Germany, France and Russia would join England. An English guarantee would be useless, while the German limitation of armaments would have a very real significance for Germany. Tirpitz's only solution was an agreement in which the relation between the two fleets was more favourable to Germany than any arrangement hitherto proposed. He admitted that Great Britain would not accept this agreement for some time to come; he thought that she would be compelled to accept it since she could not ultimately maintain the 'two-power + 10 per cent. standard'. Meanwhile Germany ought not to give up her 'trump cards'. The party

[1] D.G.P. xxviii. 55: 4 January 1909.   [2] D.G.P. xxviii. 68–9: 20 January 1909.

leaders in the Reichstag should be warned of the danger of talking too much about a limitation of armaments, and the English should be allowed to think that the Reichstag was ready to vote larger sums for the navy than it had been asked to give.[1]

It was one of Bülow's habits to content himself with a well-known quotation when he had reached the end of his persuasive powers or found himself in an awkward situation. He commented upon Tirpitz's conclusion that Germany should meet British opposition by increased armaments: 'Propter vitam vivendi perdere causas.'[2] Yet he was not prepared to fight to a conclusion a dispute which could end only in his own or in Tirpitz's resignation. He found a good deal of support in the German Foreign Office. A fortnight after Tirpitz's refusal to give way, a memorandum was drawn up showing the disadvantages of the naval policy. 'Apart from the fact that our fleet will never be strong enough to defeat England, there are economic reasons which make an agreement with England desirable.' Increased taxation resulting from a large naval programme might well bring about the introduction of Imperial preference in England. A change in the British fiscal system would damage German commerce and draw the British Empire into closer union. Even in peace time the German navy diverted money from the army and the land defences, and was harmful to German colonial policy since it made England less 'accommodating'. British support was also needed in Turkey.[3]

King Edward VII paid a State visit to Berlin in February 1909. It was unlikely that an attempt would be made on the British side to force a discussion. Tirpitz had admitted that, if the question were raised, a blank refusal would be impolitic. The King was careful not to offend

---

[1] D.G.P. xxviii. 78–80: 4 February 1909. Tirpitz had complained that Metternich had omitted to ask for compensation in return for his statement that Germany would not introduce a new supplementary law in 1912. See below, p. 208 n.   [2] D.G.P. xxviii, 80.

[3] D.G.P. xxviii. 91–2: Memorandum by Bussche-Haddenhausen, 19 February 1909.

the Emperor. He touched very briefly and lightly on the danger of panic, and said that owing to her position Great Britain must have a fleet larger than the fleets of other Powers. The Emperor agreed with his guest, and added that Germany also wanted to safeguard her interests and protect her shores. The Emperor complained that the English 'jingoes' did not understand the nature of the German programme. This programme was only following the course legally prescribed; it could not be regarded as a 'building race' with England. The King made a polite answer, and hurried from the subject.[1] Lord Crewe mentioned the question to Bülow, and added that sooner or later England would be compelled to introduce compulsory military service. Bülow made the usual answers about the German navy, and remarked that Germany would only be too pleased at the adoption of compulsory military service in Great Britain because 'compulsory military service makes nations more peaceful'.[2]

The surrender of Russia on the Bosnian question relieved Bülow of immediate anxiety. There was no likelihood of war; hence the dispute with Tirpitz could be broken off at least for a time.

Once again the latent dangers of the naval situation were to assert themselves in a manner unexpected by German observers. The Continental situation became less strained; but within a few days after Russia had given way on the Bosnian question the relations between Germany and Great Britain were disturbed by a sudden and sharp controversy over the rate of shipbuilding in Germany. A large addition to the British fleet was proposed and accepted by Parliament. The end of the long passage through the danger-zone was as far away as ever.

---

[1] Tirpitz, *op. cit.* i. 122–3.

[2] *Ib.* 122. On 18 February 1909 Mr. Byles asked in the House of Commons whether King Edward's visit to Germany had encouraged any hope of a naval agreement. The Prime Minister replied that the German Government 'adhere to the view that their programme is fixed to suit their own needs and will not be influenced by anything that we may do'. Hansard, 5th Ser. i. 224–5.

X

THE QUESTION OF GERMAN ACCELERATION, 1909

IN December 1908 Metternich thought that the favourable moment for negotiations with England had already passed. The British nation was now resigned to an increase in naval expenditure; as a practical people, they would accept this necessity.[1]

Grey had explained to Metternich that Great Britain might be compelled to lay down a number of additional Dreadnoughts in 1909, 'some to be laid down in the early part of the year, some in the summer, some in the autumn'. He added that British plans 'depended upon the pace at which the German naval programme was carried out'.[2] A month after King Edward's visit to Germany the British nation showed that it was not merely resigned to an increase of expenditure on battleships but was acutely anxious about the naval position of the country.

The question of the relative facilities for the rapid construction of ships in Great Britain and Germany had been raised earlier in 1908. The Government had given a careful answer.[3] They assumed that Germany allowed three years, the United States three to three and a half years, and France four years for the completion of a large battleship. The possibility of a reduction in the German times had been taken into account; the estimates given by German firms of their potentialities of output showed that there was a great increase in the capacities of German yards, and that the limits of expansion had not yet been reached. On the other hand, it was taken for granted in public discussion of the question that Germany would keep to her published time-table, and that

---

[1] D.G.P. xxviii. 44.

[2] B.D.D. vi. 173: 18 December 1908; D.G.P. xxviii. 34–5.

[3] See above, pp. 160 and 164–6.

no preparations would be made for laying down ships in advance of this time-table.

Within twelve months British Ministers had changed their views, and admitted that they were not sure of the rate at which Germany was building her ships, and that they did not know when these ships might be ready for service. Their embarrassment was greater because they had discovered certain facts which pointed to an acceleration of the German programme; that is to say, the Germans had not merely speeded up their ordinary rate of construction, but were taking steps which would enable them, if they wished to do so, to complete a number of their ships well in advance of the dates announced in their time-table. These facts, of which the British Government possessed incontrovertible evidence, were not easy to reconcile with the official information received from Germany. It was equally difficult to understand the reason for the divergence between the facts and the official statements about German construction. Yet upon the solution of this problem might depend the safety of Great Britain at sea.

The whole matter was complicated by the considerations to which Sir William White had referred in 1906.[1] The time taken to build a large warship could not be stated without a number of qualifications. The statement accompanying the British naval estimates for 1909–10 mentioned—for the first time in an official document—some of these qualifying factors.

'The estimated time for the completion of a battleship is now taken as two years; but this period does not cover the whole time during which work is being done in obtaining necessary materials and in the manufacture of certain parts of the ship's equipment, such as gun-mountings. Three months' notice in advance ought to be given to contractors to ensure completion within two years from the date of the order of the hull, and if an exceptionally heavy demand were to be made on the contractors, much longer notice would be required. The actual

[1] See above, pp. 161–2.

date of "laying down" can indeed be postponed for some time without delaying the final completion of the ship, provided that work is proceeding in the manufacture of guns, gun-mountings, machinery, and armour, and that the materials for the hull are all collected at the yard ready for immediate building. It is on an estimate of time in which allowance is made for these facts that the period of construction of a battleship is reckoned at two years.'

This statement showed that for the punctual execution of a programme, certain steps were necessary before the keel of a ship was laid down. The work of completion would be delayed if these steps were not taken, and if the component parts of the ship were not manufactured, transported, and assembled in due time and order. Yet one might draw another inference. If sufficient notice were given to contractors and manufacturers, would it not be possible to complete a ship in advance of the 'normal' time? If a contract were assigned to a yard some time before the keel of a ship were laid down, materials and equipment might be assembled, and the rate of building thereby accelerated. An acceleration of this kind could be kept secret for some time. Sooner or later it would be detected; but a lead of several months could be obtained without much difficulty. Secrecy was easy, and usual, in the preparation of drawings and specifications. Tenders might be arranged without public notice. Unless rival firms became suspicious or talked injudiciously, the facts would not be discovered until after the work had been put in hand. Even so, a foreign Government might take some weeks to discover any anticipation of a published programme. The naval attachés were not given access to factories or building yards; there were indirect ways of noticing any sudden increase of activity, but information would only be collected slowly. It was particularly difficult to discover the accumulation of material—guns, turrets, and armour—in an establishment as large as Krupp's works at Essen. Moreover, a certain amount of time might be gained, as far as guns were concerned, by drawing upon the reserves, and filling up the stores again as new guns were turned out by the factories.

The Krupp works at Essen occupied the attention of the British Admiralty in the winter of 1908–9. There was nothing secret about the main problem. The increase in the capacity of German shipbuilding yards had been accompanied, since the middle of 1908, by a large extension of Krupp's works and trial grounds. This extension directly affected the question of naval construction because the greater part of the armour and armaments of ships of war were made at these works. The details of the new extension were not known to the British public, but some of the facts could not escape notice. The firm had floated a loan of £2,500,000 (their existing capital amounted to £9,000,000) in July 1908. The money had been advanced at least two months earlier by the Berlin banks. A portion of the loan was spent on enlarging the Germania shipbuilding yard at Kiel, but the greater part, possibly £2,000,000, was used for the extension of the Essen works. The result of this extension was an increase of about 30 per cent. in the capacities of the works. It was thought by some British engineers that the firm could make the primary and secondary armament of eight large ships in one year, in addition to the armament of small craft. Even if this estimate were incorrect, there was evidence that the firm could begin work, in advance of the published time-table, upon the material needed for the German 1909–10 programme of four capital ships without delaying the completion of orders for the ships of the 1908–9 programme, or the armament of smaller ships.

These figures had a significance of their own. If Krupp's worked at full pressure, and if the necessary material were accumulated in advance, Germany might suddenly accelerate her programme of construction and take Great Britain by surprise. The guns, armour, and gun-mountings might be prepared in secret; the British

Admiralty would know nothing of these preparations until the ships were actually laid down, or proposals for immediate construction brought before the Reichstag. The Reichstag was likely to accept any such proposals and condone irregularities of procedure. It was not impossible that the extension of Krupp's had been planned in order to provide for the acceleration of naval construction. In any case, the British Admiralty thought that the extension reduced the time necessary for the construction of capital ships by 'upwards of nine months', and that henceforward the normal period of construction in Germany must be reckoned at two years and six months, including the time allowed for the collection of materials.[1]

The margin of British superiority in shipbuilding was now so very narrow that the Admiralty could no longer count upon overtaking a large and unexpected German programme for which material had been ordered and made in advance. For a few months the German fleet, as far as ships of the Dreadnought type were concerned, might be equal or superior in numbers to the British fleet.

Germany could take steps to bring about this relationship between the two fleets without any breach of faith. She had not agreed to an exchange of information about naval plans. The programme publicly announced in Germany was only a declaration of intention, and obviously not binding. The German Naval Law of 1900 had already been modified; every modification had increased the striking power of the German fleet. In an emergency naval construction might outrun legal or constitutional formalities. At any time Krupp's might work ahead of the credits voted by the Reichstag. Nominally, the firm would be acting at its own risk; in fact, the risk would be small.

In considering the margin of safety required by Great Britain the Admiralty had to take into account not merely

[1] Hansard 5th Ser. 1909, ii. 1454.

German statements of intention[1] but the full possibilities of German construction, and to ask whether there was any evidence of a change of intention, and of an attempt to accelerate the construction of ships already laid down or to anticipate the dates on which ships of the current year, or the next year's programme were to be laid down. According to the official programme the three battleships and one large cruiser authorized in 1908[2] would not be laid down before August 1908, and would not be completed, i.e. ready for use in battle, before February 1911. In the spring of 1908 the Admiralty had decided that the margin of superiority could be maintained if Great Britain laid down only two ships of the Dreadnought class. This provision would give Great Britain, in February 1911, twelve Dreadnoughts to nine possessed by Germany, at a time when the large British superiority in pre-Dreadnought ships could still be taken into account. Was there any evidence of acceleration in the rate of construction of these ships? A second question arose. Four more capital ships were to be laid down under the German programme of 1909–10. Was there any evidence that work was in progress upon these ships, or upon material intended for the ships, in advance of the scheduled time? The productive capacity of Krupp's and the shipbuilding yards was amply sufficient for an anticipation of this kind; Germany might accelerate the time-table of the 1908–9 and 1909–10 ships. In this case thirteen, not nine, German Dreadnoughts would be ready for battle before the end of 1911. If there were similar acceleration of the time-table of the four ships to be laid down under the programme of 1910–11, seventeen German ships

[1] This point may be explained in Bülow's own words. Tirpitz complained on 20 January 1909 of an assurance given by Metternich without any demand for 'compensation' that Germany would not introduce a supplementary naval law in 1912. Bülow's comment on this complaint includes a reference to his own statement in the Reichstag about German intentions. 'Like all parliamentary statements, this statement is only binding within the limits of our own *salus publica* and the needs of defence.' (D.G.P. xxviii. 68–9.) This was the view of the British Admiralty about 'declarations of intentions' made to them by Foreign Powers.   [2] i.e. the '1908–9 programme'.

would be ready in the spring of 1912, while it was not thought impossible for Germany to have completed twenty-one ships by the end of 1912.

The British Government, in the course of the winter of 1908–9, believed itself to be in the possession of evidence that Germany was building ahead of her published time-table. Some of the facts were common knowledge. If this evidence did not imply acceleration, it was open to the German Government to give another explanation of the facts. The British Government, in their anxiety to keep down their own naval expenditure, put definite and plain questions to the German Ambassador. The German answers were not merely unconvincing; they were misleading. Certain admissions were made, but made only after no escape was possible.

These were the facts known in Great Britain. (1) Material had been collected in advance for the four ships to be laid down in 1908. These ships were not to be laid down before August 1908, but, if material for their construction were collected in advance, they might be ready for action in the autumn of 1910. (2) Material was also being collected in advance for the four ships to be built under the 1909–10 programme. (3) Contracts had been given in advance for two of the ships of the 1909–10 programme before the necessary credits had been voted by the Reichstag. This allocation of contracts was mentioned in the German and British press in October 1908. The Berlin correspondent of *The Times* reported that

'according to various journals the German government has already placed contracts with the Vulkan works at Stettin and the Schichau works at Danzig for two of the three battleships of next year's programme. While it is explained that the action of the government will require ratification by the Reichstag, the provisional placing of contracts is described as timely in that it enables the builders to make the necessary preparations for laying down the ships and so to avoid delays which have occurred in previous years.'[1]

[1] *The Times*, 15 October 1908. *The Times* pointed out on 30 November

Mr. McKenna took the opportunity of putting a direct question about these reports to the German naval attaché in London. On 15 December Captain Widenmann[1] gave Mr. McKenna a copy of the German naval estimates for 1909–10. Mr. McKenna asked when the programme of new construction came into effect. Widenmann answered: '1 April 1909 at the earliest, that is to say, at the beginning of the new financial year, and assuming that the programme is accepted by the Reichstag.' Mr. McKenna then asked: 'Why is it that the ships of the 1909 programme have already been allotted?' Widenmann answered that he had read this erroneous conclusion a few days earlier in the press, and that he could only say that the information was based on mistaken inferences (*falsche Orientierung*) and was being exploited in a tendentious and anti-German manner. There could be no giving of contracts by the German Admiralty; individual firms might calculate for themselves the number of slips which would be occupied until the summer of 1909, and the yards which would be taken into consideration; they might therefore make an approximate guess about the allocation of the contracts. This step had clearly been taken by the person responsible for the statement, and his statement was now being accepted in England as authentic. Widenmann did not think that Mr. McKenna as the Minister responsible for the British estimates would seriously attribute unparliamentary action to Admiral Tirpitz who was responsible for the estimates in Germany.[2] Mr. McKenna could ask no further questions.

1908 that 'it is believed that German builders at least—and possibly the same remark applies to those of other countries—frequently begin this preparatory work some months not only before the actual grant is made by Parliament, but before the contracts have been officially placed'.

[1] Widenmann's rank was that of Korvettenkapitän.

[2] D.G.P. xxviii. 30–1. For Tirpitz's later admission that the contracts had been given, see below, p. 228. It is remarkable that Tirpitz seems to have forgotten the fact that the announcement about these contracts had appeared in German newspapers. On 30 March 1909 the British naval attaché told Tirpitz that he first read of the allocation of the contracts in a German paper. The Admiral found it hard to believe this statement

Nevertheless the British Admiralty knew the facts, and had reason to believe that the contractors had already begun to lay down the two ships in question.[1] Widenmann's denials therefore increased the suspicions of the Admiralty. It was also thought that money had been advanced to the contractors by German banks under the guarantee of the German Admiralty. If this latter surmise were true, no value could be put on the German assertions that money could not be spent in anticipation of a vote in the Reichstag and that for this reason acceleration was impossible.

The British Government also had before them in December 1908 the German estimates for the year 1909–10. The payments for capital ships were made in four annual instalments. The estimates showed a great increase in the first two instalments for the four ships of the 1908–9 programme. The figure—£1,130,000—was only £90,000 less than the total amount of the first three instalments for the capital ships of the 1906–7 programme.[2] This increase might mean larger ships or acceleration of construction; it might mean larger ships and acceleration of construction. The *Kölnische Zeitung* thought that the larger figures were due to increased rapidity of construction.

From the beginning of January 1909 until the publication

until it was confirmed by his own adjutant. (B.D.D. vi. 256.) Tirpitz had also found it convenient to forget Widenmann's dispatch of 15 December.

[1] In July 1911 Mr. McKenna told Widenmann that one of his friends had crossed the ice at Danzig on a winter's night and had actually seen the keel and first ribs of the ship in one of the Schichau slips. Widenmann's comment assumes that the ship might have been seen. (D.G.P. xxviii. 425–6.) It was believed in Germany that information had been given to Great Britain by members of a special naval mission from the Argentine. Schön wrote that Tirpitz had been 'extraordinarily open-hearted' in his talk with the members of the mission (in the hope of getting orders for German yards). (B.D.D. vi. 252 and D.G.P. xxviii. 109.) Goschen reported to Grey that Schön's surmise was 'more than probable' since the mission had seen 'nearly everything in the way of ships under construction'. See also Appendix V.

[2] In 1908 the second instalment for each of two battleships was £430,000. A year later the figures were £525,000 for each of three battleships. The second instalment for a large cruiser had been £450,000 in the 1908 estimates. In the 1909 estimates the figure had risen to £550,000.

of the British naval estimates on 12 March, and indeed until 16 March, the first day of the debate on the estimates, Grey did his utmost to get from Germany a plain statement about the German naval programme. He asked Metternich certain questions which gave every chance of solving the problem. He pointed out that the only way of settling differences of opinion between experts was to allow the naval attachés to see the number of ships laid down, and the stages of construction which they had reached. The Emperor had already refused to agree to this plan.[1] Neither Grey nor Metternich was a naval expert; Metternich indeed was surprised that Grey mentioned thirty-three, and not thirty-eight, as the number of Dreadnoughts with which Germany intended ultimately to equip her fleet.[2] Metternich on his side was not

[1] F. Uplegger, in *Die englische Flottenpolitik vor dem Weltkrieg*, p. 121, n. 33, still regards this suggestion as an attempt to discover the secrets of German construction. It is quite impossible, from the evidence, to doubt that Grey made the proposal (i) in order to avoid misunderstanding, (ii) in the hope that it might lead to a limitation of armaments by agreement. An Admiralty memorandum to the Foreign Office of 12 December 1911 also shows that the British proposal was not intended as an indirect means of espionage. (B.D.D. vi. 647–9.) For the history of this plan see above, pp. 130–1 and below, pp.

[2] D.G.P. xxviii. 95. Grey gave this same figure in Parliament on 29 March 1909. (Hansard, 5th Ser. iii. 54.) Two years later he repeated the figure. The fact was pointed out by the German naval attaché in London in one of his reports. (D.G.P. xxviii. 396.)

A week after Grey's speech of 13 March 1911, Lord Charles Beresford and Mr. G. Lambert pointed out the mistake. Mr. McKenna explained that Grey's statement was meant to refer to the strength of the German fleet in battleships and cruisers of the Dreadnought type in 1920: i.e. 22 battleships, 11 cruisers. Mr. McKenna said that he gave Grey these figures 'immediately before he rose'. (Hansard, 5th Ser. xxiii, 61–2, 97, 153–4.) Grey's words were: 'The German Naval Law when complete means a navy of 33 capital ships, including "Dreadnoughts" and cruisers, as well as pre-"Dreadnoughts".' (Hansard, 5th Ser. xxii. 1987.) The sentence is ambiguous, but, in view of Grey's earlier mistake, it would appear that he was still confused about the figures. In any case he found it necessary to ask Mr. McKenna for these figures as late as March 1911. Mistakes of this kind were frequent in parliamentary discussions about the German navy; they were likely to occur unless there were a precise statement about numbers and types of ships and the approximate dates on which the ships would be commissioned. See also Hansard, 5th Ser. xxiii. 887, 2490–1, and 2570–1.

told the secrets of the German Admiralty, and, in any case, was bound only to give the information sent to him officially from Berlin.

The first conversation took place on 4 January 1909. In a later reference to this conversation, when Metternich was explaining to his Government the reasons for the British mistrust of the German official figures, he spoke of 'three sphinx-like riddles' put to him by Grey concerning the 'acceleration of our shipbuilding beyond the terms of our programme'.[1] There are two versions of the conversation. According to the German version[2] Grey said that the English Admiralty reckoned that, at the normal rate of building, Germany would have thirteen Dreadnoughts ready by February 1912. The Admiralty believed that the material for four Dreadnoughts under construction had been collected six months in advance of the official time-table. If this advance collection also took place in the case of the next four ships Germany would have seventeen Dreadnoughts completed by February 1912. If, apart from financial reasons, Germany built up to the limit of speed and capacity, she might have twenty-one Dreadnoughts completed by April 1912. The British programme in March would have to take account of these possibilities. These figures were given to Metternich in a written statement which included a reference to the collection of materials in advance.[3] Metternich answered that the German shipbuilding programme was laid down by law, and that a sudden use of the whole shipbuilding capacity of the country to shorten the time of construction was thereby excluded. It is clear from a later reference that Metternich had accepted the first of Grey's figures—thirteen Dreadnoughts by February 1912—but not the second and third calculations.[4] According to the English report of the conversation[5] Grey said that he wanted Germany to

---

[1] D.G.P. xxviii. 124: 23 March 1909.
[2] D.G.P. xxviii. 57–8.   [3] D.G.P. xxviii. 99.
[4] B.D.D. vi. 240: 5 March 1909. See below, p. 216.   [5] B.D.D. vi. 237–8.

understand that if England had to propose a large shipbuilding programme, 'it was not because we had not been
ready to discuss the matter, or to compare estimates in
advance'.[1]

On 3 February Grey had another conversation with
Metternich.[2] Metternich now agreed that material for
four ships under construction had been collected in
advance; in the case of other ships not allocated to
particular firms this collection in advance would not
take place unless any of the firms cared to act at their
own risk. There would be no acceleration; the rate of
expenditure on shipbuilding was fixed by law, though this
rate might be increased by a vote in the Reichstag.
Metternich had thus admitted that some of the information obtained by the Admiralty was correct; but he gave
no further explanation. The British Government were
left to decide whether they would or would not press for

---

[1] Metternich had shown Grey's figures to Captain Widenmann: Widenmann answered that materials had been collected for the first two German
Dreadnoughts voted in 1906 some months before these ships were laid down.
These ships were voted by the Reichstag before the plans were completed;
the yards to which the ships were allotted after the Reichstag vote had been
able to begin collecting material before laying down the keels. Widenmann
was given a statement by the naval authorities in Berlin that no acceleration was intended. (D.G.P. xxviii. 96.) Widenmann's reference to the first
two German Dreadnoughts was not relevant, since there was unusual delay
in laying down these ships. He said nothing about the collection of materials
for ships of the 1908–9 programme. The statement from Berlin did not
mention the allocation of contracts or collection of materials for ships which
had not been voted by the Reichstag, and took no account of any possible
change of intention. Grey had pointed out to Metternich that, in view of
the increased facilities for naval construction in Germany, the British
Admiralty must take account of 'possibilities' in framing the British programme. It would appear (from D.G.P. xxviii. 96–7) that Metternich
assumed that Grey was referring to the collection of material for ships of
the 1906 programme, i.e. the 'first two Dreadnoughts' of which Widenmann
had spoken. For this reason he told Grey that the circumstances which had
made possible the collection of material for the earlier ships would not be
repeated. (B.D.D. vi. 240.) This statement, and Metternich's obvious and
confessed unfamiliarity with the details of naval construction, added to the
perplexities of the British Admiralty.

[2] B.D.D. vi. 239–40. This conversation is not reported in D.G.P. because
Metternich left London for Berlin within a few hours after he had seen Grey.

further statements. In any case Metternich had conceded the possibility of acceleration. On 3 March Metternich reported[1] to his Government that the British Government believed, and were seriously alarmed by the belief, that Germany intended to accelerate her rate of building, and to complete her capital ships at earlier dates than those officially announced. The information upon which this belief was founded was already appearing in the press.[2] According to Metternich Sir John Fisher, sincerely or insincerely, supported the general view, and was influencing the Cabinet. Grey had mentioned the fears of the British Government, and the information upon which these fears were based, to Metternich, without putting a definite question. The subject would certainly be raised in Parliament during the debate on the naval estimates. Metternich thought it important that the German Government should make a statement on the matter. From the British version of the conversation it is clear that Grey had repeated his remark of 3 February that Germany would have thirteen Dreadnoughts by February 1912,

[1] B.D.D. vi. 240–1; D.G.P. xxviii. 93–9.
[2] *The Times*, 23 February 1909. *The Observer*, 28 February 1909. The relevant passages from *The Times* and *The Observer* were included in Metternich's dispatch, but are not printed in D.G.P. The paragraph in *The Times* summed up very accurately the factors which the Admiralty had to take into consideration. 'The rate of ship-building in Germany has been and is being accelerated, and not only the rate of ship-building, but still more the rate of producing those accessories of ship-building—such as armour plates, guns, and gun mountings, and the like—on which the rate of ship-building depends much more closely than is generally known to those who are not directly concerned in the matter. It is not the mere putting of a ship together on the stocks or in the fitting basins that determines the rate of construction. It is much more the rate at which guns and gun mountings and the like can be produced for her equipment; and unless we are misinformed this rate has of late been very greatly accelerated in Germany—so greatly indeed as to compel the Admiralty to insist on exceptional efforts to make up for lost time.'
On 2 March *The Times* referred to the report published in October (see above, p. 209) about the placing of contracts for German ships of the 1909–10 programme. A day earlier *The Times* had insisted that Great Britain should lay down six ships without delay. 'We can no longer rely upon assured superiority in rapidity of construction, since it is well known that other people have very nearly, if not quite, as great facilities as ourselves.'

and might have seventeen by February 1912, or twenty-one by April 1912. Metternich had answered that the first statement was correct, the second and third incorrect. Grey had also suggested that each side should allow the other to see the number of ships under construction and the stages which they had reached.

On 10 March Metternich gave the official statement which he had regarded as highly necessary to reassure Great Britain.[1] Germany would not have thirteen ships until the end of 1912. Grey pointed out that these figures 'qualified' Metternich's earlier assent to the statement that Germany would have thirteen ships in the spring of 1912. Metternich again repeated the figures—thirteen ships for the end of 1912—as authoritative and added that there would be no acceleration. Grey was now in a difficult position. The Admiralty knew of the giving of contracts for two of the second batch of ships. This fact was still not told to them by Germany. The collection of material for the four earlier ships had been admitted, but it was denied that there would be any acceleration in their construction. Why, then, was the material collected in advance? Grey could not accuse the German Government of giving false information; yet the facts of which the Admiralty had positive knowledge contradicted this information. Grey therefore said that the Admiralty believed that thirteen capital ships were under construction 'or being prepared in some form or another' in Germany. Metternich answered that he was assured that this was not the case, and that if materials were being collected in advance for the next batch of four ships, certain contractors were doing so at their own risk. Once more Grey suggested an exchange of information between experts. The Emperor annotated with a refusal the mention of this plan in Metternich's dispatch.

The results of Grey's attempts, over two months, to get an explanation from Metternich were: (1) that the German Government denied the accuracy of figures pre-

[1] B.D.D. vi. 241–2; D.G.P. xxviii. 103–5.

viously admitted by their own Ambassador;[1] (2) the German Government had only admitted the collection of material for four ships after the British Government had stated its knowledge of the fact;[2] (3) the German Ambassador had not denied that materials were being collected in advance for four other ships, but had said that if this collection were taking place it was at the risk of the contractors; (5) no reference was made to the facts— known to the British Admiralty—that contracts had been promised for two ships of the 1909–10 programme in the autumn of 1908, and that the keel of one of these ships was laid down at least as early as January 1909.

Finally, on the day of the publication of the British naval estimates, and four days before the debate in the House of Commons, the Prime Minister explained to Metternich the basis upon which the British programme was calculated.

'According to information received by the British Admiralty three of the four Dreadnoughts of the financial year 1909–10 have been under construction for several months. Not only has the material been collected, but the keel of one Dreadnought of the 1909–10 programme has been laid down in the Schichau yards. If preparations are made for building, and ships are actually begun some months before they are voted (on 1 April), it is clear that the completion of these ships can be antedated by a corresponding number of months. Mr. Asquith had no wish to complain, and had no justification for any complaint, about this procedure. Germany alone had the right to determine the rate of her shipbuilding, and no responsible persons

[1] It would not be clear from Metternich's reports in D.G.P. that he had actually stated that Germany would have thirteen Dreadnoughts in February 1912, i.e. that he had assented to the first of Grey's three figures, the three 'sphinx-like riddles'. Metternich gave the impression in his reports that he neither denied nor assented to Grey's figures. Tirpitz was angry that he—Metternich—had not given a categorical denial. (D.G.P. xxxviii. 69.) The fact that Metternich's positive assent was not known to the German Government added another element of confusion.

[2] In any case, it would appear (see above, p. 214, note 1) that the German Admiralty believed that they were making this admission only in the case of the first two Dreadnoughts of 1906, about which the facts were publicly known.

in England would have the right to object; but the British Government . . . (in estimating their own programme) could not avoid taking account of the development of the German programme. The British Government would only use its authority to lay down the four Dreadnoughts conditionally sanctioned by Parliament[1] if they considered it necessary to build these ships in view of the progress in naval construction (in Germany) during the course of the year.'[2]

No answer came from Berlin to this clear statement. The Emperor was already angry with Metternich, and agreed with Tirpitz that no detailed information should be given.[3] Metternich waited four days, and then telegraphed to ask whether he might contradict the statement that material had been collected and ships of the 1909–10 programme laid down in the yards.[4] The Emperor commented on the telegram: 'I think it would be better for Metternich to hold his tongue. He is incorrigible.'[5]

Within twenty-four hours after the debate in the House of Commons, and in spite of the 'allerhöchsten Marginalien' Tirpitz agreed that Metternich should admit the allocation of contracts for two ships.[6]

---

[1] See below, pp. 222–3.   [2] D.G.P. xxviii. 106 n.: 12 March 1909.
[3] D.G.P. xxviii. 102–3.   [4] D.G.P. xxviii. 107.
[5] Tirpitz, *op. cit.* i. 134.
[6] Bülow also agreed, with the comment: 'Fiat! Unverzüglich'. D.G.P. xxviii. 107 n. See below, p. 228.

XI

THE DEBATE ON THE BRITISH NAVAL ESTIMATES, MARCH 1909

THE British Government decided to meet a difficult and possibly dangerous situation by laying down four Dreadnoughts at once, and by asking for the consent of Parliament to the laying down of four more ships, if these were necessary for the maintenance of an adequate lead in capital ships. This decision was itself a compromise reached only after much discussion in the Cabinet. The decision was likely to be challenged by the Opposition and by the left wing of the Liberal party. The Opposition would ask for more ships; the left wing of the Liberals would ask for greater economy and a smaller programme. A programme of eight Dreadnoughts in a single year, with another four in prospect for the estimates of 1910–11, could not be justified without an explanation of the circumstances leading to this drastic decision. A full explanation was impossible without reference to the plans of Germany, and without a discussion which would have extremely disturbing effects upon public opinion in Germany and in Great Britain. Grey had explained these difficulties to Metternich, and Metternich had warned the German Government that there would be an outburst of feeling which would seriously affect Anglo-German relations.[1]

Public opinion in Great Britain was already uneasy. The mere fact that the German estimates for the year 1908 had included four Dreadnoughts while Great Britain had decided only to lay down two capital ships was disquieting to those who did not take into account the relative strength of the two countries in 'all-big gun' ships. One can observe the moves and countermoves of each party. In 1907 a motion had been brought forward to

[1] D.G.P. xxviii. 97.

reduce the shipbuilding vote. A memorial signed by a hundred and thirty-six supporters of the government was presented to the Prime Minister in favour of a reduction of armaments. In 1908 an Amendment was moved to the Address, and a committee of Liberal members of Parliament issued a manifesto, asking for a further reduction. On 24 July 1908, another memorial, signed by a hundred and forty-four members, was presented to the Government. On 4 November 1908, the National Council of Peace Societies passed two resolutions. The first resolution demanded that Great Britain should take the earliest opportunity of resuming discussions with Germany about an understanding on naval armaments. The second resolution declared that the existing predominance of the British navy was such as to forbid, as wasteful and needless, any increase in the shipbuilding vote for 1909.

A few days later, the Prime Minister, at the Lord Mayor's Banquet, said that it was undesirable to state the shipbuilding programme for the next year, but that the Government intended to maintain the naval supremacy of the country. On 12 November Mr. Lee put the Prime Minister a direct question whether the Government accepted as a definition of the Two-Power standard a preponderance of 10 per cent. over the combined strength, in capital ships, of the two next strongest Powers. The answer was 'Yes'.[1] This answer was repeated on 23 November.[2] Three days earlier, in a speech at Scarborough, Grey had used plain words about the question of British naval supremacy: 'There is no half-way house, as far as we are concerned, in naval affairs, ... between complete safety and absolute ruin.' The German estimates for 1909 were published on 20 November. Four days later, in the House of Lords, Lord Cawdor complained that there was a dangerous delay in laying down British ships. The ships were sometimes delayed until the beginning of the year following their authorization, and in any case were

---

[1] Hansard, 4th Ser. cxcvi. 560. See also Appendix II.
[2] Hansard, 4th Ser. cxcvi. 1768.

rarely laid down for some months after the vote of credit. Lord Cawdor wanted immediate action, and thought that for two successive years Great Britain would find it necessary to lay down six or seven capital ships.[1] On 26 November the Reduction of Armaments Committee sent a third memorial to the Prime Minister in favour of further economies in the Naval Estimates.

Meanwhile rumours of the acceleration of the German programme had reached the public. The statement in *The Times* of 15 October,[2] together with the facts of Krupp's extension—well known in engineering circles—had begun to cause anxiety. On 10 November a question was asked in the House of Commons whether the large armoured vessels of the German 1908 programme were laid down or were in process of being laid down. The answer was a little ambiguous. 'We have no official information on the subject.' A similar answer was given to a further question whether any accumulation of material had taken place for work on the ships of the 1908 programme.[3]

Early in the New Year there were stories of Cabinet dissensions. *The Times*, on 22 January 1909, referred to these differences of view in a leading article. At this time, however, it was generally assumed that there would be an increase in the estimates. The matter was put beyond doubt by a statement in the King's Speech on 16 February; it was none the less clear that within the Liberal party there would be strong opposition to any large increase. The National Liberal Federation, at the end of February, did not commit itself to any definite line of action, but passed a resolution that further evidence was necessary before agreeing to an increase in naval expenditure.

The seriousness of the international situation in the winter of 1908–9 increased public anxiety.[4] If the British navy were involved in war, little help could be expected from France. French naval experts for some time past had

---

[1] Hansard, 4th Ser. cxcvii. 28–9.   [2] See above, p. 209.
[3] Hansard, 4th Ser. cxcvi. 35.   [4] See above, p. 188–9.

concentrated upon smaller craft and neglected the building of capital ships. French naval administration was in a bad state. There was a general shortage of stores and ammunition, and according to one estimate made in November 1908, France possessed only twelve ships—at most fifteen—capable of going into the first line. It was recognized in France that the policy of a 'cheap navy' had failed; reforms would, however, take time. The rate of construction in France was slow, and it was unlikely that any of the six Dreadnoughts which had been authorized would be completed before the middle of 1911, and possibly not before 1913.[1] In December 1908 the Austro-Hungarian Government invited the submission of designs for three 20,000-ton battleships. These ships would not be laid down before the end of 1909, at the earliest, but their construction would seriously affect the balance of power in the Mediterranean, and, consequently, the strength of the British navy in the North Sea.

Finally, there was not the least hope of reaching an agreement with Germany on the question of a limitation of armaments. The German Navy League was agitating for another increase in the shipbuilding programme, and the Emperor was as firmly resolved as ever to make no concessions.

The British naval estimates were published on 12 March. They included provision for laying down two ships of the Dreadnought class in July and two in November 1909. There was a further provision. 'His Majesty's Government may, in the course of the financial year 1909–10, find it necessary to make preparations for the rapid construction of four more large armoured ships, beginning on April 1 of the following financial year. They therefore ask Parliament to entrust them with Powers to do this effectively, i.e. to enable them to

---

[1] The French battleship *Vérité*, completed in 1908, had been under construction for six years. Two Dreadnoughts had been laid down in 1907, and four in 1908. Only the 1907 ships were launched before March 1909. A new French programme was under consideration.

arrange for the ordering, collection, and supply of guns, gun-mountings, and armour, machinery, and materials for ship-building', so that the ships would be ready for service in March 1912.[1]

These estimates were brought before the House by Mr. McKenna on 16 March. Mr. McKenna explained that in March 1908 the British Government had decided that provision for two capital ships in addition to those under construction would give the British navy ten Dreadnoughts to five German ships completed by Germany at the end of 1910, and twelve to nine German ships completed in the spring of 1911. This decision had been reached after a calculation of the probable rate of construction in Germany. The situation had changed since the spring of 1908.

'The difficulty in which the Government finds itself placed at this moment is that we do not know, as we thought we did, the rate at which German construction is taking place. . . . We anticipated that work on the (German) 1908–9 programme would begin on four ships in August, 1908. The preparation and collection of materials began some months earlier. We now expect these ships to be completed, not in February 1911, but in the autumn of 1910. I am informed, moreover, that the collection of materials, and the manufacture of armament, guns, and mountings, have already begun for four more ships, which, according to the Navy Law, belong to the programme of 1909–10, and we have to take stock of a new situation, in which we reckon that not nine but thirteen ships may be completed in 1911, and in 1912 such further ships, if any, as may be begun in the course of the next financial year or laid down in April 1910.'

Two years earlier Germany had only one or two slips capable of carrying a Dreadnought. The number had risen to fourteen; three more were under construction. 'Two years ago, any one familiar with the capacity of Krupp's and other great German firms would have

---

[1] Then followed the paragraph quoted on pp. 204–5 above, explaining the nature of the preparations which had to be made if a battleship were to be completed within two years of the laying down of the keel.

ridiculed the possibility of their undertaking to supply the component parts of eight battleships in one year. To-day this productive power is a realized fact.'

Mr. McKenna's speech was a clear statement of the facts which had disturbed the Admiralty; but facts and estimates about the shipbuilding programme of 1908, 1909, and 1910, which were common knowledge at the time are better understood now if they are put in tabular form. The British estimates of the relative strength of the British and German fleets in ships of the Dreadnought class (including large cruisers) were as follows:

1. *Admiralty forecast made in the spring of 1908.*

	Great Britain	Germany
December 1910 . .	10	5
February 1911 . .	12	9
August 1912 . .	12+ships laid down under the estimates of 1909–10	13

2. *Admiralty forecast made in the spring of 1909, and including four British ships to be laid down in 1909.*

	Great Britain	Germany
December 1910 . .	10	9
February 1911 . .	12	9
April 1911 . . .	12	11
July 1911 . . .	14	11
August 1911 . .	14	13
November 1911 . .	16	13

This forecast assumed an acceleration of the German programmes of 1908–9 and 1909–10. If there were also an acceleration of the programme of 1910–11, and if the four 'contingent' ships of the British programme of 1909–10 were laid down on 1 April 1910, the forecast for March 1912 was:

Great Britain	Germany
20	17

Notes:
1. It will be noticed that Mr. McKenna did not refer in his speech to the months between (a) December 1910 and February 1911, (b) April and July 1911, and (c) August and November 1911. During these periods the British margin of superiority was only one ship.
2. On 30 March 1908 Captain Dumas, the British naval attaché at Berlin, had reported that 'taking the earliest probable date for the completion of the ships voted during the next few years', Germany would have completed 4 Dreadnoughts and 2 Invincibles in March 1910, 7 Dreadnoughts

and 3 Invincibles in March 1911, and 10 Dreadnoughts and 4 Invincibles in March 1912. Cf. B.D.D. ii. 120.

3. Mr. McKenna's account of the Admiralty forecast in the spring of 1908 does not wholly agree with the forecast given by Mr. Robertson to the House of Commons in March 1908 (see above, p. 164). Mr. Robertson estimated that in the autumn of 1910 Great Britain would have 12 ships of the Dreadnought class, Germany 6. At the end of 1910 Germany might have ten ships; in this case Great Britain would have completed the 2 ships of the 1908–9 programme, and therefore have 14 ships of the Dreadnought class. The difference between these estimates and the figures given by Mr. McKenna in 1909 is due (i) to the inclusion of the *Lord Nelson* and the *Agamemnon* in the British figures; (ii) apparently to the inclusion of the *Blücher* in the German figures; (iii) to the omission of a reference, in Mr. McKenna's speeches on March 1909, to Mr. Robertson's statement about a 'possible acceleration' of the German programme. In 1908 Mr. Robertson was thinking of a reduction in the 'normal' period of construction in Germany. In 1909 Mr. McKenna had to deal with a possible acceleration resulting from an anticipation of the authorized time-table for commencing work on ships.

These tables show that in March 1908 Great Britain had ten ships of the Dreadnought class afloat or under construction. Germany had none afloat, and five under construction. The British estimates of 1908–9 provided for two, the German for four ships. The British Admiralty thought in 1908 that the British and German ships already under construction would be completed by December 1910. The two British and four German ships of the 1908–9 estimates would be completed by February 1911. In December 1910 the relative strength of the two fleets in ships of the Dreadnought class would be 10 : 5 in favour of Great Britain, and, in February 1911, 12 : 9 in favour of Great Britain.

According to the estimate made in March 1909 the relative strength in the autumn of 1910 would only be 10 : 9, unless two British ships of the 1908–9 estimates were completed before December 1910. In February 1911 (or a little earlier) the British figures would rise to 12. On the forecast of 1908 no more German ships would be completed in 1911; but if the construction of the German 1909–10 ships were accelerated, the date of completion might be some time in the autumn of 1911. On 18 March 1909 Mr. McKenna thought that two of these German ships would be ready in April 1911 and two in August 1911. Two of the ships which the British Government proposed to lay down in 1909 would be completed in July 1911 and two in November 1911. The ratio between the two fleets would be 14:13 between August and November 1911 and 16:13 in November 1911.

The German programme of 1910–11 included four more ships of the Dreadnought class. If this programme were accelerated, Germany might have seventeen Dreadnoughts in the spring of 1912. If there were no acceleration these four Dreadnoughts would not be completed before the autumn of 1912, i.e. thirty months after the voting of the first credits for the ships in March 1910. The British Government had no means of knowing whether there would or would not be any acceleration of this programme. They were bound to take steps to meet the possibility that Germany might have seventeen Dreadnoughts in the spring of 1912. They decided to collect materials for four ships in addition to the ships which they proposed to lay down in 1909. These ships would be laid down in April 1910 if there were evidence of German acceleration during the winter of 1909. The British strength in March 1912 would therefore be twenty Dreadnoughts to seventeen completed by Germany. If there were no acceleration of the German programme of 1910–11 Great Britain would not lay down the four 'contingent' ships as early as April 1910.

The Conservative opposition in the House of Commons at once took the chance of attacking the Government.[1] Mr. McKenna's figures showed that the British margin of superiority was not large. If two or three ships

---

[1] Labour members attacked the Government from a different point of view. Mr. Henderson refused to accept the Admiralty estimates on the ground that these figures were denied by Tirpitz. Mr. Henderson quoted two lines of Tennyson to remind the House of Mr. Gladstone's speeches on 'peace, retrenchment, and reform', and said that the Labour members proposed to vote against the proposals of the Government 'for the simple reason that if this policy is not checked we may say "Ta-ta" to all social reform'. Hansard, 5th Ser. ii. 1133–8.

of the Dreadnought class were temporarily disabled, this superiority in numbers might disappear. Public opinion had learned to reckon in terms of Dreadnoughts, and tended unduly to depress the value of pre-Dreadnought battleships. Moreover, there was room for all manner of conjectures about the possibility of German acceleration.

Mr. McKenna's figures were challenged. Mr. Balfour assumed that Germany might have twenty-one—even twenty-five—Dreadnoughts in 1912. The Prime Minister supported the estimate made by the Admiralty and Mr. McKenna gave a more detailed statement about the 'anticipated' ships of the 1909–10 German programme.[1]

'I think it is desirable to tell everything to the House. . . . All I can say is that I know that two (ships of the 1909–1910 programme) are not laid down, although for these two materials I believe have been collected and armaments are in course of construction. Two are not actually laid down. As regards the other two, I know one is actually laid down, and with regard to the fourth ship I know nothing. . . . As regards the completion of these four ships, I have no doubt that those which are not laid down will not be completed before August, 1911.'

Mr. McKenna's speech and the attacks of the Opposition upon the delay of the Government in taking action after they had received information about German acceleration had two immediate results. The first result was an excitement in the whole country verging upon panic. Neither Lord Rosebery nor Mr. Frederic Harrison were likely to be affected by hysterical jingoism, yet each of them wrote letters to *The Times* on the need for immediate action. *The Times* made strong comments upon the danger of a German hegemony in Europe, and asked for the inclusion of the four 'contingent' British ships in the substantive programme. The Conservative press was unanimous in supporting a large programme. Most of the Liberal papers accepted Mr. McKenna's

[1] For the debates on the estimates of 1909–10 see Hansard, 5th Ser. ii and iii.

arguments. The· *Manchester Guardian* thought that the Admiralty must be put in as favourable a position as Germany, but that the four 'contingent' ships need not be laid down before 1 April 1910 and could be included in the 1910–11 programme. The *Liverpool Daily Post* was 'filled with despair', but could not deny 'the force of Mr. McKenna's plea'. The debate had a similar effect in the Dominions. On 22 March the Governor of New Zealand telegraphed to the Secretary of State for the Colonies an offer from the people of New Zealand to bear the cost of one, and if necessary, two Dreadnoughts.[1]

The second result was an admission by Tirpitz that the contracts for two ships of the 1910–11 programme had in fact been given in advance of the normal date. Metternich protested to Grey about Mr. McKenna's estimate of German construction. Grey answered that Mr. McKenna had come to him on the evening before the speech and had 'at first been astounded' at Metternich's figures, since the Admiralty 'had positive information that more ships than were consistent with Count Metternich's statement were already under construction, indeed had actually been seen'. Mr. McKenna assumed that Metternich meant to exclude the large armoured cruisers. Grey asked Metternich whether his statement included these cruisers.[2] Metternich had already telegraphed for authority to deny that preparations had been made for ships of the 1909–10 class by the collection of materials and laying down keels in several yards.[3] On 17 March Tirpitz told Bülow that 'two ships of the 1909 class had been assured by contract to private yards, subject to the approval of the Reichstag, in order to secure better prices and to prevent the formation of a trust'. Tenders for the other two ships of this class would not be put out before the autumn of 1909.[4]

If this admission had been made two months earlier in

---

[1] See Hansard, 5th Ser. ii. 1777–8.

[2] B.D.D. vi. 242–3. See also Hansard, 5th Ser. xxii. 2510–11. D.G.P. xxviii. 108–10. Grey again suggested an exchange of information through the naval attachés.

[3] See above, pp. 217–18.   [4] D.G.P. xxviii. 107.

answer to Mr. McKenna's question to Widenmann, or Grey's questions to Metternich, the explanation might have carried more weight. The facts were told to Grey on 18 March.[1] Grey answered that 'this [giving of contracts for two ships] was exactly what the Admiralty had told me had happened with regard to all four ships'. He added that

'getting information in this way was very confusing. With regard to two of the earliest ships I had been told that materials had been collected in advance before the laying down, because the designs were not ready. From another source—I thought it had been from him [Metternich], but he said it was not—I had heard that the building of ships had been accelerated in order to provide against unemployment. Now I had just learned that, with regard to two of the most recent ships, contracts had been promised in advance in order to prevent the formation of a Trust.'

Once again Grey suggested an exchange of information through the naval attachés.[2]

The German explanation was accepted by the British Government, though Grey noted that the problem of reconciling the German statement with 'other information or statements given to the Admiralty' remained to be solved.[3] On 17 March a debate on the German naval estimates was opened in the Reichstag. Tirpitz said that the British forecasts were wrong, and claimed that Germany would only have completed thirteen Dreadnoughts in the autumn of 1912. The German press did not publish a full account of the debate in the House of Commons, but Count Reventlow, in the *Tägliche Rundschau* of 19 March, spoke of acceleration in the rate of building the ships of the 1908–9 and 1909–10 programmes as a 'matter of common knowledge'. Colonel Gädke wrote a few days later in the *Berliner Tageblatt* that 'beyond any doubt it

[1] B.D.D. vi. 244–6. There is no reference to Grey's remarks in the account in D.G.P. xxviii. 113–14 of a conversation between Grey and Metternich on 18 March. See Appendix VI for a conversation on 19 March.

[2] Bülow had told Metternich not to raise the question of an exchange of information. D.G.P. xxviii. 114–15.   [3] B.D.D. vi. 244.

is possible that the German navy in 1912 will number not less than thirteen Dreadnoughts and three battle cruisers (i.e. Invincibles) even without further acceleration' (i.e. three more ships than the number announced by Tirpitz in the Reichstag).

The first semi-official statement about the giving of contracts for the German ships appeared in the *Kölnische Zeitung* on 21 March. It was said that the contracts had been promised for 'industrial-financial', not for 'military', reasons. The Government could get better terms, and the firms would not have to dismiss any of their workmen. Only two contracts had been promised, and the date for the completion of the ships was put at three years from the voting of the estimates in the Reichstag. As tenders had not, apparently, been invited for the remaining two large ships, their completion might be delayed until the winter of 1912. The 'average' date of completion, therefore, would be the autumn of 1912. *The Times* pointed out that, according to the admissions of the *Kölnische Zeitung*, two of the ships might be completed in the spring of 1912, i.e. three years from the voting of the credits, and the 'average date' might be the summer of 1912.[1]

On 29 March a vote of censure on the shipbuilding policy of the Government was moved in the House of Commons.[2] Grey made the most important speech in the debate. He dealt with the question of acceleration, but also covered a wider field. On the general question of armaments Grey spoke plainly.

'The great countries of Europe are raising enormous revenues, and something like half of them is being spent on naval and military preparations. You may call it national insurance, that is perfectly true, but it is equally true that half the national revenue of the great countries in Europe is being spent on what is [*sic*], after all, preparations to kill each other. Surely the extent to which this expenditure has grown really becomes a satire, and a reflection on civilisation. Not in our generation, perhaps, but if it goes on at the rate at which it has recently

---

[1] *The Times*, 22 March 1909.　　　[2] Hansard, 5th Ser. iii. 39–146.

increased, sooner or later I believe it will submerge that civilisation. . . . Is it to be wondered that the hopes and aspirations of the best men in the leading countries are devoted to trying to find some means of checking it?'

Grey could find no way of escape from the competition in armaments by the unilateral disarmament of Great Britain.

'If we alone, among the great Powers, gave up the competition and sank into a position of inferiority, what good should we do? None whatever, no good to ourselves because we cannot realize great ideals of social reform at home when we are holding our existence at the mercy, at the caprice if you like, of another nation. That is not feasible. If we fall into a position of inferiority our self-respect is gone, and it removes that enterprise which is essential both to the material success of industry and to the carrying out of great ideals, and you fall into a state of apathy. We should cease to count for anything amongst the nations of Europe, and we should be fortunate if our liberty was left, and we did not become the conscript appendage of some stronger Power. That is a brutal way of stating the case, but it is the truth. It is disagreeable that it should be so, but in matters like this I know of no safe way except to look at what is disagreeable frankly in the face, and to state it, if necessary, in its crudest form.'

From this standpoint Grey considered the place of the navy in British policy.

'There is no comparison between the importance of the German Navy to Germany, and the importance of our Navy to us. Our Navy is to us what their Army is to them. To have a strong Navy would increase their prestige, their diplomatic influence, their power of protecting their commerce; but as regards us—it is not a matter of life and death to them that it is to us. No superiority of the British Navy over the German Navy could ever put us in a position to affect the independence or integrity of Germany, because our Army is not maintained on a scale which, unaided, could do anything on German territory. But if the German Navy were superior to ours, they, maintaining the Army which they do, for us it would not be a question of defeat. Our independence, our very existence would be at stake.'

Grey did not think that German and British interests were necessarily hostile.

'As regards our future diplomatic relations with Germany, I see a wide space in which both of us may walk in peace and amity. Two things, in my opinion two extreme things, would produce conflict. One is an attempt by us to isolate Germany. No nation of her standing and her position would stand a policy of isolation assumed by neighbouring Powers. . . . Another thing which would certainly produce a conflict would be the isolation of England, the isolation of England attempted by any great Continental Power so as to dominate and dictate the policy of the Continent. That always has been so in history. The same reasons which have caused it in history would cause it again. But between these two extremes of isolation and domination there is a wide space in which the two nations can walk together in a perfectly friendly way; and just as there is no reason to apprehend on our part that we shall pursue a policy of isolation of Germany, so also I see just as little reason to apprehend that Germany will pursue a deliberate policy of isolation of this country.'

Although there was no reason to assume an inevitable conflict of interests between England and Germany, the competition in naval armaments between the two countries was disturbing Europe.

'Public opinion in Germany and in the world at large increasingly measures the probable relations of England and Germany by their respective naval expenditure. An increase in naval expenditure on both sides is undoubtedly viewed by public opinion with apprehension. On the other hand, a decrease of naval expenditure will immediately produce a feeling of increased security and peace. If I was asked to name the one thing which would mostly reassure the world—or reassure Europe—with regard to the prospects of peace, I think it would be that the naval expenditure in Germany would be diminished, and that ours was following suit, and being diminished also.'

The British Government wanted to come to an agreement which would end the competition. There was, however, a difficulty in the way of an arrangement of this kind.

'On what basis would any arrangement have to be proposed? Not the basis of equality. It must be the basis of a superiority of the British Navy. No German, so far as I know, disputes that that is a natural point of view for us. But it is another thing to ask the German Government to expose itself before its own public opinion to a charge of having cooperated to make the attainment of our views easier. That is the difficulty which it is only fair to state.'

For this reason Grey had limited his suggestion to an exchange of information satisfactory to the naval authorities on each side. The anxiety which had arisen from uncertainty about the rate of German construction would be removed if each country had clear knowledge that the other was not secretly preparing a surprise.

From the problem of avoiding public and acrimonious discussions Grey turned to the particular difficulty with which the British Government had been faced in the absence of full information about German plans. He had taken the precaution of telling Metternich what he proposed to say about German intentions.[1] He explained to the House that

'we have been informed verbally, but quite definitely, that Germany will not accelerate her naval programme of construction, and will not have 13 ships of the "Dreadnought" type, including cruisers, till the end of 1912. . . . I understand this to mean 13 ships will, or may be, ready for commission as distinct from trial, by the end of 1912. We have also been told that contracts for two ships for the financial year 1909–10 were promised in advance to certain firms provided the money were granted by the Reichstag afterwards. In addition to this we are informed that these two ships for which orders have been promised in advance, will be ready for trial trips at the earliest in April, 1912, and will not be ready for commission before October, 1912. As regards the remaining two ships of the 1909–1910 programme, not covered by this, we are informed that tenders will be called for only late in the summer, and the orders will be given two or three months later. . . .'

[1] B.D.D. vi. 253–4.

These declarations of intention were accepted by the British Government. How far did they affect the problem of deciding the number of ships to be laid down in Great Britain? Grey pointed out that Germany allowed six months for trials. It would therefore be possible, 'in case of great emergency', to use newly constructed ships six months before the estimated time of completion, since this estimate included the six months during which the ships were at sea undergoing their trials. Furthermore, the German declarations did not contain any reference to the type of ship. If the ships would not be ready for trials until April 1912, a very large sum had been allowed for their construction in the estimates of the current year. 'The slow rate of construction of these ships cannot, in our opinion, absorb all the money to be or being allocated unless there is some change of type.' For this reason the British Admiralty had decided to wait until the German ships were launched before laying down the four 'contingent' ships in their programme.

Finally, there was the possibility of a change of intention on the part of Germany. The German declaration said nothing about the collection of material which would enable construction to be accelerated if there were a change of intention. In Grey's words:

'Another point which the German declaration does not cover is the extent to which turrets may be prepared in advance, without orders being given for definite ships. It means this, that your intention to accelerate is one thing, while your power to accelerate is another. The German intention not to accelerate their programme we perfectly accept, but in all good faith, without any breach of undertaking, even if it were an undertaking, they could accumulate the power of increasing gun mountings, of increasing plant necessary for "Dreadnoughts", and they could accumulate the power to accelerate, supposing the European situation changed and with it their intention.'

In other words, although the ships under construction in 1909–10 might not be completed before 1912, the ten

Dreadnoughts of the programmes of later years 'might appear very rapidly in 1913 and 1914'.

At a later stage in the debate the Prime Minister repeated Grey's arguments in a shorter form and more polished language. He explained once more that Great Britain was ready to come to an understanding about shipbuilding.

'There is really no satisfactory way in the long run of dealing with this most deplorable competition in naval shipbuilding except . . . either by agreement on both sides to slacken the rate of construction, or, if that be impossible, at any rate by the grant of reciprocal facilities to authorised persons for the ascertainment of the actual progress of shipbuilding, both in one country and in the other. I am sorry to say that both these ways of escape appear for the time—I trust not permanently— to be blocked. That being so, while we pay every regard to declarations of intention . . . we cannot build upon them. . . . We are obliged by the most simple and elementary requirements of precaution to act as though the present intention of Germany may peradventure be subsequently modified, but to take also into account that their present productive facilities will certainly not be diminished.'[1]

[1] The excitement which the debates on the naval estimates and vote of censure had aroused in England was not merely reflected in by-elections. *The Times* of 30 March contained a full-page advertisement of Eno's Fruit Salt headed 'The Command of the Sea and British Policy'. After quotations from Goethe and Spenser Wilkinson, the question was asked: 'What is 10,000 times more terrible than war? Answer: 'outraged nature. Eno's Fruit Salt . . . etc.' On the following day another large advertisement appeared with a rough sketch of a Dreadnought, and the words 'The two-Power standard—the Dreadnought of disease—Wincarnis.' Early in July a Dreadnought was introduced as one of the set pieces in the Crystal Palace Fireworks. On 17 March an experiment, previously arranged between the War Office and the Automobile Association, for the transport of a battalion of troops by private cars from London to the coast and back, had revived the interest of the 'sensational' press in the question of a German invasion. There were absurd stories in May of mysterious airships floating above British towns at night. These were subsequently explained as small balloons sent up to advertise a firm of motor-car manufacturers. Another rumour described a large store of German rifles and ammunition within a quarter of a mile of Charing Cross station. This rumour was traced back to a purchase of old rifles by the Society of Miniature Rifle Clubs; the rifles in question were temporarily stored by the Society's bankers near the Law Courts.

The Prime Minister also repeated Grey's assurance that the country would maintain a sufficient lead in the machinery and plant necessary for the production of armour and armaments. The Cabinet had taken action between November 1908 and February 1909 to secure adequate preparations on the part of private firms for a 'large additional output of gun-mountings'.[1]

Tirpitz also made a statement on 29 March about the allocation of contracts.[2] He told the Reichstag that two ships had been promised to private yards. The promise had been made for business reasons, and the prices obtained had been comparatively low. The Imperial yards could only undertake two of the four ships of the 1909–10 programme. If the contracts for four ships were put out simultaneously, it would be known that the Imperial yards could only undertake two of the four; the private yards would then be able to raise their terms. If the contracts for two ships were already allocated to private yards, the Imperial yards would be able to compete for the remaining two ships; the shipbuilding firms could not raise their terms above the prices at which the work could be done in the Imperial yards. There was no question of accelerating the construction of the two ships already allocated. No money had been obtained even indirectly from German banks for the contractors through the agency of the German Admiralty.

The explanation was not wholly convincing. It left out of account any change of intentions. It did not give any reason why the amount of the instalments for the ships

---

[1] This statement was questioned in Parliament at the time, but confirmed, as far as the Elswick Ordnance Works and Vickers' were concerned, by Mr. McKenna on 5 April 1909. The Coventry Ordnance Works had also laid down a new plant. Hansard, 5th Ser. iii. 714–16.

[2] For Tirpitz's speech, see D.G.P. xxviii. 136–7, n. 2. Tirpitz had given a similar explanation to the British naval attaché on 28 March. When Captain Heath mentioned the possibility of a change in the German intentions, 'this statement rather started the Admiral off again; he said that to talk of possibilities was nonsense, the possibilities of either nation were incalculable, and in any case " I have stated our fixed intention, and my word ought to be trusted "'. B.D.D. vi. 255–6.

should have been increased. No reference was made to the questions put by Grey to Metternich. If the allocation of contracts had been made simply for business reasons, why had the facts been concealed? Tirpitz did not mention that one of the ships had already been laid down. This fact was admitted three months later in the *Kölnische Zeitung*. According to this paper, the ship was laid down at the beginning of March. The British Admiralty had reason to believe that it had been laid down at an earlier date. Furthermore, as *The Times* pointed out, Tirpitz's statement that none of the ships would be ready for service before the autumn of 1912 contradicted the semi-official notice in the *Kölnische Zeitung* of 21 March.[1]

The value of Tirpitz's assurances was not increased for British readers by his remarks on the larger question of a naval agreement. Mr. Asquith had explained in Parliament on 16 and 29 March that attempts to reach an understanding with Germany which would reduce expenditure on armaments had not been successful.[2] Tirpitz denied that any offers had been made to Germany.[3] The British Government was ready to publish Grey's conversations with Metternich, but to this proposal the German Government would not agree. Grey then asked what Germany would suggest. 'Count Metternich demurred to the German Government being asked to say anything.'[4] Schön, however, told the Budget Committee of the Reichstag that while the British Government had expressed a general readiness to enter into a naval understanding, no formal proposal had been made. Bülow himself used practically the same language.[5] The German statements were technically right; from the British point of view they did not encourage a belief in the reliability of German explanations. Even the half-hearted statements of Schön

---

[1] See above, p. 230. [2] Hansard, 5th Ser. ii. 956–7.
[3] B.D.D. vi. 250–1. [4] B.D.D. vi. 244–5.
[5] B.D.D. vi. 244–58, *passim*. For the draft of Bülow's statements, see D.G.P. xxviii. 137–8.

and Bülow that a formal offer had not been made because it was known that this offer would have been refused did not reveal the fact that all the suggestions had come from Great Britain and all the refusals from Germany.[1]

Tirpitz continued his complaints against Mr. McKenna, and the Emperor wrote to Bülow early in April about the English 'Dreadnoughtschweinerei'.[2] It is therefore worth while summarizing the situation from the British point of view in the language used by the German Ambassador in an attempt to explain this point of view to his own Government.[3]

'Until November last (1908) the British Government believed that in our naval law it possessed a standard of reasonable accuracy with which to regulate its own annual shipbuilding requirements. On January 4 Sir E. Grey put to me three sphinx-like riddles which concerned the acceleration of our ship-building beyond the terms of our programme. He came back more than once to the point. . . . Two months later . . . I was authorised to state that we did not propose any acceleration and that we should have the 13 Dreadnoughts only at the end of 1912. A week ago I was authorised to tell Sir E. Grey that two ships of our 09/10 programme had already been secured by contract for private yards. As far as is known here, the money for their construction has been obtained by the firms concerned from our banks under the guarantee of the Admiralty.[4] Until last November it was assumed here that the execution of our programme depended on the annual financial vote of the Reichstag.

[1] During the debate on the vote of censure Grey explained in Parliament that there was at least three possible 'arrangements': (1) A general agreement to limit or diminish naval expenditure; (2) an annual understanding about naval budgets; (3) exchange of information about naval construction with mutual control. (Hansard, 5th Ser. iii. 59–60.) Grey had pointed out in December 1908 that Bülow was scarcely fair to Great Britain in stating that 'no proposals had been made to Germany'. The statement might be technically correct, but it did not show that overtures made by Great Britain were not well received by Germany. B.D.D. vi. 172–3.

[2] For Tirpitz's complaints see B.D.D. vi. 255–6. For the Emperor's language see a curious letter to Bülow in D.G.P. xxviii. 145–7, 3 April 1909.

[3] D.G.P. xxviii. 123–6.

[4] This fact was denied by Tirpitz. (B.D.D. vi. 255.) Metternich's dispatch was peppered with annotations by the Emperor. ('Nonsense'—'This is absolutely not so'—'No', &c.) There is no Imperial annotation to this sentence.

This security has now disappeared. The present Government has indeed our assurance that we do not wish to accelerate our "tempo" and that we shall have no more than thirteen Dreadnoughts in the year 1912; but the Government maintains that, although these may be our intentions at present, we have every right to change them at any moment we may wish to do so. The Government feels that in this important question it is groping in the dark in respect to our ship-building, and that it must not be dependent upon the good intentions of a foreign government—intentions which may change. Sir J. Fisher, e.g., believes that the ordinary money votes for the German navy are sufficient for us to have seventeen Dreadnoughts in 1912.'

XII

LATER HISTORY OF THE QUESTION OF GERMAN ACCELERATION, 1909–12

THE sequel to this stormy controversy may be told very briefly. There was no acceleration of the German programme after March 1909. No more contracts were allotted in advance of the votes in the Reichstag. In the absence of documentary evidence on the German side it is impossible at present to write the last word on the subject. Opinion in Great Britain to which value must be attached was unconvinced by Tirpitz's explanations, and remained certain that an attempt at acceleration had been made. According to this view the attempt was abandoned for an obvious reason. The discovery of the essential facts defeated the object of the plan. The decision to anticipate the published programme had been taken at a moment when there was some chance of success. The margin of British superiority was already lessening. The British programme for 1908–9 was only two ships to four German ships. The Liberal Cabinet might give way in 1909, as they had given way in 1908, to the pressure of their own supporters. Even if they decided to double the programme of the previous year, they would not neutralize the effects of German acceleration. Then came the discovery of the facts. This discovery was followed by the statement that any German acceleration would be followed by an overwhelming increase in British construction. The plan had failed. It had caused almost a panic in Great Britain, and a building programme of eight ships in a single year. The German ships of the 1908–9 and 1909–10 programmes were not completed in advance of the 'normal' time; but this is no evidence of German intentions in the winter of 1908 and the spring of 1909. Once the idea of acceleration had been repudiated, it would have been more than foolish to make another attempt. There was always, in German minds, the fear of a preventive war.

This explanation was put forward by the British naval attachés at Berlin. Captain Heath came to the end of his period of service as attaché in August 1910. His last report was a summary of his impressions during his two years' residence in Germany. He mentioned the collection of material and provisional placing of contracts in the autumn of 1908. He added: 'The German Naval authorities did their best to show that this meant no acceleration of the building programme, but there is no getting over the fact, that work on at least one of these ships was commenced in the Schichau Yard before the estimate had received the approval of the Reichstag.' Captain Heath also discussed Tirpitz's assertion that German yards could not complete ships in less than three years.

'The German Naval Authorities state officially, that their ships are built, viz. are ready for steam trials in from 36 to 42 months, from the first of April of the year in which they are authorised. An endeavour was made to shew that this meant, that no ship would be completed in less than 36 months. This fable was dispelled last year when it was officially stated that neither the plans nor the contracts for the battleships "E(rsatz) Heimdall" and "E(rsatz) Hildebrand" had been completed before the Autumn of 1909, and yet these ships must be completed in 36 to 42 months from the 1st of April that year. . . . Again, . . . it is stated that the cruiser "G" is to be delivered in 33 months, presumably from the 1st of April 1908, although the contract was only completed in September of that year.'[1]

Captain Watson, who succeeded Captain Heath as naval attaché, reported in January 1912:

'Evidence that has come to me during the past 17 months goes

[1] B.D.D. vi. 508-9. In November 1910, the German Admiralty said that these ships would be completed, respectively, in the summer and autumn of 1912. Mr. McKenna stated in the House of Commons that the *Nassau*, the first of the German Dreadnoughts, was commissioned for trials within two years and two months of the laying down of the keel in August 1907. (Hansard, 5th Ser. xviii. 664.)

to show that during the years in which the British Naval Estimates were reduced and prior to the introduction of the additional 4 British Armoured Ships being laid down (making 8 in one year), the activity in German Naval circles, Ports, and Yards, was extremely great.[1] During this period the German Naval Officers appear to have had an idea that they might be able to build sufficiently near to the British Naval strength as to be able by means of Allies and assiduous work on their part to successfully compete with the British Fleet. . . . Up to the last it was thought in German Naval circles that the 8 Armoured Ships, voted in one year, would not be laid down; and when they actually were, evidence in Germany goes to prove that the before prevailing [sic] general Naval activity was greatly diminished.'[2]

Captain Watson had already reported that there had been 'acceleration and anticipation' of the official German programme in 1909, and that 'strong evidence existed to show that . . . two ships were commenced some three months before the estimate year 1909 began'. In spite of Tirpitz's denials, Captain Watson noted the report that the firms to which the contracts for these ships were allotted had been 'assured financially by allocation of Savings Bank Funds'.[3] The Correspondent of The Times in Berlin believed that the attempt at acceleration had been given up only after the announcement of the large British programme. 'As soon as they (the Germans) saw the result of their giving an earlier order for the Oldenburg was to quicken action on this side, they determined not to continue a course which could only lead to ruinous competition.'[4] This view was held by the Conservative press, and carried with it a criticism of the Liberal

---

[1] Goschen also held the view that 'the activity in German dockyards has a tendency to increase or decrease in inverse ratio to that of Great Britain', see below, p. 292.

[2] B.D.D. vi. 656–7.　　　　　　　　　　[3] B.D.D. vi. 555–6.

[4] The Times, 17 February 1911. On 4 March 1911 the possibility of further German acceleration was mentioned in The Times. The question whether German acceleration was given up as a result of the four 'contingent ships' was 'perhaps rather a matter of debatable opinion rather than a positive matter of demonstrable fact'. Germany had the power and the right to accelerate her programme, if she wished to do so.

Government. If the Government had maintained the programme laid down in the Cawdor memorandum, the German Admiralty would never have begun to accelerate their programme.[1] The reductions made by the Liberals were not an economy, because they had encouraged the Germans to speed up their rate of construction and anticipate their programme.

The programme of eight ships had a reassuring effect upon British public opinion. In March 1909 *The Times* began a series of articles on German and British facilities for shipbuilding and armament manufacture. These articles were continued in the *Engineering Supplement* of *The Times* for more than twelve months, and were followed by an account of similar resources in Austria-Hungary. The information was of a general kind; but it left no doubt that Great Britain still held a very considerable lead over other Powers.

The excitement did not die down at once, and the comfortable belief that Great Britain could always afford to wait until other Powers had shown their plans was given up by experts as well as by the general public. The competition between Great Britain and Germany appeared a little sharper, while the heavy financial cost of the 1909–10 programme of eight ships added to the exasperation of Liberals and the difficulties of the Government. It was necessary to justify every increase in naval expenditure by reference to Germany, and every reference to German plans and intentions produced angry criticism in the German press.

In the early summer of 1909 there was further discussion about the four 'contingent' ships. The Government was not finally committed to these ships. The Conservatives wanted them to be laid down as quickly as possible; the left wing of the Liberals, which was more ready to accept German than British estimates and assurances, believed that Tirpitz's statement made a programme of eight ships

[1] This view was expressed in plain words by Lord Charles Beresford in the House of Commons on 4 July 1910. Hansard, 5th Ser. xviii. 1383.

unnecessary, and refused to take into account the possibility of a change of plan in Germany. On the other hand it was difficult to make accurate comparisons between German and British rates of construction or to calculate the dates upon which ships would be completed. For these reasons the way was open for the most exaggerated calculations. Ministers were faced on the one hand with charges of surrender to panic, and on the other hand with all manner of alarmist statistics. The question of maintaining the two-Power standard was raised in the House of Commons on 26 May. The answers of the Government, though they were reasonable in themselves, were hardly consistent with the statement made more than once by the Prime Minister in the winter of 1908–9 that this standard required 'a preponderance of 10 per cent. over the combined strengths in capital ships of the two next strongest Powers, whatever those Powers may be'.[1] In any case the emphasis laid by members on each side of the House upon the extreme unlikelihood of an Anglo-American war showed that the German fleet alone was causing uneasiness.

In July the naval estimates were voted.[2] On 26 July Mr. McKenna announced, when the shipbuilding vote was under discussion, that the four 'contingent ships' would be included in the programme. The main reason given for their inclusion was that Italy and Austria proposed to build four Dreadnoughts. One Italian ship had already been laid down; the second was to be laid down within a short time, and the remaining two before the end of the year 1909. The Austrian naval authorities had prepared two large building slips, and were constructing a large floating dock. These facts were already known to the public. It was also known that Russia intended to build four Dreadnoughts; the Russian plans had been delayed owing to political reasons, and to a long discussion about designs. The Russian Admiralty considered Italian

---

[1] For the discussions upon the two-Power standard, see Appendix II.
[2] Hansard, 5th Ser. viii. 855–970.

and German designs; finally they accepted British plans and arranged that the ships should be built at St. Petersburg with assistance from the firm of John Brown & Co. In France a committee of naval inquiry was producing disquieting evidence upon the state of the French navy; at the end of April the *Petit Parisien* commented that 'it looks almost as if our naval authorities were depending on our friends in order to assure the safety of our Channel and Atlantic coasts'. On 28 June the French commission issued its report. The report was very long (220 pages of text and 730 pages of evidence); it included references to the execution of shipbuilding programmes. Serious delays had occurred between the sanctioning of new ships in the Chamber and the settlement of plans and contracts. 'Months and generally years' passed between the allotment of contracts for different parts of a vessel, with serious effect upon the homogeneity of the ship. The report caused indignation in France. A month after its publication all the heads of departments in the naval service were changed; Admiral Boué de Lapeyrère was appointed Minister of Marine with a mandate to carry out thorough-going reforms. It was clear that the British Admiralty would have to take into account the possibility of Austrian Dreadnoughts in the Mediterranean without reckoning also upon the certainty of a counterbalancing number of French ships, and that for some time to come the Russian fleet in the Baltic would not draw away many new units of the German fleet.

Mr. McKenna still maintained that there had been an acceleration of one ship in the German programme, 'an acceleration which is admitted, and of which the only possible explanation that can be given is, that it was desirable, in the opinion of the German Government, to have the ship completed as early as possible.' Later in the debate Mr. McKenna was more explicit:

'I gather from interruptions that there is a belief that Admiral Tirpitz has contradicted in some essential matter something I stated. Last March I said with regard to the German programme of 1909–1910 that the programme had been anticipated, that at the date of which I spoke one ship had been actually laid down, beginning 1st April, 1909;[1] that, as regards two more ships, they had not been laid down; and that, as regards the fourth, I did not know whether it had been laid down or not. That statement I then made is admittedly true. I stated also that orders had been given for certain parts of ships for the 1909–1910 programme before 1st April. I adhere to that statement.'

Mr. McKenna said nothing about the large increase in the instalments voted for German ships under construction. The Admiralty had been given no explanation of this increase; but it was thought more tactful to make no reference to the question in the debate.[2] Grey had already mentioned the point in his speech of 29 March.[3]

In November 1910 Bethmann-Hollweg gave the British Government the official dates for the completion of German ships. The question of acceleration was not raised from the German side. Grey mentioned the possibility, and pointed out that the period of time allowed for the completion of each ship allowed a considerable margin for delay. The interruptions caused by strikes, for example, had not made it necessary to move forward the dates of completion of any ship under construction.[4] The German figures were shown to Captain Watson. He thought that, in view of the measures taken in 1908 and 1909, 'the probable and possible date of completion of certain ships would be three months earlier than the dates in the timetable.'[5] Nevertheless Kiderlen-Waechter still refused to recognize that the British Admiralty was bound to take account of potentialities of construction as well as declarations of intention, and that the British Government could not let the safety of the country rest upon declarations of intention which might at any time be changed, and changed without notice.[6]

---

[1] See above, p. 227.   [2] See below, p. 250–1.   [3] See above, p. 234.
[4] B.D.D. vi. 544–5; D.G.P. xxviii. 376–7, and 350–1.
[5] B.D.D. vi. 555–7.
[6] D.G.P. xxviii. 378–9   The editors of D.G.P. in their editorial comments

When the estimates for the year 1910-11 were laid before Parliament in March 1910 the subject of German acceleration was again raised. In answer to questions about the shipbuilding programmes of Italy and Austria the Government had replied somewhat indefinitely; on 10 March Mr. McKenna said that one Dreadnought had been laid down and that another was shortly to be laid down in Italian yards.[1] The British estimates provided for five capital ships. The Conservatives thought that the ships should be laid down as soon as possible. The left wing of the Liberals wanted fewer ships because the Austrian programme had not been realized and that no acceleration had taken place in Germany. On 15 March Mr. McKenna was asked to give an estimate of the number of German ships which would be completed by March 1913.[2] Once more he said that he could not name the precise date upon which a ship would be ready. If construction were accelerated in Germany and if a completed ship were put into commission at once without allowing six months for trials, Germany would have seventeen ships ready in the course of 1912, and twenty-one in 1913.

'I do not know that Germany will have seventeen ships commissioned in 1912. I have no means of saying, but I do say that the power of construction is such that she is capable of having seventeen ships so far advanced as to be available for war in the course of the year 1912. Consequently I say she will have on the same footing twenty-one similarly available in the course of the year 1913. . . . What the Germans will do in 1911 is open to everyone to conjecture.'

On 31 March Mr. McKenna again said that, in his opinion, 'a German vessel of the "Dreadnought" type could, if it is desired, be built in a less time than thirty-six months'.[3]

tend to ignore the reasons for the British attitude. Thus in a note in xxviii. 386-7, Mr. McKenna is represented as saying in October 1910 the opposite of what he had said in March 1909; no account is taken of the facts behind the speech of 1909 or of the distinction between 'actual' and 'possible' acceleration.   [1] Hansard, 5th Ser. xiv. 938, 1057-8, 1435, 1641.
[2] Hansard 5th Ser. xv. 246-7.   [3] Hansard, 5th Ser. xv. 1451.

Tirpitz protested against Mr. McKenna's figures. Grey pointed out that Mr. McKenna was not doubting Germany's word, but only explaining that if circumstances made it desirable for the German Government to accelerate their programme, it was in their power to do so.[1] Tirpitz wanted an official complaint to be made. Bethmann-Hollweg's answer is interesting.[2] The Chancellor quoted a report of Mr. McKenna's speech in *The Times* of 16 March 1910: 'He (McKenna) did not say that Germany would have 17 of these ships in commission in 1912. He had no means of knowing. What he said was that Germany's power of construction was such that she was capable of having 17 ships so far advanced as to be available in the course of the year 1913.' Upon this statement Bethmann-Hollweg commented:

'I am unable to judge the accuracy of this statement, or of the latest statement . . . of Mr. McKenna that a German ship of the Dreadnought class can, if so desired, be built in a shorter time than 36 months. If the statement is wrong, I should regard it desirable to bring the fact to the notice of the British Government if it is again necessary for us to take any official notice of Mr. McKenna's statements. If there are any reasons against giving the British government an explicit declaration . . . or again if the German yards can actually accelerate construction, then I think it is better not to raise the matter.'

The forecast given by Mr. McKenna in March was confirmed by the Prime Minister at the voting of the naval estimates in July.[3] The Prime Minister pointed out that the 'acceleration or anticipation' of the German programme of which Ministers had spoken in the debates of 1909 had taken place, and that the facilities in Germany for the rapid construction of Dreadnoughts had also increased. Germany now built ships in a period not less than two years and two months and not more than two

[1] D.G.P. xxviii. 308–9. There is no reference to the subject in the short account of the conversation in B.D.D. vi. 442.

[2] D.G.P. xxviii. 312.

[3] Hansard, 5th Ser. xix. 636–45.

years and nine months, excluding the period of trials. The British programme of five ships would provide the country with twenty-five Dreadnoughts in the spring of 1913; Germany would certainly possess twenty-one in 1913 or early in 1914. These figures did not include the two Dreadnoughts offered by Australia and New Zealand, and took no account of ships which were being laid down in Italy and might be laid down in Austria. After the financial year 1911–12 the German programme fell to two large ships a year. The British number depended on the annual estimates.

The Liberal and Labour members in favour of naval retrenchment raised the question of German acceleration several times in the spring of 1911,[1] but little general interest was aroused. On 13 March 1911 Mr. J. M. Macdonald brought forward in the House of Commons a motion to reduce expenditure on the army and navy. The motion had no chance of success, and the mover himself admitted that Great Britain ought to possess 'an adequate superiority of Dreadnoughts'. One of the main charges against the Government was that they had been entirely mistaken in their estimate of German construction, and that they had caused unnecessary panic, and undertaken unnecessary construction in 1909. To this charge Mr. McKenna was able to give a full answer.[2] The answer is worth quoting at length, since it summarizes the policy of the British Government in the period between 1909 and 1911. Mr. McKenna pointed out that the statements of fact which he had made to the House in March 1909 had not been disputed. The attack rested upon the inferences which the Admiralty drew

---

[1] 9, 13, and 20 February and 6 and 13 March 1911.

[2] For the debate, see Hansard, 5th Ser. xxii. 1877–1999. The motion was amended as follows: 'That this house views with profound anxiety and regret the continued necessity for the maintenance by this Country of large armaments, and would welcome the establishment of international arrangements under which the Great Powers would simultaneously restrict their warlike preparations.' In this form the motion was accepted without a division.

from the facts. Furthermore, it was alleged that, after the German Government had explained the facts, the Government still laid down the four 'contingent' ships.

'I must ask the House to remember that German capital ships are paid for by four annual instalments. In the winter of 1908–9 I had before me the German estimates for the year 1909–10. I saw in those Estimates that the first two instalments for the four ships which were laid down in 1908–9, and belonging to the programme of 1908–9, amounted to close on £1,300,000—that is to say, that the two instalments were within £90,000 of the amount of the first three instalments for the ships belonging to the 1906–7 programme. The fact of this great increase in the amount of money which has been devoted to the building of the ships might mean either of two things, or it might mean both of them. It might mean that the ships were going to be built earlier and quicker, and in consequence larger instalments would be necessary in the first three years, or it might mean that the ships were going to be of a much greater size and cost. . . . With these alternatives before me . . . what did I know? I knew, as is admitted to be the fact, that two of the contracts for the year 1909–10 programme had already been promised in the year 1908, and I knew as well that one of the ships was laid down and a considerable amount of work done upon it, and on the other of the two ships for which the contract was promised, although it was not actually laid down the material was gathered and all was ready to be laid down. I described the condition of affairs at that time as being this, that one ship was laid down and two ships were not laid down, and as to the fourth I could not say whether it was or was not. I knew these facts. Was I justified in venturing to think that perhaps this larger amount of money voted in the first two years was intended to pay for the ships for which contracts had been promised in anticipation of 1st April, 1909? That was the inference I drew. . . . I believed it was the intention to finish the ships earlier. I had no information to the contrary. The representative of the Admiralty in Germany had no means of getting information to the contrary, and I could only draw such conclusions as the facts permitted me to do. Thirteen days after I made my statement to the House as to my belief as to the time when the German ships would be delivered I corrected it, and I gave the House the official German figures as to the date when the German ships would be delivered. . . . Why did I not withdraw my request for the four contingent ships when I knew that these other ships were not going to be built? The House will remember that if the larger amount of the first instalment did not mean quicker building it meant larger ships. What are the facts about the ships? We know now that the whole amount is in the Estimates. . . . The first four German battleships of the Nassau class (the first German Dreadnoughts) cost £1,800,000 each; the three battleships laid down in 1908—and these were the ships I had in view—cost £2,300,000 each. . . . The difference in cost is ten times the difference in cost between the "Dreadnoughts" and the "Lord Nelson".[1] What could I do? I should have come down to the House in the month of July, 1909, and stated this fact. I should have told the House that I had accepted the statement made on behalf of the German Government, but that my inference was wrong as to dates, and my inference as to size and cost must be right. Would that have been useful at the time? . . . I was really unwilling to say anything at the time which could be calculated to cause a scare . . . but I had . . . to consider that Germany would have six of these (larger) ships probably completed in April, 1912, and that we should have two of these larger types. I availed myself of the power to build four more, and I laid down four more large ships, which would give this country six, as against the German six in the spring of 1912.'

The explanation given, or rather repeated, to the House satisfied most members, but the old charges of deliberate misrepresentation were raised once more against the Government during the discussion of the naval estimates a few days later.[2] One new fact was contributed to the subject. Mr. McKenna said that, in March 1909 he could only explain Metternich's figures by assuming that they referred to battleships and excluded large cruisers.[3]

After Mr. McKenna ceased to be First Lord of the Admiralty, there was no occasion for bringing up garbled and unfair references to his speeches on the shipbuilding question. Mr. Churchill had taken no part in the public

---

[1] This figure is incorrect. The difference between the cost of the *Dreadnought* and the *Lord Nelson* was £181,000.

[2] Hansard, 5th Ser. xxii. 2457–2558.   [3] *Id.* 2510–11.

discussions of 1909 on the naval question; he came to the Admiralty in 1911, when the question of acceleration was no longer a living issue. There were other and more topical arguments at the disposal of those who wished to attack the Government for building too few or too many large ships. Comparisons were made, and questions asked, about the relative speed of construction in Great Britain and Germany, but the public now understood that this problem could not be answered in simple terms, while the Admiralty always claimed that their plans took full account of German 'potentialities' of construction.

Two later references to the subject may be mentioned. In February and March 1912—the months which had been the subject of much discussion three years earlier— Mr. Churchill answered questions in the House of Commons about the time taken in the construction of capital ships in Great Britain and Germany since the laying down of the *Dreadnought* in October 1905. The average German time was 39–41 months from the date of order to the date of the completion of trials. The average British time was 28 months. Mr. Churchill said that the figures did not necessarily give 'an adequate criterion for judging the comparative rapidity of construction in the two countries', and the Admiralty annotated the figures: 'The above table relates to facts and is not necessarily a measure of capability.'[1]

Some months earlier[2] *The Times* had quoted a statement by the Kiel correspondent of the *Kölnische Zeitung* congratulating the German yards on 'the noteworthy achievement of completing three Dreadnoughts—*Ostfriesland, Helgoland,* and *Thüringen*—in a period ranging from $31\frac{1}{2}$ to $33\frac{1}{2}$ months', in spite of strikes lasting two months. 'With the increase in displacement there has been a constant reduction of the period of construction' of a German battleship. *The Times* was 'unwilling to speculate what would be the results of construction under pressure, or of a further progress in the "constant reduction" of the time necessary for building German ships'.

---

[1] Hansard, 5th Ser. xxxiv. 1331–2 and xxxv. 170–4.   [2] 14 August 1911.

XIII
NEGOTIATIONS AT CROSS-PURPOSES
I. APRIL–JUNE, 1909

THROUGHOUT the difficult period in which the British Government was trying to discover the facts about German shipbuilding Grey never allowed the question of a naval agreement to recede into the background. In his interviews with Metternich he had kept in view the possibility of such an agreement.[1] He had suggested in Parliament a general discussion between the two countries upon the naval question, a comparison of naval estimates, an exchange of information which would avoid misunderstandings on questions of fact. Metternich continued to report that the German navy, and not German trade competition, alarmed and exasperated British opinion. Finally, the announcement that Great Britain would build eight Dreadnoughts as an answer to the German programme made it clear that for the time at least Germany would remain in the 'danger-zone'. At enormous cost Germany was building a battle fleet with which she dared not engage the fleet of Great Britain. This German fleet had not the 'alliance value' for which its builders had hoped. The first Moroccan crisis had not destroyed the Anglo-French entente; the Bosnian crisis had not affected the solid results of the Anglo-Russian agreement.

On the other hand, with the evidence of fact pointing in the opposite direction, the naval party in Germany still expounded the 'risk' theory as though the relations of the Great Powers had remained unchanged since the end of the nineteenth century. The *Jahrbuch für Deutschlands Seeinteressen*—commonly known as *Nauticus*—may be taken as representing the views which the naval party put before the German people. The *Jahrbuch* was first

[1] B.D.D. vi. 237–8 (4 Jan. 1909), 239–40 (3 Feb.), 240–1 (5 March), 241–2 (10 March), 242–3 (17 March).

published in 1899. It contained a descriptive account of the fleets of the world, and a number of articles on current political questions. The volume for the year 1910 opened with a survey of the ten years since the passing of the first naval law. The writer put forward the philosophy which had long been associated with a particular school of German publicists and political writers.

'The political events of the last ten years shew above all else that the wise remark of Karl Benedict Haase still holds good: "Force is the decisive factor in the world; nations maintain themselves by strength in combat [*Streitbarkeit*] and unity of purpose [*Sinneseinheit*] and not by superiority of civilisation [*Überlegenheit der Kultur*]." All living and active nations therefore attempt with all their power to obtain or maintain for themselves armed forces suited to their circumstances and their economic interests. Without an instrument of this kind a strong policy is impossible over any length of time.'[1]

Hence the creation of a powerful German fleet. During the ten years since the passing of the naval law of 1900 the German fleet had not overtaken the British fleet, and was still unable to defeat this fleet on the high seas. Could the German fleet be described as an effective instrument for the support of a 'strong policy'? Once more the arguments of ten years ago were brought forward. The political circumstances of the twentieth century were no longer those of the seventeenth and eighteenth centuries. Great Britain, at any particular time in these earlier centuries, had never been faced with more than one naval Power which was also a commercial rival.

'Today, when the political factors at work tend towards the creation of a general world balance, a war between England and one of her commercial rivals for the exclusive domination of the markets of the world might end in an English victory, owing to the enormous superiority of English seapower. Yet this conclusion would only be a Pyrrhic victory, since the commercial rivals of England would take the chance of her inevitable exhaustion to deliver attacks which Great Britain could hardly meet.'[2]

[1] *Nauticus*, 1910, p. 24. [2] *Nauticus*, 1910, p. 45.

The supporters of this view of German policy and English 'embarrassments' would hardly accept, or even understand, the English standpoint. The old-fashioned mercantilism which did duty for economic theory in German military, naval, and court circles failed to realize that the 'world conditions' doomed any war for commercial purposes as a Pyrrhic victory, and might lead to a coalition of other Powers against a state known to consider such a war as a possible source of profit. Political theorists who justified German warship construction as a 'profitable undertaking' on the ground that if the money had remained in the taxpayers pockets, it would have been spent to a large extent in speculations outside Germany,[1] naturally enough, regarded disarmament as an insult to human nature. Here again one-sided deductions were made from science.

'Eternal peace, of which there has recently been much talk, contradicts the ancient and still valid generalisation that change, and not quiet, war and not peace, are part of the nature of things and of life itself. The idea of perpetual peace assumes that all conflicts of interest and all differences of outlook can be reconciled, and thereby contradicts the nature of man, and is incompatible with human societies.'[2]

There were men in Germany wise enough to feel doubts about the completeness of this philosophy, and disquiet at the political consequences which would follow from the moral isolation of Germany, at least among the democratic countries of the world. German policy was not controlled by those who shared the views of English or French liberals and socialists. Discussions with the British Government about a naval agreement were therefore little more than talk at cross-purposes. On the German side the discussions were based upon the view that the main purpose of Germany was to gain time and avoid a preventive war until the danger-zone had been

---

[1] *Nauticus*, 1912, p. 295. This view is developed in an article on the beneficent effects of the Navy Law upon German industry.

[2] *Nauticus*, 1911, p. 53.

passed. On the British side there was a belief that by agreement among themselves the great Powers might lessen the burden of armaments in a world where war for aggressive purposes would defeat its own ends. Grey and his colleagues looked upon the Anglo-French and Anglo-Russian *ententes* as measures of defence against possible aggression. The Germans assumed that the new grouping of the Powers was a measure of positive hostility directed against Germany; a limitation of armaments was mere folly unless this combination were dissolved. Hence the insistence upon a political agreement with Great Britain which would break the circle of German enemies. After the Moroccan and Bosnian crisis Great Britain could have no wish for a political agreement with Germany which would destroy the balance of power on the Continent, but the naval party believed that they might ask a high price for their 'recognition' of British naval superiority, and that for financial and political reasons this price would be paid. If it were not paid Germany must continue, in Tirpitz's words, 'to arm with all her might'.

The idea of a 'bargain'[1] was taken up again by Bülow immediately after the controversy about German acceleration in March 1909. His first task was to persuade the Emperor to listen to any talk of naval concessions. The Emperor was excited and angry. He complained that Metternich had already made an important concession without asking anything in return.[2] The 'important concession' was a statement that no German supplementary law would be introduced in 1912; the Emperor's complaint was made at a time when official Germany was indignant that England had not taken as binding for the future all German statements about the fixity of their naval plans and the dates of completion of their ships. Bülow, while on holiday in Italy, was sent a new proposal that Germany would agree to a 3 : 4 ratio with Great Britain, but would withdraw her promise not to

---

[1] See above, pp. 178–81. [2] D.G.P. xxviii. 145–6.

increase her programme. Bülow realized that this 'concession' would not be accepted by Great Britain, especially at a time when the Austro-Hungarian Government was announcing a programme of four Dreadnoughts. Bülow pointed out that the proposal increased the danger of a preventive war. He wrote to Tirpitz: 'In this case I must make Your Excellency responsible before Emperor, country, and history if the consequences should be unexpected and serious.'[1] Bülow discussed the whole question with the Emperor in Venice, but Metternich's illness delayed any decision.

Bülow's summary of the Emperor's views, after a certain calmness had been restored, shows the development of the new German plan; the attempt to use the 'trump card' and to turn English anxiety about the German fleet to the advantage of Germany. Bülow himself had said to Tirpitz in January 1909 that England was not threatening Germany, but was approaching her as a 'petitioner'.[2] Germany might therefore strike a bargain. The Emperor proposed that a naval agreement should be accompanied either by a general declaration of neutrality on the part of Great Britain in the event of a war in which Germany was involved, or by a far-reaching colonial agreement, or again by a general agreement between England and Germany not to damage each other. The naval agreement would be made on the basis of the existing German programme.[3]

The German Foreign Office, had suggested a 'bargain' with special reference to colonial 'concessions'.[4] The plan

---

[1] D.G.P. xxviii. 148.   [2] D.G.P. xxviii. 60–1.

[3] D.G.P. xxviii. 148–52. The Emperor stated once again that he had no thought of building a fleet as strong or stronger than the fleet of Great Britain. It is not easy to understand why he should have held so firmly to the view that the advantages of ending a competition in Dreadnoughts were altogether on the side of England, and that the 'concession' made by Germany entitled her to counter concessions of a political or territorial kind. If the difference between the English and German fleets were, according to the Emperor's view, to remain constant, then Germany as well as England would gain from economy in naval expenditure.

[4] See above, pp. 179 and 201.

was supported by the colonial enthusiasts. Dernburg, the Secretary of the Colonial Office, suggested an African agreement. An attempt was made to combine every form of advantage in Europe and elsewhere. Schön, the Foreign Secretary, drew up a draft agreement, or rather a series of agreements on the lines of the Emperor's proposals, and sent Baron von Stumm to London at the end of April to discuss colonial questions.[1] The draft agreement provided for three possibilities: (1) a military alliance providing for mutual assistance if either Power were attacked by one or more Powers; (2) a 'neutrality' agreement in which neither Power would join any alliance or make any engagement directed against the other, and would remain neutral (with certain exceptions intended to cover acts of aggression by Germany or Great Britain) in any war in which the other Power were engaged; (3) an *entente* based upon the maintenance of the territorial integrity of each Power. The political agreement would be accompanied by commercial and naval agreements, an understanding over the Baghdad railway, the capitulations in Egypt, and the right of capture at sea.[2]

These drafts do not appear to have been shown to the British Foreign Office. Stumm found that Grey insisted on talking about the naval question. Stumm did not even want to raise the question, but Grey said to him almost at once: 'Well, we have not come to a naval understanding yet.' Stumm's conclusion was that Great Britain would not readily compromise her relations with France and Russia, but would make very great concessions in return for a naval agreement.[3]

---

[1] Baron von Stumm was First Secretary at the German Embassy in London from 1906 to 1908, and chargé d'affaires at intervals during these years.

[2] D.G.P. xxviii. 156–8.

[3] D.G.P. xxviii. 159–65. Stumm remarked more than once on Grey's silences. When Stumm pointed out that a naval agreement would be useful only if it were followed by a general understanding between the two countries, 'Der Minister schwieg wieder längere Zeit.' When Stumm explained German policy in the crisis after the annexation of Bosnia, 'Der Minister verfiel dann in ein längeres nachdenkliches Schweigen.'

While Stumm was fencing with Grey and Hardinge, Kiderlen-Waechter had already explained to Goschen his views about a political understanding. Kiderlen-Waechter, was acting temporarily as Secretary for Foreign Affairs.[1] Goschen reported that he had made himself indispensable to Bülow, and that, according to Kiderlen himself, Bülow wanted him in Schön's place in Berlin.[2] This fact has a certain significance. Kiderlen's character and career throw light on the German diplomatic service and the conditions under which men rose or fell during the reign of William II. Kiderlen was not a young man in 1909. He was born in 1852; his father, Herr Kiderlen, was Director of the Königliche Hofbank at Stuttgart; his mother was ennobled after the death of her husband, and took the name of Kiderlen-Waechter. Alfred von Kiderlen-Waechter fought in the Franco-Prussian War, and entered the consular department of the Foreign Office in 1879. A year later he was transferred to the diplomatic side of the service. From 1881 to 1885 he was at St. Petersburg. He went for a short time to Paris, and was then recalled by Bismarck to the Foreign Office. In 1895 he was appointed Ambassador at Copenhagen. Four years later he came under the strong disapproval of the Emperor. More than once Kiderlen had been one of the holiday company on the Emperor's yacht. A holiday cruise with William II was a trying experience. There was a great deal of false heartiness, noise, and exuberance, mixed with dirty stories, schoolboy pranks, and all the intrigue of a court entourage. The Emperor's prisoners could find relief only in their own private correspondence. They did not know that their letters might be opened by the secret police.[3] Kiderlen, in particular, could not guess that Marschall would leave some private letters in his office when he was moved from Berlin to Constantinople. These letters, written by Kiderlen on the Imperial yacht, were found by Bülow. They contained

[1] Goschen became more friendly to Kiderlen during the later negotiations.
[2] B.D.D. vi. 261.   [3] Jäckh, op. cit. i, p. 101.

jokes about the Emperor, and to the Emperor they were shown by Bülow.[1]

Kiderlen's letters ruined his career. He was sent as Minister to Bucharest in January 1900, and remained there in exile for nearly ten years, with intervals in 1907–8 when he acted as chargé d'affaires at Constantinople and in 1908–9 when he was acting Secretary for Foreign Affairs. After ten years his tactlessness was partly forgiven him, and his abilities were too great to be overlooked at a time when German diplomacy had not been very successful. It is said that Holstein advised Bülow to bring him back to Berlin. He became Secretary for Foreign Affairs in June 1910, and died on 30 December 1912.[2]

Kiderlen was a rough Swabian, a man whom Bismarck alone would have known how to use and to control. He was a curious mixture of kindliness and brutality; a lover of animals—his letters are full of talk about his dogs—and a man who enjoyed watching his tame vultures tear their living prey to pieces. Kiderlen hated the apparatus of court life, and was out of place in the Byzantine atmosphere of Imperial Germany. From his forty-first year he had lived with a woman two years younger than himself. Upon her he spent the limited amount of romance of which his coarse-grained temperament was capable. He wrote to her daily when he was away from home; his letters show the sarcastic, quick, massive personality which could not but impress, favourably or unfavourably, those who met him. There is indeed something likeable about the man who could turn an awkward situation when an angry crowd came to break the win-

[1] Kiderlen, like Eckardstein, thought that the Emperor was ill-mannered and interfering in his behaviour at Cowes regatta and in his relations with the Prince of Wales.

[2] Five days after Kiderlen's death Jules Cambon wrote from Berlin to Poincaré: 'Par malheur pour elle, l'Allemagne manque étrangement d'hommes.' Poincaré, *Au service de la France*, iii. 25. The Austro-Hungarian Ambassador thought it would be extremely difficult to find any one capable of taking Kiderlen's place. O.A.P. v. 454.

dows of the German Embassy at Copenhagen, by mixing with the crowd and throwing the first stone—at the wrong windows!

Kiderlen's views on the foreign policy of the German Empire were a characteristic mixture of astuteness and lack of imagination. He knew little of England, and did not like Englishmen. He had been away from Berlin too long to understand the political reasons which had brought England and Englishmen to accept the policy of the Anglo-French and Anglo-Russian ententes. He realized the danger of the uncompromising plans of the German naval party. When he heard the rumour that Tirpitz might succeed Bülow as Chancellor, he wrote that Tirpitz's naval plans would be a heavy burden on German foreign policy.[1] He described himself in February 1912 as an enemy of Tirpitz because the naval party would bring war with England.[2] He was not unwilling or unable to learn from experience, though he could never look at a German question from the point of view of other Powers. Towards the end of his Foreign Secretaryship he realized that, whatever the reasons which might compel Germany to refuse a naval agreement with England unaccompanied by political concessions of a far-reaching kind, Great Britain would never fall in with an 'all-or-nothing' policy. In 1909 Kiderlen had not learned this lesson. Goschen described him as 'brutally frank when it serves his purpose'.[3] With this frankness Kiderlen talked to Goschen.

It is possible that Bülow himself knew nothing of the conversation. On the other hand, Goschen could hardly assume that in a matter of such importance the Foreign Secretary was speaking without the Chancellor's knowledge or consent. Goschen, in fact, described Kiderlen as 'Bülow's mouthpiece in questions of policy'.

Kiderlen's suggestions were therefore given careful attention. Kiderlen wanted a political understanding, or a naval convention, in which the two Powers 'should

[1] Jäckh, op. cit. ii. 31.   [2] Jäckh, op. cit. ii. 155.   [3] B.D.D. vi. 261.

bind themselves for a fixed period (1) not to make war against each other, (2) not to join in a coalition directed against either Power, (3) to observe a benevolent neutrality should either country be engaged in hostilities with any other Power or Powers'.[1]

This plan was commented on most unfavourably by the British Foreign Office. Crowe summed it up as 'patently absurd'. Under the terms of the agreement:

'Germany would be able (a) to increase her fleet to any size desired; (b) to fall upon France or Russia without fear of English interference; (c) to impose her hegemony on any of the less powerful States,[2] and in case this provokes resistance, actually to count upon British "benevolent neutrality" in the struggle; (d) to interfere in any part of the world whilst England would be precluded from offering any serious resistance. It is true that analogous advantages would simultaneously be secured to this country. But as we have no desire whatever of carrying on a policy of aggression, these paper advantages are in fact null for us.'

Grey himself thought that 'an entente with Germany such as M. Kiderlen sketches would serve to establish German hegemony in Europe and would not last long after it had served that purpose. It is in fact an invitation to help Germany to make a European combination which could be directed against us when it suited her so to use it'. Hardinge held similar views.[3] He thought the proposal 'a trap'. Germany would use the period of the

[1] There is no reference to Kiderlen's conversations in D.G.P. According to Goschen, Kiderlen mentioned the subject more than once. Goschen's account of the conversation is very short. B.D.D. vi. 265–6. Cf. ib. 321–2. The F.O. comments follow Goschen's letter, ib. 266.

[2] For the Emperor's views about the relation of Germany to her less powerful neighbours, see below, p. 296.

[3] B.D.D. v, App. 3, 823–6. For the date of Hardinge's memorandum (4 May 1909) see B.D.D. vi. 311, n. 9. Hardinge was discussing the general political situation in the light of the German attitude towards the Bosnian and Serbian questions, and attempting to frame an answer to a possible question from Russia whether England would take part in a war between Russia and Germany and Austria-Hungary. Hardinge thought that it would be dangerous to give a definite promise to Russia.

agreement 'to consolidate her supremacy in Europe while England would remain as a spectator with her hands tied. At the termination of the agreement Germany would be free to devote her whole strength to reducing the only remaining independent factor in Europe.'

Neither Stumm's diplomacy nor Kiderlen's frankness brought the results which Bülow wanted. At the beginning of June Bülow held a conference in Berlin to discuss the naval question. He invited to the conference Bethmann-Hollweg, Tirpitz, Moltke (Chief of the General Staff), Admiral Müller (Chief of the Naval Cabinet), Metternich, and Schön.[1] The point which strikes the English reader of the proceedings at this conference is that neither Bülow nor Tirpitz was thinking of a permanent agreement with England. They considered once again the old question; how could Germany get through the 'danger-zone' without a preventive war? Bülow used the words: 'An understanding is advisable in order to get over the danger zone between the present time and the time when our fleet is built.' It is interesting to compare this sentence with the British comment on Kiderlen's proposals: 'What would happen to the "understanding" when the German fleet was safely out of the danger zone?' Three weeks before the Conference met the German naval attaché in London had given his opinion that a preventive war would not be declared by a Liberal Government. The danger might come in 1911 with the return of the Conservatives to power.[2] Germany would be stronger in 1911 than in 1909, but the 'danger period' would not have been left behind until about 1915 when the Kiel canal had been widened and the fortifications of Heligoland completed. 'That is all very well', said Bülow, 'but how is the present danger to be got out of the way?' Tirpitz suggested an understanding on the basis of a 3:4 ratio between the German and English fleets; but he would not propose a formula, and refused

---

[1] For an account of the conference see D.G.P. xxviii. 168–78 and notes.
[2] Tirpitz, *op. cit.* i. 153–5, 11 May 1909.

to take into account the Austrian Dreadnoughts or to allow the initiative in any proposals to come from Germany. Bülow pointed out that no diplomacy in the world would persuade Great Britain to accept a formula which appeared to threaten her existence, while Metternich complained that Tirpitz wanted to defy the laws of arithmetic. He accepted the principle of slowing down the rate of building, and yet refused to allow any real diminution in the German programme. His plan meant only a temporary decrease, followed by an increase, in the building programme. The effect of this proposal on Great Britain would not be favourable.[1]

Bülow resigned on 14 July 1909. The British Parliament accepted the naval estimates in the same month; the programme of eight Dreadnoughts was an ironic comment on Bülow's metaphor of the Long Walls. The Spartans were not waiting idly for the walls to be completed. The danger-zone was prolonged indefinitely.

[1] Before the Conference Metternich discovered the Emperor's attack upon his statements to the British Government. Metternich justified himself in a letter to Bülow. He pointed out that he had had no knowledge of any plan to introduce a supplementary naval law in 1912, and added that he knew how much the Emperor disliked his reports that Anglo-German relations were poisoned by the naval question. 'It is not pleasant for our naval authorities to hear that there is a definite connexion between our rate of naval construction and our relations with England. But I should be falsifying the facts if my reports were other than they are, and I cannot barter my convictions even for the favour of my Sovereign.' D.G.P. xxviii. 166–7.

XIV
NEGOTIATIONS AT CROSS-PURPOSES
II. AUGUST–NOVEMBER, 1909

THE new Chancellor, Theodor von Bethmann-Hollweg, was a stranger to diplomacy. Bethmann-Hollweg was in his fifty-third year in the summer of 1909. His official career had been steady and successful; there had been little scope for originality or for personal initiative in the duties of a civil servant born and trained in the heart of Prussia. Bethmann-Hollweg had followed the regular *cursus honorum*; he became Prussian Minister of the Interior in 1905 and, two years later, Secretary of State for Home Affairs in the Imperial Government. He was promoted to the Chancellorship mainly for reasons of internal policy. He knew the domestic situation, and was likely to handle it with tact and confidence. In the event, he was far less competent in debate and obtained far less prestige than his friends foretold in 1909. He was the first German Chancellor to submit to a vote of censure in the Reichstag. Of foreign affairs he knew little or nothing.[1] The Ambassadors and Ministers of his own and other countries were strangers to him. For all his honesty and straightforwardness, there was a certain narrowness about him, a strain of pedantry and unadaptiveness. He was unlikely to look between the lines of official reports and to judge a situation from the point of view of other Powers. The fact that he came as a new man to the direction of German foreign policy had many advantages. He escaped responsibility for the conduct of this policy in the period of Bülow. If there were to be a change in German policy, the moment had come for new aims and new methods. Bülow's semi-Italianized cleverness had deceived no one; he made the mistake of forgetting that

---

[1] It is said that, in writing to an Hungarian official in 1909, Bethmann-Hollweg made the elementary mistake of giving Francis Joseph the title of 'King' instead of the correct title of 'Emperor and King'.

he was dealing with people as clever and as worldly wise as himself, and the airs of *faux bonhomme* which might have impressed a provincial assembly were out of place in the discussion of important matters of state with the Ministers or Ambassadors of the Great Powers.

On the other hand, Bethmann-Hollweg's inexperience and unfamiliarity with the business of the Foreign Office left him more dependent than Bülow upon the permanent officials. He did not realize the extent to which German methods had caused irritation and distrust in Europe. He knew nothing of the Holstein era, or, rather, his knowledge was only at second hand.

Bethmann-Hollweg was overworked. The business of the Chancellor was far too great for any man of ordinary talents—even Bismarck had found the work too heavy. It was impossible for a single man to decide, from direct knowledge, every question of importance which was submitted to him. It was difficult for the Chancellor even to distinguish between questions of major and minor importance. The subject-matter of foreign affairs was particularly complicated. The permanent officials of the Foreign Office knew the history of every problem brought forward for solution. A Chancellor who had served for many years in the civil service was accustomed to giving due weight to the opinions of the senior members of the bureaucratic hierarchy. There is nothing surprising in the fact that Bethmann-Hollweg was influenced by the views of those who had spent years in considering the questions which faced him for the first time. Kiderlen-Waechter was one of the ablest and certainly the most dominant of these permanent officials. For this reason Kiderlen's judgements affected Bethmann's decisions, and Kiderlen's strength of character, as well as his knowledge and experience, enabled him to impress upon Bethmann a definite view of German policy.[1] Bethmann's tempera-

---

[1] Szögyény, Austro-Hungarian Ambassador in Berlin, wrote, after Kiderlen's death, that he (Kiderlen) was the real author of Bethmann-Hollweg's parliamentary speeches on foreign affairs, O.A.P. v. 454.

ment did not incline him to any sudden change of mind. He chose a particular line of policy, and was inclined to be a little obstinate in keeping to his choice, in spite of the resistance of facts.

Finally, if Bülow had gone, the Emperor and Tirpitz remained. The Chancellor was handicapped by his civilian position. The Emperor had personal knowledge of the sovereigns and most of the leading statesmen of Europe. William II, with his exaggerated consciousness of the duties of the Heaven-sent ruler of Germany, had controlled the foreign policy of his Empire for nearly twenty years before he thought fit to appoint Bethmann-Hollweg as Chancellor. No other Chancellor had been so remote from the issues of European policy. Bismarck was the outstanding figure of his age. Caprivi was at least a general, Hohenlohe a *grand seigneur* who knew the world of princes and ambassadors. Bethmann-Hollweg, in spite of his military rank, was neither a soldier nor a member of the high aristocracy. The Emperor's private Cabinets had already become dangerously important; the military and naval chiefs possessed direct access to William II, and, in the social atmosphere of the Imperial court, countless indirect ways of influencing high policy. A great deal of Bethmann-Hollweg's time and energy was spent in attempts to counteract the effect of the naval party upon the Emperor. These attempts were not very successful.

The new Chancellor found at once that among the 'civilians', as the Emperor called them, there was serious alarm about the growing estrangement between Great Britain and Germany. Among the first memoranda prepared for him by the Foreign Office was a short statement of the desirability of better relations with Great Britain. The memorandum touched upon the question of a preventive war, but the writer was more afraid that Great Britain might encourage France and Russia to go to war with Germany. In another draft by the same hand King Edward was introduced. In the first draft Grey was coupled with Isvolsky as anxious to take revenge upon Germany for defeat in the Bosnian question.[1]

Bethmann-Hollweg was also approached through private channels. Ballin thought that a discussion between naval experts, conducted without reference to political complications or compensations, would lead to a naval agreement. Ballin had talked with Cassel on the subject, and had laid his proposal before the Emperor. The Chancellor, to Ballin's disappointment, would not separate the naval from the political question.[2] In his exposition of policy to the Emperor Bethmann-Hollweg thought that for the moment there was no need to decide whether Germany would require a general promise of neutrality.[3]

'At least, however, England must promise at the very outset of the negotiations for a naval agreement that her policy will become peaceful and friendly towards us, and we must secure a definite statement that the treaties and ententes concluded by England are not directed against us.'

This declaration was given, and given repeatedly by Grey. It was not enough. Bethmann-Hollweg indeed mentioned the idea of a general assurance in a covering letter to Schön, and decided that it was too indefinite.

'Undoubtedly the best thing would be a treaty of neutrality, in which England promised to remain neutral if we were attacked by France and Russia singly or together, or if we came to the help of Austria . . . in the event of a Russian attack. . . . If England does not accept this proposal, we shall be justified in concluding that she has already made her arrangements with one or both of these Powers for eventualities of this kind, or has decided that in the event of such a war she would join our enemies. We must put a direct question to England. If she assures us that neither the one nor the other course has been taken, but that she wishes to keep her hands free, the question then arises; can we content ourselves merely with the assurance that England will adopt a friendly and peaceful policy towards

[1] D.G.P. xxviii. 201–4: 15–16 July 1909.
[2] Huldermann, *Ballin*, pp. 222–3.
[3] D.G.P. xxviii. 211–16: 13 August 1909.

Germany. I do not think that we can altogether give up the idea of political compensations.'

The naval offer to Great Britain was a reduction of three ships in the German programme before 1914, and a proposal that German and British new construction should be in the ratio of 3 : 4.[1] This proposal was very much to the advantage of Germany. The German programme for the year 1909–10 would remain untouched, while the four 'contingent' ships would disappear from the British programme. The German 'concession' therefore required Great Britain to give up a programme of construction which had been accepted by Parliament as necessary for the safety of the country.

It is not surprising that Schön was less hopeful than the Chancellor that Great Britain would accept a political agreement on these terms. Schön thought that Germany would have to content herself with a general declaration of friendship.[2] Nevertheless Bethmann-Hollweg saw Sir E. Goschen on 21 August, and suggested that negotiations might be opened for a naval agreement which would be accompanied by assurances of mutual friendship in matters of general policy. He mentioned the friendly speeches of the Prime Minister and Mr. McKenna.[3] Bethmann-Hollweg's report of the conversation is shorter and more optimistic than the two telegraphic reports of Goschen.[4] In Goschen's report Bethmann-Hollweg spoke plainly on the question of a political understanding. The Chancellor assumed, for example, that if Germany were forced to come to the help of Austria in the case of an unprovoked attack by Russia, England would not join Russia. Grey's comment on the conversation was that Great Britain 'could agree at once to receive proposals for a naval agreement. . . . The wider proposals would go beyond anything we have with France or Russia. . . . If

---

[1] D.G.P. xxviii. 217–18.   [2] D.G.P. xxviii. 218–19.
[3] D.G.P. xxviii. 221–2. For the speeches of the Prime Minister and Mr. McKenna, see Hansard, 5th Ser. viii. 878–80 and 967.
[4] B.D.D. vi. 283–4.

any general political understanding is to be arranged it should be one not between two Powers alone but between the two great groups of Powers.'[1] Hardinge thought that Great Britain might make a general declaration of policy stating that 'her guiding principles were the preservation of peace and the maintenance of the balance of power'. Under the first principle, she would never make an unprovoked attack on another Power, and do her utmost to prevent any one else making such an attack. Under the second principle she would oppose the domination of Europe by any one Power or group of Powers and prevent the absorption of the weaker European States.[2] The British answer was therefore non-committal on the political side, though 'cordially welcoming' any naval proposals, and other proposals 'not inconsistent with the maintenance of the existing friendships of Great Britain'.[3]

Before the detailed negotiations were opened Tirpitz had slightly modified his plan. His first suggestion had provided for a ratio of 4:3 in capital ships on the basis of thirty-two British ships to twenty-four German ships completed or under construction in 1914. He now suggested a relationship of twenty-eight British to twenty-one German ships in 1913. On the main issue the new plan made little difference. Great Britain would still give up the four 'contingent' Dreadnoughts, while Germany would make no change in her 1909–10 programme. Bethmann-Hollweg himself pointed out that Germany was asking England to make a considerable sacrifice, since her existing programme would give her in 1913 twenty completed Dreadnoughts to Germany's thirteen ships.[4]

During a pause in the negotiations the Chancellor consulted Kiderlen. Kiderlen drew up a memorandum which confirmed the Chancellor in his wish not merely

---

[1] B.D.D. vi. 284.   [2] B.D.D. vi. 285–6: 25 August 1909.
[3] B.D.D. vi. 288: 1 September 1909.
[4] D.G.P. xxviii. 227–32. The Chancellor pointed out that Tirpitz's proposal was more favourable to Germany, since it reduced the time-limit of the agreement from 1914 to 1913; Germany would therefore be free a year earlier to begin an increased programme.

for a naval but for a political understanding.[1] According to Kiderlen's views England was unlikely to attack Germany, or to obtain an offensive alliance against her. The greatest danger came from English opposition on questions of a secondary order in which Germany could be forced to accept a diplomatic defeat as France had been forced to accept Fashoda. These strained relations with England were not due merely to the shipbuilding question; a purely naval agreement would not bring complete relief. Such an agreement, apart from English suspicion that Germany was not keeping its terms, would mean for Germany a formal acknowledgement of British naval supremacy. This acknowledgement would not be accepted by German public opinion without a political agreement.[2] A naval agreement offered technical difficulties. England would have to take into account the increase of fleets with which Germany might co-operate in war.

Nevertheless Kiderlen thought it necessary to announce that Germany was ready to make a naval agreement. Germany should let Great Britain take the initiative, and should avoid affronting other Powers. She must 'play fair', and not try to overreach England—'the English are fully informed about German shipbuilding'. If the negotiations failed, Kiderlen suggested a mutual agreement not to enter into any combination which had in view or in preparation a hostile attack on the other party. Germany could give this undertaking because she would never want to enter into an offensive alliance against Great Britain, while she would be protected by the agreement against any plans of her eastern and western neighbours. The details of the agreement mattered little; they were paper questions. Above all, the technical, naval question must be kept in the background as much as possible, since the experts would disagree. 'The political sphere is more elastic than the military.'

[1] Jäckh, *op. cit.* ii. 48–59, and a note in D.G.P. xxviii. 239–40.
[2] It is interesting to compare this view with Hardinge's statement of the position. See above, p. 180.

Kiderlen did not consider the impression which his proposals would make upon British public opinion. He did not take account of the fact that Great Britain possessed 'naval supremacy', whether this fact was or was not admitted in Germany and by the German people. His political agreement gave nothing to Great Britain; on his own showing, Germany would not join an alliance against Great Britain. Furthermore, it was most unlikely that any Power or Powers would propose such an alliance to her. On the other hand, Great Britain was asked to promise more than she had promised France and Russia in return for substantial concessions from these Powers.

One comment of the German Foreign Office is worth mention. Flotow, who was in close relations with Bethmann-Hollweg, wrote that there would be some danger in assuring Great Britain, as Kiderlen suggested, that Germany did not intend to make proposals conflicting with English ententes.

'The English ententes have been concluded through fear of us, and are pointed against us. . . . If we are to proceed later on to ask for neutrality against France and Russia, this proposal can scarcely be harmonized with the ententes. It may be, however, that by clever management of the negotiations we can allow our political demands to rise in such small and easy stages that the English will not be scared [*verprellt*]. In my opinion we must give the English a quiet time for reflection so that, after weighing the advantages offered by France and Russia against the security offered on the German side, the latter appears the more desirable. If one takes into account the clever and businesslike way in which Englishmen think, this conclusion does not appear impossible.'[1]

It is interesting to compare this plan of action with Grey's sentence: 'I want a good understanding with Germany, but it must be one which will not imperil those we have with France and Russia.'[2]

---

[1] D.G.P. xxviii. 239–40 note.
[2] B.D.D. vi. 289: 1 September 1909. The British Government informed France and Russia that conversations were taking place with Germany.

The negotiations were continued in October. Goschen had a conversation with Bethmann-Hollweg and Schön on 15 October.[1] The German point of view was that a political agreement must accompany a naval agreement, and that in a naval agreement Germany could not consent to any alteration in her naval law, but only to a slowing down in the rate of building.[2] A reduction in the programme embodied in the naval law might follow in a few years. Goschen pointed out in reply that England had no formal 'understanding' with France and Russia, and could hardly go farther with Germany. He also explained that from the British point of view a retardation of the rate of construction would be only a temporary advantage. When Goschen asked for more details about the political assurances which Germany would require, Schön answered that they might be similar in wording to the Baltic agreement.[3] To the British Foreign Office this statement meant that Germany would want a formal recognition of the territorial *status quo* as far as Germany

B.D.D. vi. 291 and 313–14. The German Government discovered that the fact of the conversations was known to Russia. As they had asked for secrecy they believed that Nicolson, not Grey, had told Russia what was happening. Bethmann-Hollweg was much troubled by this breach of confidence because he had not mentioned the negotiations to Aehrenthal. See D.G.P. xxviii. 271–2, 275–7. It may be remembered that the German Emperor had informed the Tsar of Chamberlain's offer of an alliance in 1898. The British Foreign Office was afraid of indiscretions on the part of the Emperor. Mr. L. Mallet (Assistant Under-Secretary of State) wrote to Grey on 26 August 1909: 'It seems to me that we must tell the Russians of these overtures; otherwise the German Emperor will tell the Tsar that we originated them.' B.D.D. vi. 287.

[1] For this conversation see B.D.D. vi. 293–302, and D.G.P. xxviii. 239–43.

[2] Goschen never understood what the Chancellor really meant by a 'reduction in the *tempo*'. He could not see how the Germans could reduce their programme after 1911 and at the same time carry out this programme as laid down by law. He thought that Bethmann-Hollweg was himself uncertain; when asked to give a detailed explanation, the Chancellor answered that the question must be left to the naval experts. (B.D.D. vi. 510 and 513.) Metternich had described the proposal as a defiance of the laws of arithmetic.

[3] The Baltic agreement, guaranteeing the territorial *status quo* in the states bordering the Baltic Sea, was signed by Russia, Germany, Sweden, and Denmark in April 1908.

was concerned,[1] and therefore a formal recognition of the German possession of Alsace and Lorraine. Great Britain would neither encourage nor support France to fight Germany for these provinces, but a guarantee on the other side would mean the end of the entente. The naval concessions came to very little, and did not constitute a claim for political 'counterconcessions'.[2]

Metternich was therefore given a general reply on 26 October 1909 that Great Britain awaited the German proposals for a naval agreement.[3] The Chancellor was dissatisfied with any general assurances. He still wanted a promise of neutrality, even if he were compelled to use some other term.[4]

Once again, it is interesting to compare the cleverness of Delcassé and Cambon, with the lack of subtlety in the policy of Bethmann-Hollweg and Kiderlen. It is equally interesting to notice how far Great Britain had travelled on the road towards continental obligations since Lansdowne arranged a settlement of extra-European questions with France. The question of the German possession of Alsace-Lorraine did not affect, directly, any British interest. Germany was now insisting upon a guarantee of this possession, and Great Britain was refusing to give such a guarantee. Yet there had not been one word concerning Alsace-Lorraine in the discussions between England and France. No British statesman could have brought his country into a European war for the recovery of these provinces by France, and there was little serious fear in Great Britain that France would provoke a European war in order to regain Alsace and Lorraine.

Bethmann-Hollweg went on his way, honest in intention, never looking at the situation from a wider view of the historical place and function of Great Britain in the

---

[1] The draft agreements which Schön had drawn up in May included a reference to the maintenance of the territorial *status quo* even in the weakest of the three 'formulae'. D.G.P. xxviii. 158.

[2] In this context Hardinge wrote the view about British naval supremacy quoted above, p. 180.

[3] B.D.D. vi. 302 n., and D.G.P. xxviii. 243–4. [4] D.G.P. xxviii. 245–7.

grouping of the Powers, never considering the reasons for the increasing solidarity of the ententes. He had his own difficulties in Germany. The Emperor was changeable and uncertain; Tirpitz and the experts were in closer touch with the Emperor's moods. Bethmann-Hollweg was, after all, a civilian, and a civilian could never fathom the wisdom of the decisions of the Supreme War Lord. It is significant that Bethmann-Hollweg, though reporting to the Emperor, was careful to emphasize the need for keeping the Emperor's name out of the negotiations in the preliminary stages; a tactful way of preventing indiscretions by 'William the Sudden', as Kiderlen called him. In November, when delay was certain, Flotow wrote to Kiderlen: 'the troublesome thing is that we are not sure, whether, if the thing takes time, we may not let His Majesty and Tirpitz slip out of our hands'.[1]

On 29 October 1909 Kiderlen was sent a draft agreement in which each Power gave a promise of 'benevolent' neutrality in a war in which the other Power were attacked by one or more enemies. The Austro-German and Anglo-Japanese alliances were provided for in a special note. Germany was pledged not to join Russia if England supported Japan against a Russian attack and England was pledged not to join Russia if Germany supported Austria against a Russian attack. Germany and England would promise mutual friendship, with its logical implications in European and colonial policy.[2] The draft was almost identical with the second of the three proposals drawn up by Schön in May 1909; Bethmann-Hollweg had rejected the idea of a defensive alliance as too far-reaching from the English point of view, and the idea of an entente, with a recognition of the territorial *status quo*, as insufficient for Germany. The explanatory note, providing for neutrality in case one of the contracting parties was drawn into war through existing alliances, was an addition to Schön's draft.[3]

---

[1] Jäckh, *op. cit.* ii. 74.   [2] D.G.P. xxviii. 247–50.
[3] For the earlier drafts see above, p. 258. The new proposals also referred

Kiderlen's comments are interesting. He thought that 'it would be almost incomprehensible to serious opinion in Germany that we should lose the advantage of a friendly rapprochement with England for the sake of a few ships more or less, as long as the defence of our coasts is assured'. Kiderlen did not expect that the draft proposals would be accepted at once by Great Britain. He suggested that they should not be given to Great Britain *en bloc*, but that Germany should go slowly: *tropfenweise*, drop by drop. The proposals went beyond the terms of the ententes; 'England would suspect that Germany wanted gradually to detach her from these ententes.'[1]

Meanwhile Grey had explained to Metternich that Great Britain would be ready to say that she had no hostile intentions towards Germany, and no understandings with other Powers directed against her. On the other hand, it would be difficult to find 'any formula going beyond this which did not give the impression that we were entering into closer relations with Germany than we had previously entered into with any other Powers'. Great Britain had 'no such general formula' with any other Power. Once again Grey suggested an exchange of naval information, and pointed out that British public opinion would not be content with a general understanding which did not reduce naval expenditure.[2] Metternich told Bethmann-Hollweg that the British Ministers were unlikely to accept a ratio of 3:4 between the German and British shipbuilding programmes, but that they might agree to a ratio of 2:3.[3]

In these circumstances progress was difficult. Germany would not negotiate a naval agreement until a political formula had been accepted. Great Britain insisted upon a naval agreement as the first stage on the road to a political agreement. The difficulties were not only difficulties of procedure. The German Foreign Office maintained

---

to the possibility of mutual concessions outside Europe, e.g. the Baghdad railway. [1] Jäckh, *op. cit.* ii. 64–7.
[2] B.D.D. vi. 303–4: 28 October 1909.   [3] D.G.P. xxviii. 251–3.

that Germany did not want a naval agreement. 'If the English, as they tell us, want a naval agreement, they must pay a price for it in the political sphere. We have no wish for a naval agreement. For this reason we cannot accept Sir Edward Goschen's and Sir Edward Grey's arguments that England cannot give us more than she has given France and Russia. England wants something from us, and must pay for it.'[1]

On 4 November Bethmann-Hollweg had another long interview with Goschen.[2] At the outset Goschen explained once more that, in the British view, the 'sacrifice' entailed in a naval agreement was no greater for Germany than for England. Bethmann-Hollweg proposed a curtailment of naval construction for three or four years, and again Goschen pointed out that this suggestion did not mean any real reduction in the German naval programme and therefore brought no ultimate relief to British taxpayers. The Chancellor repeated his words about the impossibility of accepting any modification of the naval law, or any proposals for the exchange of information which implied the idea of control. On the political side Germany already knew that the Anglo-French and Anglo-Russian understandings were not directed against her. Something further was required. Bethmann-Hollweg then administered one or two of the 'drops' suggested by Kiderlen. He put forward the plan of a mutual assurance that neither Power entertained any idea of aggression, and that neither Power would join in an attack on the other. Goschen said that England was being asked for something more definite than she had promised France and Russia. The Chancellor answered that England wanted a naval agreement, and that such an agreement could

---

[1] Memorandum written by Schön. D.G.P. xxviii. 253–4.

[2] B.D.D. vi. 304–12; D.G.P. xxviii. 259–62. At the previous interview Goschen had been a little taken aback by the Chancellor's insistence that full notes should be taken of an informal conversation. The same proposal was made at the interview of 4 November. In each case Goschen pointed out that Schön's version did not make his (Goschen's) points with sufficient clearness.

be made only between friends. Schön, in a separate memorandum, noted that he (Schön) had emphasized this point.[1] England had asked for a naval agreement, and thereby had introduced a new factor into the situation; for this reason Germany required a political agreement more far-reaching than the ententes with France and Russia. Schön himself thought that the 'neutrality' agreement would be difficult to draft. He wanted to avoid the 'naked words "war" and "neutrality" '.

The British Government could not, and did not, avoid naked words. Crowe wrote that it was difficult at first sight to take the German proposals seriously. England would be tied in her shipbuilding not only against Germany but against the rest of the world. Germany would have a free hand in Europe. Hardinge pointed out that the proposals were none other than those made by Kiderlen and rejected by the Foreign Office. England had no probable enemy except Germany, and a pledge from Germany that she would not join an anti-English coalition had no value. Hardinge suggested that the British Government should use the internal situation (the campaign against the House of Lords was at its height, and a general election was in prospect) as an excuse for dropping the question politely, but that if an answer were necessary, His Majesty's Government might explain that Germany had now transferred the discussion from the naval question to the larger problem of a political understanding. The clearest answer came from Metternich himself.[2]

'The English friendship with France would be almost worthless if England were to say plainly that under no circumstances would she help the French against us. Similarly, though not to the same degree, Anglo-Russian relations would be affected, and—here is the main point as far as England is concerned— England could no longer count on help from either of these two Powers, if assistance were needed against us. England would abandon this hope only if she felt secure in her relations with us. This security is possible only on the basis of a naval agreement.

[1] D.G.P. xxviii. 262-3.   [2] D.G.P. xxviii. 266-8.

... I cannot conceal my view that the English Government will not obtain this sense of security from the naval formula which we are suggesting. . . . We must reckon that this formula will not be accepted. . . . We should content ourselves with the advantages we can obtain on the principle that the best is sometimes the enemy of the good.'

Grey took the excuse suggested by Hardinge. On 17 November he told Metternich, and Goschen told Schön that the elections must mean delay, and that in any case the naval agreement did not go far enough in the reduction of expenditure.[1] Meanwhile Grey wanted to begin discussions on the question of the Baghdad railway.

[1] B.D.D. vi. 312–13, 314–15; D.G.P. xxviii. 273–5.

XV

GREY'S PROPOSAL FOR AN EXCHANGE OF INFORMATION. I. 1910

F OR some time the negotiations were not continued. The general election in Great Britain gave the Liberals a small parliamentary majority, though the Ministry depended upon the Labour and Irish vote. Early in February the French Government announced a large naval programme.[1] The Conservatives had brought the naval question into the foreground during the British election campaign;[2] there was, in Metternich's opinion, less chance that the British public would accept a 4:3 ratio between the British and German fleets. Germany had allowed the favourable moment to pass. Great Britain was seriously alarmed; the two political parties might unite in making the shipbuilding programme a non-party question. 'For years past the view has been generally, if not universally, held in Germany that the period of anxiety in England over the building of our fleet would be only temporary, and would be followed by a patient surrender to the inevitable, and therefore by better relations.'[3] This belief was proved wrong by the facts. It was more probable that, instead of 'patient surrender' there would be an increase of effort which would entirely outstrip Germany.

The British naval programme was announced on 10 March. There was an increase in expenditure of £5,000,000; five new capital ships were to be laid down.

[1] Briand had told his colleagues that France ought to spend more money on her navy in order to be able to fulfil her obligations to England. Grey thought that this attitude of Briand 'might raise some embarrassing questions later on'. France would say that 'what she has spent on her Navy for the sake of her obligations towards us adds force to our obligations towards her'. B.D.D. vi. 489–90.

[2] Robert Blatchford also carried on an active and sensational anti-German campaign in *The Clarion*, a Socialist newspaper.

[3] D.G.P. xxviii. 284–91: 3 February 1910.

Until these ships were completed the two Dreadnoughts voted by Australia and New Zealand would be kept in Home waters. A visit by Prince Henry of Prussia to England in February 1910 did not improve the chances of an agreement. The Prince talked of the impossibility of German naval disarmament and the numerical inferiority of the German fleet.[1] Metternich thought, from the Prince's words, that the Emperor and Tirpitz were now opposed to any naval understanding. The action of Germany over the Bosnian question seemed to British observers, for the time at least, to end any hope of a genuine change of policy on the part of the German Government towards the friends of Great Britain.[2] Nevertheless Metternich again mentioned the negotiations to Grey on 22 March.[3] Grey pointed out that Germany had given no indication that her naval programme would be modified; Metternich answered that there had never been any talk of modifying the programme. On 31 March Grey told Kühlmann, who was acting as chargé d'affaires in Metternich's absence, that he had been thinking over the question. Grey spoke again of his plan for an exchange of naval information. He also suggested that while any 'general' arrangement seemed impossible, in view of the German refusal to alter the naval law, the relations between the two countries might be improved by an understanding over the Baghdad railway.[4] The German proposals on this question seemed entirely inadequate, and the British Government was astonished that, even without a naval agreement, the Chancellor still hoped that the German terms might be included in a general political arrangement.[5] These negotiations had been carried on secretly between the British and German Governments. All chance of reaching an agreement

---

[1] D.G.P. xxviii. 302–4. Prince Henry also expressed himself strongly about the Yellow Peril—to the European ally of Japan.

[2] See above, c. ix.

[3] B.D.D. vi. 442, and D.G.P. xxviii. 309–10.

[4] B.D.D. vi. 442–3, D.G.P. xxviii. 313–14.

[5] B.D.D. vi. 454–61 and 463–5.

would have been lost if secrecy had not been kept. The Ministers of a Liberal Government were bound to use methods of secret diplomacy; they could not leave without an answer questions asked in Parliament about the possibility of a naval understanding with Germany. The Prime Minister told the House of Commons on 26 July 1909 that the Government had been doing its utmost for three years past to reach an agreement.

'Some people think we have overstepped the limits of what is prescribed by what is called "national dignity" in the efforts which we have made in that direction. . . . If our efforts have hitherto been frustrated, it has been through no want either of zeal or of effort on our part, . . . not only is the door still open, but we are anxious and even eager, if we can, to come to some arrangement as between us and other Powers, which will prevent us year by year from coming to the House of Commons, and making demands which are as unwelcome to us as they can be to any Member sitting on these benches. When I make that statement I am stating what is historically indisputable.'[1]

The comments of the German press upon the Prime Minister's statement were not favourable. The suggestion of an agreement was dismissed as without present significance. It was pointed out that Germany was still being asked to recognize a permanent British supremacy at sea. The *Kreuz-Zeitung* thought that the time would come for an agreement when the German programme of construction had been carried out.

In September 1909 a question was again asked in the House whether the Government would not make fresh efforts to reach an agreement. The Prime Minister answered that any intimation that the German Government desired to make an agreement would be met 'with a cordial response'. To a further question whether Great Britain could not take the initiative the Prime Minister answered: 'We have taken the initiative.'[2] *The Times* correspondent in Berlin thought that the revival of the

---

[1] Hansard, 5th Ser. viii. 878–80. For the German Chancellor's view of this speech, see above, p. 269.   [2] Hansard, 5th Ser. x. 1093.

subject was taken in Germany as a sign of weakness. The matter was, however, discussed in the German press; the *Kreuz-Zeitung* hinted at the negotiations by saying that a naval agreement would be possible only if England were ready to 'do justice on all questions to the international position of Germany'.[1] On the other hand, a protest against the refusal of Germany to make an agreement came from a curious quarter. The *Deutsche Revue*[2] reported that Holstein, three months before his death, had spoken of 'the lying and treacherous fallacy . . . that every fresh ship is an addition to the power of Germany, when every fresh ship causes England, to say nothing of France, to build two ships'. Holstein had also described in December 1907 the 'navy fever now raging in Germany' as a 'dangerous disease fed upon fear of attack by England'. The naval expansion was dangerous from a financial as well as from an international point of view. Germany could not compete with France and England, and the consequences would be particularly serious after the return of a Conservative government to power in England. A few days later Count Reventlow discussed Holstein's views in the *Deutsche Tageszeitung*. Reventlow admitted that in 1900 the naval experts had been wrong in thinking that Great Britain would not be able to concentrate an overwhelming force in the North Sea. The formation of the Triple Entente had altered the position. On the other hand, the growth of the navies of the United States and Japan would limit British concentration.[3] In December a semi-official *démenti* was given in Germany to rumours that an agreement had been reached on the question of the limitation of armaments. The *Frankfurter Zeitung* explained that Bülow had hoped for such an agreement in the last days of his Chancellorship, but that this agreement would have been made after the provisions of the Navy

---

[1] *The Times*, 8 September 1909.
[2] *Deutsche Revue*, October 1909. The article in the *Deutsche Revue* on 'Reminiscences of Holstein' was written by Herr von Rath, a retired official.
[3] *The Times*, 7 October 1909.

Law had been carried out, and would have been confined to the exchange of information.[1] At the beginning of 1910 the German Navy League published a 'New Year greeting to the German people' with a warning against the 'siren song' of agreements with England. It was the duty of every patriot to suppress all endeavours which could be interpreted in foreign countries as weakness. 'What party could have regard to the next Reichstag elections, and yet undertake to represent a policy of diminishing our forces at sea . . . in the vain hope of composing an antagonism which lies in the conditions of existence of the two peoples?'[2]

The limitation of construction was not mentioned in the debate on the German estimates in the Reichstag at the end of February, but questions were asked on 4 and 10 March in the House of Commons upon the expediency of reopening negotiations with Germany. The references of Mr. Lloyd George to 'mythical armadas', and 'the building of Dreadnoughts against nightmares', had little positive significance, but they showed the exasperation of the left-wing Liberals at the diversion of money from measures of social reform. The Labour opposition even described the issue as one between social reform and naval armaments. For this reason the Prime Minister repeated in July 1910 the statement which he had made a year earlier about the refusal of Germany to come to an agreement.[3]

'I see quite as clearly as my right Hon. friend the Chancellor of the Exchequer that every new Dreadnought that you build postpones *pro tanto* the achievement of some urgent work of social reform; but national security, national insurance, after all is the first condition of all social reform. You may say "Is it not possible to come to some kind of arrangement between the nations of the world, particularly between ourselves and the great friendly Empire of Germany, by which this kind of thing might be brought to a close?" I wish it were. The German

---

[1] *The Times,* 29 December 1909.   [2] *The Times,* 1 January 1910.
[3] Hansard, 5th Ser. xix. 644–5.

Government told us—I cannot complain, I have no answer to make—their procedure in this matter is governed by an act of the Reichstag under which the programme automatically proceeds year by year. . . . We are now, we may hope, at the very top of the wave. If it were possible even now to reduce (the) rate of construction no one would be more delighted than His Majesty's Government. We have approached the German Government on the subject. They have found themselves unable to do anything. They cannot do it without an Act of Parliament repealing their Navy Law. They tell us, and, no doubt, with great truth, they would not have the support of public opinion in Germany to a modified programme. These are the governing and unalterable facts of the situation for the moment.'

On the very day before this speech fifty members of parliament met to condemn the increase in naval expenditure; they resolved, in view of the general political situation, not to vote against the naval estimates. The Prime Minister's care to disclaim any hostility to Germany was well received in the German press; but the subject of a limitation of armaments by mutual consent was not raised. No further question was asked in the House of Commons during the year 1910. At the Lord Mayor's banquet the Prime Minister referred to his hope that an international agreement might be reached on the problem of armaments; but there was no public response from Germany to this suggestion.

The Prime Minister was not free to state the terms upon which Germany offered a general agreement. Public opinion would certainly have supported the Cabinet in the refusal to accept those terms. Bethmann-Hollweg did not want the German conditions to be discussed in public; but he was afraid that the plain words of the Prime Minister might misrepresent the German standpoint before public opinion. The British Government replied by a memorandum which recapitulated the story of the negotiations.[1] Germany had refused to alter the

---

[1] B.D.D. vi. 501–2; D.G.P. xxviii. 351–4.

naval law. Any 'retardation' of the rate of building would not reduce expenditure, though Great Britain would consider proposals made to her for this 'reduction of *tempo*'. The German proposals for a political understanding offered a difficulty owing to British relations with other Powers. There remained the possibility of an agreement, on the basis that the German naval programme would not be increased, for the mutual exchange of information to the satisfaction of the two Admiralties.

Grey was not hopeful about the result of proposals for the 'reduction of *tempo*', but the Cabinet wanted him to try at least for some arrangement.[1] The Emperor now consented to an exchange of information, but insisted that a political agreement should have precedence. Bethmann-Hollweg wanted to know what reductions England would make in her naval programme.[2] Goschen answered that it was difficult to lay down a standard, but that the more Great Britain knew of the programmes of other Powers 'the nearer we should get to having a fixed programme'. It was easier for Germany to fix a programme since the army, not the fleet, was the German first line of defence; German ships were built merely for the protection of the coasts and commerce of Germany.

The German answer to the British memorandum was given on 12 October.[3] The German Government accepted in general terms the proposal for an exchange of information and mentioned the possibility of retardation. They asked what 'equivalent' was offered in return for an

---

[1] B.D.D. vi. 511. There is no account in D.G.P. of the conversation between Goschen and Bethmann-Hollweg reported in B.D.D. vi. 511–13. The British memorandum is printed in D.G.P. with the Emperor's marginalia and comments, but without any notes by the Chancellor or by officials of the Foreign Office.   [2] B.D.D. vi. 512–13.

[3] D.G.P. xxviii. 367–8; B.D.D. vi. 524–5, and comments, 525–8. The German memorandum of complaints is printed in B.D.D. vi. 564–6 and 572–5, and D.G.P. xxviii. 368–73. For the history of this memorandum see below, pp. 288–90. Goschen's account of the conversation of 12 October is contained in an official letter to Grey (B.D.D. vi. 521–4) and in private letters to Grey and Nicolson (B.D.D. vi. 528–30; cf. *ib.* 536–7).

engagement to renounce an extension of the naval law.
They also insisted on a political agreement. The short
written statement was accompanied by a long disquisition
from Bethmann-Hollweg upon the grievances of Germany
against England. This series of complaints was read to
Goschen from notes, in the form of a memorandum
drawn up by Kiderlen. Goschen thought that the Chancellor was more friendly than his language implied, and
that he slurred over many of the severer criticisms in
Kiderlen's memorandum. On the other hand, the Emperor was as wild as ever in his talk when Goschen presented his official letters of credence on 16 October. He
would never consent to bind himself not to extend the
naval law.[1]

The difference between the Emperor's refusal to give
up the possibility of a further extension of the naval law,
and the Chancellor's question about the equivalent Germany might obtain for such a renunciation were noted
by the British Foreign Office. At the same time Crowe
drew up a full answer to the memorandum of complaints,
and suggested that the Admiralty, for the guidance of
the Foreign Office, should say 'exactly what we desire
to stipulate for and what we are prepared to undertake'
in a naval agreement.[2] Crowe thought that the German
Chancellor was in a sense right in thinking that the question of naval armaments was not the main cause of Anglo-
German estrangement. 'The building of the German
fleet is but one of the symptoms of the disease. It is the
political ambitions of the German government and nation
which are the source of the mischief.' Grey himself felt
that, however desirable German friendship might be,
Great Britain could not go back to the condition of things
under which Germany was openly on good relations

---

[1] B.D.D. vi. 530–3. The Emperor's conversation is less violent in tone
(except for the usual attack on Mr. McKenna) in a report of the conversation in Tirpitz, *op. cit.* i. 182–4. According to Tirpitz's report Kiderlen was
present throughout the interview and nodded his assent to the Emperor's
remarks ('nickte mir immer beifällig zu).

[2] B.D.D. vi. 533–6.

with England, but was always driving hard bargain after hard bargain.[1]

The British answer to the German list of complaints was given to the Chancellor in the beginning of December.[2] The answer took the form of a memorandum discussing the charges in detail, and a covering letter to the British Ambassador in Berlin explaining Grey's attitude to the German complaints. The details belong to the history of the Turkish loan of 1910, the Baghdad railway, and the Algeciras Conference.[3] In the covering letter Grey protested against the Chancellor's statement that British public opinion had been taught by the British Government to regard Germany as an enemy. Grey pointed to the anti-English character of German naval propaganda, and added that if charges of such a kind were made, discussion would become impossible.

The sequel to this complaint is interesting. On 5 December Goschen reported by telegram that the German Government was seriously troubled by the British reference to the phrase that the British Government had 'taught' the English people to regard Germany as an enemy.[3] Four days later Goschen sent to the Foreign Office a summary of the conversation of 12 October in which the German statement had occurred.[4] This sum-

[1] B.D.D. vi. 538–9.
[2] B.D.D. vi. 546–54 and 557–60; D.G.P. xxviii. 379–82. It would appear that Goschen, at an interview with the Chancellor on 1 December, presented the British memorandum. The Chancellor asked Goschen to give him a copy of his notes. On 2 December Goschen sent a *compte rendu* of the general conversation and the detailed memorandum. The latter is referred to in a footnote (pp. 380–1) but is not printed in D.G.P. though the draft of a German answer to the points discussed is given on pp. 382–4. This German answer was handed to Goschen on 16 December (B.D.D. vi. 568–72; D.G.P. xxviii. 382–4). D.G.P. does not include any account of the conversation of 16 December. The *compte rendu* of the conversation of 1 December is printed in D.G.P. xxviii. 380–2. It is not accompanied in D.G.P. by any summary of the conversation from the German side. This omission is unfortunate in the light of the discussion whether the Chancellor did or did not use the words of which Grey complained.
[3] B.D.D. vi. 561–2.
[4] B.D.D. vi. 564–6. For Kiderlen's explanation, see B.D.D. vi. 562–4.

mary was dictated in French by Kiderlen to Mr. Seymour, a secretary at the British Embassy, two days after the interview of 12 October. The dictation was made from the German notes prepared by Kiderlen for the Chancellor, and used in the conversation. The summary contained the words: 'Si le peuple anglais n'avait pas appris par ses gouvernants de considérer l'Allemagne comme l'ennemi, il ne serait pas ému de l'agrandissement de la flotte allemande. Les grands progrès de la flotte des États Unis le laissent calme.' An official of the German Foreign Office had read through Mr. Seymour's version of the document dictated to him.

Goschen was sure that Bethmann-Hollweg, speaking from notes, had said the same thing 'with great emphasis, and a little more strongly'. Moreover, in the interview of 1 December, Bethmann-Hollweg at first doubted that he had used such words, but, when pressed by Goschen, said that 'the speeches of prominent statesmen like Mr. McKenna and others, had justified him in drawing such a conclusion.[1] Nevertheless Kiderlen denied that he had written the phrase in his memorandum, or dictated it to Mr. Seymour, even though Goschen pointed out the extreme unlikelihood that Mr. Seymour would or could have interpolated a whole sentence while a document was being dictated to him.

On 16 December the Chancellor assured Goschen that he had not used the words in question. Goschen referred him to the dictated version. Bethmann-Hollweg answered that Kiderlen denied that the words had been dictated. Goschen was given the document from which Kiderlen's dictation had been made.[2] The document did not contain the sentence of which the British Government had complained. There was only a sentence: 'that a powerful German fleet in the hands of a friendly Power need not be a cause of anxiety for England is shown by

---

[1] B.D.D. vi. 558.
[2] B.D.D. vi. 568–72. A translation of the German document is printed in B.D.D. vi. 572–4. There is no account of this interview in D.G.P.

the equanimity with which England regards the growth of the fleet of the United States'. It is not surprising that Grey described the German explanation as 'obviously irreconcilable with the facts'.[1] Grey decided that it would be unwise to press the German Government any further about the original document. Crowe commented on 'the sorry shifts to which even the highest German officials stoop'.[2] The incident, like the discovery of the facts about the naval contracts in 1909, was unlikely to increase British trust in the statements given to them by the German Government.

[1] B.D.D. vi. 566–7.

[2] The treatment of this question in D.G.P. is not satisfactory. D.G.P. contains (xxviii. 368–73) a version of Kiderlen's memorandum for the Chancellor's use on 12 October. This version does not contain the sentence of which Grey complained. A footnote on p. 368 states that 'extracts' from the memorandum were dictated to a secretary of the British Embassy on 14 October, and that the whole text was given to Goschen in December. The only reference to Grey's complaint in D.G.P. are in the *compte rendu* of the conversation of 12 October drawn up by Goschen (pp. 380–2) and the German denial that the phrase in question had ever been used (pp. 382–3). Unless the British documents were consulted, it would be impossible to discover that the British Government had the strongest reasons for suspecting that the phrase had been cut out of the version shown to them. On the other hand, D.G.P. states that a copy of Kiderlen's memorandum was sent to Metternich on 15 November 1910. It would be interesting to see whether this copy, which was sent away before the controversy arose, contains the sentence. It is remarkable that the German Government did not produce the copy of the document which had been sent to London, since this copy, if it did not contain the sentence, would have been an excellent piece of evidence.

A comparison of the three versions—the version taken down in French by Mr. Seymour, the version in German given to Goschen on 16 December, and published in B.D.D. in translation, and the German version printed in D.G.P.—shows other important differences. The French version is shorter than the others, and is obviously a summary dictated with some freedom. The versions in German and English agree save for omissions from the version given to Goschen of certain passages which appear in the version printed in D.G.P. The omissions are (1) a paragraph in D.G.P. (370) to the effect that Germany would be ready to continue a discussion of the proposal for a 'reduction of *tempo*', (2) a reference to the sacrifices which England was prepared to make for Russian friendship, while she put no value upon the friendship of Germany (371), (3) specific references to matters in the Far East (annexation of Corea, Russo-Japanese treaty) in which Germany and England had common interests, and might have worked together (372).

Two further steps were taken before the end of the year. The British Admiralty laid down the conditions necessary for the exchange of information between Great Britain and Germany,[1] and on 16 December Metternich told Grey that Germany was now ready to agree to an exchange of information without reference to the political agreement. Grey took this chance of explaining the difficulty of finding a political 'formula' which would improve Anglo-German relations without impairing Anglo-French and Anglo-Russian relations.[2] Metternich noticed that Grey once more used the word 'understanding'; his usual word was 'formula'; he never spoke of an 'agreement'. Metternich told his Government that Grey was not a man who tried, for reasons of 'opportuneness', to awaken hopes in which he did not believe, or to promise more than he thought he could perform', but that he had never shown so clearly his desire for a *rapprochement*.

[1] B.D.D. vi. 560–1.   [2] B.D.D. vi. 575–6; D.G.P. xxviii. 385–9.

XVI

GREY'S PROPOSALS FOR AN EXCHANGE
OF INFORMATION. II. 1910–11

THE general election in Great Britain delayed the negotiations but on 7 February Goschen was able to give the German Chancellor the English proposals for the exchange of naval information.[1] Grey wanted a document which could be made public. 'I desire this because it would have some effect in dissipating an impression in the public mind here, in Germany, and in third countries that either nation is preparing for a sudden spring upon the other.'[2] Meanwhile Captain Watson, the British naval attaché in Berlin, had reported that there were rumours of a supplementary law which would increase the German shipbuilding programme in 1912. Goschen believed that Captain Watson was right in thinking that the scope of the law would depend on the British programme of naval construction for 1911–12. Goschen wrote that

'the activity in German dockyards has a tendency to increase or decrease in the inverse ratio to that of Great Britain. If, proceeding on this system the German government should wish to take advantage of a reduced British ship-building programme to meet the wishes of the "Strong Navy" Party, there are no reasons, financial or otherwise, except perhaps an adverse public opinion, to prevent them from doing so.'

The increase of British shipbuilding in 1909 and 1910 had checked the extreme activity which prevailed in German dockyards in the preceding years. In Goschen's opinion, 'a British ship-building programme showing a steady rate of increase in 1911–12, and a determination to continue on that basis annually' would probably convince Germany that competition was useless.[3] The German answer

---

[1] B.D.D. vi. 579–87. The written proposals were actually given to the Chancellor on 8 February. D.G.P. xxviii. 390–1.

[2] B.D.D. vi. 579.   [3] B.D.D. vi. 581–3; cf. *ib.* 588–9.

to the British proposal was delayed until 24 March; Nicolson wondered whether the German Admiralty was waiting to hear the British naval estimates.[1] The German reply was based upon a memorandum of Tirpitz's suggesting that information should be exchanged simultaneously, and that the programme of the two countries should be limited for the next year by the figures which they had communicated.[2] The Chancellor explained that the desire for 'simultaneity' implied that neither country would take advantage of the knowledge of the other's plans to 'go one better'. Kiderlen also laid stress upon the condition that the programmes exchanged should be binding for one year.[3]

The British naval attaché commented at once that the German plan went beyond the British proposals. The Admiralty had suggested nothing more than a statement of information about work projected or under construction. Captain Watson suggested that the 'exchange' should take place after the publication of the naval programmes and should be limited to the dates of laying down ships, and other general facts, e.g. dimensions of ships.[4]

The British Foreign Office and Admiralty agreed with Captain Watson's view.[5] They thought that Bethmann-Hollweg was now proposing, not an exchange of information, but a limitation of armaments, and a limitation in the German interest. The British naval programme was largely dependent on that of Germany and Austria; the German proposals would compel the Admiralty to decide upon a naval programme without knowledge of German and Austrian plans. These facts were well known to Germany, and had often been pointed out to the German

---

[1] B.D.D. vi. 603.

[2] D.G.P. xxviii. 400-1. It is curious, in relation to his earlier views on the subject, that Tirpitz should have described this readiness to exchange information as a blow to British naval prestige, and a recognition of the great military importance of the German fleet (ib. 401).

[3] B.D.D. vi. 608-13; D.G.P. xxviii. 402.

[4] B.D.D. vi. 613-14.   [5] B.D.D. vi. 614-15, 629-30.

Foreign Office; the German Emperor and the naval party were always saying that the number of ships laid down by Great Britain was a matter of indifference to them. There was a further delay before an official answer was given to Germany. This answer explained the difference between the original proposal made by Great Britain and the suggestions made by Germany. The British Government, however, agreed that, 'there should be no variation of the programme . . . made known without previous and further information being given to the other party'.[1] Bethmann-Hollweg, 'in view of the general political situation', was anxious to give a favourable answer.[2] The answer was an acceptance of the British conditions; it was given on 27 June 1911.[3] On 1 July the German Government sent the *Panther* to Agadir.

Even before this sudden act the possibility of a general agreement was receding. The reply to the German memorandum of 12 October was given to the Chancellor on 24 March—the day on which he had accepted in principle the idea of an exchange of information. Grey told the French and Russian Governments confidentially that the negotiations were reopened; he also told the German Chancellor that France and Russia knew that Anglo-German discussions were taking place.[4] The British answer again insisted that no political formula could be accepted which might impair British relations with France and Russia. Grey once more suggested an agreement on certain outstanding questions—notably, the question of the Baghdad railway; the method of settling particular subjects of difference had been used with success in the negotiations with France and Russia. The British Govern-

[1] B.D.D. vi. 636–7; D.G.P. xxviii. 419–20; 9 June 1911.
[2] D.G.P. xxviii. 420–1.
[3] B.D.D. vi. 640–1; D.G.P. xxviii. 423–4. For the later history of his proposals for exchange of information, see below, pp. 305–7.
[4] It might be assumed, from a note in D.G.P. xxviii. 403 that the British Government concealed from Germany the amount of information given to France and Russia. It is clear from B.D.D. vi. 602–4 and 609 that this was not the intention of the British Government.

ment, however, agreed to the simultaneous conclusion of a political and a naval understanding.[1] Upon this last proposal—which was a surrender of the earlier position that a naval agreement should precede any political agreement—Kiderlen commented: 'Yes—if they will recognize reciprocity there also—equal strength'.[2]

The Chancellor's comments on receiving the memorandum, were not hopeful.[3] His official answer was given on 9 May 1911.[4] He explained that Germany could no longer discuss the question of slowing down the rate of shipbuilding. For financial reasons it was now impossible to postpone the regular expenditure laid down under the naval law; it was also impossible, from the point of view of German shipbuilding yards, to cut down the building programme. The German Government wanted a general political agreement which would make a purely naval agreement superfluous. An agreement excluding all possibility of attack by either party might be extended to France and Russia.

It is necessary to take into account not merely this official statement, but also a draft of 5 April, in which the Chancellor wrote down his 'ideas about England', and a letter to Metternich in which these ideas were developed.[5] The Chancellor still held to four assumptions which could not be accepted by Great Britain. These assumptions were: (1) that England was unnecessarily nervous about German shipbuilding intentions. Germany had declared that she had no aggressive intentions; (2) that the German naval programme took no account of the British programme; this German programme could not be cut down, but would not be increased unless there

---

[1] B.D.D. vi. 598–600; D.G.P. xxviii. 403–6.

[2] D.G.P. xxviii. 406. Kiderlen's note to the word 'simultaneous' was 'No'. The note quoted above may be regarded as a certain qualification of the 'No'.

[3] B.D.D. vi. 608–10. There is no account of the conversation of 24 March in D.G.P. xxviii.

[4] B.D.D. vi. 625–7; D.G.P. xxviii. 409–10.

[5] D.G.P. xxviii. 407–9 and 411–15.

were 'a change in the political constellation' unfavourable to Germany; (3) that England could give to Germany a promise of neutrality in a war in which Germany
was engaged with France and Russia without affecting
British relations with these two latter Powers; (4) that
on the question of the Baghdad railway and Persia the
Germans were in the position of 'beati possidentes'. Any
recognition of the wishes of England on these questions
would be a concession on the part of Germany, and would
therefore require 'counterconcessions'.

The British comments on the Chancellor's statement
were unfavourable.[1] The British Government had begun
by insisting that a naval agreement should precede a
political agreement, and that no naval agreement would
be accepted unless it brought a real reduction in naval
expenditure. These two points had been surrendered;
Great Britain had agreed to consider the simultaneous
conclusion of naval and political agreements, while Germany still refused to modify the naval law, and therefore
to offer any real diminution of naval expenditure. Germany had manœuvred Great Britain into a discussion
of a political agreement, and then withdrawn even her
limited and vague proposal for a retardation of naval
construction within the limits of the naval law. Of the
two reasons given for the withdrawal of this proposal, the
financial reason was clearly insufficient, and the reference
to the need for continuous employment in the German
shipbuilding and armament works was 'ominous'. The
German political proposals would still leave Germany
free to continue the indirect pressure which she was
exercising on the smaller European States.[2] The distrust

---

[1] B.D.D. vi. 622–3 and 627–9.

[2] The question of German pressure on the smaller Powers deserves a more
thorough study than it has yet received. It is interesting, in this context,
to notice a remark of the Emperor's about an article in the *Westminster Gazette*
at the end of the year 1911. The article was sent to the Emperor by Ballin,
and returned to Ballin with the usual marginalia and a final comment:
'Very good as far as the ridiculous statement that we are aiming at the
hegemony of Central Europe. We actually are Central Europe, and that

was not lessened by rumours of a further increase in the strength of the German navy.

Thus a deadlock had been reached in the negotiations. After two years of conversations, exchange of notes, and drafting of memoranda, the German Chancellor had not receded from the point of view that Germany could not afford to make any concessions in her naval programme unless Great Britain would give in return a promise of neutrality. The British Government could not give this promise without destroying the ententes with France and Russia. On one point indeed agreement had been reached, though even here a good many difficult questions of detail had still to be settled. The German Government had agreed in principle to an exchange of information about the work actually in hand or projected in their shipyards. Grey had looked upon an exchange of information as the first step to a wider agreement for the limitation of armaments. The German attitude showed that this hope was not likely to be realized. The first information to be exchanged would probably be the news of another supplementary naval law in Germany.

Meanwhile the Liberals in Parliament and outside Parliament were becoming more restive. The Liberal party stood for economy in armaments; every year there was an increase in the cost of the navy. A programme of eight capital ships had been followed by a programme of five ships. There seemed no end to this competition in shipbuilding. The naval architects designed larger and more expensive ships; the ordnance factories turned out heavier guns. The submarine was becoming an important war vessel; the airship and aeroplane were about to add to the complications and charges of army and navy.

The Prime Minister had explained in 1909, and again in 1910, that Great Britain was anxious to come to an

other states should lean upon us or come into our circle of influence through the law of gravity, especially when they belong to the same race [*Stamm*], is quite natural. The English don't want this, because it destroys their theory of the balance of power, i.e. playing off the European great states against one another *ad libitum*.' Huldermann, *Ballin*, p. 245.

agreement with Germany to limit this burden of armaments. The story of the negotiations with Germany could not be told without aggravating the situation. The British public would have thought, with some reason, that Germany was trying to detach Great Britain from the ententes. There would have been an outburst of anger, and all hope of an Anglo-German agreement would have been at an end. The Liberal enthusiasts for disarmament on almost any terms knew very little about German views and German policy. It is difficult to escape from the conclusion that many of them made no effort to learn the facts or to understand the significance of the European situation.

The attacks upon Ministers for their failure to ease the position by a settlement with Germany were peculiarly unfair to Grey. He could not use his knowledge to the full; he was bound to give his answers in general terms. He felt deeply and sincerely the seriousness and danger of the growth of naval armaments. He believed that there was some hope of a change for the better. He was convinced that this change could only come about through careful and deliberate action by all the Powers. He thought that there were signs of goodwill in Europe. Three months before the dispatch of the *Panther* to Agadir he told the House of Commons that there had been an improvement in international relations.

'The Great Powers of Europe are spoken of as being in separate groups. Yes; but gradually, in the last five years at any rate, things which might have brought these groups into opposition with each other, have been disappearing. . . . I am speaking not of our particular (foreign) relations only, but of the relations of France with Germany, and Russia with Germany.'[1]

Grey was unwilling to meet the attacks of the disarmament party in the House of Commons by an appeal to jingoism, or by references to supposed German designs and dangers which might threaten Great Britain. His speeches were never sensational; they were entirely free

---

[1] Hansard, 5th Ser. xxii. 1984. For this speech see below, pp. 299-303.

from debating points. Grey never doubted the sincerity of his critics. He agreed with the purpose they had in view. He could only point to the despotism of fact, the importance of adapting means to ends, the limited power of action possessed by one nation.

In the early spring of 1911 Mr. J. M. Macdonald, the leader of the 'reduction of armaments' group in the House of Commons, brought forward a motion in favour of a diminution of armaments. Grey's answer to Mr. Macdonald's speech is an important statement of his own views about disarmament and the aims of British foreign policy in the years before the War.[1] The German Chancellor replied to Grey in the Reichstag. A comparison between the British and German views is instructive. Grey described the paradox that the armaments of Europe were increasing rapidly at a time when there was an improvement in the relations between the Great Powers.[1] He quoted extracts from speeches made by Bethmann-Hollweg and others.

It might be thought that, as armaments increase, these opinions could not be sincere. I believe they are sincere. . . . Yet the armaments increase. . . . There is a much greater paradox. It is that this growing and enormous burden of Naval and Military expenditure is coinciding not merely with friendly relations between the Powers, but with the growth of civilisation as a whole. It is a fact that it is in the most civilised nations of the world that the expenditure is greatest. If civilisation means all that we imply by it, surely the growth of civilisation should have softened and not increased Naval and Military expenditure. Some Naval and Military expenditure the most highly civilised nations necessarily must have until the world is all equally civilised. The most highly civilised nation must, of course, have in all circumstances the power to protect themselves against those who remain less advanced. But the paradox remains, that their expenditure on armaments is not directed against nations less civilised than themselves, not against more backward nations but it is directed—I will not say directed against,

[1] Hansard, 5th Ser. xxii. 1977-91: 13 March 1911. The motion was seconded by Mr. Ponsonby.

but it is entered upon in rivalry with each other. This paradox
—unless the incongruity and mischief is brought home not only
to men's heads generally, but to their feelings, so that they
resent the inconsistency and realize the danger of it—if this
tremendous expenditure on and rivalry of armaments goes on,
it must in the long run break civilisation down. . . . If you are
to have these great burdens of force piled up in times of peace,
as it has been in the last generation, it will become intolerable.
There are those who think it will lead to war precisely because
it is becoming intolerable. I hear it said that as the burden
grows it will be felt so strongly that some nation will seek relief
in war. I think it is much more likely that the burden will be
dissipated by internal revolution—not by nations fighting against
each other, but by the revolt of the masses of men against taxation. But it does not follow from that that one nation can . . .
put a stop to the rivalry by dropping out of the race. . . . On the
contrary, it might very well be that if one nation dropped out
of the competition it might momentarily give a spurt in expenditure in some other. . . . I spoke of a revolt against naval and
military expenditure. That revolt will not come until the taxation presses directly upon the classes for whom existence at best
must be a struggle. When you begin to make hunger by taxation, as sooner or later every country will come to make it if
naval and military expenditure goes on increasing, then you will
be within measurable distance of that revolt which will put a
stop to it. That is the direction in which the great countries are
heading. There is a greater danger than that of war—the
danger which I once outside this House called bleeding to death
in time of peace. . . . I would fain hope that some way out may
be found. . . . Agreement with other nations? I believe that
agreement may do something. Agreement with Germany has
been spoken of. It needs very careful handling. I have always
avoided the phrase "limitation of armaments", because limitation of armaments is often construed abroad as if we intended
or were endeavouring to impose some limit on another country.
No country would stand that, and, least of all, Germany.
"Mutual reduction of expenditure" is the phrase I have always
endeavoured to use. Remember that in any possible naval agreement with Germany we have been given to understand that the
German Naval Law must in the long run be carried out. That
German Naval Law when complete means a navy of thirty-

three capital ships, including "Dreadnoughts" and cruisers, as well as pre-Dreadnoughts.[1]

'That is a very serious Naval expenditure for any Power; but I am sure that if I held out any hope to the House that by agreement Germany would part with her naval law, or alter it, I should at once be contradicted by the German Government. Within the limits of that declaration I think agreement may do something.'

Grey then came back to his plan of mutual exchange of information.[2]

'I have always held that frank exchange of information between the two Governments, through their Naval attachés, would guard against surprise. It would convince each nation and the world that neither was trying to steal a march upon the other, and it would have a pacific effect. It may be that within the limits of the German Naval Law some retardation of naval expenditure may be effected. It may be that agreement would make it certain that there would be no addition to the present programme in Germany.

'All that is a subject for discussion between the two Governments. It would be to the good if any agreement could be reached between them. But remember, it must always be within those limits! So far as this agreement is concerned, it must be remembered that the German Naval Law has been laid down by Germany to fulfil what she thinks necessary for her own purposes. She believes it within her power to have a strong navy, and due to herself. That is a position that nobody can resent Germany taking up. Germany has never regarded our Navy Estimates as a provocation to herself. Agreement may do something, but it is a small matter compared with the whole question.'

Grey then turned to what he thought to be the real remedy for the race in armaments.

'What we have to look for is any beneficent movement which will go to the root of the matter, and so affect public opinion, not in one country but in all. That may lead to first of all the

---

[1] It will be noticed that Grey was not very clear about the number of capital ships to be provided under the Naval Law. See above, p. 212.

[2] For the previous statements of Grey upon this plan see above, *passim*.

tide ceasing to flow, then turning, then, I hope, ebbing. I can conceive of but one thing that will really affect this Military and Naval expenditure of the world on the wholesale scale in which it must be affected if there is to be a real and sure relief. You will not get it till nations do what individuals have done, come to regard an appeal to law as the natural course for nations, instead of an appeal to force. Public opinion has been moving. Arbitration has been increasing. But you must take a large step further before the increase of arbitration will really affect this expenditure on armaments.'

Grey quoted two speeches of the President of the United States. He pointed out that no official proposal had followed these speeches, but that, if public opinion would discuss large proposals in a spirit which looked beyond the immediate gains of this or that nationality, there was some hope of success.

'Supposing . . . two of the greatest nations in the world were to make it clear to the whole world that by agreement such as that, that in no circumstances were they going to war again, I venture to say that the effect on the world at large of the example would be one which would be bound to have beneficial consequences. It is true that the two nations who did that might still be exposed to attack from a third nation who had not entered into such agreement. I think it would probably lead to their following it up by an agreement that they would join with each other in any case in which one only had a quarrel with a third Power by which arbitration was refused. And more and more the tendency which is growing in the world to recognise that war between two great countries must not only be a serious thing for them but must be a serious thing for neutral Powers through the disturbance it causes, the more and more they would join and nations would come to the conclusion as between themselves, that they were not going to fight, but that it was their interest to join together to keep the peace of the world. . . . Entering into an agreement of that kind there would be great risks entailed. You must be prepared for some sacrifices of national pride. . . . I know that to bring about changes of this kind public opinion has to rise to a high plane, higher than it can rise in ordinary times . . . but the times are not ordinary with this expenditure, and they will become less ordinary as this expenditure increases. The minds of men are working up on this, and if you look back into history you will find there do come times at favourable moments when public opinion has risen to heights which a generation previously would have been thought impossible. It was so when public opinion abolished slavery with all its vested interests. . . . I think it is not impossible, though I admit that in a case of such an enormous change progress may be slow, that the public opinion of the world at large may insist, if it is fortunate enough to find leaders who have the courage, upon finding relief in this direction. Some armies and navies would remain, no doubt, but they would remain then not in rivalry with each other, but as the police of the world. . . . The great nations of the world are in bondage, in increasing bondage, at the present moment, to their armies and navies, and it does not seem to me impossible that in some future years they may discover, as individuals have discovered, that law is a better remedy than force, and that all the time they have been in bondage to this tremendous expenditure, the prison door has been locked on the inside.'

Grey's speech was more favourably received in England than on the Continent. A representative body of nonconformist ministers spoke of the 'gleaming goal' towards which Grey had pointed in his references to disarmament and arbitration, but the general view in France was that England had everything to gain from an arbitration treaty with the United States since Canada was defenceless. German opinion on the whole regarded the speech as a sign that Great Britain was at the end of her financial resources. The German naval attaché in London concluded a report on the speech with the words. 'Grey's surrender is due to the Naval Law alone and the unshakable resolution of the German nation not to allow any diminution of this important instrument.'[1] The Emperor's comment was equally simple. 'If we had followed the advice of Metternich and Bülow for the last four or five years and ceased to build we should now have had the "Copenhagen" war upon us. As it is, they respect our firm resolution and surrender to the facts.

[1] D.G.P. xxviii. 396–8.

So we must go on building undisturbed. And when our higher *tempo* comes to an end instead of building two battleships and one cruiser, we must build one battleship and two cruisers.' Metternich reported in full the most important paragraphs in Grey's speech. The Emperor's comment upon the reference to the beneficent influence of an exchange of information on shipbuilding was 'Nonsense'.[1] To the suggestion that there might be a slowing down of German construction the Emperor remarked 'No'.

On 31 March the German Chancellor gave in the Reichstag a direct answer to Grey's speech. He pointed out that no practical proposals for disarmament had been suggested. The question was extremely difficult. It was not easy to define the relative position of each nation. 'Perhaps the procedure used in the formation of industrial syndicates can be adopted.' Bethmann-Hollweg said that he could not himself suggest any draft scheme.

'England is convinced, and has repeatedly declared that, notwithstanding all her wishes for a limitation of armaments and for the composition of disputes by arbitral procedure, her Fleet must in all circumstances be a match for, or even superior to, any possible combination in the world. To aim at this state of things is England's perfect right . . . but it is quite a different matter to make such a claim into the basis of an agreement which by peaceful assent is to be accepted by other Powers.'

An attempt at control would lead to 'nothing but perpetual mistrust and excitement'. Disarmament would remain impracticable as long as men were men and states were states.

On the question of an exchange of information Germany was ready to agree with any practical plan. The introduction of arbitration on all points, including those affecting the 'honour and interests' of a nation, meant nothing more than an assertion that a serious breach of the peace was unthinkable between the two nations making such an agreement.

'The condition of peaceableness is strength. The old saying still holds good that the weak will be the prey of the strong. When

[1] D.G.P. xxviii. 398–400.

a people will not or cannot continue to spend enough on its armaments to be able to make its way [*sich durchzusetzen*] in the world, then it falls back into the second rank, and sinks down to the role of a "super" on the world's stage. There will always be another and a stronger there who is ready to take the place in the world which it has vacated.'

The radical and socialist newspapers in Germany disapproved of the Chancellor's speech. Otherwise there was little press comment. The *Frankfurter Zeitung* pointed out that the emphasis of the speech was on the difficulties of finding a way out of the impasse. The German Government looked at things from the point of view of a conservative, military caste and the interests of armament manufacturers. The press took no notice of the suggestion of an exchange of information on the shipbuilding programmes.[1]

At the end of May the German Navy League held its annual meeting. The League again wanted an increase in the number of large cruisers.[2] Some protests were made, notably in the *Vossische Zeitung*, against this demand and against the close association of the German Admiralty with the meetings of the Navy League, but the protests had no sequel. On 20 June—less than a fortnight before the dispatch of the *Panther* to Agadir, the Emperor described Germany as a block of steel forged by the hammer of God, and added that the development of German trade and shipping was possible only behind German armed forces, 'above all, behind a respected German navy'.

NOTE TO CHAPTER XVI

Proposals for the Exchange of Naval Information; Negotiations after 27 June 1911

The later history of this plan upon which Grey had placed great hopes can be told in a few words. The German letter of

[1] Count Reventlow referred to the subject, but pointed out that the information to be exchanged concerned matters which were already clear.

[2] The League asked for six additional cruisers between 1912 and 1917, i.e. an increase of one capital ship a year in the building programme. B.D.D. vi. 644-7. See also, above, p. 284.

acceptance suggested that the details should be settled by the naval authorities. The Foreign Office thought this proposal unsatisfactory. Crowe noted that 'we have had repeated and unhappy experience of concluding agreements and leaving some essential part to be arranged subsequently. It is to my mind an absolutely unsound method, and almost invariably leads to Great Britain being jockeyed out of what she thought had been settled.'[1] During the Agadir crisis Grey felt that relations between the two countries were so very much strained that more harm than good would be done by continuing the negotiations. The German press would certainly describe an agreement for mutual inspection of shipbuilding yards as an insidious piece of espionage on the part of Great Britain. Captain Watson reported on 27 September that the German Government intended to change the date of the publication of their naval estimates from November to March, in order to take away any advantage which the British Admiralty might obtain from knowing the German estimates before the British estimates were published.[2] On 3 November the Chancellor told Goschen that he was still waiting for an answer to the German letter of acceptance.[3] Grey was uncertain whether the time was favourable for reopening the question. Crowe was afraid the Germans might think that Great Britain was trying to discover whether they had any plans for an increase in construction.[4] Goschen saw no objection to sending a detailed answer to the note of 27 June.[5] This detailed answer was given to Kiderlen on 28 January 1912, immediately after the elections to the Reichstag. The British Admiralty suggested an extension of the 'information' to include 'all cases of the arming of merchant or passenger vessels'. They also explained that they had no wish to inquire into details which the naval authorities would rightly regard as professional secrets. They did not 'seek to know the intentions of the German Government so far as the future is concerned, or to lead that Government into any arrangement which would fetter reciprocally the free discretion of either Power to alter, vary, diminish or extend their naval programme. They are concerned with the exact situation, in fact at given and agreed periods in each year. They would desire to know how many vessels of each class or type are being constructed at

[1] B.D.D. vi. 641.   [2] B.D.D. vi. 644–7.
[3] B.D.D. vi. 647.   [4] B.D.D. vi. 649.   [5] B.D.D. vi. 653–6.

such given times in all the yards, public or private, of the German Empire, whether for the German Government, or for foreign sale. They are prepared similarly to satisfy the German Government beyond doubt or question as to the general position of all warship construction within the United Kingdom. What is desired, indeed, is an exchange of simple and easily verifiable facts.'[1] Haldane's visit followed within a few days of the presentation of the British detailed proposals. No further correspondence on the subject is printed in the British or German documents; the German Government apparently let the matter drop after the failure of the negotiations for a political agreement. Mr. Churchill referred to the proposals in April 1912, but no further suggestions were made by Great Britain.[2]

[1] B.D.D. vi. 662–3; D.G.P. xxxi. 50–3.

[2] Widenmann's comments on the British proposals were extremely unfavourable, and to some extent justified Crowe's fear that these proposals would be misinterpreted, and connected with the rumoured proposals for an increase in German naval construction (D.G.P. xxxi. 56–61). Metternich did not agree with Widenmann's opinions; as usual the Emperor paid no attention to Metternich (D.G.P. xxxi. 55).

The editors of D.G.P. assume that the renewal of the discussions by Great Britain in January 1912 was caused by the desire to create a favourable atmosphere for Haldane's visit. It is clear from the British documents that the only reason why the British answer had been delayed was, in Grey's words to Cambon, 'the electricity in the air during the discussion of the question of Morocco'. (B.D.D. vi. 664.) Reference to the German press during the autumn of 1911 shows that Grey's words were not exaggerated.

XVII

THE AGADIR CRISIS, 1911

IN 1898 and 1900 Tirpitz had launched a naval programme on a strong tide of anti-British feeling in
Germany. He had taught the German people to think
that they were helpless before the rapacity of England
because they could not resist England at sea. This lesson
was driven home at every succeeding crisis in international
affairs. Whatever the general gain or loss to Germany,
there was always a harvest to be reaped by the naval
party. New financial burdens could be imposed upon the
German taxpayer in the cause of national defence.

A serious crisis occurred in the summer of 1911; again
the German people were warned that they could not
expect fair treatment by Great Britain until the German
navy had reached its proper development. There was an
important difference between the situation in 1900 and
in 1911. In 1900 Bülow supported the naval party. His
enemies have said that he owed his place to this support.
In 1911 the German Chancellor and the Foreign Secretary
were doing their utmost to restrain the Emperor and the
naval party from taking a step which would endanger
German relations with Great Britain.

From this point of view the action of Germany is not
easy to understand. The Chancellor and Kiderlen—it is
better perhaps to say Kiderlen and the Chancellor—were
anxious to improve Anglo-German relations. Within
Germany they tried to prevent anything which would
counter this policy. Outside Germany they destroyed the
effect of their own work by employing the 'shock tactics'
which always roused the suspicions of the Powers.
Kiderlen had insisted that Germany should do nothing
to offend British susceptibilities. He had used the phrase
'drop by drop' to describe the methods whereby he hoped
to persuade Great Britain to side with Germany rather

than France. The dispatch of a warship to a port on the Atlantic seaboard of Morocco was likely to strengthen the Anglo-French entente; yet Kiderlen himself seems to have been responsible for this drastic measure. The suggestion did not come from the Chancellor. The Emperor doubted whether the step was wise.[1]

The circumstances leading to a revival of the Moroccan question were extremely complicated; a great deal of financial intrigue lay behind the official policy of the Governments of France and Germany. A full explanation of the facts must wait until further evidence is produced—if it is ever produced. The settlement reached at Algeciras in April 1906 had broken down before the end of 1907, largely owing to the weakness of the Sultan and the unwillingness of his subjects to accept and enjoy the benefits of European control. A rebellion in favour of the Sultan's brother, Muley Hafid, did not improve the position. Muley Hafid was faced with large claims, mainly French and Spanish, for damages during the rebellion. In 1909 these claims and other liabilities reached a total sixteen and a half times as large as the annual revenue left to the Sultan. The French and German Governments had reached an agreement in 1909; France promised to allow Germans equal standing with Frenchmen in financial and commercial matters, and Germany recognized the special political position of France. Unless the financial troubles of the new Sultan were settled, there would be no commercial privileges for any one, and the lives and property of Europeans would be endangered. The German Government therefore allowed the Sultan to receive a French loan of 107,000,000 francs.[2] The Sultan's creditors obtained greater hold of

---

[1] There is no confirmation of the statement made by the King of Rumania on 20 September 1911 that the Emperor himself was responsible and that Kiderlen knew nothing of the fact until after the *Panther* had been sent to Agadir (O.A.P. iii. 342). Kiderlen may possibly have given this version of events to the King of Rumania.

[2] The loan was sold to a syndicate of French banks at 89; the bankers sold it to the public at 97.

the revenues of the country, but within a short time Muley Hafid was again without money. He tried to impose new taxes; the taxes were farmed out to local chiefs, and caused great discontent among the tribes which recognized the Sultan's authority. Finally, in April 1911 the tribes near Fez revolted against Muley Hafid. The French Government sent an expeditionary force to protect the Europeans in Fez, and promised to withdraw the troops after the restoration of order. Great Britain had made a similar promise a generation earlier, in Egypt. The German Government could not refuse to allow the troops to go to Fez; the Europeans in the city were certainly in danger. On the other hand, the agreement of 1909 was not working well. The French suspected an attempt at political control in every demand made by Germany. They knew the close connexion between finance and policy in Germany; a similar connexion existed in France. They could not divide railway and other concessions between their own and German firms because the British Government objected to any infringement of the principle of open competition laid down in the Algeciras settlement. From the German point of view the agreement seemed to have assured French political control without giving economic advantages to Germany. The matter was complicated by a dispute about rival French and German trading companies in the French Congo near the border of German territory. M. Caillaux, at this time French Minister of Finance, and M. Messimy, Minister of the Colonies, tried to arrange by secret negotiation a general settlement of the questions in dispute. The Germans would not name their price for leaving Morocco in French hands; the French Cabinet was afraid of popular criticism.

The French Ministry fell in 1911, and M. Caillaux became President of the Council, but French opinion was unwilling to support his policy of a Franco-German *rapprochement*. M. Caillaux's position was not strong; the opposition groups in the Chamber suspected his motives.

The dispatch of the expeditionary force to Fez brought matters to a head. The German Foreign Office was pressed by the colonial enthusiasts, and gave way to them, although the reopening of the Moroccan question might easily have endangered the peace of Europe. On 21 June Kiderlen told the French Ambassador that Germany was prepared to receive 'offers', but he gave no general warning that German interests required immediate satisfaction. A gunboat—joined later by a cruiser—was sent to the port of Agadir, nominally to protect German interests. There were no German interests of any importance within range of Agadir. On the other hand, a strong body of opinion in Germany was known to favour the annexation of a portion of the Atlantic seaboard of Morocco. The plan was discussed at public meetings and canvassed in the press. Kiderlen himself made remarks to Cambon, and, according to German evidence, to prominent pan-Germans which could not easily be reconciled with a claim to territorial disinterestedness.[1] It was also known to the public that German syndicates had tried to obtain coaling stations in Teneriffe or Madeira. The evidence however seems to show that Kiderlen was merely trying to force a settlement of claims for 'compensation' elsewhere, without much thought that his action would be interpreted in the light of the past history of German policy and German methods. Furthermore, M. Caillaux's negotiations were not known to the British Foreign Office; some of these negotiations were not even known to the Minister of Foreign Affairs in M. Caillaux's own Government. Unless the British Ministers were given a more explicit statement of the reasons why the *Panther* had been sent to Agadir, they would be likely to assume, or at least to suspect, that Germany had some far-reaching territorial aims. No other explanation seemed

---

[1] *The Times*, 20 January 1912. It was alleged in Germany that Zimmermann, Under-Secretary of State for Foreign Affairs, had tried to prevent the German press from asking for 'compensation', since Germany wanted not 'compensation', but a position in Morocco.

adequate. At a moment when the German Government was trying to persuade Great Britain to sign a political agreement the German Chancellor would hardly destroy all chance of this agreement and even risk a European war over a few square miles of territory in the hinterland of the Congo.

The *Panther* was sent to Agadir on 1 July. Three weeks passed; Kiderlen followed the 'sphinx-like attitude' taken six years earlier by Bülow, and maintained the fiction that the ship was protecting German interests in the neighbourhood of Agadir. Only on 23 July was an explanation given. Two days before Metternich came to Grey with this explanation Mr. Lloyd George (with Grey's approval) had spoken in strong terms at the Mansion House. Mr. Lloyd George said nothing which had not been said about German interests by German statesmen a score of times. The fact that the language of British Ministers was usually less assertive in tone gave Mr. Lloyd George's words a particular importance.[1] Moreover, these words were spoken by a Minister whose general wish for an Anglo-German understanding was well known; the speech was received with applause, and was approved by most British newspapers. The attitude of the German press towards this speech was at first uncertain. The *Kölnische Zeitung* at first denied that there was any menace in a statement of principle, applicable to the Great Powers, which might have been delivered by any non-English

---

[1] The most important passage in Mr. Lloyd George's speech followed a reference to the services rendered by Great Britain in the past in safeguarding the liberties and at times the existence of continental nations. 'I would make great sacrifices to preserve peace. . . . But if a situation were to be forced upon us in which peace could only be preserved by the surrender of the great and beneficent position Britain has won by centuries of heroism and achievement, by allowing Britain to be treated where her interests were vitally affected as if she were of no account in the Cabinet of nations, then I say emphatically that peace at that price would be a humiliation intolerable for a great country to endure. National honour is no party question. The security of our international trade is no party question; the peace of the world is much more likely to be secured if all nations realize fairly what the conditions of peace must be.'

statesman. . . . 'Similar truths have been spoken from the
tribune of the German Reichstag and have not been held
to contain warlike tendencies or threats against other
people.'[1] The reception given to the speech in England,
and the highly nervous state of opinion in Germany soon
produced a different impression, and Mr. Lloyd George's
speech was regarded as an unnecessary provocation. A
week later (27 July) the Prime Minister explained more
fully the British standpoint. Great Britain had not interfered, and would not interfere, 'to prejudice negotiations between France and Germany', but she had a right
to be consulted in matters affecting her obligations. 'It
would have been a grave mistake to let the situation drift
until an assertion of our interest in it might, owing to
previous silence, cause surprise and resentment at the
moment when this assertion became most necessary.'[2]

The resentment of the German press was turned mainly
against Great Britain. Throughout the summer, and particularly in July and August, there were rumours in
Germany and Great Britain of sinister movements of
fleets.[3] In September the British Admiralty made the
experiment of sending coal for the fleet by rail from South
Wales to Scotland. About the same time there were signs
of panic on the Berlin Stock Exchange, and a deputation
of bankers visited the German Foreign Office, where they
were at once reassured. At the end of July the rate of
insurance in London against war risks at sea rose from 5s.
to 10s. or 15s. per cent.; in September the rate was 10s.
per cent.

The crisis lasted for several months. The German terms
were very high; the first demands included the whole
of the French Congo. Kiderlen's action had increased
the difficulties of the French Government. Concessions
which might have been made by France without much

[1] *Kölnische Zeitung*, 23 July 1911. On 12 September a writer in the
Kölnische Zeitung thought that 'the ambitious soul of Sir E. Grey' wanted
revenge for the humiliation of Great Britain on the Bosnian question.
[2] Hansard, 5th Ser. xxviii. 1827–8.
[3] An English railway strike in August added to public anxiety.

opposition now appeared as a humiliating surrender to a German ultimatum. Finally the surrender was made by Germany. In return for a strip of French African territory running from the Cameroons to the Belgian Congo, Germany recognized French political influence in Morocco. It was difficult to believe that this African concession was worth the risk which had been taken, or that Germany would have given up all claim to Moroccan ports if France and Great Britain had not stood firm. Kiderlen's tactics had failed; the failure affected the rest of his policy. Great Britain and France had been alarmed; the military conversations between the two Powers were renewed. There was nothing binding in these conversations. They were held for reasons of common prudence. They did not 'threaten' Germany; yet they were bound to affect the relations between Germany and Great Britain. If British Ministers took particular care to let the French Government understand that they reserved full freedom to decide whether they would or would not take part in a Franco-German war, they would be equally careful not to give away their freedom to Germany in a political formula.

Kiderlen had also increased his difficulties within Germany. He had given the naval party a new opportunity. During the height of the Moroccan crisis Tirpitz decided to use the excited state of public opinion to secure a new supplementary naval law.[1] The Emperor shared this view, and on 27 August 1911 made a speech at Hamburg in which he referred to the enthusiasm of the people of Hamburg as evidence that they wished for a further increase in the German fleet, 'so that we can be sure that no one will dispute our rightful place in the sun'.[2] Tirpitz

---

[1] Tirpitz, *op. cit.* i. 200.

[2] D.G.P. xxxi. 3–4, note. It is clear from D.G.P. that this speech was made to prepare German public opinion for a further increase in the navy.

In November 1911 Captain Faber gave, in a speech at Andover, an ill-informed and exaggerated account of the precautionary measures taken by the British Admiralty during the crisis. Captain Faber was a Conservative Member of Parliament; his speech was intended to show that the naval

had two interviews with the Chancellor at the end of
August. It was decided to postpone the decision about
the supplementary law until the settlement of the Moroccan question. Before September was over Tirpitz had
persuaded the Emperor that the German people ought to
be told that their Government aimed at a 2 : 3 ratio
between the German and British fleets. This announcement would be made early in 1912,[1] and in the autumn
of 1912 a new naval law would be introduced. The
Emperor thought that British finances were in a bad
condition and that Great Britain would accept his proposal. He saw signs of surrender in the moderate British
naval estimates of 1911, and in the willingness of Mr.
McKenna to accept a ratio of 30 : 21 in capital ships in
1914.[2] In September 1911 Italy declared war on Turkey
over the question of Tripoli. The war was not desired by
Germany. Turkish relations with Germany were not
improved by the action of one of Germany's allies in
attacking Tripoli at a moment of Turkish weakness.
There was also a danger that the Balkan States might take
the chance of attacking the Turks, and bring about a
difficult Austro-Russian conflict of interest. Tirpitz, as
usual, turned the situation to good effect for his propaganda. The war showed the importance of sea-power.
Italy was able to control the eastern Mediterranean and
prevent the Turks from bringing any reinforcements to

and military arrangements of the country were insufficient to meet an
emergency and that the British fleet would have been caught unawares in
the event of a sudden German attack. The speech was widely reported in
Germany as evidence of British plans of aggression. On the day before
Captain Faber's speech Mr. A. H. Ponsonby, M.P., had stated, in a paper
read at the New Reform Club, and apparently on good authority, that in
September the British squadrons in the North Sea were cleared for action.
A few days earlier the Chancellor's exposition of the Franco-German agreement in the Reichstag was received almost in silence, and was followed by
a violent attack on Great Britain by the leader of the Conservative party.

[1] Tirpitz wanted immediate publication. The Emperor was ready to
wait until February 1912. D.G.P. xxxi. 5–6, note.
[2] For Mr. McKenna's speech, see Hansard, 5th Ser. xxii. 1920–1. This
speech was made without reference to the possibility of a further increase in
the German programme.

defend their African possessions. Moreover, the German press was ready to print the wildest reports that Great Britain had encouraged Italy to attack the Turks. The *Post* acknowledged with regret that 'England had accomplished a master-stroke of policy'. The moral drawn was that Germany had shown her intellectual inferiority in the international arena, and must therefore appeal to the only weapon left to her—the German sword. Large naval increases were therefore necessary.[1] Meanwhile a French naval programme foreshadowed the construction of sixteen 'improved Dreadnoughts' between 1912 and 1920, while the Russian naval estimates rose from nine and a half million almost to seventeen million pounds. The explosion in the French battleship *Liberté* in November showed that the much-needed reforms in French naval administration had not been fully carried out, but the French and Russian programmes more than balanced any gain to Germany from the Dreadnoughts of Austria-Hungary. The Italian Dreadnoughts could not be counted as assets and might be used against Austrian or German ships.

With the Emperor on his side, Tirpitz was determined not to give way. He still maintained as his official view that the German fleet must be strong enough to make England think that war with Germany would be too great a risk. In private discussion Admiral von Heeringen, the Chief of the Naval Staff, went beyond this view, and admitted that there was a larger aim. The 'risk' theory was poor comfort for the navy. Something more positive was necessary than a conception which implied the defeat and destruction of the German fleet. 'Our fleet needs for the maintenance of its morale as well as for external success a reasonable [*brauchbares*] chance against England.'[2]

The Chancellor was unconvinced. The financial question was difficult. The Emperor's belief that England was ready to 'surrender' was not supported by the

<hr>

[1] *Die Post*, 8 October 1911.   [2] Tirpitz, *op. cit.* i. 221.

evidence. Mr. Winston Churchill succeeded Mr. Mc-
Kenna as First Lord of the Admiralty in October 1911.
He made his first important speech on naval questions at
the Lord Mayor's Banquet. He admitted the strain
caused by the heavy expenditure on the navy. There was
some hope of relief if the German programme were not
increased. If there were no relief, 'Great Britain would
be found best able to bear the strain'. Mr. Churchill
added that it was 'futile' to say that naval competition
was not at the root of the troubled relations between
England and Germany.

Metternich continued to report that a new supplementary law would bar the way to any reconciliation with England.[1] The Chancellor wrote almost an appeal. He said
that the Emperor wanted the law; public opinion was in
favour of another increase in the fleet. A declaration that
Germany intended to build eighteen instead of twelve
capital ships in the next six years did not strengthen the
fleet in 1911; but the German people would not see the
matter from this point of view. Bethmann-Hollweg
thought that he could not control public opinion unless
England would make a political agreement.[2] Metternich
looked at the question as it would appear to Great
Britain, and answered that

'if we now state bluntly to the British Government the alternatives: either you remain neutral, or we increase our fleet, the
result will be an even closer attachment to France—if the relations between England and France could be closer than they
are at present. If this increase is made by a law, that is, if it
exists for the time merely on paper, we shall need extraordinary
care to secure the interval for carrying through our programme
without war. . . . We may succeed; we may not' . . .[3]
'Is an increase of one ship after four years so valuable that we
ought to sacrifice for it the reasonable hope of better relations
(with England) and the hope of an agreement of a far-reaching
kind?'[4]

[1] D.G.P. xxxi. 29–31.   [2] D.G.P. xxxi. 31–3.
[3] D.G.P. xxxi. 33–4: 24 November 1911.   [4] D.G.P. xxxi. 43–4.

While Metternich and the Chancellor discussed the question from the wider point of view of Anglo-German relations, Wermuth, the German Minister of Finance, stated he was seriously alarmed at the imposition of new and heavy charges without careful examination of their effect. He was afraid that the army might be starved for the benefit of the fleet. He did not believe that Great Britain could not support higher naval charges; on the other hand, for Germany, 'the financial difficulties in the way of a new naval law are insurmountable'.[1]

The struggle between the Chancellor and his financial and diplomatic advisers on the one side, and the Emperor and his naval advisers on the other side, lasted until the end of January.[2] The strongest pressure was brought to bear on the Emperor by the naval party. Müller was still working closely with Tirpitz. Metternich was already discredited in the Emperor's opinion. He was a civilian; he was too much affected by the 'dear English'.[3] He was 'absolutely unteachable on naval questions'. It was 'useless to listen to him'.[4] Kühlmann, who supported his Ambassador, was only 'a docile pupil of Metternich'.[5] The 'civilians' found it impossible to control the reports sent by the naval attaché in London directly to the Emperor. These reports were described by Kiderlen as 'systematic attempts to increase hatred'.[6] The efforts made by the Chancellor of the Empire and the German Ambassador in London to check the intrigues of a subordinate member of the Embassy staff throw a good deal of light upon the confusion in the highest regions of German political life, and the place which the military and naval experts had obtained in the direction of policy. At the end of November 1911 the Chancellor reminded Metternich that naval and military attachés were required to avoid political reflections not directly bearing

---

[1] D.G.P. xxxi. 35–42. Wermuth resigned in March 1912 over the question of the supplementary law.

[2] For Tirpitz's disputes with the Chancellor, see Tirpitz, *op. cit.*, *passim*.

[3] D.G.P. xxxi. 24 and 9.   [4] D.G.P. xxxi. 55.

[5] D.G.P. xxxi. 87–92.   [6] D.G.P. xxxi. 17.

on their technical subjects. Captain Widenmann had frequently disregarded these instructions.[1] Metternich thought that the only way of silencing Widenmann was to get him recalled before his time expired. 'He feels himself completely secure under the protection of Herr von Tirpitz and H.M. the Emperor. . . . He thinks it his duty to employ the rest of his time here [Widenmann's appointment was due to expire in May 1912] in ceaseless warnings against the danger from England.' Yet nothing could be done. If Metternich asked Widenmann to leave off sending 'tendencious' reports, Widenmann would refuse. If Metternich himself refused to forward the notes, Widenmann would complain to Tirpitz, and Tirpitz would send the complaint to the Emperor. The Emperor would ask to see the reports, and would support Widenmann. A conflict would follow between the Emperor and the Chancellor.[2] The Chancellor did not think it possible to obtain Widenmann's recall. He wanted Metternich to contradict the reports, though he knew well enough that the Emperor would not listen to Metternich's contradictions. Metternich, who was a stronger man than the Chancellor, talked to Widenmann without letting him know that he was aware of his (Widenmann's) disloyalty.[3] On 19 February 1912 the Chancellor was bold enough to complain to the Emperor about statements made by Widenmann to Admiral Jellicoe. The Emperor supported Widenmann. No reprimand was sent as a result of this or a later complaint.[4] The Emperor said that Widenmann was an officer, and 'could only be reprimanded by the Supreme War Lord, never by civilian officials'. Tirpitz thought Widenmann might be congratulated.[5] A few weeks later Metternich, not Widenmann, lost his post.

In spite of their control of the Emperor, and of the Emperor's contempt for 'civilians' the naval party did not

[1] D.G.P. xxxi. 42–3.
[2] D.G.P. xxxi. 47: 10 December 1911.   [3] D.G.P. xxxi. 49–50.
[4] D.G.P. xxxi. 66–7. Tirpitz, *op. cit.* i. 294.   [5] Tirpitz, *op. cit.* i. 295–6.

win a complete victory. They had asked for three battle-ships and three large cruisers; they had to content them-selves with three battleships. The official announcement was made in the Speech from the Throne at the opening of the Reichstag on 7 February 1912. The question had been discussed openly in the German press for several months before the official statement. The *Frankfurter Zeitung* had warned its readers in November 1911 that, if Germany increased her programme, the British pro-gramme would probably be doubled. The Liberal Government wanted to spend money on social reforms, and might be forced to introduce revenue duties which would be the first stage in a tariff. The *Frankfurter Zeitung* described the naval agitation in Germany as 'the most effective means of making impossible for ever a sensible understanding with England'. The *Germania*—a journal of the Centre party—was afraid that a new Navy Bill would be so sharp a provocation of England that it might lead to a preventive war. The first answer to the new supplementary law came not from England but from France. The discussions in Germany were not lost upon the French Chamber. A week after the Speech from the Throne in Berlin, the deputies in Paris voted for a pro-gramme of construction which would bring the strength of the French navy up to twenty-eight ships of the line in 1920.

Meanwhile Bethmann-Hollweg and Metternich, with the help of Kühlmann, had attempted a diversion, if not a counter-attack, on the naval party. They tried to develop the idea of a colonial agreement with England. The attempt failed, though it was renewed again in the conversations of 1912. The main feature of the plan was an extension of German power in Africa. On 28 Novem-ber 1911 Grey said in the House of Commons that, if Germany wanted 'a place in the sun' in Africa, Great Britain would not block the way. Great Britain would not be 'an ambitious competing party' for more African possessions. 'In my opinion the wise policy for (Great Britain) is to expand as little as possible, and certainly no further [*sic*] the African possessions.'¹ Bethmann-Hollweg came directly to the point.

'Had he [Grey] the Spanish Muni territory in mind? That would not mean much. In any case, sooner or later it will fall of itself into our lap. The Belgian Congo is not yet ripe for partition. Furthermore it is inexpedient to raise the question now because we should thereby throw Belgium into the arms of France, and we want on military grounds to avoid doing this. Therefore there remain only the Portuguese colonies, about which we already have an agreement with England.'²

Grey had not intended anything so definite; but Metternich entered into the Chancellor's plans. He also thought that the Portuguese colonies might be obtained. Portugal did not deserve any consideration. Pressure could be put upon her, by means of her creditors, to part with her colonies. If necessary, a monarchical pretender could be subsidized on condition that he promised to give up the colonies.³ Metternich's suggestions throw a curious light on the attitude of Germany towards small States, and the results which the British Foreign Office feared if Germany should obtain a free hand in Europe. This plan of a great African Empire, stretching from the Indian Ocean to the Atlantic, was also described attractively by Kühlmann;⁴ but the suggestions were not encouraged either by Grey or by the Emperor. Grey took the proposals seriously, and wanted the Cabinet to think about them, but raised the question of the Baghdad railway before he reached the map of Africa. He also pointed out that Belgium 'did not show any disposition to part with the Congo'.⁵

¹ Hansard, 5th Ser. xxxii. 61–2. Grey made minor exceptions in the case of lands bordering British possessions, especially in South Africa.
² D.G.P. xxxi. 71–2: 6 December 1911.
³ D.G.P. xxxi. 72–6: 9 December 1911.
⁴ D.G.P. xxxi. 87–91: 8 January 1912.
⁵ B.D.D. vi. 650–1. A sentence about Belgium in one of Metternich's reports has an interest of its own. 'The Belgians have long known from which side their neutrality in a Franco-German war is primarily threatened. But if we guarantee the integrity of their possessions (*Besitzstand*), they will not hasten to throw themselves into the arms of France.' D.G.P. xxxi. 74.

The Emperor's criticisms were extravagant and foolish; sentence after sentence of rhodomontade upon the way in which Germany and the German Empire ought to be treated. Germany could buy or take any colonies she might want without England's consent. . . . There was, however, one sound piece of criticism among much bombast. The Emperor remarked that England was giving away land which did not belong to her. The criticisms affected Bethmann-Hollweg and Metternich more than Grey, since it is clear from subsequent negotiations that Grey had in mind the surrender of portions of territory in British hands, or land allotted to Great Britain, if the Anglo-German agreement about the Portuguese colonies came into effect through the action of the Portuguese themselves; but it was difficult for the opponents of a naval increase to counter the Emperor and Tirpitz by vague hopes of colonial expansion.[1]

[1] The Emperor's moods were not easy to follow. He had spoken about Germany's place in the sun. Yet he annotated Kühlmann's memorandum with the words, 'We have colonies enough.' D.G.P. xxxi. 91.

XVIII

THE HALDANE MISSION, 1912

A<small>T</small> the end of 1911 Germany and Great Britain were as far away as ever from a settlement of those questions which disturbed the relations between the two countries. More than two years had gone by since Albert Ballin had tried to bring about a meeting between German and British naval experts to discuss the possibility of a reduction in naval expenditure. The Chancellor, to Ballin's disappointment, had transferred the question to the 'political sphere'.[1] Within the political sphere, the dispatch of the *Panther* to Agadir, the speeches of the Emperor, and the violent outburst of anti-English feeling in the summer and autumn of 1911, had increased British distrust of Germany and made it extremely difficult for the German Chancellor to accept a compromise either on the naval or on the political side. The naval party had used the excited state of public opinion to ask for a further increase in the German naval programme. The naval party was supported by the Emperor; the 'civilians' counted for little in the old Prussian scheme of things under which the Emperor had been trained, and to which he was inclined by temperament.

Nevertheless Ballin still hoped that a meeting between German and British statesmen would result in a reasonable compromise. Ballin's hopes came to nothing. His biographer puts in a few words the reasons why he supported a compromise, and failed to move the Emperor.

'His long business relations with England, extending over many years, and his knowledge of the psychology of the English people convinced him that the English argument against the building of the German fleet was—at all events from the English point of view—right, and therefore would be upheld by England to its most extreme consequences; a nation which possessed a third

[1] See above, p. 268.

of the inhabited world, and wanted to hold what it possessed could not abandon a dominant position on the seas. Therefore a compromise in the form of an Anglo-German understanding seemed the solution. This solution was not accepted because—apart from personal questions—the idea of "compromise" was not the dominant idea in Germany; the dominant factors were an ignorance of other countries and their characteristics, and an exaggeration of German power. These two factors were typical of the two ruling powers of Germany at that time, the old Prussian mentality (Altpreussentum) and the so-called "heavy industry".[1]

[1] Huldermann, *Ballin*, pp. 202–3. Huldermann (*op. cit.*, p. 248) found no written material for the first stages of the plan. He suggests that Ballin and Cassel decided in conversation what action they would take. It would appear that in order to start the negotiations Cassel allowed the British Government to think that he was repeating an informal message sent through Ballin from the Emperor. The wording of Mr. Churchill's letter of 7 January shows that the British Ministers certainly believed that they were dealing with an invitation which could have come only from the Emperor himself. The Emperor, on the other hand, seems to have been told by Ballin that he—Ballin—was repeating a suggestion made by the British Government through Cassel. This hypothesis provides the simplest and most straightforward explanation of the fact—which astonished the British Ministers—that within a very short time the Chancellor said that the initiative had not been taken by Germany. Cassel was used by the Cabinet as an intermediary because he had brought the first message to Mr. Churchill, but on 7 February Grey told Metternich that he now wanted to exclude 'private channels of communication'; for this reason Haldane was being sent to Berlin. On 8 February the Chancellor explained to Goschen that the original suggestion had not come from the Emperor. The Emperor was surprised that the British Government had used Cassel as an intermediary when they might have used Metternich. The Chancellor denied that Ballin had acted with authority. Goschen was taken aback at the Chancellor's statement, and did not believe it. Haldane thought that the Chancellor 'was only trying to save Metternich's face'. Stumm also asked Haldane: 'Why on earth did His Majesty's Government employ Cassel?' (B.D.D. vi. 672 and 674). Metternich was told to tell Grey that the Emperor had not encouraged communications through unofficial channels (D.G.P. xxxi. 107). When Ballin and Cassel were preparing to leave Berlin on 8 February, Haldane said that he needed Cassel's advice; the Emperor then agreed that Cassel should stay in Berlin (D.G.P. xxxi. 111–12). Grey, in answer to Metternich's statement, replied that the first intimation—'an invitation, or at least a desire or suggestion' had been conveyed from the Emperor through Ballin and Cassel early in January, and therefore the same channel had been used for a reply (B.D.D. vi. 689; D.G.P. xxxi. 121–2). The Emperor annotated as 'nonsense' the statement that he had sent the message to Mr. Churchill. The Emperor wrote to

Ballin and his friend Cassel therefore revived the idea of direct conversations between English and German states-men. Ballin suggested that Mr. Winston Churchill, who had succeeded Mr. McKenna as First Lord of the Admiralty, should come to Berlin. Cassel was more closely in touch with leading political and diplomatic circles in Lon-don than Ballin was in touch with the Emperor, Chan-cellor, and Foreign Office in Berlin; he agreed with the suggestion, and wrote to Mr. Churchill. Mr. Churchill answered on 7 January 1912 that it would be inexpedient for him to make a special journey to Berlin.[1] A journey of this kind could not remain a secret. If no agreement were reached, the tension between the two countries would only be increased. Mr. Churchill also thought that nothing could be done 'till Germany dropped the naval challenge'. The Prime Minister was out of Eng-land, but Mr. Churchill consulted Grey and Mr. Lloyd George. On the Prime Minister's return it was agreed to send Cassel to Berlin with a special memorandum. Mean-while Cassel had shown Mr. Churchill's reply to Ballin, and Ballin had shown the letter to the Emperor. The Emperor sent a message assuring Mr. Churchill of a welcome, but saying that there would be additions, in the near future, to the strength of the German army and navy. This message was given to Mr. Churchill on 20 January.[2]

Cassel was received by the Emperor on 29 January. He brought with him a memorandum containing three clauses.[3] The first clause—described as 'fundamental'—consisted of two sentences. 'Naval superiority recognized as essential to Great Britain. Present German naval pro-gramme and expenditure not to be increased but if possible retarded and reduced.' The second clause dealt with the colonial question. 'England sincerely desires not to interfere with German Colonial expansion. To give

Ballin an account of his interview with Haldane, and concluded with the words 'Cassel informieren mit Grüssen' (Huldermann, *Ballin*, p. 257). In September Kiderlen had complained of alleged false and indiscreet state-ments made by Cassel about the discussions in 1909 (D.G.P. xxviii. 359).

[1] B.D.D. vi. 666.   [2] B.D.D. vi. 666–7.   [3] D.G.P. xxxi. 98.

effect to this she is prepared to discuss forthwith whatever the German aspirations in that direction may be. England will be glad to know that there is a field or special points where she can help Germany.' The third clause stated that 'proposals for reciprocal assurances debarring either Power from joining in aggressive designs or combinations directed against the other would be welcome'.

Metternich was told of the British statement; he did not think that it would meet the situation. 'Even a platonic recognition of (English) naval supremacy would scarcely find support in Germany without a real guarantee against an aggressive policy on the part of England.'[1] The Emperor was more hopeful. He believed that he had in his hands an offer of neutrality in return for naval concessions.[2] Cassel brought back with him a short memorandum and a short summary of the new German shipbuilding proposals. The German answer was friendly, but stipulated that the 1912 programme—the new supplementary law—must be included in a calculation of German naval plans. It was suggested that Grey himself should go to Berlin.[3] Cassel thought that the Germans 'did not seem to know what they wanted in regard to colonies'.[4] The naval proposals were clear enough. In Mr. Churchill's words, 'the spirit may be good but the facts are grim'.[5]

Nevertheless the British Ministers receded still farther from their original position. They had given up their insistence upon a real diminution of naval expenditure; they now accepted an increase in the German programme,

[1] D.G.P. xxxi. 100–1.
[2] William II, *Ereignisse und Gestalten*, pp. 122 ff.　　[3] D.G.P. xxxi. 98–9.
[4] Churchill, *The World Crisis, 1911–1914*, i. 96.
[5] *Ib. The Times* of 15 January 1912 had printed a note from the *Reichspost* of Vienna about the supplementary law. The *Reichspost* announced 'from an absolutely trustworthy source in Berlin' that a third active squadron would be formed to enable a fourth squadron to remain in reserve. There would be an increase of 5,000 in personnel, and a moderate increase in armed cruisers. See also *The Times*, 20 November and 21 December 1911, 19 January and 5 February 1912.

but suggested that there should be a slower rate of increase. In other words, they would accept the supplementary law, if the programme which it contained could be spread over twelve instead of six years.[1] Cassel telegraphed to Berlin that negotiations would be 'difficult, if not impossible' unless some retardation were promised, but that the British Government was ready to enter into further discussions if the question of naval expenditure were open to discussion, and if there were fair prospects of settling this question favourably.[2] The Cabinet decided that Haldane, not Grey, should go to Berlin. The Emperor, who was not present at the meeting of the British Cabinet, makes a long story about this decision.[3] It is clear, however, that the British Ministers, whose previous experiences had not made them very hopeful of success, were thinking mainly of the possible consequences of a break-down. A study of the German documents shows that Grey's pessimism was nearer the mark than the hopefulness of some of his colleagues.[4] The Emperor's own points for discussion included the maintenance of the

[1] *Ib.* i. 97.   [2] *Ib.* 98 and D.G.P. xxxi. 102–3.

[3] William II, *op. cit.*, pp. 126 ff. A serious division in the Cabinet is implied in a report sent by Metternich on 5 February (D.G.P. xxxi. 107). Mr. Churchill denies that there was any serious division. Grey was as anxious as ever for an improvement in Anglo-German relations, though more sceptical than those of his colleagues who knew less about the previous negotiations. Grey wrote to Sir G. Buchanan on 7 February. 'It is very desirable that we should also [the reference here is to the Russo-German discussions at Potsdam in December 1910] settle some of our questions, if possible, or present relations with Germany may get worse' (B.D.D. vi. 668). Haldane emphasized the political side of an agreement as strongly as any of his colleagues who were said to be in the opposition group (B.D.D. vi. 674). There is no foundation for the suggestion in D.G.P. xxxi. 101–2, note, that anxiety about Anglo-Russian relations on the Persian question contributed to English willingness to reopen the question of an agreement with Germany. It is clear from the British sources that the Cabinet wanted to make another attempt to avoid an increase in naval expenditure and to prevent the recurrence of a European crisis as dangerous as the crisis following the dispatch of the *Panther* to Agadir. See also below, p. 339.

[4] An editorial note in D.G.P. xxxi. 109 remarks that the negotiations had scarcely a chance of success, since after 4 February the Emperor, under Tirpitz's influence, had decided not to make any concession on the question of the supplementary law.

supplementary law and 'a clear treaty of alliance, or at least a neutrality treaty'.[1] The Chancellor laid down the condition that the two Powers 'would agree not to take part in any plans, combinations, or developments resulting in war [*kriegerische Verwickelungen*] directed against each other'. Otherwise Germany could not discuss the question of naval concessions.[2] The introduction of the word 'war' had been suggested by Metternich, on the ground that the term 'aggressive designs' did not give Germany enough security.[3] Bethmann-Hollweg himself told Metternich that he thought it out of the question to expect Grey to negotiate on this basis. He could not judge whether 'a Liberal Cabinet would do so after throwing overboard their Foreign Minister. At all events our attitude on the naval question has been so very conciliatory that such a result is not out of the range of possibility.'[4]

The Chancellor was calculating upon the possibility of a change in the attitude of Great Britain as a result of German concessions on the naval question. It is therefore necessary to look at the matter from the British point of view. On 10 February Goschen summarized the offer made to Haldane.

'What does it amount to? That if what has been suggested is carried out the Germans get what, under Grey's instructions, I have been opposing for two years, namely a political understanding without a naval agreement. For I cannot regard a relaxation of the *tempo* of a brand new and additional Naval Programme as a naval arrangement. We more or less rejected a relaxation of the *tempo* of the original naval law as a rather worthless concession, and now it is proposed that we should accept the relaxation of the *tempo* of a new Law, which will add a number of ships to the German Navy and bring up its personnel up [*sic*] to about 80,000 men as a *quid pro quo* for the realization of Germany's dearest wish viz. a political understanding, an agreement which however carefully drawn up as regards the "aggressive" point . . . is only too likely to hamper

[1] D.G.P. xxxi. 104.   [2] D.G.P. xxxi. 105–6.
[3] D.G.P. xxxi. 100.   [4] D.G.P. xxxi. 106.

us in the future. . . . Recent events have shown that our position, unhampered by a political understanding, is a strong one, and our price should therefore have been raised not lowered.'[1]

Haldane arrived in Berlin on 8 February;[2] he saw the Chancellor at once. He said that he had no authority to do more than talk over questions; he could not commit himself or his Government. After some general conversation in which Haldane denied that Great Britain had secret agreements with France and Russia, and explained the character of British military preparations in the summer of 1911, the Chancellor proposed a 'formula of neutrality'. Haldane pointed to the difficulties in the Chancellor's formula. Great Britain would be ready to promise not to join combinations for attack or aggression; but if he—Haldane—looked first at the 'formula of neutrality' from a German point of view, he might ask: 'Suppose Great Britain were to attack Austria or Denmark. Germany would certainly have to attack Great Britain. Similarly, if the formula was considered from the British

---

[1] Goschen to Nicolson: B.D.D. vi. 674–5.

[2] Haldane's diary of the interviews and the memorandum drawn up at the last interview with Bethmann-Hollweg are printed in B.D.D. vi. 676–84. Goschen's comments are given on pp. 672–5, and Foreign Office minutes on the diary and memorandum on pp. 684–6. The account of the first two interviews was written on the 8th and 9th (up to the end of the interview with the Emperor) within two hours of the conversations which are recorded. The account of the last conversation with the Chancellor was written on the morning of 11 February. A note in B.D.D. vi. 676 states that Part III of the Diary was written on the morning of 10 February. This date is impossible, since Part III contains an account of the conversations of the afternoon of 10 February. The mistake is due to a misinterpretation of the three conversations mentioned by Haldane in B.D.D. vi. 709. There is no continuous account in D.G.P. of the first interview between Haldane and the Chancellor though there is a later notice written in 1917. There are short notes by the Emperor recording his interview with Haldane in D.G.P. xxxi. 112–13 and Huldermann, *Ballin*, pp. 256–7. For a later account of this interview, drawn up in 1917 by Tirpitz, see D.G.P. xxxi. 221–7. Notes of the last interview with Bethmann-Hollweg appear in D.G.P. xxxi. 117–20. Haldane's long note correcting various misrepresentations is given in B.D.D. vi. 709–10 (11 March 1912), cf. *ib.* 722–4 and 746. Haldane has also written an account of his visit in *Before the War*, pp. 57–66. The Haldane mission is described, with a full bibliography, in Kraft, *Lord Haldane's Zending naar Berlin*.

point of view, suppose Germany joined in an attack upon Japan or Portugal or Belgium[1]—he [the Chancellor] then interposed "or Holland"—but I said I really hadn't all our treaties sufficiently in my head to be as sure about Holland as I was about the others. Or if Germany were to pounce upon France and proceed to dismember her . . .?' Bethmann-Hollweg said that these cases, and the hypothesis of an attack upon France, were unlikely, 'but he admitted that they were fatal to his formula'. The Chancellor said that it was difficult to leave the assurance from Great Britain in vague terms; one could not easily define 'aggression' or 'unprovoked attack'. Haldane answered: 'You could not define the number of grains which it took to make a heap, but one knew a heap when one saw one.'

The conversation turned to the naval law. Haldane said that if Germany added a third ship every second year to her programme, Great Britain would have to lay down two keels to every one of the additional German ships. The Chancellor asked whether this would really be the case. Haldane answered that the Government would be turned out unless they laid down two keels to one, even though they might be forced to add a shilling to the income tax.

Haldane suggested a 'slowing down';[2] the programme might be spread over twelve years. The Chancellor mentioned eight or nine years. Finally the colonial question

---

[1] D.G.P. xxxi. 109–10 quotes a denial by Bethmann-Hollweg that the possibility of a German attack upon Belgium was discussed. Haldane's diary reports clearly that this possibility was mentioned. See also, *Before the War*, p. 65.

[2] The proposal for 'slowing down', as suggested by Haldane, was free from the ambiguities which Metternich and Goschen had noticed in its earlier form. The proposal was not connected with the German programme already defined by law and accepted by the Reichstag; a 'slowing down' would only affect the terms of the supplementary law—as yet unpublished —and would not be counterbalanced by a subsequent increase in the rate of construction. Nevertheless it is important to notice how far the British Government had travelled from the position which they had taken up in the earlier stages of the negotiations.

was discussed. Again Haldane said that he could not make any definite proposals, or commit his colleagues; but that, 'if we agreed on the two great topics, he [the Chancellor] would find us in an excellent mood for discussion'.

On 9 February Haldane lunched with the Emperor, and had a discussion in the presence of Tirpitz. Haldane again said that he could not be bound by the conversation, and that the remarks on each side must be taken 'ad referendum'.[1] The Germans explained that the new naval law had been cut down from six extra ships beginning in 1912 to three extra ships in the same period. The German programme would be an alternation of three and two ships a year. Haldane pointed out that the ship-building question was all-important. If there were to be an increase in the German programme a political agreement would be 'bones without flesh. . . . The world would laugh at the agreement, and our people would think we had been befooled.' Haldane therefore insisted upon a modification of the new programme; otherwise an agreement could not be considered. Tirpitz would not hear of any alteration; but the Emperor was 'really disturbed'. Haldane first suggested dropping one ship; Tirpitz would not accept the idea. Haldane then proposed 'slowing down'. The first ship might be laid down in 1913, the second in 1916, the third in 1919. To this plan the Emperor and Tirpitz finally agreed. Tirpitz wanted Great Britain to give some pledge about shipbuilding. 'He thought the two-Power standard a hard one for Germany, and, indeed, Germany could not make any admission about it. I said it was not a matter for admission. Germany must be free, and we must be free,

[1] In B.D.D. vi. 710 and *Before the War*, p. 60 Haldane says that at this meeting he was given by the Emperor a copy of the new supplementary law, but refused to study it in detail. In D.G.P. xxxi. 146 and B.D.D. vi. 723 the copy appears to have been given to Haldane shortly before he left Berlin. The two versions are not incompatible. The editors of D.G.P. regard it as a 'tactical mistake' to have given Haldane the detailed information about the law. D.G.P. xxxi. 111, n.

and we should probably lay down two keels to their one. In this case the initiative was not with us but with them.' It was then suggested that nothing should be said in the agreement about shipbuilding, but that the Emperor should announce, when the agreement was made public, that the new ships could safely be 'spread over' a longer period of years.

Later in the day (9 February) Haldane again discussed the shipbuilding question with Bethmann-Hollweg. The Chancellor was 'depressed' that Haldane thought the German concession too small. On 10 February Stumm gave Haldane a hint that the Chancellor did not want the negotiations to break down through the obstinacy of Tirpitz on the naval question, and that his (Bethmann-Hollweg's) chances of getting a further concession from the Emperor would be much improved if Haldane 'took a very strong line to the effect that there must be further naval concessions'.[1] Haldane therefore took this stronger line at an afternoon interview with the Chancellor, and Bethmann-Hollweg promised to do his best with the naval experts. The Chancellor himself reported Haldane's doubt whether the Cabinet would be content merely with an additional three years' 'spread over'.[2] Haldane and Bethmann-Hollweg then drew up a general memorandum. 'We sat down at a table with pencils and paper and went on a voyage of discovery.' The 'formula' which the Chancellor proposed had been rewritten by Kiderlen and himself from a draft made by Kiderlen.[3] Kiderlen still believed that, with sufficient naval concessions, Great Britain could be persuaded to sign a political agreement promising unconditional neutrality; that is, neutrality, in

[1] Haldane was entirely convinced of Bethmann-Hollweg's sincerity. 'The attitude of the Chancellor was that of a high-minded, sincere gentleman, and left me nothing whatever to desire' (B.D.D. vi. 682. Jules Cambon, French Ambassador at Berlin, reported that Haldane spoke of Bethmann-Hollweg as 'a splendid fellow'; 'il apprécie moins M. de Kiderlen', D.D.F. 3rd Ser. ii. 16. In *Before the War*, p. 59, Haldane described Bethmann-Hollweg as 'an honest man struggling somewhat with adversity'. Relations with the Emperor were 'very agreeable' and with Tirpitz 'a little strained'.

[2] D.G.P. xxxi. 119.   [3] D.G.P. xxxi. 114-17.

case Germany were involved in war, without any reference to the question of aggression. On 22 February Kiderlen told Tirpitz that the Anglo-French entente would collapse of itself if Germany and England made an agreement.[1] The draft which the Chancellor first suggested to Haldane contained a promise of unconditional neutrality, although Haldane had already pointed out the difficulties in the way of British acceptance of any formula of neutrality. Haldane explained at once that 'there was not the least prospect that we could accept the draft formula which he had just proposed. . . . We should find ourselves . . . precluded from coming to the assistance of France should Germany attack her and aim at getting possession of such ports as Dunkirk, Calais, and Boulogne.'[2] On the other hand, the Chancellor would not accept the formula suggested by Haldane. The British formula consisted of a single clause. Neither Power 'will make or prepare to make any unprovoked attack upon the other or join in any combination or design against the other for purposes of aggression, or become a party to any plan or naval or military enterprise alone or in combination with any other Power directed to such an end.'[3] Haldane then suggested a compromise in which the term neutrality was used but safeguarded by limitation to cases in which the 'Power involved in war' was not the aggressor.

[1] Tirpitz, op. cit. i. 291. Kiderlen complained that he was kept away from the discussions (Jäckh, op. cit. ii. 155). The editors of D.G.P. think (xxxi. 114–16) that Kiderlen was referring to the negotiations with Cassel which preceded Haldane's visit. It is difficult to put this interpretation upon Kiderlen's words. Kiderlen was in Berlin during Haldane's visit. Although he worked with the Chancellor on the political formula, he took no part in the conversations. He met Haldane at dinner on 9 February; Haldane had previously called on him, but avoided any detailed political conversation because he thought the Chancellor did not wish Kiderlen to be brought into the discussions. B.D.D. vi. 681.

[2] Haldane, Before the War, p. 65. There is no mention of the political side of the conversation of 10 February in Haldane's diary, though the political proposals are enclosed as memoranda. Haldane did not enclose the Chancellor's first draft of a political agreement.

[3] This formula should be compared with the formula offered by the British Government on 14 March. See B.D.D. vi. 713–14, and, below, p. 346.

He drew up a 'sketch of a conceivable formula' in these terms:

'If either of the High Contracting Parties becomes entangled in a war in which it cannot be said to be the aggressor, the other will at least observe towards the Power so entangled a benevolent neutrality, and use its utmost endeavour for the localization of the conflict. The duty of neutrality which arises from the preceding article has no application in so far as it may not be reconcilable with existing agreements which the High Contracting Parties have already made. The making of new agreements which render it impossible for either of the High Contracting Parties to observe neutrality towards the others [*sic*; other] beyond what is provided by the preceding limitation is excluded in conformity' [with the general promise of non-aggression, i.e., the original British formula].

The Chancellor also noted that the suggested compromise did not commit either party (*selbstverständlich unverbindlich*).[1] The discussions were not binding; Germany was as free as England to report, on mature consideration, that the formula was not acceptable.

The Chancellor gave Haldane a memorandum about the Baghdad railway. There followed a discussion of possible territorial agreements. Haldane's version of the conversation differs from that of the Chancellor on one important point. Haldane wrote that 'Germany would like to have Zanzibar and Pemba'. Bethmann-Hollweg noted: 'England will hand over Zanzibar and Pemba if we meet her wishes on the question of the Baghdad railway.' Haldane later denied that he had *offered* to 'cede Zanzibar and Pemba'. He had merely stated that they were places which might very well come into a general arrangement.[2] A similar confusion arose over other

[1] D.G.P. xxxi. 118.

[2] B.D.D. vi. 709–10: 11 March 1912. Cambon wrote from London on 13 February that Grey had given him an account of Haldane's report to the Cabinet. 'M. de Bethmann-Hollweg a demandé la cession de Zanzibar et de Pemba. Les visées de l'Allemagne sur ces deux îles ne sont pas nouvelles et le Chancelier les a réclamées sans allusion à la moindre compensation, comme si l'affirmation des bonnes dispositions du Gouvernement allemand au sujet des dépenses navales et du golfe Persique valait un pareil abandon.

colonial questions. Finally Haldane noted the Chancellor's words. 'I am not here to make a bargain with you. We must look at this thing on both sides from a high point of view, and if you have any difficulties, tell me, and I will see whether I can get round them for you.'[1]

In the recriminations which took up, from the German side, a good deal of the later negotiations, the German Government insisted that Haldane was negotiating with full powers, and that all his suggestions were 'firm offers'. The Emperor wrote to Admiral Müller, after hearing an account of the colonial discussions, in almost child-like terms: 'The Chancellor showed us on the map what England will help us to obtain: i. all Angola—that is, something bigger than the whole of South-West Africa; ii. the section of Mozambique allotted to us; iii. Zanzibar, and Pemba also, if we want it; iv. the southern half of the Congo State (later) so that East Africa can be connected with South-west Africa. As payment for all this the island of Timor.'[2] Bethmann-Hollweg himself telegraphed to Metternich on 12 February that, in return for concessions in the matter of the supplementary naval law and the Baghdad railway, Haldane had offered a neutrality agreement, the alteration of the Anglo-German agreement about the Portuguese colonies to suit German interests, the cession of Zanzibar and Pemba, and participation in Persian railway schemes. Haldane had also proposed, while not binding himself, neutrality in case of aggression by a third party.[3]

Lord Haldane, peu au courant des questions africaines, n'a formulé aucune observation. Sir E. Grey a fait remarquer qu'une offre de compensation territoriale serait indispensable et que la France possédait encore à Zanzibar des droits et des privilèges qui rendraient son assentiment nécessaire.' D.D.F. 3rd Ser. ii. 25–6. Two days later Cambon telegraphed to the French Foreign Office that Nicolson had been authorized by Grey to state that the demand for the cession of Zanzibar and Pemba 'ne paraissait mériter aucune suite et que le Gouvernement britannique ne pourra faire accepter [par] l'opinion un abandon de ce genre', ib. 34.　　　　[1] B.D.D. vi. 684.

[2] Tirpitz, op. cit. i. 285–6. Müller was on the side of the naval party, and the Emperor's letter may have been an attempt to persuade him that Germany was making a good bargain in return for a minor naval concession.

[3] D.G.P. xxxi. 120.

It is difficult to understand why Bethmann-Hollweg should have gone so far in his estimate of the 'firmness' of Haldane's offer. He knew that the British Government, and Haldane himself, for that matter, had not read the details of the naval proposals. It must be remembered that neither Haldane nor Bethmann-Hollweg was familiar with the methods of diplomatic negotiation.[1] Both men were sincerely, almost feverishly, anxious to reach an agreement. Haldane's conversation about a colonial 'bargain' came at the end of a long and very exacting series of conversations and social engagements which had begun within a few hours of his arrival in Berlin. Yet Haldane said explicitly that he had not come with full powers, and that his remarks and suggestions were merely 'ad referendum'. He had refused to look at the naval proposals, and had explained that the British public would think themselves 'befooled' if the political agreement were not accompanied by far-reaching naval concessions. The Chancellor himself had reserved his freedom in the important question of the political formula.

Nearly two months later (25 March), when it was clear that no far-reaching concessions would be made by Germany on the naval side, and that Great Britain would not use the term 'neutrality' in a political agreement, the Chancellor talked freely to Goschen.[2]

'Saying that he was not talking as Chancellor to the British Ambassador, but as Bethmann-Hollweg to Goschen, he . . .

[1] This point may be illustrated by two comments of a 'technical' kind made by Nicolson on the 'sketch of a conceivable formula' drafted by Haldane and the Chancellor. The formula contained references (i) to 'benevolent neutrality' (ii) to the obligation upon each of the contracting parties 'to use its utmost endeavour for the localisation of (a) conflict' in which the other might have become 'entangled'. Nicolson pointed out (i) that the Foreign Office had 'always consistently maintained that there is no such thing as a "*benevolent* neutrality"' as it involves a contradiction in terms. If a country is neutral it is neutral and nothing else—*benevolence* towards one country is distinctly a violation of that neutrality'. (ii) the use of 'best endeavours' for localizing a war might very conceivably involve belligerent operations. B.D.D. vi. 686. See also Metternich's comments, p. 345, below, on the conduct of diplomatic negotiations by 'amateurs'.   [2] B.D.D. vi. 731-3.

quite admitted that Haldane had observed that all his remarks were *ad referendum*. Nevertheless he had given him [the Chancellor] the impression that in what he said he was speaking the mind of the King and the Cabinet. Lord Haldane's words were, he continued, "We are ready [*wir sind bereit*] to hand you over Zanzibar and Pemba". The Chancellor added that he could not forget those words, as they had caused him such intense surprise, because never in his wildest dreams had he expected such an offer. But he had certainly regarded the offer as definite. . . . Such an explicit statement could only mean that His Majesty's Government had authorized him to make the offer.'[1]

Haldane's comment on Goschen's report of this conversation was that he (Haldane) was possibly speaking in English when he mentioned Zanzibar, and that the Chancellor had misunderstood him. 'But from the rest of the conversation—even if this were so—he must have gathered that I was merely discussing possible parts of a great all-round bargain every part of which depended on the rest, and the whole on what the two governments and the Parliaments and public might say when the entire scheme was brought before them. Indeed he agreed with this view himself.'[2]

[1] The Chancellor told Goschen at this interview that he could not understand why British opinion was so much affected by the supplementary law. According to Goschen, 'he spent some time in trying to prove . . . that the "Novelle" is well *inside* the existing Fleet Law'.

[2] B.D.D. vi. 746: 10 April 1912.

XIX

LAST ATTEMPTS AT A POLITICAL AGREEMENT

In his review of Haldane's 'offers' Bethmann-Hollweg made no allowance for the effect upon British Ministers of a detailed knowledge of the supplementary law. When the terms of the law had been examined by the British Government, the question of a political formula seemed almost academic. On 14 February the Cabinet reviewed the draft proposals of the law. These proposals went far beyond the establishment of a third squadron primarily for purposes of training. There was a large increase in personnel and in the number of ships to be kept at full strength throughout the year. Full permanent crews were authorized for nearly all, instead of a quarter, of the number of torpedo-boat destroyers. An increase of fifty or sixty submarines was contemplated.[1] Even Widenmann reported in March that this increase in personnel and in the number of ships at full strength was really a more serious consideration for England than the relatively small increase in the number of capital ships.[2]

In any case, the Foreign Office thought that the German demands in the colonial field were very large, and their offers very small. On 22 February Grey and Haldane had an interview with Metternich in which Haldane was the chief speaker.[3] Haldane pointed out the significance of the naval proposals, and the difficulty of getting the British public to accept a political agreement which would mark a new and better era in Anglo-German relations at a moment when Germany was increasing the size of her fleet, and therefore compelling Great Britain to add to her own naval expenditure. He commented

---

[1] Churchill, *op. cit.* i. 102–3. The final text of the supplementary law for the addition of 72 submarines by 1920.

[2] D.G.P. xxxi. 163.   [3] B.D.D. vi. 696–7; D.G.P. xxxi. 128–30.

on the difficulty of defining neutrality. Metternich answered by a comment upon the difficulty of defining aggression; but he realized at once, and told Bethmann-Hollweg, that the naval law was the great stumbling-block.[1]

Two days later (24 February) Grey gave to Metternich a memorandum on the supplementary law, and explained that Great Britain could not regard the German concessions on the Baghdad railway as an equivalent for the cession of Zanzibar. The railway concessions would be made not by Germany but by Turkey. Recognition of British rights in the Persian Gulf would only be an acceptance of the *status quo*. The British Cabinet thought that the questions of naval expenditure and a political formula should come before colonial questions, although they would not rule out a discussion on the latter point.[2]

Metternich's dispatch put the Emperor into a bad temper.[3] Where were now the 'proposals' of Lord Haldane? The Emperor thought that Metternich ought not to have allowed any discussion of the supplementary law, since this discussion implied an interference with the German right to free self-determination, and an invasion of the sphere of the Supreme War Lord.[3] Haldane had negotiated as a representative of the whole Cabinet. The negotiations were now disavowed. Bethmann-Hollweg was scarcely less indignant.

'The whole basis of discussion is changed. England offered us through Haldane, who, though without full powers to conclude an arrangement, nevertheless spoke for the whole Cabinet, (1) a political agreement, (2) Angola, (3) support in acquiring the Belgian Congo, (4) Zanzibar and Pemba, and asked in

---

[1] D.G.P. xxxi. 131–2. There is no foundation in any British document for the assumption in D.G.P. xxxi. 131, note, that Great Britain was less inclined to an agreement with Germany owing to the improvement in Anglo-Russian relations in Persia. On the other hand, there was some fear in British diplomatic circles that the German Emperor was trying to disturb British relations with Russia and France. For a 'studied indiscretion' of the Emperor, see B.D.D. vi. 711.

[2] B.D.D. vi. 697–9; D.G.P. xxxi. 132–5.   [3] D.G.P. xxxi. 136–7.

return for (1) slowing down in the rate of building the three Dreadnoughts of the naval law, (2) Timor, (3) consideration of English wishes in the Baghdad railway question. Haldane . . . recognized the necessity of the third squadron and increase of personnel. According to his definite statement, this measure would not trouble England.'

'England now withdraws part of her offer, makes no further mention of a political agreement, criticizes the increase in personnel and submarines, although in the question of slowing down we promised to meet her, and would stand by our promise. We cannot but recognise a complete disavowal of Haldane.'[1]

The Emperor instructed Kiderlen that Metternich must refuse to discuss the naval question until England had given Germany her proposals for a political agreement —including a clause about neutrality. 'The first English verbal note [sic] spoke expressly of tempo of building, and nothing else. This formed the basis of my negotiations with Haldane. To this basis he and I remained constant.'[2]

If the Emperor and Chancellor had forgotten that Haldane had not examined the naval law, and that the summary given to Cassel before Haldane's visit did not make clear the extent of the law, the English supporters of a friendly arrangement with Germany were under no delusion. Lord Morley, who was one of the strongest supporters of an Anglo-German agreement, told Metternich on 29 February that the whole Cabinet shared Grey's view, and that the Government would be regarded as foolish if it agreed to a cession of territory, and yet had to increase the naval expenditure of the country. Ten days later Morley repeated that the Ministers would be 'idiots' to take such a line of policy.[3] Mr.

---

[1] D.G.P. xxxi. 139–40.   [2] D.G.P. xxxi. 141.

[3] D.G.P. xxxi. 142–4 and 174. Morley denied that French pressure had made Grey change his view. The editors of G.D.P. are inclined to doubt the value of Morley's denial (D.G.P. xxxi. 144–5, note; cf. ib. id. 182, note 2). On 13 February Grey gave Cambon 'a résumé of what had passed in connexion with Lord Haldane's visit'. Cambon made no important comment. Two days later Cambon gave to the Foreign Office Poincaré's

Spender, the Editor of the *Westminster Gazette*, and another supporter of Anglo-German friendship held the same view.[1] Kiderlen-Waechter was doing his best to persuade Tirpitz to make some concessions.[2] Tirpitz refused, and drew up a memorandum which was shown to the Emperor. Tirpitz was consistent in his views, and knew what he wanted. 'We ask from England a new orientation of her general policy in the sense that she should give up her existing ententes, and that we should take the place of France.'[3] The Emperor, less clear in his mind, repeated Tirpitz's words, with a difference: 'we should more or less take the place of France.'[4] Tirpitz maintained that England wanted to be secure against the German fleet, while Germany dared not give up her naval programme; this programme was the only guarantee that the change in English policy would be lasting. Hence a vicious circle, from which, according to Tirpitz, 'there could be no escape',[5] and from which, according to the Emperor, 'an escape was difficult, and upon which [*sic*] it was still more difficult to build up a satisfactory agreement.'[6] The Emperor therefore refused any further naval concession. Bethmann-Hollweg did not agree with this refusal, but at this point the British note[7] arrived, with Metternich's account of his conversation with Grey and Haldane. The Emperor asked for the publication of the new naval and military proposals. On 28 February

thanks for the communication made to them. 'The French government made no comments.' (B.D.D. vi. 692–3.) Sir F. Bertie, who thought the Haldane mission a foolish move, reported on 11 February that this mission had not created suspicion with Poincaré, though it might have alarmed others in France (B.D.D. vi. 687). On 15 March Grey showed Cambon the 'formula' proposed by Great Britain. 'M. Cambon read the words, and seemed satisfied with them.' (B.D.D. vi. 716.) The British formula was also communicated to the Russian and Japanese Governments. The Japanese Government raised the question whether the formula was consistent with the terms of the Anglo-Japanese alliance, but were satisfied with the British answer (B.D.D. vi. 721–2). See below, pp. 358–61.

[1] D.G.P. xxxi. 145.

[2] Jäckh, *op. cit.* ii. 155–8; Tirpitz, *op. cit.* i. 290–3.

[3] Tirpitz, *ib.* 299.   [4] *Id. ib.* 301.

[5] *Id. ib.* 299.   [6] *Id. ib.* 301.   [7] See above, p. 339.

the Chancellor agreed that the proposals should be published within a few days.[1]

On 1 March Haldane had another conversation with Metternich. He reminded Metternich that he (Haldane) had not examined the draft of the naval proposals, and was not competent to do so. He had not gone to Berlin with any formal proposals, but only with certain broad suggestions. Among these suggestions was an exchange of territory in which Germany would receive Zanzibar. Haldane also explained that the British Government would introduce supplementary estimates after the German naval proposals were published, and would increase the concentration of the British fleet by bringing ships from the Mediterranean to the North Sea.[2] This last announcement alarmed the Emperor so much that he ordered Metternich to tell Haldane that Germany would consider such an act a *casus belli* (*Kriegsfall*), and would answer it not merely by withdrawing all concessions about reduction of *tempo*, but also by mobilization.[3] The Emperor repeated his order to the Chancellor on 5 March and telegraphed directly to Metternich[4] that the withdrawal of British ships from the Mediterranean to the North Sea would be regarded by Germany as a threat of war, and would be answered by a stronger supplementary law, and eventual mobilization. This act of the Emperor brought a letter of resignation from the Chancellor.[5] Bethmann-Hollweg raised the constitutional point that instructions to Ambassadors could not be given directly by the Emperor, and insisted that negotiations ought to be continued, even after some delay, and that the blame for failure must be laid on England. The Emperor was now faced with a political crisis. If

[1] Tirpitz, *op. cit.* i. 308.   [2] D.G.P. xxxi. 145–8.

[3] D.G.P. xxxi. 148. Tirpitz thinks that the Emperor meant 'Threat of war'—*Kriegsdrohung*, not *Kriegsfall*. Tirpitz, *op. cit.* i. 310, note.

[4] D.G.P. xxxi. 155–6, where the Emperor used the term *Kriegsdrohung*.

[5] For the details (as far as they are known) of this constitutional crisis, see D.G.P. xxxi. 157–8, note, and references therein to Jäckh and Tirpitz, *op. cit.*

he made concessions to Tirpitz, the Chancellor would resign. If he made concessions to the Chancellor, Tirpitz would resign. The crisis lasted until 22 March. On this day the naval proposals were published, and the Emperor went to Corfu for his holiday. Meanwhile a memorandum had been sent to Great Britain (6 March). The Chancellor persuaded the Emperor to postpone the publication of the naval law until an answer had been received. The memorandum repeated the view that Haldane had made a 'firm offer'.[1] 'Although without full powers to conclude a binding arrangement, but still under authority from the whole British Cabinet', Haldane had declared that the British Government was prepared to conclude a general political agreement precluding an aggressive policy, to support the German acquisition of Angola and parts of the Congo Free State, and to cede Zanzibar and Pemba to Germany; Germany in return would 'slow down' the building of the three new ships provided by the new naval law, renounce her claims to Timor, and take account of the wishes of Great Britain in the matter of the Baghdad railway. Haldane had said nothing about the increase in personnel; Zanzibar and Pemba were offered 'unconditionally'. Germany still offered a reduction of *tempo*, if Great Britain would continue the political conversations. The German Government would make a further concession, and refrain from naming any date for the commencement of the third new ship.

The German memorandum thus repeated previous statements without taking any account of Haldane's contradictions or of the change in the British attitude after a fuller knowledge of the naval proposals. Metternich, in conversation with Grey, mentioned a number of technical points upon which the German naval authorities could not accept the British interpretation of the supplementary law; Grey said that he must refer these

---

[1] B.D.D. vi. 704–6; D.G.P. xxxi. 150–2. For the British answer to the German memorandum, see below, pp. 354–5.

questions to the Admiralty.[1] Haldane thought that the
memorandum had not been written by the Chancellor;
he said once more that he had explicitly and frequently
stated in his conversations that he had no binding authority and was communicating no offers; in any case, he
was not considering particular questions in isolation.[2]
As there was nothing new in the German statement, it
is unnecessary to repeat at length the Foreign Office
comments. There appeared to be deliberate distortion
of Haldane's words; deliberate denial that Germany had
taken the initiative, and that Haldane had gone to Berlin after an invitation to British Ministers from the Emperor himself. The bargain proposed was absurdly one-
sided. It is important to remember that the Foreign
Office believed that they had had previous examples of
the distortion of words spoken in conversation. Crowe
wrote that

'It is of course possible that Lord Haldane did not make his
meaning so clear to the German Chancellor as in his own
written record of his visit. But a reference to the several passages
(in the written record) . . . make [*sic*] this difficult to believe.
I am afraid this will prove another instance of the well-known
practice of the German Foreign Office to make profitable use
of the ambiguities which so easily glide into confidential and
unguarded conversations, in order to tie the other party down
to statements and promises and engagements never made. We
need only remember the incidents of the "Yangtse" agreement,
the occupation of Kiao-Chow, the alleged promise of Great
Britain not to seek a connexion between the Sudan and South
Africa through the Belgian Congo; the alleged assent of the
Powers to the Waldersee appointment in China; the recent
assertion that the Emperor obtained, when in London, the
formal approval of the King and H.M.'s Government to the
German occupation of Agadir etc.'

In spite of the difficulties, Grey wanted to continue the
discussions. He invited Metternich to meet Harcourt,

[1] B.D.D. vi. 707–8: 6 March 1912.
[2] B.D.D. vi. 709–10. See also above, p. 337, and below, p. 354.

the Colonial Secretary, though he was careful to say that the discussion of colonial questions was 'informal and non-committal'.[1] Metternich again spoke of Haldane's 'offers', and the British Ministers again denied that Haldane had been given powers to make definite or final offers. In his report to the Chancellor Metternich commented on the result of the conduct of negotiations by well-meaning intermediaries who were only amateurs in diplomatic business.

'In the wish to bring their mission to a conclusion generally satisfactory to all parties promises are made which cannot later be kept. Consequently misunderstandings and disappointments arise. The best intentions therefore come to nothing owing to mismanagement—a fault more common among amateurs than among professional (diplomatists). Trained negotiators do not so easily allow themselves to be deceived by their hopes, or misled by the favourable atmosphere of the moment. They know that later on their words will be weighed in the balance.'[2]

Bethmann-Hollweg could have no more doubt about the position. He made one further effort which puzzled the British Ministers. On 12 March he wrote to Metternich that the naval proposals were still being kept back in the hope that England would meet Germany on the political question. In this case, if a formula could be reached, Bethmann-Hollweg would ask the Emperor to make further concessions on the naval side.[3] Kühlmann was in Berlin at the time, and was given a new formula, not apparently for immediate transmission to Grey, but as a basis for negotiations.[4] The formula differed little from the 'sketch of a conceivable formula' drawn up at the last interview with Haldane. Metternich carried out his instructions at once. He saw Haldane late in the evening of 12 March. He said that time pressed, and that he wanted an answer as soon as possible.[5] He told

---

[1] B.D.D. vi. 708–9. [2] D.G.P. xxxi. 255–60.
[3] D.G.P. xxxi. 166–7.
[4] D.G.P. xxxi. 164–7. The German formula, which was given to Grey on 15 March is also printed in B.D.D. vi. 715. [5] B.D.D. vi. 710–11.

Haldane 'privately and informally' that, according to his information from Berlin, 'if the British Government would offer a suitable political formula the proposed Fleet Law as it stood would be withdrawn. Some Fleet Law there must be, but one of less magnitude would be introduced.' Grey was occupied with the dispute in the coal industry,[1] but Metternich's appeal was too important to be postponed. Nicolson wrote to Goschen that he would do his utmost to find a formula. Grey himself produced a draft on 13 March. He proposed to submit the draft to the Cabinet on 14 March.[2] The formula was accepted by the Cabinet, and given to Metternich on 14 March.[3] It was short, and contained the words which Grey had used again and again in the course of the discussions. 'England will make no unprovoked attack upon Germany and pursue no aggressive policy towards her. Aggression upon Germany is not the subject and forms no part of any Treaty understanding or combination to which England is now a party nor will she become a party to anything that has such an object.'[4] Metternich wrote to Grey later in the day (14 March) that he was afraid the formula would not be sufficient since it did not mention the word neutrality.[5] On 15 March he showed Grey the German formula, and suggested an addition to the British formula to the effect that 'England will therefore observe at least a benevolent neutrality should war be forced upon Germany', or, as an alternative wording, 'England will therefore as a matter of course remain neutral if a war is forced upon Germany'. Grey said that the British formula exactly expressed the situation. The French Government knew clearly that 'if France was aggressive towards Germany, or attacked Germany, no support would be forthcoming from us, or would be approved by British public opinion'.

[1] A coal strike began on 26 March and ended on 11 April 1912.
[2] B.D.D. vi. 712.
[3] B.D.D. vi. 713-14; D.G.P. xxxi. 178. See above, p. 333.
[4] There is a comma between 'Treaty' and 'understanding' in the version of the formula in D.G.P.   [5] B.D.D. vi. 714.

On the other hand, Metternich's proposed addition 'would give an impression going beyond the literal sense of the words, and might be taken to mean that under no circumstances, if there was war on the Continent, could anything be expected from us'. Metternich again spoke of the need for haste. 'He was afraid that if the Novelle were proceeded with, the negotiations would come to an end. He gave me to understand that this would be due to a change of "personnel" in Berlin.'[1] In other words, Grey was told indirectly, but plainly, that, if an agreement could not be reached at once, Bethmann-Hollweg would be forced to resign. There is no report of this conversation in the German documents; it is therefore impossible to say whether the Chancellor knew that this hint had been given to Grey. It is unlikely that the Emperor knew anything about it. For this reason a step which the British Government now took was misunderstood in Germany, and particularly by the Emperor. Grey saw Metternich again on 16 March.[2] He was ready to add a short preface to the formula which he had suggested. The draft would then read: 'The two Powers being mutually desirous of securing peace and friendship between them, England declares that she (will make no unprovoked attack &c.).'[3] Grey also proposed to

[1] B.D.D. vi. 714–15. Metternich received two telegrams on 16 March asking urgently for an answer from the British Government. There is no indication that the British Government had any information—other than the rumours current in Germany—of the political crisis caused by the Chancellor's threat of resignation. Goschen reported on 22 March that nearly all the people he had seen in Berlin 'seem to think it by no means improbable that if the Chancellor goes he will be succeeded by Tirpitz. Personally I can hardly believe this.' B.D.D. vi. 726. Herr von Roederer (a high court official) told Goschen on 28 March that 'Tirpitz had made a strong bid for the Chancellorship, but had failed'. B.D.D. vi. 733.

[2] B.D.D. 718–19; D.G.P. xxxi. 181–3.

[3] A footnote in B.D.D. vi. 718 (note 2) assumes that the 'formula' to which Grey was referring was the German formula. It is probable from the context, and from Metternich's report in D.G.P., that Grey was referring to the English formula. The German formula had been described by Metternich as 'the formula which the German Chancellor had sketched to Lord Haldane as being what he would like'. (B.D.D. vi. 715.) Metternich reported that Grey would not take this German formula as the basis of discussion; and

substitute the words 'will neither make nor join in any unprovoked attack' for the words 'will make no unprovoked
attack'. The British Government could not agree to use
the word 'neutrality', since the use of this word 'would
convey an impression that more was meant than was
said'. Grey said that the exchange of a 'formula' would
be of no use 'if a naval increase was impending, because
the naval increase would destroy the good effect produced by the formula. But, if public opinion had been
excited by the naval increase, we might afterwards consider the territorial questions, and exchange some formula
which would have a calming effect.' In other words,
the British Government was prepared to continue the
negotiations, even if they were not given concessions on
the naval question. Grey then took the hint given him
by Metternich about a change of 'personnel' in Germany.
He saw no reason why the wording of the British formula
should affect the position of the Chancellor, 'since there
was no dispute between him and Admiral von Tirpitz'
about the supplementary law. Grey spoke of the confidence which he and Lord Haldane felt in Bethmann-
Hollweg. 'As long as he [Bethmann-Hollweg] remained
German Chancellor, he might rely upon our co-operating with him to preserve the peace of Europe, each of us
not only abstaining from aggression upon the other, but
each also using what influence we had with others to
prevent war. If this was likely to be of use in personal
questions now pending in Berlin, Count Metternich
might certainly report it.' Grey went on to point out
that a formula could not be personal, and that the
British Government could not make promises which depended merely upon goodwill. 'If we were to exchange
with Germany now a formula which made relations between us and any other country more distant, we could
have no security that Herr von Bethmann-Hollweg might
not be overthrown a month or two hence: when we

that he (Metternich) had therefore tried to introduce the word 'neutrality'
into the British formula.

should be in the position of having gained nothing as regards the policy of Germany, and we should have lost something elsewhere.'

It is difficult to avoid thinking that Metternich reported this conversation a little clumsily. He could not explain that he had mentioned to Grey the possibility of Bethmann-Hollweg's resignation. He could only say that the British Ministers trusted the Chancellor. He was not content to leave well alone, but added a few sentences which did not give the real explanation of Grey's reference to the Chancellor, and were only too likely to upset the Emperor's temper. 'Grey is also strongly convinced that any difficulties arising between the two Governments would reach no unpleasant dimensions as long as German policy is directed by the Chancellor.' The German Foreign Office took care to add —before the report reached the Emperor—'directed by His Majesty on the lines advocated by the Chancellor.' Even so, the Emperor noted 'He means of course the other way round.' Metternich added another paragraph.

'He [Grey] would go further, and guarantee that British policy would be framed in accordance with the . . . agreement proposed by him as long as the Chancellor were responsible for German policy, even though the conclusion of an agreement was impossible for the moment owing to the supplementary law, since an agreement could not coincide with a large increase of armaments in each of the two countries. The effects of a neutrality agreement would however be independent of personalities. The English Government must consider what would happen if, with a change in the personnel, there were also a change in the responsible direction of German policy.'[1]

Grey had told Metternich that he might report the confidence which the British Cabinet felt in the Chancellor; he had not suggested that his other remarks might be reported in their plain and blunt form to the Emperor himself. The Emperor might have remembered some of his own letters and comments about British statesmen;

[1] D.G.P. xxxi. 182.

but William II would never allow to others the liberties which he took for himself. He annotated the suggestion that new Ministers might change the direction of German policy with a remark that German policy depended not upon the Ministers but upon himself. 'Therefore *I* am distrusted.' His general conclusion was typical of his over-sensitiveness and of his attitude towards constitutional rule. 'I have never in my life heard of the conclusion of an agreement with one particular statesman, without reference to the sovereign. . . . It is clear that Grey has no idea who really rules here, and that *I* am the master. He dictates to me in advance who is to be my minister, if I conclude an agreement with England.'[1]

On receiving Metternich's telegraphic report of the conversation the Chancellor pointed out to the Emperor that England still appeared ready to sign a political agreement, if the naval proposals were modified. If the proposals were published, the way would be closed, and 'the signal given for a race in armaments and therewith the possibility of a war between Germany and England and, as a necessary consequence, wars on land, within the present or the coming year'.[2]

The Emperor would not continue to discuss proposals which in his opinion ought to have been rejected at sight. He ordered a plain statement to be made to England that Germany offered an offensive and defensive alliance in which France might be included.[3] Bethmann-Hollweg could hardly take this plan seriously. He did not follow the Emperor's instructions. Metternich was not told to suggest this alliance to Great Britain. According to Tirpitz, the Chancellor proposed on 17 March that negotiations should be broken off. This statement is impossible to reconcile with the Chancellor's plea for further delay in the publication of the supplementary law. Tirpitz's assertion that on 18 March the Chancellor accepted the plan of an offensive and defensive alliance is equally hard to reconcile with the facts, as well as with

[1] D.G.P. xxxi. 183.   [2] D.G.P. xxxi. 185–7.   [3] D.G.P. xxxi. 187–8.

Bethmann-Hollweg's common sense. The Chancellor's instructions to Metternich on 18 March contain no mention of the proposal. On the other hand, the Emperor seems to have believed that action was being taken to propose a triple alliance on the lines he had suggested. As late as 8 May he telegraphed on his return from Corfu: 'I expect to receive in Karlsruhe a report from Kiderlen about the draft of the proposal for an alliance which I have ordered to be drawn up.'[1] The Emperor wrote a letter (in English) to King George V on 18 March, as an appeal from sovereign to sovereign. The letter went over the history of the Haldane mission from the German point of view, and included a protest against the suggestion that 'the agreement could only be made with His Exc. the Chancellor H. v. Bethmann as long as he remained in office and provided I followed the policy dictated by him. . . . Your Minister labours under an illusion [sic]. The Chancellor as well as the Foreign Office are both purely officials of the Emperor. It is the Emperor, who gives them the directions as to [sic] which policy is to be pursued and they have to obey and follow his will.' The Emperor suggested 'an offensive and defensive alliance with France as a partner and open to other powers to enter ad libitum'. It is uncertain whether this draft was ever shown to the Chancellor, and, if it were shown, whether the Chancellor pointed merely to the effect which such an alliance would have on German relations with Austria.[2] In any case the Chancellor took his own precautions. On 26 March Metternich told Grey not to pay any attention to suggestions from 'a very high quarter' in Germany that 'something in the nature of (the British) alliance with Japan' would be required in return for any naval concessions. Grey was asked to take

[1] D.G.P. xxxi. 188. When Grey suggested (19 March) that negotiations might be resumed after public excitement about the naval law had died down, the Emperor annotated Metternich's report: 'But not about the agreement; on another basis, alliance.' D.G.P. xxxi. 193.

[2] Tirpitz, op. cit. i. 331–2. There is no mention of this draft in D.G.P.

no notice of any expression of opinion which did not come to him through Metternich himself.[1]

The Chancellor's instructions to Metternich show, however, that Bethmann-Hollweg was losing his nerve.[2] He raised his demands. Grey was to be told that the English formula was useless. The Chancellor added, with some rudeness, that 'the formula left room for the idea that an unprovoked attack by England was an eventuality with which Germany might hitherto have had to reckon.' The assurances necessary for Germany, if she were to give up her means of defence against the fleets of the Triple Entente, must go beyond the suggestions made by Great Britain. Grey's reference to the possibility of a change in the direction of German policy was answered by a reference to the possibility of a change in the policy of England after Germany had surrendered the security which the naval law would give her.

'Apart from this consideration' (and the fact that Germany would be bound by an agreement), 'the person of His Majesty the Emperor is a guarantee that German policy will not leave the peaceful path which it has never abandoned under the direction of His Majesty. . . . I must ask you to leave no doubt . . . in Sir E. Grey's mind that I must be absolutely certain of an agreement guaranteeing the neutrality of England and approximating to a defensive alliance with us before I can advise His Majesty to surrender important sections of the . . . supplementary naval law.'[3]

It is curious that, on the same day, Kiderlen telegraphed to Metternich to discover what concessions on

[1] B.D.D. vi. 728–9.

[2] D.G.P. xxxi. 188–9.

[3] The fact that the Chancellor referred in such definite terms to the direction of policy by the Emperor, and spoke of an agreement 'approximating to a defensive alliance', as well as the discourteous remark about the 'eventuality with which Germany might hitherto have had to reckon' give the impression that this dispatch was written under the influence of the Emperor, and may have been a compromise between the more violent and unpractical letter which the Emperor had drafted to H.M. the King, and the letter which the Chancellor himself would have written to Metternich.

the naval question would satisfy Great Britain.[1] There is no record in the German documents of any answer from Metternich to this question. An answer was unnecessary. Metternich realized that the Chancellor's latest move would mean the end of the negotiations. He did not point out that Bethmann-Hollweg was raising his terms, but suggested that it might be wiser to let the matter rest for a time; the discussions could be resumed, as Grey had suggested, some months later.[2] From a note by Kiderlen it would appear that he was told to carry out the instructions already sent to him.[3] Metternich saw Grey on 19 March, and fulfilled his instructions to the letter.[4] He used the Chancellor's own words, and added that Mr. Churchill's speech introducing the naval estimates would not have a 'soothing effect'.[5] Grey pointed out that the Chancellor had increased his demands. 'What (he) now asked amounted to an agreement of absolute neutrality, which was more than conditional neutrality. Count Metternich said that the Chancellor had not used the word "absolute", but in effect his wish amounted to that.' Grey still doubted the 'exact extent' of the Chancellor's meaning. Metternich confirmed the interpretation that 'failing a guarantee of absolute neutrality, the *Novelle* must proceed'. Grey promised to consult his colleagues, though he thought that 'if the Chancellor meant to infer that, failing a guarantee of absolute neutrality, the relations between the two Powers could not be cordial or satisfactory . . . such an idea would be unreasonable'.

Three days later (22 March) Grey had another interview with Metternich.[6] Metternich had received instructions from the Chancellor to say that 'an agreement about

---

[1] D.G.P. xxxi. 189–90. There is no note in D.G.P. to explain why, at the time when the Chancellor was sending instructions which could only close the discussion, Kiderlen should have asked what concessions on the naval question would be satisfactory.   [2] D.G.P. xxxi. 190–1.

[3] D.G.P. xxxi. 191.   [4] B.D.D. vi. 719–21; D.G.P. xxxi. 191–2.

[5] For Mr. Churchill's speech, see below, pp. 368–70.

[6] B.D.D. 724–5; D.G.P. xxxi. 203. Cf. *ib.* 200–1.

neutrality of a far-reaching character' was not 'merely a one-sided present from England, but would be no less valuable to England than to Germany'. Grey did not argue this point; Metternich himself knew that, in the general European situation, Germany would not be asked to join in an unprovoked attack against England. Grey was still uncertain whether the Chancellor was asking for 'absolute' or 'conditional' neutrality. Metternich again confirmed the view that, 'though the word "absolute" neutrality was not used it represented in effect the sort of neutrality for which the Chancellor was asking'.

The German naval proposals were published on 22 March, and the Emperor left on this day for Vienna, Venice, and Corfu. The die was cast.

The negotiations did not end at once. A memorandum in answer to the German statement of 6 March[1] was presented by Goschen to the Chancellor on 25 March.[2] The answer, which was drafted by Haldane,[3] contained a full and clear statement of the British point of view about the informal and 'non-binding' character of the conversations between Haldane and the 'high personages' whom he met in Berlin. Haldane had no technical knowledge of naval questions; he did not mention the details of the supplementary law because he had not read the law. He disclaimed any suggestion of putting pressure upon Belgium or Portugal to part with their colonies. He had made no offer to cede Zanzibar and Pemba. These places were mentioned as 'suitable assets for consideration in a general settlement'. Finally, Haldane had pointed out the difficulties in the way of accepting a formula of unconditional neutrality.

The Emperor's annotations were as violent as ever. The English plan had been based on the hope of persuad-

---

[1] See above, pp. 343–4.

[2] B.D.D. vi. 722–3; D.G.P. xxxi. 205–8. The Emperor's marginalia and long final comment follow the memorandum in D.G.P.

[3] Haldane made use of a draft prepared by Nicolson.

.ing Germany to give up the naval law, in return for an African empire made up of other people's territories. The Emperor had saved the German people, and the English had 'bitten on granite. . . . I hope that my diplomatists will learn from this experience the lesson that henceforward they should pay more attention to their Rulers and to the orders and wishes of these Rulers, particularly in questions concerning England. They don't understand how to deal with England, and I understand quite well.'

The Emperor was not in Berlin, and the Chancellor seems to have been influenced by Kiderlen and by the friendly tone of the British answer.[1] On 21 March he had asked Metternich to allow Kühlmann, who had just come back from Berlin, to talk to the British Ministers.[2] Metternich answered that he must keep the control of the negotiations in his own hands, and that he had already forbidden Kühlmann to see Haldane. He added that 'Sir E. Grey is most anxious to reach an understanding with us; in this respect he is more friendly now to Germany than many of his colleagues. He needs no stimulation from these colleagues, and would be displeased if any attempt were made by (Kühlmann) to influence them.' The Chancellor replied: 'I am unable to conceal the fact that the result of the negotiations up to the present time, and the facts reported by you, cannot be reconciled with that strong desire for an understanding which you find in Sir E. Grey.'[3]

On 25 March, however, the Chancellor sent a message to say how much he appreciated the friendly tone of the British answer.[4] Kiderlen telegraphed on the same day to point out that the formula given to Kühlmann[5] was based upon the proposal drawn up by Haldane in Berlin and did not go beyond this formula in respect to neutrality. The Haldane proposal was a compromise between

---

[1] For the Chancellor's remarks to Goschen on 25 March about Haldane's 'offers', see above, pp. 336–7.

[2] D.G.P. xxxi. 201.   [3] D.G.P. xxxi. 201–2.

[4] B.D.D. vi. 727. There is no reference to this message in D.G.P.

[5] See above, p. 345.

the first German formula[1] asking for absolute neutrality and the formula which Haldane brought with him. Metternich was asked to explain the facts to Grey.[2] In other words, the demand for absolute neutrality was given up—after the publication of the naval law, and therefore too late. The British Government had made it clear that a political formula would be useless if there were no modification in the naval proposals.

Metternich now telegraphed for further instructions. 'I have asked here for absolute neutrality. I could put no other interpretation upon "an agreement securing the neutrality of England, and approximating to a defensive alliance with us". I will go at once, before the Cabinet comes to a decision, and explain that our formula does not go beyond the compromise suggested by Haldane and that it provides only for relative (i.e. conditional) neutrality. This brings the chance of an understanding once more within the range of possibility.'[3] On 27 March Kiderlen answered Metternich's inquiry about a form of words which would satisfy Germany.[4] 'The importance lies not in the form of words but in the content of the English assurances. We must be certain that we shall not be attacked by England directly, or in a war forced upon us by a third Power. Clear expression must be given to this assurance.'

Metternich had seen Grey on 26 March and explained that, though the neutrality required by Germany would 'have to be of a very far-reaching character', the Chancellor still held to the formula given to Great Britain on 15 March.[5] Three days later (29 March) Metternich again spoke to Grey about the formula. Grey answered that the British formula could not be changed or extended without risk of ambiguity or misconstruction. The German formula contained ambiguities, and went beyond any agreement made by Great Britain with any European

[1] See above, pp. 332–4.　　　　[2] D.G.P. xxxi. 203–4.
[3] D.G.P. xxxi. 204.　　　　[4] D.G.P. xxxi. 205.
[5] B.D.D. vi. 728–9. For the formula of 15 March, see *id. ib.* 715.

Power, with the exception of the long-standing treaty of alliance with Portugal. Thereupon Grey and Metternich went over the ground again, without coming any nearer to an agreement. Finally Grey hoped that the failure to reach a naval understanding would not lead to a complete break-down in the negotiations. There might be an examination of colonial and territorial questions, and after some interval, a political agreement on the lines of the English formula might be reconsidered. Grey spoke of the improvement in Anglo-French and Anglo-Russian relations which had followed a settlement of practical questions, although neither settlement had included a political agreement as far-reaching as the formula proposed to Germany. Metternich said that Germany could not regard the British formula as likely to bring the favourable results to which Grey looked forward.[1]

The Chancellor and Metternich regarded this interview, for the time at least, as the end of the discussion about a political agreement. On 3 April Bethmann-Hollweg told Metternich that 'the refusal of the English Government to offer us a satisfactory agreement about neutrality means that we can no longer hope to meet English wishes by modifying our supplementary naval law'. On the other hand, Germany was ready to continue the discussions about colonial and territorial questions. The Chancellor suggested a single agreement which would include the Portuguese colonies, minor colonial questions, the cession of Zanzibar and Pemba, the Baghdad railway and southern Persia.[2] The Chancellor's instructions were carried out by Metternich on 10 April.[3] Bethmann-Hollweg's last word was that

---

[1] B.D.D. vi. 730; D.G.P. xxxi. 210–13. Kühlmann, who wanted a colonial agreement, told Mr. Tyrrell on 3 April 1912, that, in his opinion, the British formula 'did in substance insure the neutrality of (Great Britain) for all legitimate purposes. He said that he quite understood our reluctance to use the word "neutrality" in such a formula, as it might cause legitimate apprehensions in the minds of other Powers with whom we wished to remain on friendly terms.' (B.D.D. vi. 740.)

[2] D.G.P. xxxi. 264–7.   [3] B.D.D. vi. 746; D.G.P. xxxi. 267–70.

Germany, in offering to limit her naval expenditure, was making an unprecedented concession.[1]

The interview of 29 March had not appeared as decisive to Grey as it had seemed to Metternich. Grey had told Metternich that the British Government 'did not see, and would like to have explained . . . what it was that Germany wished to have beyond what was covered by the words we had suggested'.[2] After 29 March the Cabinet was considering the formula. As late as 10 April, the Prime Minister wrote to Grey that he was 'becoming more and more doubtful as to the wisdom of prolonging these discussions with Germany about a formula. Nothing, I believe, will meet her purpose which falls short of a promise on our part of neutrality: a promise we cannot give. And she makes no firm or solid offer, even in exchange for that.'[3] The Chancellor's final refusal was therefore received with a certain relief.

The relief was based on the fact that the negotiations had been opened by the British Government four or five years earlier, for a settlement of the race in naval armaments between England and Germany. This competition in shipbuilding had become more serious. With every international crisis and every increase in the German naval programme, British fear of German intentions also increased. The negotiations had drifted from the concrete subject of naval expenditure to the vaguer and more indefinable political sphere. The discussions had now reached a point at which the Powers of the Entente might well take alarm. Step by step Great Britain had surrendered conditions which she had regarded as essential. France and Russia knew the general history and trend of the negotiations. The French and Russian Governments feared that the 'drop by drop' methods[4] of the German Foreign Office might succeed, and that

---

[1] D.G.P. xxxi. 213, note.   [2] B.D.D. vi. 730.

[3] B.D.D. vi. 745. Each party was thus left with the belief that the discussion had been brought to an end by the other party.

[4] See above, p. 276.

Great Britain might sign a 'neutrality' agreement with Germany. In this case Germany would be free to attack France. This attack would not take the form of direct aggression; but France might easily be driven into a position in which she might appear, technically, as an aggressor.[1] It would be difficult to convince British public opinion of the true interpretation of the facts in time for British help to be of any use. There was no general defensive alliance between France and England; England was entirely free to judge whether French action was directly or indirectly aggressive. On the other hand, the French Government had seen the efforts made by Germany to break up the Entente. Direct action and 'shock tactics' had failed. There was a chance that more delicate methods might succeed. Until the last days of March the French Government had merely watched events. They began to show their anxiety when they knew that the British Cabinet was considering the question of a promise of neutrality.

On 22 March Grey told Cambon that Great Britain had refused this promise. Cambon's comment to Poincaré was short: 'ainsi s'évanouissent les espérances ou les craintes que des esprits peu avertis avaient fondées sur la visite de Lord Haldane à Berlin.'[2] The closing of the discussion from the German side set French fears at rest for the time, but an irregular step taken by the British Ambassador in Paris reopened the question.[3] Sir F. Bertie

[1] The French Government might well remember the manœuvres of Bismarck in 1870.

[2] D.D.F. 3rd Ser. ii. 247. See also above, p. 334.

[3] D.D.F. 3rd Ser. ii. 262–5, 276. Poincaré repeated Bertie's warning to the Russian Ambassador at St. Petersburg. *Id. ib.* 328–9. See also Poincaré, *Au service de la France*, i. 170–2. In March [no precise date is given] 1912, probably in connexion with the Anglo-German conversations, Poincaré asked Joffre, as Chief of the General Staff, to draw up a report 'résumant les ententes établies entre les États-majors français et anglais et indiquant sous quelle forme ces ententes ont été traduites en vue d'une exécution prévue'. Joffre's report mentioned the stipulation that 'les pourparlers engagés sont "dépourvus de tout caractère officiel et ne peuvent lier en rien les Gouvernements anglais et français" '. D.D.F. 3rd Ser. ii. 267–71. Cambon had been a little disturbed at the effect upon French opinion of any strong campaign

went to see Poincaré on 27 March in great disturbance of mind, and asked him to speak firmly to Grey on the dangers of a declaration of neutrality. The matter was settled before the French stated their case;[1] but it is important to notice two facts. In the first place, the British Government refused—before any pressure was put upon them by France—to promise even conditional neutrality. In the second place, Grey and the Prime Minister thought the French 'unduly nervous'.[2] Grey pointed out to his own Foreign Office that 'Russia and France both deal separately with Germany and . . . it is not reasonable that tension should be permanently greater between England and Germany than between Germany and France and Germany or Russia'.[3] On 13 May 1912 Grey wrote to Goschen that Jules Cambon (the French Ambassador in Berlin), who had spoken to Goschen of his anxiety about Anglo-German discussions, 'ought to bear in mind that the French have more than once negotiated with the Germans. . . . Russia has done the same on occasion. We cannot keep Germany at arm's length. . . . So long as France is informed of anything of importance that takes place, and we do nothing with Germany that is really of detriment to France, the French must not complain'.[4]

Cambon suggested to Nicolson on 15 April that France would welcome a statement from England upon the British attitude in the event of a Franco-German war. Nicolson answered that

'he doubted extremely if His Majesty's Government would be

in England in favour of an agreement with Germany; but he did not think that a new attempt would be more successful than previous efforts in the same direction. English opinion was determined by the facts of German rivalry and would only be modified by a change in the facts. 'Depuis 1906 plusieurs campagnes germanophiles ont été entreprises. . . . Elles semblèrent tout d'abord porter quelques fruits, mais elles échouèrent toujours à la suite d'incidents qui dévoilèrent brutalement le caractère de la politique allemande.' D.D.F. 3rd Ser. i. 632. See also below, p. 363, n. 1.

[1] B.D.D. vi. 729–45 *passim*; and D.D.F. 3rd Ser. ii. 267.
[2] B.D.D. vi. 745.
[3] B.D.D. vi. 739.   [4] B.D.D. vi. 753.

at all disposed to tie their hands in any way as to the line of
action they would adopt in any possible contingencies. They
would . . . desire to preserve complete liberty of action. . . . If
at this moment France were to come forward with proposals so
to reshape our understanding as to give it more or less the
character of an alliance, I felt pretty sure that neither the
Government as a whole nor large sections of British public
opinion would be disposed to welcome such proposals, which
would be regarded by many as offering umbrage and a
challenge to Germany. It would be far wiser to leave matters
as they were.'[1]

Grey approved of Nicolson's language.[2]

How far was the course of these negotiations known to
the public? What effect, if any, did their failure have
upon public opinion? The fact of Haldane's visit could
not be kept secret. As early as 9 February—while Haldane was in Berlin—*The Times* doubted the expediency
of his mission, and feared that its effect would not be to
relieve the strain. On 10 February *The Times* published
a note from its Berlin correspondent that Haldane was
'engaged in an authoritative though unofficial discussion
of Anglo-German relations in order, as far as possible to
understand the true nature of the German, and to explain
the true nature of the British policy'. The question of the
competition in armaments would be included in the discussion, although 'political circles in Germany think
there is now no suggestion of a limitation of armaments
by agreement'. The German press thought that Haldane
would make some 'African offers'. The Berlin correspondent of *The Times* also pointed out that the difference of
opinion between the Emperor and the Chancellor was
no longer a secret. The *Frankfurter Zeitung* protested
against the agitation of the Navy League, and declared
that Tirpitz had deliberately fostered excitement on the
Moroccan question in order to carry through a naval
increase beyond the terms of the Navy Law. The Foreign
Office Press Bureau gave practically no information to

---

[1] B.D.D. vi. 747–9.   [2] *Id. ib.* 749.

the German Press, and the first official statement about the visit came from the British side.

The debate on the Address was begun in the House of Commons on 14 February 1912.[1] Mr. Bonar Law spoke of Haldane's 'mysterious mission' to Berlin and doubted the value of 'amateur diplomacy'. The Prime Minister answered in general terms.

'Lord Haldane was going sooner or later to Germany on business connected with the London University Commission, and in the circumstances we thought it well, and I doubt whether anybody would say we were ill-advised, that he should hasten his visit and take advantage of it to engage in friendly and confidential communications with those who are responsible for the control and guidance of German policy. This involved, I agree, upon both sides a departure from conventional methods, but upon both sides it was felt that frankness of statement and communication would be easier in the first instance if it was a question of informal and non-committal conversations rather than what I might call full-dress diplomatic negotiations. These anticipations have been completely realized. There was perfect freedom of statement and frankness of explanation over a wide area of discussion'. The Prime Minister hoped for good results 'without . . . in any way sacrificing or impairing the special relationships to which each of us stands to other Powers'.

A day later the German Chancellor read a statement to the Reichstag. He explained that Haldane discussed 'without authorization to enter into binding agreements, but nevertheless at the instance (*im Auftrag*) of the British Cabinet, the points at which the interests of the two countries come into contact, with the object of establishing a basis for relations of greater confidence'. Only the chauvinist papers in Germany disapproved of the statement; elsewhere there was a fairly uniform desire for the improvement of relations.

Lack of information about the discussions, and the publication of the new German shipbuilding programme soon diverted public interest from the subject of Haldane's

[1] Hansard, 5th Ser. xxxiv. 21–3 and 31–3. For the discussion in the House of Lords, see *ib*. xi. 21–3 and 39–41.

mission.¹ Questions were asked in the House of Commons on 30 April, and 1 and 21 May 1912, but no detailed answers were given.² During the parliamentary recess Haldane went for a short holiday to Germany. The fact was noticed, and a question asked in the House. Grey answered that Haldane 'had had no conversation, correspondence, or communication with any political personage'.³ The subject of the February visit was again raised in July 1912, during the discussion of the Foreign Office

¹ On 22 April the *Daily News* published an article stating that Germany had offered important naval concessions in return for certain concessions—not known to the *Daily News*—on the British side. The *Daily News* thought the British refusal was due to pressure from France. Cambon believed that the German Foreign Office was trying to obtain attacks on Grey's policy in the British press. D.D.F. 3rd Ser. ii. 378–9. He had explained to Poincaré on 7 February that German influence upon the British press was a factor of considerable importance. 'C'est surtout dans la presse que la campagne pro-germanique trouve son appui et elle est secondée par l'action des agents officiels et officieux de l'Empire. Ces agents ne sauraient guère exercer d'action sur les propriétaires des grands journaux, personnages considérables par l'influence et la fortune, mais ils peuvent agir et ils agissent sur les rédacteurs, plus sensibles à leurs arguments de toute nature et dont beaucoup sont d'origine allemande.' D.D.F. 3rd Ser. i. 632. Cambon thought German (and, by implication, anti-French) sympathies were to be found among the high aristocracy ('des aristocrates endurcis auxquels l'Allemagne apparaît comme le type de la Monarchie'; *id.* 631) and among socialists. He believed that Radical and Labour opinion was not in favour of an entente with Germany rather than an entente with France. 'Ils sont simplement hostiles à toute politique étrangère active et à cet impérialisme qui distingue au contraire leurs adversaires unionistes. Leurs prédécesseurs ou eux-mêmes prônaient, il y a quinze ans, un rapprochement avec la France pour les mêmes raisons qui les amènent aujourd'hui à désirer une entente avec l'Allemagne; ce qu'ils veulent, c'est réduire les dépenses militaires et navales, et éviter toute chance de conflit avec les États étrangers.' Cambon thought that the Germans were better placed than the French for turning British opinion to their advantage. 'Ils disposent dans le Royaume-Uni de moyens d'action dont nous manquons, grâce au nombre et à la richesse de leurs compatriotes naturalisés anglais et restés attachés à leurs pays d'origine; nous devons donc suivre de près une campagne dont le but avoué est de remplacer l'Entente cordiale par une Entente anglo-germanique.' (D.D.F. 3rd Ser. i. 192: 24 November 1911.)

² Hansard, 5th Ser. xxxvii. 1679 and 1855; xxxviii. 1726–7.

³ Hansard, 5th Ser. xxxix. 8. Grey's answer ended with the words: 'It was, in fact, a real holiday, free from any taint of politics, though I am credibly informed that he went with a friend who by the cut of his beard was identified in Germany as being either the Prime Minister or myself.'

vote. The Prime Minister made a general statement on
25 July. 'Our relations with the great German Empire
are . . . relations of amity and goodwill. . . . Lord Haldane . . . paid a visit to Berlin early in the year. He
entered upon conversations and an interchange of views
which have been continued since in a spirit of perfect
frankness and friendship both on one side or [*sic*] the
other.'[1] Finally, the break-down of the political negotiations increased the Emperor's dissatisfaction with Metternich. Bethmann-Hollweg agreed to Metternich's recall.[2]
There was a good deal of plain speaking on the subject
in the German Press. The *Frankfurter Zeitung* on 14 May
said that Metternich was being dismissed because 'the
views which he has expressed in his reports for a long
time past and up to the last concerning the political
effect of German naval armaments upon the relations
between the two countries have not won the approval of
very influential persons and of the quarter which ultimately decides'. A week later (19 May) the *Frankfurter
Zeitung* was even more direct in its language. Metternich
had insisted upon the danger of any further increase in
the German navy.

'The dispatches of the naval attaché may have had quite a
different tenor. . . . The authentic saying "You go on hitting
Wolff-Metternich just as the peasant hits the barometer which
points to a level which he does not like" is now many years old,
and dates from the Bülow era. Several people have been
hitting this barometer because it did not change, and because
they fancied it wrong. So it has been taken away. Will the
weather change now?'

[1] Hansard, 5th Ser. xli. 1393.
[2] The naval attaché had written to Tirpitz on 9 March 1912: 'If only
Metternich were gone from here. He is a national misfortune for us.'
D.G.P. xxxi. 233 n. For the recall of Metternich see D.G.P. xxxi. 231–6.
Grey spoke of his regret at Metternich's departure in the House of Commons
on 14 May 1912. On 6 June Metternich was entertained by the Lord
Mayor at the Guildhall, and on 10 June by Grey at the Foreign Office.
For Grey's view of Metternich, see *Twenty-Five Years*, i. 245. A leading
article in *The Times* of 15 June 1912, described the value of the information
which Metternich had sent to his Government.

The *Münchener Neueste Nachrichten* also commented upon Metternich's 'involuntary retirement as due, in part, to his emphasis on the obstacles which the naval policy of Germany had put in the way of an Anglo-German agreement'. Baron Marschall von Bieberstein was appointed in Metternich's place.[1] The appointment led to considerable excitement in the German Press, though the news was more coolly received in England. The British Government had indeed some reasons for believing that Marschall's removal from Constantinople was partly due to the resentment felt by Italy at his policy during the Italo-Turkish war.[2] Marschall himself made no secret of his wish to establish better relations between Great Britain and Germany. He had criticized the policy of Bülow, frankly and openly, to his French colleague at Constantinople. He was disappointed that he was not chosen to succeed Bülow. After Kiderlen's Moroccan failure Marschall would have accepted the Foreign Secretaryship; but Kiderlen was not dismissed. There remained the London Embassy.[3] Marschall was no more convinced than at The Hague Conference that Great Britain and Germany could come to an agreement on the subject of armaments. He thought that such an agreement would lead to dangerous suspicions and recriminations. He described the correspondence dealing with Anglo-German relations and the attempts at an understanding as 'fatras et logomachie'; he was sarcastic over the number of people—soldiers, civil servants, diplomatists, industrial magnates, politicians, and the Emperor himself—whose interference had confused the issue.[4]

Marschall was too clever to commit himself to any definite line of policy immediately after his arrival in London. He went out a great deal in society, and talked mainly about Turkey and the young Turks. From

---

[1] On 11 February 1912 the French chargé d'affaires at Constantinople had reported rumours of Marschall's appointment to the London Embassy. D.D.F. 3rd Ser. ii. 18.　　　　[2] B.D.D. vi. 755.

[3] D.D.F. 3rd Ser. iii. 2–4: 12 May 1912.

[4] D.D.F. 3rd Ser. iii. 23–5: 19 May 1912.

this point of view he did not greatly impress people with his abilities. Mr. Balfour found him commonplace.

On his second meeting with Grey Marschall 'headed rather in the direction of the exchange of some formula'.[1] He also spoke to the Prime Minister and Haldane on the subject. The conversation with Grey had no result. 'We expressed the opinion that to keep frankly in touch with Germany about each question as it arose was a more sure way of avoiding difficulties than the exchange of any formulae.' Marschall again referred to the matter on 4 July.[2] The discussion was again short and non-committal. Marschall died in August 1912.

Marschall was succeeded by Lichnowsky. Lichnowsky's diplomatic career had not been brilliant; he had held no post of any kind for eight years before his appointment to the German Embassy in London; but in July 1912 he had published an article defending the naval policy of the German Government. The article attracted the Emperor's attention; Lichnowsky was evidently a man who could be trusted not to repeat the mistakes of Metternich. Yet within a few months this new Ambassador was convinced that Great Britain had no aggressive intentions, and that Germany had no reason to fear either a direct attack by Great Britain or British support of France or Russia unless these countries were victims of German aggression.

[1] B.D.D. vi. 758–9.   [2] B.D.D. vi. 759–60.

XX

MR. CHURCHILL AND A 'NAVAL HOLIDAY'.

I. 1912

THE rumours of a further increase in the German building programme, the announcement of this increase,
and the evident failure of the Haldane mission, once
more brought the problem of naval competition before
public opinion in England. From the British point of
view the facts were as follows. On 1 March 1912 Great
Britain still held a superiority of 13 per cent. in battleships
and armoured cruisers over the combined fleets of Germany and the United States. This superiority had
diminished by a quarter since 1909, and was given mainly
by the older and pre-Dreadnought ships. The British
margin of superiority in completed Dreadnoughts was
only 4 per cent. In March 1915—the date to be considered in relation to the shipbuilding programme of
1912–13—Germany would have added to her fleet twelve
more Dreadnoughts which were actually under construction, and two, or more, ships, which would be laid down
in 1912–13. Five old German battleships and two old
cruisers would be struck off the list. The United States
would add eight and lose six ships. Great Britain would
therefore need to lay down seven large ships if she were
to secure a 10 per cent., four large ships to secure a
5 per cent. superiority.[1] *The Times* expected that the
British estimates would provide for four Dreadnoughts if
there were no increase in the German programme. If
Germany laid down more than two ships the Admiralty
would build two ships for every additional German ship.[2]
A problem not wholly unlike the problem of acceleration
in 1908–9, though on a much smaller scale, had already
arisen in the case of torpedo-boat destroyers. A report

[1] *The Times*, 1 March 1912. [2] *The Times*, 9 March 1912.

appeared in the German Press in November 1911 that the Schichau works at Elbing had begun to build twelve destroyers of a type similar to those built for the German navy. It was stated that the firm was not building these ships in anticipation of the 1912–13 programme, but had laid them down for a foreign purchaser—Turkey or China. Questions were asked on the subject in the House of Commons on 28 February and 4 March 1912.[1] Mr. Churchill explained that Germany was not anticipating her programme, but that the British Admiralty had taken the precautionary step of asking for tenders for twenty destroyers so that work could be commenced upon them as soon as the expenditure had been sanctioned by Parliament.

The British naval estimates for 1912–13 were published on 12 March 1912. The statement accompanying the figures began with the words: 'These estimates have been framed on the assumption that the existing programmes of other naval Powers will not be increased. In the event of such increases, it will be necessary to present supplementary estimates, both for men and money.' The estimates provided for four large armoured ships, eight light armoured cruisers, twenty destroyers, and an unspecified number of submarines.

Mr. Churchill introduced the estimates in the House of Commons on 18 March.[2] His speech covered a great deal of ground, and included a new proposal for relieving the strain of competition in shipbuilding. Mr. Churchill's speeches were more vivid, more detailed, and more direct than those of his predecessor. He explained that the Admiralty was not 'prepared to recommend at the present time the two-keels-to-one standard against Germany. The time may come when that will be necessary, but it is not necessary now.' The two-Power standard, which had been adopted at a time when France and Russia represented 'the most probable adverse diplomatic combina-

---

[1] Hansard, 5th Ser. xxxiv. 1340–1, and xxxv. 35.
[2] For the debate, see Hansard, 5th Ser. xxxv. 1549–1654.

tion', was no longer a suitable rule of measurement. The standard became unreal and theoretical with the inclusion of the navy of the United States. The actual standard taken by the Admiralty was a superiority of 60 per cent. in vessels of the Dreadnought class over the German navy. For the smaller vessels a higher standard of superiority was necessary. This superiority of 60 per cent. in Dreadnoughts was, however, adequate only during the lifetime of the most recent of the pre-Dreadnought ships. 'Every addition which Germany makes, or may make, to the new ships she lays down each year must accelerate the decline in the relative fighting value of our pre-Dreadnoughts, and, therefore, requires special measures on our part.' If there were no increase in the German programme of two ships a year for the next six years, an alternating programme of four and three ships for six years would give Great Britain slightly over 60 per cent. superiority. If Germany added two more ships to her programme for the next six years, Great Britain would meet this addition by laying down four additional ships during the same period. If Germany added three ships, Great Britain would add six.

'Let me make clear, however, that any retardation or reduction in German construction will, within certain limits, be promptly followed here . . . by large and fully proportioned reductions. For instance, if Germany elected to drop out any one, or even any two, of these annual quotas . . . we will at once, in the absence of any dangerous development elsewhere not now foreseen, blot out our corresponding quota, and the slowing down by Germany will be accompanied naturally on our larger scale by us. Of course both Great Britain and Germany have to consider, among other things, the building of other Powers. . . . Take as an instance of this proposition which I am putting forward for general consideration, the year 1913. In that year . . . Germany will build three capital ships, and it will be necessary for us to build five in consequence. Supposing we were both to take a holiday for that year. . . . The three ships that she (Germany) did not build would therefore automatically wipe out no fewer than five British potential super-"Dreadnoughts", and that is more than I expect them to hope to do in a brilliant naval action.'[1]

Mr. Churchill also outlined a new organization of the fleet. The ships available for home defence would be divided into three fleets. The first fleet would include a flagship and four battle squadrons of fully commissioned ships. Two of these squadrons would be composed of ships already in home waters; the Atlantic fleet, hitherto based on Gibraltar, would be brought to home ports as a third squadron. The battleships now stationed at Malta would be moved to Gibraltar and form a fourth squadron. The second fleet would be composed of two squadrons of vessels with half their ratings on board, and half in the schools and barracks on shore. The third fleet, which would also consist of two squadrons, would be manned with nucleus crews. When the reorganization had been completed the first and second fleets together would include forty-nine battleships. It was expected that the German fleet would then include twenty-nine battleships ready, without mobilization, for war.

Further details about the reorganization of the British fleet were published in the beginning of May. The first three battle squadrons, each of eight ships, of the first fleet would be composed of Dreadnoughts, Lord Nelsons, and King Edwards. The Lord Nelsons would be replaced by Dreadnoughts at present under construction. Until these ships were ready the fourth squadron would only have four ships. As soon as this squadron reached full

[1] On 9 February Mr. Churchill had made an important speech at Glasgow on the naval question. He said that Great Britain would welcome any 'retardation or slackening of naval rivalry'. If this retardation were not possible, 'we shall not only have to increase the number of ships we build, but the ratio which our naval strength will have to bear to other great naval Powers, so that our margin of strength will become larger, and not smaller, as the strain grows greater. Thus we shall make it clear that other naval Powers, instead of overtaking us by additional efforts, will only be more outdistanced in consequence of the measures which we ourselves shall take.' The speech was badly received in Germany because Mr. Churchill had described the German fleet as 'something in the nature of a luxury'. *The Times* thought that the term was not well chosen.

strength Great Britain would have in home waters thirty-three battleships in full commission, and eight with nucleus crews; each fleet would have its attendant cruisers and other vessels.

Before the British naval estimates were finally voted the new German programme had been brought before the Reichstag. In 1920 the German navy would include a home fleet composed of a flagship, five squadrons each of eight ships, twelve large and thirty small cruisers, and a foreign service fleet composed of eight large and ten small cruisers. A flagship, three squadrons of Dreadnought battleships, eight large and eighteen small cruisers would form the active fleet. Two squadrons of pre-Dreadnought battleships and four large and twelve small cruisers would make up the reserve. All the ships of the active fleet and one-quarter of the ships of the reserve fleet would be kept in full commission. On balance this reorganization meant an increase of three battleships, three large cruisers, and three small cruisers in full commission. The three battleships and two of the small cruisers represented new construction not foreshadowed in the law of 1900 or its amendments. One battleship would be laid down in 1913, and a second in 1916. No date was given for the laying down of the third battleship. These proposals meant an additional expenditure of £10,250,000 between 1912 and 1917.[1]

The proposals were introduced to the Reichstag in comparatively short speeches. The Chancellor dissociated himself from the chauvinists and said that he saw no immediate danger of war, but insisted that German armed strength was the measure of 'the weight of (Ger-

[1] In 1920, when the new formations were complete, the German fleet would comprise 41 battleships, 20 armoured and 40 unarmoured cruisers, 144 destroyers, and 72 submarines. Twenty-four battleships and 11 cruisers would belong to the Dreadnought type. Four of the cruisers of the foreign service fleet would form a flying squadron, available for service at home or abroad. The total personnel of the fleet would be 101,500, and the annual cost of maintenance £23,000,000. In 1898 the personnel was 25,000 and the annual cost of maintenance £6,000,000.

man) opinion in international questions which affected
Germany, and of the respect which others paid to their
interests'. Herr Bassermann thought that Germany had
perhaps carried her peace policy too far in the hope of
coming to a lasting agreement with France and establishing good relations with England. In spite of some
disquiet about the financial question, the bill was passed
without much opposition. A special meeting of the
German Navy League, which had now a membership of
over one million, condemned the new proposals as inadequate. A few weeks later the League drew up its demands.
The demands were large. Five or seven additional cruisers
were wanted before 1917.[1]

The increase in the naval estimates was accompanied
by an increase in the army estimates of Germany. Mr.
Churchill's suggestion of a naval holiday was coldly
received by the German Press. The Emperor sent a
message through Cassel that an arrangement of this kind
was possible only between allies.[2] His first comments
upon the British naval estimates were that the German
programme was based upon German needs, 'and it does
not matter what counter measures England takes. England will not go to war about it, as people here have
feared for months past.'[3] Metternich's views were ignored.
He was 'hopelessly incurable',[4] and the Emperor was
waiting eagerly for his recall.

The Chancellor made the best of a situation from which
he had tried to escape. He went out of his way to give
the impression that there was no disagreement in the
highest quarters about German policy. After the passing
of the supplementary law he walked up to Tirpitz in the
Reichstag and shook him warmly by the hand. From one
point of view this gesture was reassuring. If Bethmann-
Hollweg agreed with Tirpitz, Tirpitz also agreed with

---

[1] The circulation of *Die Flotte*, the journal of the League, had risen to
350,000. Its value as an advertising medium was realized by German
business men. The weekly communiqués of the League were sent to a large
number of newspapers.   [2] Churchill, *The World Crisis*, i. 109.
[3] D.G.P. xxxi. 166.   [4] D.G.P. xxxi. 194.

Bethmann-Hollweg; but the Admiral was a stronger man than the Chancellor, and knew what he wanted. On the other hand Bethmann-Hollweg attempted to reassure foreign opinion. In the autumn of 1912 he gave Lord Granville a curious justification of the German navy.

'He quite understood that England disliked the change in the situation that had been brought about in the last thirty years. Germany had gradually grown up to be a great Power in every sense, especially commercially, and we naturally did not like her competition. But we must learn to realize that the change had taken place. A really great Power with a seaboard could not be a "Landratte"; she *must* have a fleet and a strong fleet. Her fleet was not in the least directed against us, but it was an absolute necessity for a Great Power. I said that the argument was always used in Germany that she required her fleet merely to protect her commerce and not as a threat against us, but in that case, what was the object of a mass of Dreadnoughts congregated at home.'

Bethmann-Hollweg might have answered that the naval experts agreed that a battle fleet in home waters was the best protection of German commerce. He did not use this simple and obvious argument. He said that 'Germany required her fleet not merely for the purpose of defending her commerce, but for the general purpose of her greatness. A man would be considered a fool who merely developed his legs and left his arms alone because he was a postman or something of the sort and only required the use of his legs. In exactly the same way Germany must develop her fleet as well as her army.'[1] Grey had used, at the end of July 1912, similar language about the development of German sea-power.[2] Grey was arguing in the House of Commons against the view that British foreign policy was responsible for this hostile development. He pointed out that the Germans themselves had given the reason for the 'big naval policy'

---

[1] B.D.D. ix. 2. 36–9: 18 October 1912. Lord Granville was First Secretary, and sometimes chargé d'affaires at the British Embassy in Berlin.

[2] Hansard, 5th Ser. xli. 1496–7: 25 July 1912.

begun as early as 1897. He quoted the preamble to the Navy Law of 1900, and added there was 'one very possible and obvious cause' for the building of the German fleet. 'A great and growing nation generates power not necessarily for aggression, and with no special design, but because it wishes to be powerful.' The intention of Grey's speech was good; Bethmann-Hollweg also wanted to relieve public anxiety in Great Britain. But Englishmen might well ask what use Germany intended to make of her power, and of a fleet intended 'for the general purpose of her greatness'.

This question was raised by Balfour in an article written for German readers.[1] Mr. Balfour began by repudiating any idea of a 'preventive' war, or a war of aggression against Germany. On the other hand, the average Englishman was disturbed by certain features which he observed in German policy. The German naval proposals, and the results of these proposals were a particular cause of anxiety.

'If Englishmen were sure that a German fleet was only going to be used for defensive purposes—i.e. against aggression—they would not care how large it was; for a war of aggression against Germany is to them unthinkable. . . . Putting on one side all considerations based on public morality, it must be remembered

[1] Mr. Balfour's article appeared in a symposium on the naval question published in the June and July (1912) numbers of the journal *Nord und Süd*. The other articles in the symposium contained a good deal of empty politeness on each side. One writer, Admiral von Ahlefeld, a strong supporter of Tirpitz's policy, was plain-spoken. He thought that the strained relations between the two countries was due to the fact that 'England refuses us equality (*Gleichberechtigung*) at sea, and only allows it to us on land or in the sphere of *Kultur* or the like. . . . The importance of this fact is reinforced by history: England has defeated at sea the Hansa, the Netherlands, Portugal, Spain, and France, and annexed their maritime commerce. Now she stands faced with a repetition of these proceedings, and, in comprehensible dislike of the dangers of a war, holds fast to the unnatural alliance with France . . . and by soft and flattering speeches tries to divert us from our attempt to win recognition at sea (*Seegeltung*). But we will not allow ourselves to be lulled to sleep. We want equality with England on the open sea. Only when this is granted, can there be a "détente between entente and alliance".' *Nord und Süd*, July 1912, pp. 46–7.

in the first place, that we are a commercial nation; and war, whatever its issue, is ruinous to commerce and to the credit on which commerce depends. It must be remembered, in the second place, that we are a political nation; and an unprovoked war would shatter in a day the most powerful Government and the most united party. . . . In the third place we are an insular nation, wholly dependent on seaborne supplies, possessing no considerable army either for home defence or foreign service, and compelled, therefore to play for very unequal stakes should Germany be our opponent in the hazardous game of war.'

British opinion was especially concerned with this last consideration. Germany could starve or invade England. England could neither starve nor invade Germany.

'Without a superior fleet Britain would no longer count as a Power. Without any fleet at all Germany would remain the greatest Power in Europe. The mere instinct of self-preservation therefore made it necessary for Englishmen "to weigh the motives" of those Powers who were building navies. Germany was the most important of these Powers. The external facts of the situation appear as follows:—The greatest military Power and the second greatest naval Power in the world is adding both to her Army and to her Navy. She is increasing the strategic railways which lead to the frontier States—not merely to frontier States which themselves possess large armies, but to small States which can have no desire but to remain neutral in the unfortunate case of war between their powerful neighbours. She is in like manner modifying her naval arrangements so as to make her naval strength instantly effective. It is conceivable that all this may be only to render herself impregnable against attack, though for this purpose her efforts might seem "to outside observers" excessive. Unfortunately no mere analysis of the German preparations for war will shew for what purpose they are designed.'

Few Englishmen believed that the German nation or the German Government wished to attack England.

'The danger lies elsewhere. It lies in the coexistence of that marvellous instrument of warfare, the German Army and Navy, with the assiduous, I had almost said the organised, advocacy of a policy which it seems impossible to reconcile with the peace of the world or the rights of nations. For those who accept this policy German development means German territorial expansion. All countries which hinder, though it be only in self-defence, the realization of this ideal are regarded as hostile; and war, or the threat of war, is deemed the natural and fitting method by which the ideal itself is to be accomplished.'

It was not the business of Englishmen to criticize such theories.

'Let German zealots, if they will, redraw the map of Europe in harmony with what they conceive to be the present distribution of the Germanic race; let them regard the German Empire of the twentieth century as heir-at-law to all territories included in the Holy Roman Empire of the twelfth century; let them assume that Germany should be endowed at the cost of other nations with overseas dominions proportionate to her greatness in Europe. But do not let them ask Englishmen to approve. We have had too bitter experience of the ills which follow from the endeavour of any single State to dominate Europe.'[1]

[1] General Bernhardi's *Germany and the Next War* was published in the spring of 1912. Bernhardi was one of the most influential writers on military subjects in Germany. He maintained that a war was inevitable if Germany were to fulfil her destiny, that this war would mean a change in the balance of power in Europe to the advantage of Germany, and that the main task of Germany would be the defeat of the British navy at sea, since Great Britain stood in the way of German expansion. In 1913 Bernhardi published an article on 'Ireland, England, and Germany', in which he pointed out that in an Anglo-German war Germany would have allies in the enemy's camp, and that in view of the difficulties of Great Britain in Egypt, India, South Africa, and elsewhere, Germany need not follow a 'policy of renunciation'.

THE MEDITERRANEAN AND QUESTIONS
OF IMPERIAL DEFENCE, 1912–13

M R. CHURCHILL had already said that any increase in
the German fleet would be answered by an increased
British programme. He announced on 15 May that supplementary estimates would be necessary. The naval
position in the North Sea was not the only cause of
anxiety. The proposals for the regrouping of the fleet
had aroused a certain disquiet about the strength of
British squadrons in the Mediterranean. *The Times*, in
a leading article of 30 May on the entente with France,
mentioned the 'loose talk' of the abandonment of the
Mediterranean by the British fleet. The new distribution
of the fleet took account of the Mediterranean. A cruiser
squadron would remain at Malta, and the battle fleet at
Gibraltar would serve two purposes. There was, however,
a good deal of public discussion of the importance of the
Mediterranean as a main route for the food supplies of
Great Britain. Before the debate on the supplementary
estimates the Prime Minister, Mr. Churchill, the Lords of
the Admiralty, Lord Kitchener, and Sir Ian Hamilton,
paid a visit of inspection to the Mediterranean stations.
The Mediterranean question was raised on the Foreign
Office vote on 10 July. The debate was in general terms,
and of incidental interest because Grey explained once
more his view that the 'separate groups (the triple alliance
and the triple entente) need not necessarily be in opposing diplomatic camps'.[1] Grey pointed out that the

[1] Hansard, 5th Ser. xl. 1933–2040. There was a debate in the House of
Lords on the naval position in the Mediterranean on 2 July 1912. See Hansard, 5th Ser. H. of L. xii. 298–335. On 27 June Cambon wrote an interesting report on the subject. D.D.F. 3rd Ser. iii. 176–81. Cambon thought that
the British public would have been less alarmed if the Italo-Turkish war had
not aroused interest in the question of the Eastern Mediterranean. The French
Ambassador at Rome believed that the withdrawal of British ships would
have a serious effect upon the prestige of Great Britain in Italy and Turkey.
D.D.F. 3rd Ser. iii. 278–80: 20 July 1912. There was also a certain anxiety

relation between foreign policy and naval strength was not uniform.

'You must keep up a sufficient margin of naval strength in home waters whatever your foreign policy is. If you do not, your foreign policy will become impossible, because in every diplomatic situation that arises, if you are inferior in strength in home waters to a neighbouring fleet or fleets, in every diplomatic question you will have to give way, and your position will not be that of a great Power. . . . When you get further afield into other parts of the world it is a very different matter; then foreign policy and naval strategy do and must depend upon each other to a large extent. . . . If we did anything like abandoning the Mediterranean you could not make our position there a secure one by any skilful diplomacy or foreign policy. On the other hand, it certainly is not necessary that we should keep a force in the Mediterranean which is to be able at all moments to hold its own against all the other fleets which may be there. . . . Therefore I admit that we want to keep a sufficient force available for use in the Mediterranean at any moment to count as one of the Mediterranean Naval Powers.'

Mr. Churchill announced on 22 July[1] that, as a result of the German supplementary law, during the next five years Great Britain would lay down not 3, 4, 3, 4, 3, but 5, 4, 4, 4, 4 capital ships. The construction of light cruisers would be accelerated, and there would be an annual increase in the personnel of the fleet. The cruiser squadron in the Mediterranean would be strengthened by the addition of four Invincibles to take the place of the ships withdrawn from Malta. The British ships available for the Mediterranean, 'in conjunction with the Navy of France . . . would . . . make a combined force superior to all possible combinations, and these vessels can be spared from our force at home because of our great strength and preponderance in powerful armoured

in Great Britain about the condition of the French fleet. The German Emperor put the case in his usual manner: 'The French have no powder, the British no army ready to hand.' (D.G.P. xxxi. 503: 30 May 1912.)

[1] For the debate, see Hansard, 5th Ser. xli. 835–946 and 1198–308.

cruisers over the next strongest naval Power'. This combination would be sufficient to meet the needs of the next two years.

'The time has not yet come to provide for the latter part of the financial year 1915–1916. It is not unlikely that the Mediterranean squadron will require to be reinforced towards the end of that year. I am bound to add, however, the information which has reached the Admiralty seems to indicate that one of the Mediterranean Powers . . . is contemplating another considerable naval programme. . . . It will be sufficient for me to say, if that information should prove to be correct, it would constitute a new fact requiring prompt attention, and not included in any of the forecasts I have given of future naval construction.'

Austria-Hungary was the 'Power contemplating another considerable naval programme'. The past history of Austrian construction showed that it was impossible to consider only official statements. In the spring of 1910, owing to the internal situation in Austria-Hungary, the Government could not obtain legal assent to the building of Dreadnoughts proposed in 1909; but in 1909 the Stabilimento Tecnico of Trieste had already begun to construct two Dreadnoughts on its own responsibility. In this 'childish game of hide-and-seek', as it was described by the Viennese *Neue Freie Presse*, the private firm actually worked on official plans drafted in part by Government constructors. It was admitted in November 1909 that these Dreadnoughts were not being built·for 'free sale', and that two other ships would be laid down in 1911.[1] The fact therefore that there was no increase in the Austro-Hungarian estimates for 1913 was not a guarantee that there would be no attempt to repeat the process of building 'private Dreadnoughts'. The control of the Stabilimento Tecnico, the Skoda works, and the Wittkowitz armour works was largely in the hands of the

[1] The third and fourth ships were laid down in January 1912. The first credits for the two ships laid down by the Stabilimento Tecnico were not voted until March 1911.

Austrian Rothschilds. There would be little difficulty in raising the necessary funds in anticipation of a government purchase. The Austrian authorities had announced a programme of three more Dreadnoughts in the spring of 1912,[1] but the official plans of construction were not submitted for approval until September 1912. The programme was then postponed for financial reasons. A further postponement took place in January 1913, but one ship at least was laid down early in 1913 by the Stabilimento Technico.

It was therefore impossible to forecast the needs of the future. From the point of view of France and Great Britain the balance of naval power was likely to become more favourable, whatever the action of Austria, if the Russian naval plans were put into effect. In June 1912 the long controversy whether Russia should build a battle fleet or be content with torpedo attack was settled in favour of battleships. A five years' programme was voted by the Duma. The cost of the programme would be £50,000,000. The coal capacity of the new battleships would enable them to take part in actions outside the Baltic, while a new naval base was to be constructed at Reval.

Finally the 'strategy of position', as *The Times* described the dominant phase of the naval rivalry of the Powers in European waters was affected by the announcement, in September 1912, that the French Government intended to concentrate the greater part of the navy of France in the Mediterranean.[2] Six pre-Dreadnought battleships were transferred from Brest. These ships would have been of little use against the Dreadnoughts of Germany, but were a match for the pre-Dreadnought battleships of Austria or Italy. The new French Dreadnoughts would also be stationed in the Mediterranean. This action of

[1] On the completion of this programme in 1916 the Austro-Hungarian navy would consist of three super-Dreadnoughts, four Dreadnoughts, and a second line of older ships. The Italian Government had also decided to complete six Dreadnoughts by the spring of 1915.

[2] *The Times*, 11 and 16 September 1912. The plan was known to the British Government in July.

France is one of the clearest examples of the effect of the intense naval competition upon the general political situation. It was followed at once by rumours that the Triple Entente would be transformed into an alliance.[1] The rumour was denied, but the new facts that the French were leaving their northern and western ports without adequate naval defence, and that Great Britain was welcoming the reinforcement of the French fleet in the Mediterranean, would have seemed to Bismarck a calamity of extreme magnitude from the point of view of German policy. The significance of the facts was realized by the British and French Governments. Informal conversations between the French naval attaché and the First Sea Lord and Mr. Churchill had already begun, but Mr. Churchill had expressly raised the question of British freedom of action.[2] He wrote to the Prime Minister.

'The point I am anxious to safeguard is our freedom of choice if the occasion arises, and consequent power to influence French policy beforehand. That freedom will be sensibly impaired if the French can say that they have denuded their Atlantic seaboard, and concentrated in the Mediterranean on the faith of naval arrangements made with us. This will not be true. If we did not exist, the French could not make better dispositions than at present. They are not strong enough to face Germany alone, still less to maintain themselves in two theatres. They therefore rightly concentrate their Navy in the Mediterranean where it can be safe and superior and can assure their African communications. Neither is it true that we are relying on France to maintain our position in the Mediterranean. . . . If

[1] The question had been discussed in the French and British press during the spring and summer of 1912. *The Times* and the Liberal press in England thought a change unnecessary. For the German view of the discussion, see D.G.P. xxxi. c. 248.

[2] D.D.F. 3rd Ser. iii. 270-2. On 24 July 1912 the French naval attaché in London was given a draft of a proposed convention. The preamble contained the words: 'The following agreement relates solely to a contingency in which Great Britain and France were to be allies in a war, and does not affect the political freedom of either Government as to embarking on such a war.' This preamble was not accepted by the French Government. The formula finally chosen was suggested by Cambon. For the discussions see D.D.F. 3rd Ser. iii. 506-11, 523-5, 530, 543-7, and iv. 11-13, 318-22, 535-8, 559-60.

France did not exist, we should make no other disposition of our forces. Circumstances might arise which in my judgment would make it desirable and right for us to come to the aid of France with all our force by land and sea. But we ask nothing in return. If we were attacked by Germany, we should not make it a charge of bad faith against the French that they have left us to fight it out alone; and nothing in naval and military arrangements ought to have the effect of exposing us to such a charge if, when the time comes, we decide to stand out. . . . This is my view, and I am sure I am in line with you on the principle. . . . Consider how tremendous would be the weapon which France would possess to compel our intervention if she could say, "On the advice of and by arrangement with your Naval authorities we have left our Northern coasts defenceless. We cannot possibly come back in time".'[1]

For these reasons the British Government would not go beyond an exchange of letters. The exchange took place on 22–23 November 1912. The letters mentioned the naval and military conversations, and stated that, if either Government had grave reason to expect an unprovoked attack by a third Power or something that threatened the general peace, it should immediately discuss with the other, whether both Governments should act together to prevent aggression and to preserve peace, and if so, what measures they would be prepared to take in common. If these measures involved action, the plans of the General Staffs would at once be taken into consideration, and the Governments would then decide what effect should be given to them. The freedom of action of either Government was reasserted.

'We have agreed that consultation between experts is not, and ought not to be regarded as, an engagement that commits either Government to action in a contingency that has not arisen and may never arise. The disposition, for instance, of the French and British fleets respectively at the present moment is not based upon an engagement to co-operate in war.'[2]

---

[1] Churchill, *The World Crisis*, i. 112–13.

[2] D.D.F. 3rd Ser. iv. 536–8. See also Grey, *Twenty-Five Years*, vol. i, 96–8 and Asquith, *Genesis of the War*, 82–3. Important documents on the Mediterranean question will be published in *British Documents*, vol. x.

In spite of these precautions, which were clearly recognized on the French side, the new disposition of forces made it unlikely that Great Britain would allow Germany to attack the northern and western French ports or French commerce in the Channel. Moreover, although the German war plans against France did not rely on the navy (it was hoped that the army would bring victory in six weeks), it was not easy to suppose that interference with the freedom of the German navy in a Franco-German war would not bring Great Britain into the war on land and sea. Kühlmann was in charge of the German Embassy in London during September 1912. He thought, or at all events wrote, that the redistribution of the British and French fleets was only a technical measure. 'England can say with a clear conscience that any idea of a joint Anglo-French attempt to injure Germany is nonsense. Germany has built a large fleet, has been within her rights in so doing, and is now building a still larger fleet. This fact imposes certain tasks on England which she desires to fulfil without in any way coming into conflict with Germany.' The Emperor commented on this dispatch: 'Kühlmann should know better than serve up the soft soap of the old Metternich period.'[1] Civilians never realized the dangers which were clear to experts.[2] In one sense the Emperor was right.

The German supplementary law of 1912, the concentration of the British fleet in home waters, and the failure of the attempts to reach an agreement with Germany on the shipbuilding question had effects outside Europe. The British Government had looked forward to a period of comparative calm in the competition in naval armaments; they were faced with a renewed effort by Germany to expand her fleet. The British reply would add to the burden of taxpayers in the home country, and Ministers wanted the facts to be made clear to the Dominions in order that the common burden of defence might be shared.

[1] D.G.P. xxxi. 547 [the German term is 'olle Kamellen'].
[2] Tirpitz, *op. cit.* i. 367 n.

The military strength of Germany on the European mainland hardly touched opinion beyond the European seas. The growth of the German navy directly affected the Dominions. It was impossible to deny the need for concentrating the British fleet in home waters. Yet this concentration left the growing mercantile marine of the Dominions without adequate defence.

A second reason, wholly unconnected with Germany, brought the question of Imperial defence into the foreground during the year 1912. The Panama Canal would probably be open to shipping in the autumn of 1913. The effect of the canal upon the direction of trade was extremely important. Before the opening of the Suez Canal Liverpool was nearly 500 miles nearer by sea than New York to Asiatic, Eastern African, and Australasian ports. The Suez Canal had increased the advantages of Liverpool to 1,444 miles for Asiatic and 1,142 miles for Australasian ports. The opening of the Panama Canal would not much affect traffic to Far Eastern ports south of Shanghai, but would shorten very considerably the voyage from eastern American ports to Japan and Australasia. Yokohama would be 1,805 miles nearer by sea to New York than to Liverpool, Sydney nearer by 2,382 miles, Wellington (N.Z.) nearer by 2,759 miles.[1] This change in the trade routes would be of immense advantage to the iron and steel exporting industries of the United States, and would bring the eastern American factories closer to the raw silk of Asia. The effect upon foreign, and particularly British, shipping would be even more serious if the United States persisted in the plan of exempting American coastwise shipping from the canal tolls. If this plan were carried through, the Canadian railways would lose a great deal of traffic. From the naval point of view the opening of the canal would raise,

[1] If the dues were fixed at $1 a ton, a 12,000 ton British liner would pay about £5,000 on a round voyage to New Zealand, and save nine days' steaming on the double journey. On the other hand, more coal and less cargo would be carried than on the Suez Canal route, since there were no coaling stations between Panama and New Zealand.

or rather increase, the importance of the problem of sea power in the Pacific. This problem was of special interest to Australia and New Zealand. American opinion held that the canal zone could be defended only by sea. A large increase in the American navy was necessary.

The question of the Dominions and sea power was not new. The Spanish-American and Russo-Japanese wars had affected Colonial opinion, and the visit of a strong American squadron to Australian ports after the Russo-Japanese war had caused much excitement in Australia; but the first stage of the problem of defence had been considered thirty years earlier, in relation to the navy of Russia. At the time when Anglo-Russian relations were strained, there was some danger of raids upon Australasian commerce by Russian ships from the Far East. The Australian press suggested that if Great Britain increased the number of ships in Australian waters, the colonists might help towards the cost of upkeep. In 1878 the Australian colonies decided to fortify their principal ports. A year later Lord Beaconsfield appointed a Commission to inquire into the whole problem. The Commission sat for three years, and issued a report in three volumes.[1] In 1881 an Intercolonial Conference was held at Sydney. The result was not satisfactory from the point of view of the Home Government. The colonists asked for increased naval protection, and at the same time claimed that the navy should be maintained entirely by Great Britain. In 1887 Sir George Tryon, the Commander-in-Chief in Australian waters, renewed a suggestion which had been made but not accepted in 1885 that the Colonies should hire a small force to supplement the squadron provided by the Admiralty. The Colonies now agreed to the plan. Great Britain built and equipped five third-class cruisers and two torpedo gunboats, and the colonial Governments paid a sum of £91,000 a year for their upkeep

---

[1] The report was not made public but a short abridgement was laid before the Colonial Conference of 1887. See Hardinge, *Life of the fourth Earl of Carnarvon*, iii. 38–41.

and a contribution of £350,000, spread over ten years, towards the cost of the ships. The scheme was officially accepted at the first Colonial Conference in London in 1887, and carried out under the Imperial Defence Act of 1889. The arrangement was made for a period of ten years, but there was no great change in the Australian contribution at the second Colonial Conference of 1897. In 1901 the Commonwealth of Australia took over the naval forces of the different states, and a year later, at the third Colonial Conference of 1902, the Australian contribution was increased to £200,000 a year, a contribution of £40,000 a year was added from New Zealand, and more ships attached to the squadron. In 1906 a scheme for a locally owned Australian squadron was rejected by the Committee of Imperial Defence.

Meanwhile, at the Conference of 1897 Cape Colony had offered to pay for a first-class battleship, and Natal to provide 12,000 tons of coal a year. The offer from Cape Colony was changed to an annual contribution of £30,000 a year towards the cost of the Imperial navy. The contribution was raised in 1902 to £46,000 a year, and an annual payment of £35,000 substituted for the gift of coal from Natal. At the Conference of 1902 the Canadian Government proposed to create its own naval force, and, two years later, the cruiser *Canada* was acquired as a training ship for the Canadian naval militia. In 1905 Canada offered to take over the Imperial dockyards of Halifax and Esquimault.

The fourth Colonial Conference met in 1907. The German fleet was now an important factor in British naval policy, and the Dominions wanted to create fleets of their own. In spite of the recommendations of the Committee of Imperial Defence in 1906, Australia decided to form her own navy. Canada took over the two dockyards. New Zealand raised her subsidy, after the Conference, to £100,000 a year. Cape Colony and Natal also continued their annual payments, but asked for a training ship as the first stage in providing for their own local needs. After the crisis of 1909 Australia offered one and New Zealand one, and if necessary, two Dreadnoughts to the Imperial navy.[1] A special Imperial Conference on Defence was held in London later in 1909, and the members, including the Prime Ministers of New Zealand, Newfoundland, and Natal, and Ministers of Defence and Marine from other Dominions, were invited on 19 August to attend a special session of the Committee of Imperial Defence. An agreement was reached on several important questions. The Far Eastern squadron was to be remodelled as a Pacific fleet with three units. These units, each of which would include one battle-cruiser, would be stationed respectively in the East Indian, Australian, and China Seas. Australia, with help for a time from the Imperial Government, would pay for her own unit, and would also maintain a dockyard at Sydney. New Zealand would contribute towards the China Seas unit, some of the vessels of which would patrol New Zealand waters. Canada proposed to begin the formation of local fleets in Pacific and Atlantic waters. The South African colonies were unable to take any new steps until the Union of South Africa had been completed.

In 1910 two battle-cruisers were laid down in Great Britain on behalf of Australia and New Zealand, instead of the battleships which had been offered in 1909. Contracts for two Australian protected cruisers were placed in October 1910; two Australian destroyers were launched, and a third taken out in sections for completion in Australia. Canada bought the cruisers *Niobe* and *Rainbow* for training ships, and borrowed a number of British naval officers. Sir Wilfrid Laurier's Government announced a programme of five cruisers and six destroyers. No decision was taken on the question whether the ships should be built in Canada or in Great Britain.[2]

The question of 'local' navies built, owned, and main-

[1] The Australian suggestion was changed to an offer to provide a ship in local waters.

[2] The cost of building in Canada was estimated at 22 per cent. higher than the cost in Great Britain.

tained by the self-governing Dominions introduced the whole problem of the relations between the Dominions and Great Britain. If Great Britain were at war, what would happen to the 'local' fleets? Was it possible for one of the Dominions to remain neutral? If these fleets were to be of any use in a naval war with one of the Great Powers, they must be kept in close contact in peace time with the Imperial navy. Moreover, a divided command would be impossible in war. Behind the question of control lay the wider question of the relation between the foreign policy of the Dominions and the foreign policy of Great Britain. Separate fleets might lead to separate policies, unless care were taken to secure unity of aim.

At first sight these problems did not make for unity.[1]

[1] Complaints about 'colonial apathy' on naval questions, and about the smallness of colonial contributions to the cost of Imperial defence may be read in the parliamentary debates. One instance may be given from the year 1903, i.e. after the Boer War, and before the Anglo-French agreement or the more spectacular growth of the German navy. Mr. Arnold-Foster, in a speech on the naval estimates, pointed out that 'there was a real danger that this persistent apathy . . . on the part of the Colonies was likely to have one serious result. Whatever might be the view of the Colonies, there was the danger of reaction in this country, and the growth of the feeling that it was impossible to bear this burden very much longer. He was sure that they all agreed that the idea of pressing the Colonies beyond their own desire to contribute to the naval and military establishments of this country was one which no sane person could entertain. It was a matter on which we had no power at all; and it was as certain as anything could be that if, in the future, we were to receive more generous contributions at the hands of the Colonies, it would be entirely of their own good-will, and the result of further instruction of Colonial opinion to which he attached great importance. But there was a danger that reaction might come on this side. . . . On that account he could not help feeling the fact the [sic] misconception in regard to a naval war which appeared in some of the Colonies, for it was a very serious one. It appeared to be the idea among certain Colonial circles that a naval war could be made a matter of limited liability. That was an entire delusion. If, for instance, the Australian Colonies found themselves, as they might find themselves in the event of the Imperial navy abandoning them, pressed by France in regard to the New Hebrides, pressed by Japan in regard to Japanese immigration, or pressed by Germany, which desired to establish some colony on Australian soil, then the Australian Colonies would at once find that the idea of limited liability in naval warfare was one which had no substantial foundation, and that they would not have to contend only with the foreign squadron—say the German—at present in Australian waters, but against the whole maritime strength of the foreign nation with which

Their solution was not easy. Yet in spite of temporary set-backs and differences of view, the strategical situation enforced its own logic. The German navy therefore had the indirect result of strengthening the links which bound the Dominions to the Home country.[1] The constituent parts of the British Empire were brought into closer connexion in order to meet a common danger. The 'strategy of position' affected the relations between Great Britain and the Dominions scarcely less definitely than it affected the relations between Great Britain and France.

These questions of Imperial foreign policy and Imperial defence were discussed at the first Imperial Conference (the successor of the 'colonial conferences') in London in the spring of 1911. The members of the Conference were again invited to a meeting of the Committee of Imperial Defence. At this joint session Grey made a full statement of the aims and conditions of British foreign policy.[2] Canada and Australia settled the question of the control and organization of their fleets. In time of war, when the Dominion fleets, in whole or in part, had been placed under the control of the Imperial Government the ships were 'to form an integral part of the British fleet, and remain under the control of the British Admiralty'. The Admiralty could therefore send them anywhere they are engaged.' Mr. Arnold-Foster also maintained that the policy of 'local navies' was far too expensive. 'If the Australian Commonwealth were to furnish itself with the smallest navy known in the civilized world, the mere cost of upkeep would be enormously in excess of anything which had been suggested as the contribution of Australia to our Fleet.' Hansard, 4th Ser. cxix. 1048–50: 17 March 1903. In December 1904 a deputation organized by the Imperial Federation (Defence) Committee asked the Prime Minister to give prominence, at the forthcoming Colonial Conference, to the subject of the contribution of the Colonies towards Imperial defence. Mr. Balfour answered that dictation was impossible, but that he hoped the Colonies would begin to take a large share in the cost of Imperial defence.

[1] Public opinion in Germany held a very different view. The writer well remembers his own astonishment—while staying in Germany in 1912—at the general impression that the British 'Colonies' would 'throw off' their allegiance to the Mother-Country if Great Britain were involved in a naval or continental war against Germany. See also Bernhardi's arguments, p. 376 above.

[2] The statement is printed in B.D.D. vi. 781–90.

during the continuance of the war.[1] It was also agreed that representatives of the Dominions should attend meetings of the Committee of Imperial Defence when questions affecting the overseas Dominions were under discussion, and that a Defence Committee should be set up in each Dominion.

The Australian Government decided not to ask for financial help in the formation of their fleet; but a change took place in the development of Australian plans after Admiral Henderson had visited Australia to review the question of an Australian fleet. Admiral Henderson pointed out that Australia possessed harbours of great strategic value along the northern, southern, and eastern trade routes, and that Australian oceanic and inter-state trade was rapidly expanding. He proposed that the Commonwealth should build, over a period of twenty-two years, a fleet of eight armoured and ten protected cruisers, eighteen destroyers, and twelve submarines, with a personnel of 15,000 officers and men. For many years the senior officers would be drawn from the Imperial navy, but an Australian Naval College might be founded at once. In April 1911 an Australian Naval Board was constituted. The cruisers *Melbourne* and *Sydney*, and the battle-cruiser *Australia* were launched in the course of 1911 and 1912. Another cruiser and three destroyers were begun in Sydney, and three Australian submarines were laid down at Barrow. At the end of 1912 the Union of South Africa offered to pay for the construction and upkeep of six cruisers to be stationed in South African waters.

The Dominions had not a sufficient number of trained artisans to build on an extensive scale, but the problem was not merely one of shipbuilding. A battleship could be completed in Great Britain in two years. A 'trained seaman' needed four years for his 'training'; skilled ratings also needed four years, officers from seven to ten years for their efficient instruction. The expansion of the

[1] *Parliamentary Papers*, 1911. Cd. 5746–2.

British navy had made heavy calls on the number of trained men; there was a 'dearth of lieutenants'. The Admiralty found no difficulty in recruiting boys and seamen, but the shortage higher in the scale could only be made good after some time. For this reason the development of local fleets would take several years.

From one point of view the delay was fortunate. The naval issue became a matter of serious controversy in Canadian politics. Sir Wilfrid Laurier's Government was defeated at the elections in September 1911. Sir Robert Borden, who succeeded to office as leader of the Conservatives, held up the tenders for building the Canadian ships in Canada, and at a conference of Canadian Ministers early in 1912 the Canadian programme was postponed. The Canadian Government asked the Admiralty to prepare a memorandum on naval defence requirements affecting Canada. This memorandum was presented at the end of October 1912. It contained a short and very interesting statement of the general naval situation.[1] The statement covered slightly less than four printed pages. The first two pages dealt almost entirely with the growth of the German navy, and included the words: 'This great fleet is not dispersed all over the world for duties of commerce protection or in discharge of Colonial responsibilities; nor are its composition and character adapted to those purposes. It is concentrated and kept concentrated in close proximity to the German and British coasts.' The memorandum then described the situation in British and Mediterranean waters. The last section explained the position overseas in plain language.

'Naval supremacy is of two kinds: general and local. General naval supremacy consists in the power to defeat in battle and drive from the seas the strongest hostile navy or combination of hostile navies wherever they may be found. Local superiority

[1] *Parliamentary Papers*, 1912. Cd. 6513 (December 1912). Readers of the speeches or books of Mr. Churchill will recognize the distinctive style of the memorandum.

consists in the power to send in good time to, or maintain permanently in, some distant theatre forces adequate to defeat the enemy or hold him in check until the main decision has been obtained in the decisive theatre. It is the general naval supremacy of Great Britain which is the primary safeguard of the security and interests of the great Dominions of the Crown, and which for all these years has been the deterrent upon any possible designs prejudicial to or inconsiderate of their policy and safety.

'The rapid expansion of Canadian sea-borne trade, and the immense value of Canadian cargoes always afloat in British and Canadian bottoms, here require consideration. . . . The annual value of the overseas trade of the Dominion of Canada in 1909–1910 was not less than £72,000,000, and the tonnage of Canadian vessels was 718,000 tons, and these proportions have already increased and are still increasing. For the whole of this trade wherever it may be about the distant waters of the world, as well as for the maintenance of her communications, both with Europe and Asia, Canada is dependent, and has always depended, upon the Imperial Navy, without corresponding contribution or cost.

'Further, at the present time and in the immediate future Great Britain still has the power, by making special arrangements and mobilising a portion of the reserves, to send, without courting disaster at home, an effective fleet of battleships and cruisers to unite with the Royal Australian Navy and the British squadrons in China and the Pacific for the defence of British Columbia, Australia, and New Zealand. And these communities are also protected and their interests safeguarded by the power and authority of Great Britain so long as her naval strength is unbroken. This power, both specific and general, will be diminished with the growth not only of the German Navy, but by the simultaneous building by many Powers of great modern ships of war. . . . The Admiralty are assured that His Majesty's Government will not hesitate to ask the House of Commons for whatever provision the circumstances of each year may require. But the aid which Canada could give at the present time is not to be measured only in ships or money. Any action on the part of Canada to increase the power and mobility of the Imperial Navy, and thus widen the margin of our common safety, would be recognized everywhere

as a most significant witness to the united strength of the Empire.
. . . The Prime Minister of the Dominion having enquired in
what form any immediate aid that Canada might give would
be most effective, we have no hesitation in answering . . . that
it is desirable that such aid should include the provision of a
certain number of the largest and strongest ships of war which
science can build or money supply.'

The immediate result of this statement of policy was a
proposal by Sir Robert Borden to the Canadian Parliament that the Dominion should provide three Dreadnoughts for Imperial defence. The proposal was made
early in December 1912. In November the Federated
Malay States had offered a Dreadnought to the Imperial
Government,[1] and there were wild rumours of very large
gifts from the Princes of India.

Sir Robert Borden's proposal was not well received by
the Opposition in the Canadian Parliament. In February
1913 the Lower House resolved that the three Dreadnoughts should be added to the Imperial navy; but the
motion was only carried by 115 votes to 83. The Liberals
wanted a Canadian unit to be formed out of ships built
in Canada; they obstructed the Government Bill, although Mr. Churchill pointed out, in letters to Sir Robert
Borden that there were no yards in Canada which could
take large warships. The cost of laying down plant for
building these ships would be £15,000,000; four years
would be taken in erecting the plant. The Admiralty
would find it difficult to provide crews for ships in Canadian waters. The Australian ships would relieve Imperial
ships in Australian waters; the Canadian ships would be
a new charge.[2] The Liberals persisted in asking for a fleet
which would be built in Canada and manned by Cana-
dians. Sir Wilfrid Laurier thought that the Dominion

---

[1] About twelve years earlier a scheme had been initiated in Germany for
the occupation of the valuable Pulo Lantar group of islands off the Malay
Peninsula. These islands were under the sovereignty of one of the Malayan
Rajahs.

[2] The correspondence was published in *Parliamentary Papers*, 1913. Cd.
6689.

should reserve the right to approve of any war in which Great Britain might be engaged, and that there should be closer consultation with the Home Government on matters of foreign and imperial policy. The Canadian Senate rejected the Navy Bill. The result was a deadlock lasting until the outbreak of war in 1914.

Meanwhile friction had arisen in the early part of 1914 between the Admiralty and the Government of New Zealand. Mr. Allen, the Minister of Defence in New Zealand, complained in February 1914 that the Admiralty had not carried out the promise made in 1909 to provide two new light cruisers and a number of destroyers and submarines for New Zealand waters. *The Times* commented on 'the natural wish of New Zealanders to safeguard their defence', but pointed out that the naval situation had changed since 1909. A further concentration of the fleet in home waters was necessary, while the renewal of the Anglo-Japanese alliance relieved the position in the Pacific at least for some time to come.[1] Mr. Massey, the Prime Minister of New Zealand, then suggested that the Admiralty should provide two new cruisers of the Bristol class within eighteen months. If these cruisers were sent to New Zealand waters, the subsidy would be increased to £150,000 a year. Otherwise the subsidy would be given up. New Zealand would then build at least one cruiser in Great Britain for a 'local' navy. The capital ship offered in 1909 was already in home waters. The British Government accepted the proposal of a conference on the naval question; but events moved more quickly. Before the conference met, Great Britain and the Dominions were at war with Germany.

---

[1] *The Times*, 20 February and 28 April 1914. A similar charge of bad faith was made against the Admiralty by the Australian Government. See *The Times*, 13 April 1914. The Admiralty maintained that destroyers and submarines were unsuitable for Australasian waters.

XXII

THE BALKAN WARS AND ANGLO-GERMAN RELATIONS

AT the time when Sir Robert Borden proposed that Canada should provide three capital ships for the service of the Imperial navy, the European situation was extremely serious. The first of the three Balkan wars had broken out in October 1912. Within a short time the Turks were defeated by the Balkan allies. Servian troops reached the Adriatic, and a Bulgarian army attacked the defences of Constantinople. The origin and course of the three Balkan wars lie outside the subject-matter of this history; but it is impossible to understand the political background of the last two years of Anglo-German naval rivalry without taking into account the disturbing effect of the Near Eastern Question.

In the first and second Balkan wars Servia, Montenegro, Bulgaria, and Greece attacked Turkey. The weakness of Turkey had encouraged this attack. The Great Powers warned the Balkan States that they would not allow any change in the territorial *status quo* in European Turkey. The Balkan States had heard this language many times; they counted upon the disunion of the Powers. The initiative was in their hands; the opportunity given by the Italo-Turkish war was too good to miss. The first war ended in an armistice. The peace negotiations broke down, mainly over the Bulgarian desire to capture and hold the fortress of Adrianople. After another period of fighting the Great Powers laid down a settlement which was accepted most unwillingly by the Balkan allies in May 1913. Greece received Salonika and a stretch of Macedonia which included a number of Bulgarian inhabitants. Servia was given northern and central Macedonia—again with a number of Bulgarians. Bulgaria was given the greater part of Thrace and the Aegean coast from a point east of Kavalla to the western end of the Gallipoli peninsula. Albania became an independent principality.

The settlement satisfied no one, and within a few weeks the Balkan allies were fighting one another. The Servians wanted a port on the Adriatic, the Montenegrins part of Albania. The Bulgarians refused to hand over Salonika or Kavalla to the Greeks, or central Macedonia to the Servians. The Greeks and Servians refused to give up their claims to any territories allotted to them under the settlement. Bulgaria then attacked the Servians, and the Servians and Greeks replied by a combined attack upon the Bulgarians. The Turks took this excellent chance, marched out of Constantinople, and recaptured the fortress and city of Adrianople. The Rumanians, who had taken no part in the first two Balkan wars, envied the fine prizes secured by the other States; they too attacked Bulgaria, and threatened Sofia.

The first Bulgarian attack was delivered on 29 June 1913. On 10 August the Bulgarians signed a treaty of peace with Servia, Rumania, and Greece. They had failed to retake Salonika or to keep Kavalla. They had failed to win more land in Macedonia. They were forced to cede to Rumania the fortress of Silistria and the southern part of the Dobruja. They were also compelled to allow Turkey to keep Adrianople and the fortress of Kirk Kilisse.

From the outbreak of the first Balkan war Europe lived under the fear of an extension of the area of fighting. The German Emperor, with a few candid reflections upon the history of Prussia, and a contempt for the 'eunuch-like' preoccupation of the leading statesmen of Europe with 'everlasting talk about peace', thought at first that the Balkan States should be left alone to settle their affairs. Russia and France were not likely to interfere; they were not ready for the general war which would follow their interference.

'The action of the Balkan States is described as an attempt to extort something from Turkey? Why? From the Austrian standpoint was not the action taken by the young Frederick against Maria Theresia before the first Silesian war just the same thing? The Balkan states want an increase of territory. They can satisfy their wants only at the expense of Turkey— probably a declining Power. They cannot do this without fighting, and they are doing it together in order to make possible their own growth and extension. The Great Powers simply want to stop them. With what right? In whose interest? I will keep out of it. Just as we did not allow in '64, '66, '70, any interference with our "legitimate development", so little right or intention have I to hinder others or interfere with them. . . . The war is coming right enough. Then the Balkan States will show what they can do, and whether they can justify their existence. If they smash the Turks, then they have right on their side (*dann haben sie recht*), and they are entitled to some reward. The Great Powers must keep a ring round the battle field. There must be no interference "in the name of this so-called peace" (*um des sogenannten "lieben Friedens" willen*). The Eastern Question must be settled by blood and iron! But at a time favourable to us! That is now!"[1]

This simple and revealing philosophy assumed that the 'reward' to which victory would entitle the Balkan States might be given without endangering the security of Austria. It assumed also that for a second time in four years Russia would give way in a matter which touched an age-long Russian tradition. If Austria refused to allow Servia the 'reward' which Servia claimed, and if Servia appealed to Russia, there would be difficulty in 'keeping the ring round the battlefield'.

The German Emperor used strong and sweeping language about the folly of going to war with France and Russia over a border town in the Balkans;[2] but the Chancellor and Kiderlen-Waechter knew very well that Germany could not desert Austria. They pointed out that the maintenance of Austria as a Great Power was essential to the safety of Germany, and that Austria must set limits to the growth of Servia.[3] The Emperor himself

[1] D.G.P. xxxiii. 164–6: 4 October 1912.
[2] D.G.P. xxxiii. 295.   [3] D.G.P. xxxiii. 302–4.

agreed that the dissolution of Austria-Hungary would be fatal to the position of Germany in Europe. For the time Germany was anxious to co-operate with Great Britain and France. German influence in Vienna, French and British influence in St. Petersburg, might persuade Austro-Hungarian and Russian statesmen and generals to listen to reason.

The co-operation between Germany, Great Britain, and France during the three Balkan wars impressed and indeed surprised the statesmen and diplomatists of Europe. The Concert of Europe had at last taken form. London was the centre of action, and throughout the most critical periods a conference of the Ambassadors of the Great Powers met under the presidency of Grey. The success of these meetings raised the hopes of Grey and Bethmann-Hollweg that there might be a real improvement in Anglo-German relations. Yet there was an important difference between the British and the German views of this improvement. Grey believed that the two groups of European Powers need not remain in 'opposing diplomatic camps'.[1] He thought that the method of conferences might be used to settle sharp differences, and that the influence of friend upon friend and ally upon ally would prevent the foolishness and calamity of war. He brought forward this plan of settlement by conference during the month of July 1914. Fifteen years later he remained convinced that his proposals had offered a way of escape from the Great War.[2]

Bethmann-Hollweg also hoped that Anglo-German relations had taken a turn for the better. He told Goschen on 12 January 1913 that Anglo-German co-operation on the Near Eastern Question was 'worth more than any Naval Agreement or political understanding as a starting point for future good relations'.[3] Kiderlen, who rarely paid compliments, took the chance of an interpellation in the Reichstag to speak of the close and intimate rela-

---

[1] B.D.D. ix, pt. i. 595.   [2] B.D.D. ix, pt. ii, Foreword, vi–vii.
[3] B.D.D. ix, pt. ii. 399.

tions between the two Powers. After Kiderlen's death, Zimmermann and Jagow made similar references.[1] Yet the German Chancellor and the German Foreign Office looked at this improvement in Anglo-German relations mainly from the point of view of the attitude—in other words, the neutrality—of England in a European war which seemed inevitable. Bethmann-Hollweg wrote to Berchtold on 10 February 1913. He wanted Berchtold to control the 'war party' in Austria-Hungary and to do his utmost to reach a *modus vivendi* with Servia. He spoke of the changed relations with Great Britain.

'The attitude of England is one of the many indications that the Entente policy has passed its highest point, and that we may look for a new orientation of English policy if we can get through the present crisis without any quarrels. Of course we are dealing with something which is only in the first stages of development, and a certain time must pass before the fruit ripens. But I think it would be a mistake of immeasurable consequence if we attempt a solution by force—even though many interests of the Austro-Hungarian monarchy favour such a solution—at a moment when there is even the remotest prospect of entering this conflict under conditions far more favourable to ourselves.'[2]

In other words, while Grey still hoped that the two groups of Powers might draw closer, Bethmann-Hollweg thought a peaceful solution of the Austro-Servian question impossible, and wanted to postpone an inevitable war until Germany had been able to detach Great Britain from the system of ententes.

The German Foreign Office might blame the 'stupidities'[3] of Austria, and deplore the fact that they were bound to support her even in her mistakes. Jagow told Granville in conversation that the Austrian statesmen

---

[1] Jagow succeeded Kiderlen as Foreign Secretary. Jagow was Ambassador in Rome at the time of Kiderlen's death, and only took over his office on 22 January 1913. Zimmermann, to whom the Foreign Secretaryship had been offered, acted for Jagow between 5 and 22 January.

[2] D.G.P. xxxiv, pt. i, 346–8: 10 February 1913.

[3] D.G.P. xxxiv, pt. ii. 824.

were 'hopeless bureaucrats, and not very intelligent at that'.[1] Moltke wrote to Jagow on 6 February that 'it is beyond doubt extremely inconvenient for us that our treaties and the necessity of supporting Austria make us in some measure dependent on Vienna. The chief work of Your Excellency must be to restrain as far as possible Austrian blunders—no pleasant and no easy task'.[2] Yet Moltke was sure that a European war was unavoidable. He advised Jagow to keep Austria in check, but at the same time he wrote to Conrad von Hoetzendorf:

'I was and am convinced that sooner or later there must be a European war, and this war . . . will be a battle between the Germanic and the Slav world. It is the duty of all those states which are the champions of Germanic culture to prepare for this war. The aggression must however come from the side of the Slavs. Those who see that this conflict is coming will know that they must concentrate all their resources and use every opportunity. Above all they must see that their peoples understand the significance of this "world-historical decision".'[3]

Conrad had wanted war for years past; Moltke had warned his Government in 1904–5 that the moment was favourable. One might therefore make some allowance for the military point of view, and the tendency of politically minded generals to see inevitable wars everywhere. The civilians were, however, of the same opinion as the soldiers. Tschirschky described the state of public opinion in Vienna in April 1913. 'You can scarcely form any idea of the state of opinion here. There is a feeling of disgrace, of suppressed anger, that Russia and her friends are leading Austria by the nose. The unfortunate Berchtold is being criticised in the sharpest terms.' Tschirschky added:

'do not think that I am painting too black a picture, or looking at things through Austrian spectacles. The time has at last come for the Monarchy to make it plain to Europe, and above all to its own peoples, that it is not a corpse to be disposed of

[1] B.D.D. ix, pt. ii. 930: 22 July 1913.   [2] D.G.P. xxxiv, pt. i. 318–19.
[3] D.G.P. xxxiv, pt. i. 352–3: 10 February 1913.

by others as they will. Even the very calm Avarna[1] spoke to me most seriously to-day in this sense. The internal dissolution of the Empire will make alarming progress if the Monarchy is unable at this present time to enforce its demands. General v. Conrad answered an Austrian friend who had asked whether the army was still capable of meeting an enemy: "Now, yes. Whether this will be so in a few years, I am doubtful." If the Monarchy does not get its way at this crisis, the result will be a defeat for the German element which is predominant at the moment, but would be forced to admit that it can not maintain the Monarchy as a Great Power. The Slav onrush within the Monarchy could not then be kept back, and in the long run the alliance could not be upheld.'[2]

The German Ambassador at Vienna believed that Austria must settle the Servian question in her own way if the Monarchy were to survive. The German Ambassador at St. Petersburg thought that an Austrian attack upon Servia would certainly mean war with Russia.

'The Pan-Slavist agitators form a comparatively small but powerful and very touchy group. They will carry with them the whole of public opinion and force the hands of the present leaders of the country. A war will then be at least extremely probable. In this case the question whether such a war is really in Russian interests will not be asked. No attention will be paid to the internal dangers which will certainly threaten the country in war. The one dominant factor will be the sentimental, Slavophil policy . . . The monarch, the government and the great majority of the Russian people do not want war, but war will come through the agency of impersonal forces, and when it comes, it will soon be popular . . . if it is fought against Austria.'[3]

Tschirschky and Pourtalès were thinking in terms of the immediate crisis, but their views were of general application. In the Emperor's words 'the struggle between Slavs and Germans can no longer be avoided. It is certain to come. When?'[4] The final settlement after

---

[1] Italian Ambassador at Vienna.
[2] D.G.P. xxxiv, pt. ii. 731–2: 24 April 1913.
[3] D.G.P. xxxiv, pt. i. 330–2: 6 February 1913.
[4] D.G.P. xxxiv, pt. ii. 811: 6 May 1913.

the defeat of Bulgaria had only aggravated the relations between Austria and Servia, and strained Austro-Russian relations almost to breaking-point.[1] The Emperor believed that England would join France and Russia. In December 1912 he was much excited by a dispatch from Lichnowsky describing an interview with Haldane. Haldane had explained that Great Britain was determined to maintain the balance of power in Europe, and could not allow the defeat of France. The Emperor wrote to Kiderlen that the veil was lifted at last. In the forthcoming struggle between the Germans and the Slavs and their Gallic supporters, the Anglo-Saxons would be found on the side of the Slavs. This fact must form the basis of German policy. Germany must make military conventions with Turkey, Bulgaria, Rumania. 'We must make a similar agreement with Japan. Any Power which we can get is good enough to help us. It is a matter of life and death for Germany.'[2]

The Emperor's view that England would certainly join France ruled out any chance of concessions on the naval question. The German Foreign Office was less sure that Great Britain would support France and Russia under any conditions, although Lichnowsky had no doubts about the matter. Even those who believed that there was some chance of obtaining British neutrality were inclined to put their trust in the German fleet. Tirpitz held this view; he could hold no other view. It is more surprising to find Jagow in agreement with the naval party. He wrote to Lichnowsky: 'we have not built our fleet for nothing, and I am convinced that England will ask herself very seriously whether it is altogether simple and safe to act as the guardian angel of France against us.'[3]

The improvement of Anglo-German relations was

---

[1] On 23 April 1914 Tschirschky wrote that it was useless for Germany to attempt to arrange a *modus vivendi* between Austria and Servia which would give lasting satisfaction to each side. 'A compromise of this kind, as I have frequently had the honour to report, is regarded here as unattainable.' D.G.P. xxxviii. 346. [2] D.G.P. xxxix. 119–25.

[3] D.G.P. xxxvii, pt. i. 105: 26 February 1914.

therefore less real than it appeared. The collaboration of the two Powers had done much to keep the peace of Europe. It had done nothing to remove the deep causes of unrest. The Austro-Russian difference remained, and in the opinion of leading statesmen and soldiers in Germany, Austria, and Russia could be settled only by force. The naval rivalry between Great Britain and Germany was as acute as ever. All attempts to reach a naval agreement had failed. An increased German programme had been followed by an increased British programme. Great Britain was following the advice given by Moltke to Conrad. Her forces were concentrated, and she was making an effort to explain to the Dominions that their fate as well as the fate of the United Kingdom would be decided in the North Sea.

XXIII

MR. CHURCHILL AND A 'NAVAL HOLIDAY'.

II. 1913–1914

THE offer of the Canadian Dreadnoughts caused a
certain excitement in Germany. Mr. Churchill announced in Parliament on 9 December 1912 that the
Canadian ships would have no effect upon the British
programme already laid before the House.[1] Before this
announcement Count Reventlow had asked in the *Deutsche
Tageszeitung* for an increase in the German programme
if the Canadian ships were not to be counted as part of
British programme of capital ships for the year 1912–
13. The German naval attaché in London had made the
same suggestion.[2]

The Chancellor and the German Foreign Office were
afraid that the Emperor would fall in at once with this
proposal. He had already taken steps to begin a press
campaign in favour of another supplementary law. Lichnowsky's account of the 'lifting of the veil' had moved
him to such an extent that he called a meeting of the
naval and military chiefs and ordered Tirpitz to start
work with the newspapers.[3] The Chancellor only heard
of this meeting some time after it had taken place, and
could rely only upon an indirect report of the proceedings. He telegraphed at once to the Emperor that it was
of the utmost importance to say nothing about any addition to the German army or navy during the negotiations
over the Eastern Question in London. The Emperor
gave way, but commented that 'this does not alter the
fact that demands for an increase must be made later,
and I am determined to have this increase'.[4] Early in
January the Emperor appears to have broken away again,
but once more the Chancellor restrained him, partly by

---

[1] Hansard, 5th Ser. xlv. 17. [2] D.G.P. xxxix. 6.
[3] D.G.P. xxxix. 7–8. For the Emperor's proposals, see Tirpitz, *op. cit.* i.
368–71. [4] D.G.P. xxxix. 9–11.

the argument that the naval increase ought to be postponed until 1914 because an increase in the army was more urgently needed.

The naval position was explained, shortly, and as far as Dreadnoughts were concerned, by Mr. Churchill in answer to a parliamentary question on 16 January 1913. 'On the assumption that the progress of the work on ships under construction remains normal and that there is no acceleration', Great Britain would possess twenty-nine Dreadnoughts (excluding the battle-cruiser *Australia*) on 1 April 1914, and thirty-five on 1 April 1915. Germany would have completed twenty-one on 1 April 1914, and twenty-three on 1 April 1915. On these respective dates Italy would have four and six, Austria three and four Dreadnoughts.[1] The British figures did not include the Dreadnought offered by the Malay States and the ships under discussion in Canada. Considerable discussion took place about these 'gifts' to the Home Government. Already in January 1913, *The Times* warned its readers of the fate of the Roman Empire when its citizens looked for borrowed support.[2]

Before the publication of the British naval estimates for 1913–14 Tirpitz made a speech in the budget committee of the Reichstag which caused considerable comment in Germany and in England. He said that the German Admiralty was ready to accept Mr. Churchill's figure of a relationship of 16 : 10, i.e. roughly 60 per cent., in Dreadnoughts between the British and German fleets. Tirpitz expressed the relationship in squadrons: eight British and five German squadrons.[3] Tirpitz's speech was followed, on 7 February, by an assurance from Jagow that Anglo-German relations were improving.

'The intimate exchange of opinion which goes on between us and the English Government has done a great deal to remove difficulties of many kinds which had arisen during the last few months. We have now seen that not only have we points of

---

[1] Hansard, 5th Ser. xlvi. 2277–8.   [2] *The Times*, 20 January 1913.
[3] D.G.P. xxxix. 15–20.

contact of a sentimental kind with England, but that common interests exist as well. I am no prophet, but I indulge in the hope that, on the ground of common interests, which in politics is the most fruitful ground, we can continue to work with England and perhaps reap the harvest. But I must point out to you that we are dealing here with tender plants; we must not destroy them by premature acts or words.'

Tirpitz's proposal was neither a great concession nor a fair description of the standard which the British Admiralty were taking as the basis of their policy. Mr. Churchill made two important qualifications when he suggested a superiority of 60 per cent. in Dreadnoughts. He pointed out that a margin of 60 per cent. would be sufficient only during the lifetime of the most recent pre-Dreadnought battleships. He also said that the standard of 60 per cent. superiority was intended only to meet the German programme before the passing of the supplementary law of 1912. If the German programme were increased, Great Britain would build two ships for every one ship laid down in Germany under the terms of a supplementary law.[1]

The supplementary law had been passed; Germany was building more ships, and keeping a larger number of ships in full commission. Tirpitz's suggestion therefore, so far from being a friendly acceptance of a British proposal, was an attempt, very cleverly made, to persuade Great Britain to lower the margin which the Admiralty had announced as necessary for British security. Tirpitz himself has explained in his memoirs that he made his proposal in terms of squadrons, because he knew that Great Britain could not easily increase her programme of construction by a whole squadron. The German naval attaché in London also noticed that the proposal was advantageous to Germany, because it did not include cruisers.[2] The proposal was made at a time when the German Admiralty realized that the plans for increasing the army would block any naval increase for a year.

---

[1] See above, p. 369.   [2] D.G.P. xxxix. 30.

The French Press, naturally enough, commented on this point; Germany was giving an easy satisfaction to Great Britain while large military increases were being carried through. It was also suggested that Tirpitz wanted to influence opinion in Canada.

For these reasons Great Britain could not take any official notice of Tirpitz's proposal without entering into detailed discussions. Discussions had already been held. They had led to no good result; it was useless to resume them.[1]

The British naval estimates for 1913-14 were published in the second week of March. The programme of construction included five Dreadnoughts, eight light cruisers, and sixteen destroyers. There was an increase in personnel amounting almost to 7,000 men, and an increase of £1,300,000 in the total cost of the navy. The estimates were brought before the House on 26 March 1913. Once more Mr. Churchill defined the British standard of superiority. He excluded the Colonial and Dominion ships. These ships were necessary for Imperial defence over and above the concentration in the North Sea. 'They are additional to the requirements of the 60 per cent. standard; they are not additional to the whole-world requirements of the British Empire.' Great Britain would also carry out the policy of building two ships for every additional ship laid down by Germany under a supplementary naval law. The Admiralty might find it

[1] The editors of *Die Grosse Politik*, while omitting any reference to the fact that Tirpitz was not giving a fair account of Mr. Churchill's proposal, suggest that Grey did not reopen negotiations because he feared the effect upon France and Russia. There is not the least evidence to support this suggestion. There is also no reason to suppose that the German Government either expected or desired resumption of negotiations for a naval agreement. (D.G.P. xxxix. 19-20 n. and, for Lichnowsky's views, 46-8.) In view of the Emperor's wish for another increase in the German programme, it is difficult to think that the Chancellor would have favoured a reopening of the question, and there is no evidence that Tirpitz's speech was made with this intention. After the negotiations of the past few years, a proposal involving another important concession on the part of Great Britain would not have been the most tactful way of reopening negotiations.

necessary to increase their margin of superiority after a period of five years when the pre-Dreadnought ships had lost their value. The shipbuilding programmes of other Powers might force Great Britain to increase her own programme even during this period. Naval developments in the Mediterranean might be a reason for such an increase. Mr. Churchill referred to Tirpitz's misrepresentation of the '60 per cent. standard'. He added:

'We must not try to read into recent German naval declarations a meaning which we should like, but which they do not possess; nor ought we to seek to tie German policy down to our wishes by too precise interpretations of friendly language used in the German Reichstag with a good and reassuring purpose. If, for instance, I were to say that Admiral Tirpitz had recognized that a British predominance of sixteen to ten in Dreadnoughts was satisfactory to Germany, that such a preponderance exists almost exactly in the present period, and that in consequence Germany ought not to begin any more capital ships until we did, that might be a logical argument, but it would, I am sure, do a great deal of harm.'[1]

Tirpitz had maintained that Germany was not attempting to compete with England. The proportion of 10 to 16 was sufficient for Germany because it ensured her against attack. 'It gives us such a measure of power that it is difficult to attack us.' This sentence must be taken in the general context of the 'risk' theory upon which Tirpitz had justified, thirteen years earlier, the development of the German navy, and to which he always returned. Mr. Churchill also referred, indirectly to the 'risk' theory, and to the British answer to such a theory.

'I must explicitly repudiate the suggestion that Great Britain can ever allow another Naval Power to approach her so nearly as to deflect or to restrict her political action by purely naval pressure.[2] Such a situation would unquestionably lead to war. . . . It would mean a continued atmosphere of suspicion and

---

[1] For Mr. Churchill's speech, see Hansard, 5th Ser. i. 1749-91.

[2] The Emperor's comment on this sentence was 'There are other means of pressure'. D.G.P. xxxix. 28.

alarm, with all the national antagonisms consequent upon such a state of affairs. It would mean that instead of intervening, as we do now in European affairs, free and independent to do the best we can for all, we should be forced into a series of questionable entanglements and committed to action of the gravest character, not because we thought it right, but as a result of bargains necessitated by our naval weakness. Margins of naval strength which are sufficient when the time comes to compel a victory, are insufficient to maintain a peace.'

In 1912 Mr. Churchill had suggested the plan of a 'naval holiday'. He repeated the proposal in his speech of 1913.

'If, for the space of a year . . . no new ships were built by any nation, in what conceivable manner would the interests of any nation be affected or prejudiced? The proposal . . . involves no alteration in the relative strength of the navies. It implies no abandonment of any scheme of naval organization or of naval increase. It is contrary to the system of no Navy Law. . . . The finances of every country would obtain relief.'

Great Britain, with her resources, her leadership in design, and the quality of her workmanship, could make the suggestion of a year's pause not out of weakness but out of strength. The plan was not disadvantageous to Germany, since, in the year 1914, Great Britain would be laying down four, and Germany only two, capital ships. The arrangement would involve other Powers— France, Russia, Italy, Austria; but, once an agreement had been made by the two principal naval Powers, the co-operation of the other Powers would not be improbable. If the suggestion were not accepted, 'events will continue to move forward along the path upon which they have now been set, with the result that at every stage the naval supremacy of the British Empire will be found to be established upon a more unassailable foundation'.

In the debate which followed Mr. Churchill's speech the proposal for a naval holiday was dismissed by Mr. Lee, the principal speaker on the side of the Opposition, as Utopian and unlikely to meet with support. The main part of the discussion was concerned with the question whether Mr. Churchill's programme of construction really upheld the standard which he had laid down. Mr. Churchill had balanced against the decline in the value of the pre-Dreadnought ships the British preponderance in 'improved' types of Dreadnought. He explained later in the debate that in the view of the Admiralty 'the minimum standard of Dreadnoughts which should be maintained in Home waters should be three to two as compared with Germany; that is to say, that one-sixth of the 60 per cent. superiority might be considered available for foreign service or for the general service of the Empire'. He added that 'having regard to the responsibilities of the British Empire both in the Pacific and in the Mediterranean, and having regard in particular to the new development of forces in the Mediterranean, it is clear that the margin of strength available for the whole-world service of the British Empire will not be sufficient after the first quarter of 1916 unless further steps are taken either by the Dominions or by ourselves. From this point of view, the reality of the need of the three Canadian vessels can be well appreciated. They would raise the margin of the strength available for the general defence of the Empire.'[1]

Once more Mr. Churchill's proposal for a naval holiday was badly received in the German Press. The suspension of programmes of construction would give a breathing space to English yards during a period when these yards were overcrowded with work and were affected by a shortage of skilled labour.[2] When the year's 'holiday' had gone by, and new ships were laid down, the advantage would be on the British side, since Great Britain could build more quickly than Germany. The year's

[1] For Mr. Churchill's second speech, see Hansard, 5th Ser. li. 68-90.

[2] In his speech of 31 March Mr. Churchill denied that this view was correct, and insisted that, if it were necessary, Great Britain could lay down more ships and find crews for them. The Emperor believed at this time that the crews would not be found. D.G.P. xxxix. 28.

pause would interfere with the steady development of the German navy, and particularly with the substitution of new ships for the old ships of a smaller and less powerful type. Furthermore, the 'holiday' would not affect the programmes of the British Dominions, since their ships were not to be included in the calculations of a 60 per cent. superiority. Germany, on the other hand, had to consider the naval plans of Powers other than Great Britain. Finally, what was to happen to the German shipbuilding yards during this year? Would the plant lie idle and the workmen remain unemployed?

These arguments were exactly those put forward by the naval attaché in London.[1] Captain Müller thought that the proposal was either a 'rhetorical *captatio benevolentiae*' put forward for the benefit of the left wing of the Liberal party or an attempt to fasten upon Germany the odium of responsibility for the competition in armaments. The Chancellor did not believe that the proposal was practicable.[2] He gave a friendly but not encouraging answer in the Reichstag.[3] On 20 June Captain Müller reported that Mr. Churchill intended to make a definite suggestion to Germany. The Chancellor had already mentioned to the Reichstag that Germany would await proposals of this kind. Tirpitz and the naval circles were seriously alarmed at the prospect. The Emperor's comment was: 'We are on our guard. Caveant consules.'[4] Captain Hopman, on behalf of Tirpitz, wrote to Müller[5] from Berlin:

'Your letter about the conversation with Churchill has caused great interest here, but not exactly pleasure. The fact that

[1] D.G.P. xxxix. 28–35.

[2] Lichnowsky reported a conversation with Mr. Churchill in which the latter said that 'he was completely serious in his proposals and thought them entirely practicable'. The Chancellor annotated the sentence 'Meo voto nein. B. H.' It is uncertain whether this annotation covers the whole sentence. D.G.P. xxxix. 38–9. The editors of *Die Grosse Politik* suggest that the whole plan was merely a tactical manœuvre.

[3] D.G.P. xxxix. 35–6.

[4] D.G.P. xxxix. 39–46.

[5] Tirpitz, *op. cit.* i. 395–7: 11 June 1913.

Churchill is going to bring forward his holiday proposals again in the autumn is not altogether convenient. Although every consideration of reason is against the plan, and almost the whole of the German and English press has hitherto opposed it, it is to be feared that the military proposals (i.e. the new army increases) with their heavy demands on the German taxpayer, the (forthcoming) agreement with England about Central Africa, and the general wish for a lasting agreement with England, will ease the way for Churchill's plans. According to the Secretary of State (i.e. Tirpitz) opinion in the Reichstag is not so very unfavourable to the idea. The military proposals will make people tired of the cost of armaments and this expansion will be another factor in support of the plan, and will certainly be used by the Wilhelmstrasse in their own direction.'

Hopman thought that there was even a danger in trying to influence Mr. Churchill; he might guess that the naval authorities were afraid that 'our Government (*Wilhelmstrasse*) and the Reichstag would not be unfavourable'. Tirpitz therefore advised Müller, in conversations with Mr. Churchill, not to say much about the technical arguments against the plan, but to

'act as though from our naval standpoint we were not altogether unapproachable, and to point out at the same time that the English and the German Press had given the idea an unfavourable, even a contemptuous reception, and that he, Churchill, after his "luxury" speech and other remarks of the kind, could scarcely expect that his proposals would meet with great confidence in Germany. In any case it is probable that there will be more talk about the navy in the press (*ein grosser Flottenrummel*). This is undesirable in the present situation, and may easily have the opposite effect from that which is intended. . . . In general you are recommended to treat the matter in as dilatory a manner as possible, and less as a naval than a purely political question. Therefore it is advisable that you should use the Ambassador . . . to talk to Grey about the danger of a naval discussion in the press, and to say that Churchill can only harm the tender plant of a German-English detente by his plan of a naval holiday.'

Tirpitz's fears of opposition from the German Foreign

Office were groundless. On 26 June Lichnowsky had already written privately to Jagow that he would try to prevent any official proposal about the naval holiday from reaching Berlin.[1] Three days earlier he had asked for official instructions whether he should tell Grey directly, or through a third person, that the German Government would prefer Mr. Churchill not to come forward again with his plan. The Emperor had recommended that this step should be taken; his recommendation was telegraphed to Lichnowsky.[2]

The rejection of the Canadian Naval Bill further complicated the naval controversy in Great Britain. Mr. Churchill announced in the House of Commons on 5 June 1913 that immediate action was necessary 'in order that the margins of naval strength necessary for the whole world protection of the British Empire may be adequately maintained for the autumn and winter of 1915 and in the spring of 1916'. The Government had decided to advance the construction of three of the ships of the 1913–14 programme.[3] No full discussion of the matter took place until the debate on the shipbuilding vote in July. Mr. Churchill then explained that the Admiralty had chosen to accelerate the construction of three ships of the 1913–14 programme rather than lay down three extra ships to take the place of the Canadian ships because they felt that the Canadian Government had not finally given up the idea of a contribution to the Imperial navy. It would

[1] D.G.P. xxxix. 48 n.

[2] The uneasiness of the Foreign Office over reports sent by the naval attaché had not been removed by the substitution of Müller for Widenmann. Müller reported to Tirpitz that 'Lichnowsky's political position is entirely determined by the Foreign Office. He showed some independence at first, and made a speech or two about Anglo-German relations. He then received hints from Berlin not to talk on this subject. Anglo-German relations were to be managed from Berlin. In connexion with one of the dispatches of Ostertag (the military attaché) the Foreign Office reminded him (Lichnowsky) of his right of censorship. . . . Lichnowsky himself does not agree with the Foreign Office, but he will not state his own opinion. We have told him that he should not accept these letters from Stumm . . . &c.' Tirpitz, *op. cit.* i. 383–4.   [3] Hansard, 5th Ser. liii. 1043–4.

be possible to decide after a twelvemonth whether further acceleration would be necessary, or whether three ships would be added to the 1914–15 programme.[1] Mr. Churchill's plan met with fairly general support in England. *The Times* thought that, in view of the uncertainty about the Canadian plans and the position in the Mediterranean, it was wiser to do nothing more than accelerate the construction of the three ships. Further action would have to be taken early in 1914.[2] For a time the German Emperor was much excited by the news. He proposed that there should be a similar anticipation of the German programme. Rumours of this proposal reached England, but were contradicted.[3]

There was no further public discussion, on any important scale, of the shipbuilding programme during the summer of 1913. Domestic issues occupied public opinion in Great Britain, and the country was satisfied with the precautions taken by the Government. On the other hand, the general question of European armaments could not escape notice. Austria, France, and Germany had announced large increases in their military strength. Germany was afraid of Russia, France afraid of Germany. These increases, in the words of *The Times*, had received in each country 'a large degree of popular sanction'.[4] They were not tangibly directed against aggression, but were 'the gloomy heritage of the Balkan war'. The German Emperor, in describing the German Army Bill, said that 'the best parry is the lunge'. The lunge was expensive, and required from the German people a heavy contribution which was taken in the form of a capital levy. A capital levy could not be repeated indefinitely. The peace strength of the German army would reach 870,000 of all ranks in 1915—an increase of approximately 150,000 over the peace strength of 1912. The peace strength of the French army would rise from 567,000 to 673,000 when the system of three years service was in full opera-

---

[1] Hansard, 5th Ser. lv. 1482–9.   [2] *The Times*, 18 and 19 July 1913.
[3] D.G.P. xxxix. 45–6 n.   [4] *The Times*, 5 March 1913.

tion. Improvements in the German scheme of mobilization would give the German armies two more days in which to 'rush' France before the Russian striking power could be of much effect. It was difficult to avoid the conclusion that France as well as Germany had reached the limit of military resources. *The Times* even wrote that 'France has played her last card, and must become more and more dependent upon her friends and allies'.[1] The cost of navies and the size and destructive power of their armaments had increased, and was continuing to increase more rapidly than at any previous time. The Dreadnought had been superseded by the 'super-Dreadnought'. The fifteen-inch gun and the 40,000-ton battleship, costing £4,000,000, were considered to be within practical possibilities. The range of the torpedo had increased since the time of the Russo-Japanese War from 2,000 to 11,000 yards; and the weight of the charge from 97 lb. to 330 lb. The speed of torpedoes had doubled, and experts were considering whether torpedoes might not take the place of guns. In any case the submarine had now been provided with an extremely effective weapon.

A new factor had appeared with the development of airships. The German air programme announced in April 1913 included five army airship battalions, five aeroplane battalions, two squadrons of naval airships, six groups of 'waterplanes', thirty army airships and ten naval airships. The total personnel of the air services had risen to 6,450. In the summer of 1913 *The Times* began the publication of a series of articles on the development of aeronautics in the chief countries of Europe.[2] The first article referred to the action taken by *The Times* twenty years earlier in enforcing the need for greater expenditure on the navy. In 1893 the Naval Defence Act was on the point of expiry, and a policy of retrenchment was likely to endanger the British margin of safety. *The Times* sent a special correspondent to Toulon to report on the increase in the French navy. A similar step was necessary in 1913

[1] *The Times*, 22 August 1913.   [2] *The Times*, 25 June 1913.

to arouse public opinion. 'England has ceased to be an island. . . . Her cosiness is disturbed by a menace which for the moment seems more alarming because less tangible than any naval rivalry by foreign Powers.'

In these circumstances the opening of the Peace Palace at The Hague seemed almost as ironical to contemporaries as it must appear to historians. The opening ceremony was accompanied by an informal Peace Congress, but the congress never reached any practical discussion of the problems at issue. The comments of *The Times* upon the meeting of pacifists and the value of the Peace Court at The Hague represent perhaps the 'average' view of the educated public in Great Britain in 1913 upon the problem of avoiding war.[1]

[1] *The Times*, 25 August 1913: 'A Peace Congress that knew its business would . . . seek to undermine the old idea of nations as separate and isolated units. It would shew how the ease and multiplicity of communications, the bonds of commerce, and particularly of finance and credit, the Press, the spread of education, a common restlessness under common burdens, the loosening of theological dogma, the growing solidarity of Labour—how all these facts simultaneously are working towards a cosmopolitanism of mind and outlook and interests, and render the idea of war more and more repellent to the more highly organized nations. It would utilize as an ally . . . the finer sensitiveness of the age to the more obvious forms of suffering. It would recognize . . . the curious fact that, in spite of the world-wide movement towards uniformity and interdependence, nationality was hardly ever a more stubborn or a more jealous reality than it is to-day, when all the old landmarks might seem on the very point of submergence. It would emphasize, as the younger and wiser school of pacifists is beginning to do, every argument against war that can be drawn from the complex web of mutual interests woven by international finance and commerce. It would . . . endeavour to prove that, in our modern world of credit and universal trade, aggression defeats itself, and that confiscation, indemnities, and seizure of property and territory are as injurious to the conqueror as to the conquered, and of no lasting benefit to either. It would strive to propagate the idea that war is the collapse not only of the reason but of the higher nature of humanity. It would . . . insist that human nature does change . . . and that there is nothing to prevent such a modification of its old instincts and emotions as will make an end of war. . . . But not in ten thousand years could the delegates at The Hague abolish war with their incredible Utopias, their annihilating solutions, and their imperviousness to the passions that move the common run of men. Ordinary men want peace accompanied by justice to their own nations, and do not think war the worst of evils. As for armaments and their burden, the question has never been answered "How close

A few days later *The Times* returned to the subject in two leading articles. The first article welcomed the growth of the movement in favour of arbitration, and the 'wholesome discipline' of 'the mere necessity for stating a case', but considered that there were limits to the possible work of a Peace Court. 'There are clashes and collisions of human entities which are not to be settled by a legal tribunal. They act on motives which it cannot judge, obey external impulses which press as blindly as physical necessities: they grasp where they think they have power, and yield to force only—and that with the fixed intention to try again.'[1]

The second article described the growth of an internationalism far beyond the dreams of idealists of the early nineteenth century. Among the forces making for this internationalism were the Jews, who were a power in the money-market, and 'very largely' controlled 'the newspapers and the theatres'. The writer of the article also thought that the change in the economic and political importance of women favoured the breaking down of nationalist barriers. He added that the enthusiast of the nineteenth century would be 'entirely wrong' in thinking that Europe was 'on the verge of becoming a united commonwealth. There is still one great counter-tendency pulling against the realization of his dreams—the sentiment of patriotism. It is one of the paradoxes of our times that as the world of science and literature, finance and philosophy grows smaller and more uniform, each unit or group of nations seems to grow more self-conscious and more eager to maintain its own individuality. Patriotism is proof against any purely intellectual solvent.'[2]

Mr. Churchill returned to his plan for a naval holiday in a speech at Manchester on 18 October 1913. Before this speech was made Kühlmann reported to Berlin an address given by Mr. Churchill to the Women's Liberal

is the sequence of cause and effect between armies and navies or social poverty and industrial unrest?" '

[1] *The Times*, 28 August 1913.   [2] *The Times*, 29 August 1913.

E e

Association of Dundee. The address had nothing remarkable about it. Its purpose was obvious: an attempt to show to the left wing of the Liberal party, and particularly to the women supporters of this left wing, that British naval preparations were necessary in view of the general situation, and that these preparations were neither an offence nor a challenge to other Powers. Lack of security rather than confidence in one's own strength caused distrust and unrest.

The remarks, taken out of their context, excited the Emperor. They appeared to confirm his idea of the purpose of the German fleet, and to justify the 'risk' theory. The Emperor annotated sentence after sentence of Kühlmann's short report. 'What a triumph for Tirpitz.' 'My risk theory! Best thanks for the compliment, Mr. Churchill. Thereby the McKenna-Fisher era of lies is disavowed and done with. Similarly Haldane, and the Building Holiday.' There followed a paragraph of imperial self-glorification which entirely misjudged the attitude of Great Britain.

'This is an implicit recognition—whole and complete—of German Naval Law and particularly of the "risk" paragraphs by the British First Lord of the Admiralty. A more brilliant justification could not have been dreamed of or expected by me or by those who made the naval law with me, enlarged it, and defended it from all internal and external attacks. . . . A grandiose triumph for Admiral Tirpitz before the whole world. He has deserved it, and it will give him a superlative position in the world. A new proof of my old theory that only firm, manly, and unshakeable defence of one's interests impresses the English, and at last brings them near to us. . . . England comes to us, not in spite of, but owing to the Imperial Navy!! Avis au lecteur!!'[1]

Mr. Churchill reintroduced the question of a naval holiday with a reference to Bethmann-Hollweg's speech. The Chancellor had said that Germany awaited definite proposals. The British Government would not take any

[1] D.G.P. xxxix. 51-2.

steps if Germany were unfavourable to the idea; they did not wish to give the appearance of trying to secure for themselves the laurels of a proposal for the restriction of armaments, or to force Germany into the position of giving a refusal. On the other hand, Mr. Churchill thought that the moment was not unfavourable for the renewal of the suggestion. Anglo-German relations were friendly. The question was urgent because Italy and Austria were likely to bring forward new naval programmes.

'The proposal which I put forward in the name of His Majesty's Government is quite simple. . . . Next year, apart from the Canadian ships or their equivalent, apart from anything that may be required by new developments in the Mediterranean, we are to lay down four great ships to Germany's two. Now we say, while there is plenty of time, in all friendship and sincerity to our great neighbour Germany:—If you will put off beginning your two ships for twelve months from the ordinary date when you would have begun them, we will put off beginning our four ships, in absolute good faith, for exactly the same period. That would mean that there would be a complete holiday for one year as far as big ships are concerned between Great Britain and Germany. There would be a saving, spread over three years, of nearly six millions to Germany, and of nearly 12 millions to this country, and the relative strength of the two countries would be absolutely unchanged.'

The arrangement depended upon a general agreement among the Powers, but Mr. Churchill thought that, if Germany and Great Britain took the lead, other Powers would be likely to agree.

Even in Great Britain the plan had little support. Critics pointed out that the choice of a year in which Great Britain was planning the construction of four, and Germany the construction of two ships, meant the surrender of an advantage on the British side. The limitation of the 'holiday' to the building of 'capital' ships left a dangerous loophole. Germany might spend a larger sum upon submarines and aircraft, or upon her army and land fortifications. Furthermore, what would be the effect upon the programme of the Dominions? Mr. Churchill had excluded the three Canadian ships from the 'holiday'; but would Japan be willing to allow Australia and New Zealand to lay down a battleship apiece? The shipbuilding firms might take foreign orders, or, like the Stabilimento Tecnico, build at their own risk. Finally, there was the question of making preparations in advance. Armour-plating and gun-making firms might improve their machinery or make preparations for an acceleration in the rate of construction after the 'holiday' year had passed.

The proposal was criticized once more in the 'unofficial' German Press. A 'semi-official' communiqué in the *Kölnische Zeitung* of 21 October, welcomed the friendliness of Mr. Churchill's speech, but repeated the objections to his plan. Count Reventlow, in the *Deutsche Tageszeitung*, suggested that Mr. Churchill should take a year's holiday from making speeches likely to damage Anglo-German relations. The American Press was more friendly,[1] while French papers, naturally enough, pointed out that Germany could spend on her land armaments the six millions which she would have spent on naval construction. It is unnecessary to describe at length the official German comments upon the proposal. Captain Müller supplied the usual explanation.

'Mr. Churchill is merely trying to increase by all the means in his power the military distance between England and Germany, and to get rid of the main principle of the German fleet, the

[1] A resolution in the American House of Representatives proposing a 'naval holiday' was brought forward on 6 December 1913. The Secretary of the Navy supported the motion and suggested a world conference to discuss a temporary cessation of building. The resolution was passed by 317 to 11, after a good deal of oratory upon the peace-making mission of the United States. There was no important sequel to the resolution, but in his annual report upon the navy (published in the last week of December), the Secretary referred sympathetically to Mr. Churchill's proposal, with the comment 'It is manifestly not possible for the proposed cessation in battleship construction to be declared at once. It is not a vacation we need, but a permanent policy to guard against extravagant and needless expansions.'

"risk" theory. . . . Four to five capital ships a year represent the highest possible financial effort of Great Britain over a long period without the help of her colonies. . . . If a normal "three-tempo" (i.e. three capital ships a year) were the established rule in Germany, the military distance between England and Germany would diminish, and, slowly but surely, approach the proportion 16 : 10. In any case England can scarcely maintain an overplus beyond her self-chosen superiority of 60 per cent.'[1]

Müller was on stronger ground when he pointed out that Mr. Churchill's distinction between British ships intended for the North Sea and British ships intended for the Mediterranean and the rest of the world would not be accepted by Germany. If England had Mediterranean interests, Germany had Baltic interests, and Germany, no less than England had to protect a world-wide commerce. In any case the success of the scheme depended upon its adoption by every naval Power in the world. Would it be possible to supervise the naval construction of the United States and Japan?

Kühlmann made one new contribution to the subject. He wrote to the Chancellor that Mr. Churchill's real motive was a desire to keep alive in the Dominions the belief that the burden of naval armaments was crushing the Mother country. The Dominions[2] were uninterested in the naval problem in European waters and could only be moved to make contributions in kind if they were convinced of an emergency which really threatened the Empire. As Anglo-German relations were improving, and as the Cabinet did not wish to take any steps which might hinder this improvement, it was impossible to use the German bogy. Therefore Mr. Churchill laid stress upon the threat to the Mediterranean from alleged Italian and German construction. A Russo-Japanese combination in the Pacific would have made an even better scarecrow, but Anglo-Russian relations stood in the way.

[1] D.G.P. xxxix. 65–9: 30 November 1913.
[2] D.G.P. xxxix. 58–60: 21 October 1913. Kühlmann and other German officials always used the terms 'colonies' and 'colonials' in speaking of the self-governing Dominions.

The Chancellor thought of repeating in the Reichstag, in the last week of November, his careful and guarded remarks of 7 April.[1] Meanwhile the Zabern incident, which showed the high-handed behaviour of German officers in Alsace, produced a storm in the Reichstag as well as in France, and turned public interest in another direction.[2] The speech was not made. Bethmann-Hollweg spoke on 9 December about the improved relations with England, but did not refer to the naval holiday. No official statement of the German attitude was announced until the beginning of February 1914. Tirpitz then discussed the subject in his speech to the Budget Committee of the Reichstag. He pointed out the usual German objections, and added that, if, in spite of the difficulties, Great Britain really wished to come to an agreement she would naturally have to take the initiative as the strongest sea Power in the world. If proposals of a positive kind were made, Germany would give them the most careful examination.[3] Grey answered at once that

'the sole reason why positive proposals from His Majesty's Government have not reached Germany is that His Majesty's Government had been given to understand by private intimations[4] which reached them from high German sources that such proposals would be unwelcome and would have a bad effect upon public opinion in Germany.[5] In these circumstances . . . it is essential that His Majesty's Government should know, for

[1] D.G.P. xxxix. 62–3 n. See above, p. 411.

[2] The Chancellor did his best to minimize the seriousness of the interference with civil liberty by the troops at Zabern, but the Prussian Minister for War made a violent speech defending the action of the colonel in command and his subordinates. As a result, the Reichstag passed a vote of censure on the Chancellor's handling of the question.

[3] D.G.P. xxxix. 75 n. Tirpitz's main practical objections were (1) German yards were, at the time, less occupied than British yards with new construction. (2) Great Britain was, and Germany was not, building for foreign states. (3) German financial arrangements, and the spacing out of work in the yards would be adversely affected. (4) The German programme depended upon the regular entry of ships into the battle squadrons. (5) Would France and Russia accept the plan?

[4] See above, p. 413.

[5] The Emperor's marginal comment was 'certainly'.

use in Parliament, exactly what Admiral Tirpitz meant and how proposals for a naval holiday would be received.'[1]

Grey added that, after Tirpitz's speech, the British Government was 'bound either to put such proposals forward or to furnish some explanation to Parliament . . . why they did not do so'.[2] The Chancellor consulted the Emperor about a German reply to the British Note. The Emperor refused to reopen the 'endless, dangerous chapter of the limitation of armaments', but was ready to discuss a naval agreement on the basis of a relationship of 16 : 10 expressed in terms of eight battle squadrons to five, between the two fleets. The German reply therefore stated that the Imperial Government did not consider the idea of a naval holiday as practicable, but that a proposal for an agreement on a basis of 5 : 8 squadrons, each of eight battleships, would meet with careful examination.[3]

Grey was in earnest when he said that he must give to Parliament an explanation of Tirpitz's speech. The agitation in the Liberal party against a further increase in the naval estimates was becoming stronger. At the Lord Mayor's Banquet the Prime Minister and Mr. Churchill deplored the extravagant expenditure upon armaments, but Mr. Churchill also mentioned the possibility of an increase in the naval estimates for 1914–15. This possibility disturbed the supporters of the Government. A deputation of protest went to the Prime Minister in December, and, early in January 1914 a hundred Liberal members supported a movement for the revival of the Committee for the Reduction of Armaments.[4]

[1] The Emperor's marginal comment was 'not at all'.

[2] D.G.P. xxxix. 74–6.

[3] D.G.P. xxxix. 77–80. The British note was given to Jagow on 6 February 1914; the German reply was dated 10 February 1914.

In view of the British question and the German answer the editorial note in D.G.P. xxxix. 60–1 complaining that no 'positive proposal' was made is unconvincing. The editorial note repeats, indirectly, the charge that the 'holiday proposal' was made merely in order to allow Great Britain to gain an advantage over Germany in shipbuilding. See also above, p. 420.

[4] The Reduction of Armaments Committee had been extremely active in 1908 when Sir J. Brunner and Mr. J. M. Macdonald presented a

Mr. Lloyd George, who seems to have been impressed by the unfavourable comments in the German Press upon the behaviour of the army at Zabern, allowed the *Daily Chronicle* to publish an account of a New Year's conversation at Criccieth. In this conversation Mr. Lloyd George gave three reasons for economy in the naval estimates: (1) The improvement of Anglo-German relations. (2) The fact that the Continental nations were spending more upon their land forces. Owing to the military situation, Germany could not challenge our naval supremacy, even if she wished to do so. (3) The 'revolt against military oppression' throughout the whole of Christendom, and particularly throughout the whole of western Europe.

Mr. Lloyd George's conversation was not well received in the French or German Press.[1] The French Press pointed out that the increased military burden upon France ought not to be a cause of rejoicing in England, and that any one-sided reduction in armaments would destroy the balance of power for the preservation of which the ententes had been called into existence. The general view in Germany was that Mr. Lloyd George knew nothing about the country, and that it was absurd to speak of a 'spread of revolt against military oppression'.

Mr. Lloyd George's attitude encouraged the revolt of the Liberals. On 1 January 1914 Sir J. Brunner wrote to the *Daily Chronicle* asking Liberal associations to pass motions in favour of a reduction of armaments. Meetings and countermeetings on the naval question were organized throughout the country. There were rumours, strongly denied by Mr. Churchill, of Cabinet dissensions upon the amount of the estimates, and the number of ships to be

memorial to the Prime Minister signed by 144 supporters of the Government.

[1] The Berlin correspondent of *The Times* suggested that the increase in armaments was partly due to the Liberal attempts to bring about a reduction. The campaign in Great Britain for the reduction of armaments was of the greatest possible help to the advocates of German naval expansion (*The Times*, 3 January 1914). The *Frankfurter Zeitung* agreed that Germany and England suffered equally from the burden of expenditure.

laid down as a result of the continued dead-lock in Canada. The Cabinet came to an agreement at the end of January, but the agitation continued. On 3 February a large meeting in favour of the limitation of armaments was held at the Queen's Hall. At this meeting Lord Courtney of Penwith spoke of the pressure exerted upon the Government by the 'armaments gang'.[1] The Bishop of Hereford was sanguine enough to hope that, 'if the British Government would go into conference with other nations, prepared to surrender the claim to destroy private property at sea and with proper undertakings honestly carried out', the naval estimates need be no larger than £40,000,000.[2] Grey answered the critics of the Government in one of the last of his speeches upon the armament question.[3] The speech is worth quoting at some length since it represents the considered view of the majority in the Cabinet. The causes of the great and deplorable expenditure upon armaments were

'really a cosmopolitan matter, and that is the serious side. . . . It is not a British matter alone, but one of European interest. It is the cumulative effect of the expenditure of the countries of Europe together upon the prospects of Europe. . . . It is no relief to Europe to save on its naval expenditure and increase on its military expenditure. The effect is the same in regard to one as in regard to the other. . . . Any large increase in the building programme of any great country in Europe has a stimulating effect upon the expenditure in other countries (but) it does not follow that a slackening in the expenditure of one country produces a diminution in the expenditure of others. . . . There is a general impression that there is in Europe, as a whole, an idea that this is a race with some prize to be won at the end of it. It is a most misleading idea, but supposing it exists, consciously or unconsciously, it does not follow that if the leading

[1] Mr. Ramsay MacDonald, at Dundee, on 22 January, said that the increase in the naval estimates was 'all due to the game of the armament manufacturers'. Mr. MacDonald made the same charge in Parliament on 2 March 1914. Hansard, 5th Ser. lix., 112-14.

[2] The expenditure for 1913-14 (including supplementary estimates) was £48,800,000, and for 1912-13, £45,000,000.

[3] Manchester, 3 February 1914.

horse slackened off, and that slackening was due to exhaustion, the effect would be a slackening on the part of others. It might be a stimulating one. Whilst British naval expenditure is a great factor in the naval expenditure of Europe, the forces that are making for that increase are really beyond control. . . . The increase in the expenditure on Dreadnoughts . . . is going on without reference to England at all. The ships which Germany is laying down are being laid down under a Naval Law which cannot be altered by anything we can do. . . . If we shut down our programme altogether and desist from building anything this year, or if we were to build nothing the year afterwards, I don't think it would cause any alteration in shipbuilding in Europe. . . . For us to make an enormous reduction of our naval expenditure when there was no certainty that it was going to have a corresponding influence on the rest of Europe, would be staking too much on a gambling chance. (*Cheers.*) Nevertheless I do think that this Dreadnought era is one to be deplored and very wasteful. I should like to know what verdict history will pronounce upon it in the future, and I trust it may pass in time for history to pronounce on it in our own lifetime. The feeling of dislike of excessive expenditure is especially strong in this country—stronger in this country than in many other countries in Europe at the present moment. . . . We are not calling out more loudly than others because we are most hurt. It is not that we feel the financial strain more than others. On the contrary we feel it least. . . . We are not calling attention to the excessive burden of the expenditure on armaments because the financial pressure has been felt mostly in this country. Then why are we doing it? The reason is that we are a business country and we are penetrated with the sense of the unproductiveness of the expenditure. We are shocked as business men with the sense of the waste of it, and we are filled, as business men, with apprehension of the effect it will have, not upon our own credit, but upon the credit of Europe, in which each country, however financially sound it is, has a vital interest, and because, as thinking men, we have the foreboding that, in the long run, exceptional expenditure on armaments, carried to an excessive degree, must lead to catastrophe, and may even sink the ship of European prosperity and civilization. What then is to be done? I am bound to say, at the present moment I can see very little to be done except to keep our own expenditure within the limits of national safety and our obligations to other parts of the Empire. It has been suggested we should make appeals to other countries to enter into mutual arrangements for the reduction of expenditure on armaments. We have in the course of the last few years made appeals—individual Ministers have made appeals, every one of which I endorse, some of which, indeed, have been initiated by me, and made by me to other countries. I endorse everything which has been said by my colleagues, but we must not get into the habit of thinking that, if the world does not do what it seems obvious to us it ought to do, it is our fault; that they are dying to do it, only they are so bashful as to be waiting for a proposal from us to do what seems to us so obvious. I think in foreign affairs we must modify the maxim of doing unto others as you would be done by. . . . If you wish to please foreign nations and to get on well with them, do unto them as they would be done by. That is the real maxim which operates for good relations between foreign Powers. . . . It is no good making to them proposals which they will not welcome and are not prepared to receive. We have to bear in mind that in a large part of the Continent of Europe, at any rate, in many great countries of Europe, they still regard their expenditure on armaments as an internal affair and resent as intrusion demands from any foreign country that their expenditure on armaments should be open to discussion or arrangement. It is felt by us that we must wait till other great countries in Europe are penetrated with the same feelings that we ourselves have with regard to the desirability of arresting the expenditure on armaments. . . . The pressure of finance is the one thing which will bring home to people the desirability of diminishing the probability of war and of keeping within bounds the competition in expenditure on armaments. And, if I see little that is hopeful at the present moment, I cannot help thinking that we must be approaching the time when the pressure of finance will alter the perspective and bring about a point of view in Europe generally with regard to expenditure on armaments which may produce an atmosphere, perhaps no long time ahead, which may make the chances of an agreement between the nations for an arrest of expenditure in armaments very much greater than it is at the present moment. (*Cheers*.)'

Meanwhile in Germany the Emperor had returned to the proposals for a further naval increase. Admiral

Müller wrote at the Emperor's command to the Chancellor that the proposals which had been postponed for political and parliamentary reasons must be brought up for reconsideration in the autumn of 1914, since the Emperor wanted to send as soon as possible a division of ships of the line to Pacific waters.[1] Tirpitz had already discussed the question with the Emperor, and prepared the way in the Reichstag by a general reference to the advantages of sending German ships abroad.[2] Unless more ships were available for foreign service, the German fleet could not show the flag in foreign ports. 'The aim of the next years must be, within the framework of the Navy Law, to obtain as soon as possible for foreign service what the Navy Law itself provides.'[3] It was also rumoured that the third battleship to be built under the supplementary law of 1912 would be laid down in 1915.

[1] D.G.P. xxxix. 82: 18 February 1914.   [2] 20 February 1914.
[3] i.e. the cruisers for which Tirpitz had asked in 1912.

XXIV

THE LAST MONTHS, 1914

THE speech in which Mr. Churchill introduced the naval estimates on 17 March did little more than repeat the facts about the British programme. Four new battleships were to be laid down, in order to maintain a superiority of 60 per cent. in capital ships. The construction of two ships would be accelerated because the ships expected from Canada were not forthcoming. The acceleration of two ships only was sufficient, since the general surplus over 60 per cent. would enable Great Britain to provide from existing resources the third ship for imperial defence. A battle squadron of eight ships, including six Dreadnoughts or Lord Nelsons, would be stationed at Malta by the end of 1915. Mr. Churchill did not mention any proposals for the limitation of armaments or for a 'naval holiday'.[1] The debate on the estimates was concerned mainly with the details of the figures given by Mr. Churchill, and was followed by a discussion upon the strategic position in the Mediterranean.[2]

From the German point of view Mr. Churchill's speech was hardly satisfactory. He accepted the 8 : 5 ratio as a standard only in Home waters. The line appeared to be drawn at Gibraltar. Ships stationed at Malta were not included in the fleets available for home defence, and therefore were outside the 8 : 5 ratio. Moreover, even

[1] There was an indirect reference to this proposal in the statement that 'every delay, accidental or deliberate, on the part of the next strongest naval Power in the development of its enormous fleet organization will be matched by us'.

[2] For these debates, see Hansard, 5th Ser. lix. One of the remarkable features of the debate was a violent attack by Mr. Snowden on the influence of armament firms upon the development of naval policy. Mr. Snowden mentioned by name a number of Ministers and other members of the two Houses holding shares in these firms. He referred to the 'bogus story about the acceleration of the German programme' in 1908–9 and said that Mr. Mulliner's information (see Appendix VI) was utterly false.

in Home waters the British Government did not bind itself always to accept a figure of 8:5. Mr. Churchill repeated the statement which he had made two years earlier. 'I must not be taken as agreeing that the ratio of sixteen to ten could be regarded as sufficient preponderance for British Naval strength as a whole above that of the next strongest naval Power. Even if we possessed an Army two-thirds as strong as that of the strongest military Power, we could not agree to that.' Mr. Churchill did not merely reassert his statement of 1912. He said that the British Government accepted the standard of a 60 per cent. superiority over the German fleet. This measure had taken the place of the obsolete two-Power theory. But the standard of 60 per cent. superiority was 'not eternal; still less could it be made a binding international instrument. It is capable of revision either in one direction or the other. I have always guarded myself against any inference that it could be made an absolute standard.'

The Emperor, following as usual the advice of the naval attaché in London, was as anxious as ever to introduce a supplementary law increasing the number of cruisers on foreign service, and also to begin in 1915 the construction of the third battleship voted in the supplementary law of 1912. For the first time Tirpitz took the side of the Chancellor, and pointed to the danger that Mr. Churchill would use the opportunity to raise a scare in England and increase the British programme.[1] Moreover, there was the German taxpayer to be considered. Tirpitz wrote to the naval attaché that 'the bow is overstrung here as much as in England'[2]—a confession which he had never made before the year 1914. In any case, further demands upon the Exchequer were necessary to provide for the development of submarines, aircraft, and destroyers. The estimated cost of these supplementary services was between seven and a half and ten million pounds over a period of six or eight years.

[1] D.G.P. xxxix. 98–9.   [2] Tirpitz, *op. cit.* i. 424.

Tirpitz's acknowledgement that any further increase in the German navy would be 'a great political blunder' is a curious 'last word' in the history of the naval competition between Great Britain and Germany. Fourteen years had gone by since the Navy Law of 1900. The danger-zone was not yet passed. The 'risk' theory had lost any political meaning. Great Britain might hesitate for a score of valid reasons from entering upon a naval war with Germany. These reasons did not include the calculation that even a victorious war with Germany would leave a weak British fleet open to attack from France or Russia, the United States, or Japan. The 'alliance' value of the German fleet had been one of the main arguments of the advocates of a strong navy. The effect of the fleet had been to draw Great Britain more closely to France and Russia. The fleet was one of the causes of the isolation of Germany, and yet it was not strong enough in time of war to protect German commerce or the German colonies, or to meet its main rival in battle on the open sea. Great Britain, so far from watching anxiously the development of the fleets of France and Russia, was counting upon France for assistance in the defence of British Mediterranean interests in the case of war with Germany, while Russia, upon whose lasting hostility to England Tirpitz had set much store less than twenty years earlier, was asking, in the spring and early summer of 1914, for a consultation with British naval authorities upon the question of mutual assistance at sea.[1] Finally, although the financial burden of the British navy was heavy upon the taxpayers, and although there might be complaints that this burden was unnecessarily severe, the first signs of actual exhaustion came not from Great Britain but from Germany. The cost of the German fleet from 1900 to 1914 was more than £200,000,000.

The story is incomplete without one curious episode—

[1] For the Anglo-Russian naval conversations, see Grey, *Twenty-Five Years*, D.G.P. xxxix. ch. ccc, and Poincaré, *Au service de la France*, iv.

the mission of Colonel House to Europe. This mission is
not important for its immediate results—results indeed
there were none; but it has a dramatic interest because
it took place in the last days of the period of armed peace.
It also shows a view of Europe in the year 1914 which
may well be taken years hence by a generation unfamiliar
with the psychological background, the historical forces
and the limitations set by time and place. This view, true
to common sense but false to history, could have been held
in 1914 only by an American living in splendid isolation
from the old world. There had been a time when Englishmen could think of themselves as remote from the troubles
of continental Europe. Palmerston looked at the confused politics of central and southern Europe as a detached
and critical spectator; in 1914 Great Britain could no
longer watch these struggles with the comfortable security of mid-Victorian statesmen.

Victorian security had been more of a delusion than a
reality. American security and self-sufficiency were no
more strongly founded. Within a few months the leaders
of the United States could not escape from the evidence
that America was as much affected by the troubles of
Servia and Austria as Great Britain had been affected
two generations earlier by the rise of Prussia and the
defeat of France.

The United States had become a world Power before
the passing of the German Navy Law of 1900, but
American action had been limited to the American
Continent and the Far East. The tradition of aloofness
from European conflicts was still strong, although President Roosevelt had taken a considerable part in the
Moroccan discussions of 1905 and 1906. The increasing
tension in Europe had begun to alarm those Americans
who were in close touch with high politics in the European
capitals. The position was, in a sense, exasperating. The
peace of the world was endangered by causes which
seemed trivial, ludicrously unimportant, or futile. Europe
as it appeared to an American observer was well de-

scribed by Walter Page in a letter to Colonel House eleven months before the outbreak of the Great War.

'Here are great navies and armies and great withdrawals of men from industry—an enormous waste. Here are kings and courts and gold lace and ceremonies which, without producing anything, require great cost to keep them going. Here are all the privileges and taxes that this state of things implies—every one a hindrance to human progress. We are free from most of these. We have more people and more capable people and many times more territory than both England and Germany; and we have more *potential* wealth than all Europe. They'd like to find a way to escape. The Hague programmes, for the most part, just led them around a circle in the dark back to the place where they started. Somebody needs to *do* something. If we could find some friendly use for these navies and armies and kings and things—in the service of humanity—they'd follow us. . . . There's no future in Europe's vision—no long look ahead. They give all their thought to the immediate danger. Consider this Balkan War; all European energy was spent merely to keep the Great Powers at peace. . . . The Great Powers are mere threats to one another, content to check, one the other!'[1]

Page wanted to find some other work for the armies. He suggested that they might 'clean up' the tropics. Colonel House, Wilson's chief friend and adviser, had already discussed the European situation with Page; he wished for concerted action to bring about a good understanding between England, the United States, Germany, and Japan. House was not much impressed with Page's plan for using the armies of Europe to 'clean up' the tropics; but he felt that some move might be made to bring Germany and England together. He mentioned the question to Tyrrell in December 1913.

'I told him the next thing I wanted to do was to bring about an understanding between France, Germany, England, and the United States, regarding a reduction of armaments, both military and naval. I said it was an ambitious undertaking, but was so well worth while that I intended to try it. He thought it one of the most far-reaching and beneficent things that could be

[1] *Life and Letters of Walter Page*, ed. B. J. Hendrick, 1922, i. 270–1.

done. He thought if we continued as at present, ruin would eventually follow, and in the meanwhile it would prevent us from solving the vexatious industrial problems we are all facing. He considered I had "a good sporting chance of success".[1]

Tyrrell suggested that House should go to Germany, and that he should see the Emperor and the Ministers of Foreign Affairs and Finance.

'He said I would find them responsive to the idea, but that the Minister of Marine, von Tirpitz, was a reactionary and largely responsible for the present German policy. He thought I should proceed quietly and secretly, but should secure an audience with the Kaiser and say to him, among other things, that England and America had "buried the hatchet", and there was a strong feeling that Germany should come into this good feeling and evidence their good intention by agreeing to stop building an extravagant navy, and to curtail militarism generally. Sir William assured me that England would co-operate with Germany cordially, and had been ready to do so for a long while.'

Tyrrell promised to give House all the memoranda which had passed between Great Britain and Germany upon the question of disarmament.

Wilson agreed with House's suggestion. In May House left the United States for what he called his 'Great Adventure'. He was unable to see the Chancellor—Bethmann-Hollweg had just lost his wife—but he had 'long talks' with Jagow and Tirpitz. He thought that Tirpitz had 'a decided dislike for the British, a dislike that almost amounted to hatred'. Tirpitz explained that in Germany 'the Government had absolutely no control over the German newspapers, but in England, he noticed, the English brought their papers around to the Government point of view whenever the situation required it'. It is clear from this remark that Tirpitz did not rate very highly House's general knowledge of the political conditions under which the German navy had developed. Tirpitz disclaimed any idea of conquest, and insisted that Germany wanted peace, 'but the best way to maintain

[1] For House's narrative, see *The Intimate Papers of Colonel House*, ed. C. Seymour, vol. i.

it was to put fear into the hearts of her enemies'. House pointed out the danger of this plan. Great Britain would be compelled to choose between Germany and Russia, and the choice under these conditions would be decided by fear of German naval supremacy. The Emperor talked to House for a half-hour during a military festival. House insisted upon seeing the Emperor alone. In September 1914 he told Spring-Rice that 'the Emperor's entourage and the Empress and her son were bitterly opposed to his mission, and evidently afraid lest the Emperor should be led away'. House did not leave a full account of the conversation; but he was satisfied that he had said what he wanted to say. The Emperor did most of the talking; he was much excited by the Yellow Peril. Disarmament was impossible as long as this danger to civilization existed. One need not suppose that the Emperor was deliberately leading House away from Europe to a subject which might show the question of armaments in a different light and give an American food for thought. The Emperor was scarcely less expansive in his discussion of European questions.

'He spoke of the folly of England forming an alliance with the Latins and the Slavs.' . . . He described the Latins and Slavs as semi-barbarous. House pointed out that 'there could be no understanding between England and Germany so long as he [the Emperor] continued to increase his navy. He replied that he must have a large navy in order to protect Germany's commerce in an adequate way, and one commensurate with her growing power and importance. He also said it was necessary to have a navy large enough to be able to defend themselves against the combined efforts of Russia and France. I asked when he would reach the end of his naval programme. He said this was well known, since they had formulated a policy for building, and, when that was completed, there would be an end.'

The Emperor did not add that his Chancellor and Foreign Office were holding him back from a further increase in his navy, and that this increase was only postponed—in the Emperor's view—for a few months.

His last words were: 'Every nation in Europe has its bayonets pointed at Germany. But'—and here he pointed to the officers of his entourage—'we are ready'.

From Berlin House went to Paris. He arrived in the middle of a serious Cabinet crisis, and found that nothing would be gained by discussion at such a moment though he wrote to President Wilson that 'he did not find the war spirit dominant in France'. He left Paris for London on 9 June. There was an even more serious political crisis in England over the question of Ulster, but House saw Grey and explained to him his mission. He found Grey

'very fair concerning the necessity for Germany to maintain a navy commensurate with her commerce, and sufficient to protect herself from Russia and France. I told him of the militant war spirit in Germany and of the high tension of the people, and I feared some spark might be fanned into a flame. I thought Germany would strike quickly when she moved; that there would be no parley or discussion. . . . I thought the Kaiser himself and most of his immediate advisers did not want war, because they wished Germany to expand commercially and grow in wealth, but the army was militaristic and aggressive and ready for war at any time. I told him that there was a feeling in Germany, which I shared, that the time had come when England could protect herself no longer merely because of her isolated position. . . . Sir Edward replied, "The idea, then, is that England will be in the same position as the Continental Powers". I said, "Quite so".'

House wanted Grey to meet the Emperor at Kiel. This suggestion showed how little House knew of European politics, or of the delicate susceptibilities of the European Chancelleries. Grey explained that a meeting of this kind would certainly arouse suspicion in France and Russia. The British Foreign Office knew that every English move in the direction of closer relationship with Germany was exploited by the German semi-official press as a sign of the collapse of the entente. Moreover, from House's own statements as well as from the previous history of negotiations over the naval question, it was hardly to be expected that Germany would make any concessions. If the meeting between the Emperor and the British Foreign Secretary produced no results, the situation would only become worse, and much of the progress towards better relations would be lost. The Anglo-German negotiations over the Baghdad railway were on the point of settlement; Grey and Bethmann-Hollweg realized that the way of escape from the older hostility lay through detailed agreements of this kind rather than through any spectacular gesture. Grey was however anxious that House should tell the Emperor privately the good reception which his proposals had received in England. House wrote a long letter to the Emperor[1] in which he said that he had come to England with high hopes, and had not been disappointed.

'I have met the Prime Minister and practically every important member of the British Government, and I am convinced that they desire such an understanding as will lay the foundation for permanent peace and security. England must necessarily move cautiously, lest she offend the sensibilities of France and Russia; but, with the changing sentiment in France, there should be a gradual improvement of relations between Germany and that country which England will now be glad to foster.'

House's letter was written on 7 July 1914. The Emperor had already started on his northern cruise, and did not return until after the delivery of the Austrian ultimatum to Servia. On 31 July, when the hope of European peace had disappeared, House wrote to Wilson that he had felt, during his stay in Germany, that

'the situation, as far as a continuation of peace was concerned, was in a very precarious condition. . . . I tried to convey this feeling to Sir Edward Grey and other members of the British Government. They seemed astonished at my pessimistic view and thought that conditions were better than they had been

[1] One may observe House's unfamiliarity with European conditions and European history from the fact that he addressed the Kaiser as 'Emperor of Germany'.

for a long time. While I shook their confidence, at the same time I did not do it sufficiently to make them feel that quick action was necessary; consequently they let matters drag on until after the Kaiser had gone into Norwegian waters for his vacation, before giving me any definite word to send to him. It was my purpose to go back to Germany and see the Emperor, but the conservative delay of Sir Edward Grey and his confrères made that impossible.'

One may think that before the last week of July House could not have realized the urgency of the situation. It is small blame to the British Cabinet if they inferred from the progress of their colonial negotiations with Germany that matters had improved, and that at a time of acute domestic crisis they might be allowed a few days consideration of a vast problem which they had been trying to solve for more than ten years. They had heard rumours of the proposal to introduce another supplementary law. They knew very well that an attempt to persuade the Emperor to take out one ship from his naval programme was bound to fail, and merely to cause ill will. They could not suppose that Germany had suddenly changed her policy, and that the Chancellor, who had worked for peace during the Balkan wars, would allow Austria a free hand to bring about a European war. Neither House nor, at this period, Page understood the European problem; House had been surprised and alarmed at the warlike tendencies of the Emperor's entourage, but these tendencies were well known to the Ministers of Great Britain. House, with a curious failure to realize the immense difficulties and complexities of the issue, wrote to Page on the outbreak of war: 'It is all a bad business, and just think how near we came to making such a catastrophe impossible! If England had moved a little faster and had let me go back to Germany, the thing, perhaps, could have been done.' Page, who knew a little more of Europe, replied: 'No, no, no,—no power on earth could have prevented it. The German militarism, which is *the* crime of the last fifty years, has been working for this for twenty-five years. It is the logical result of their spirit and enterprise and doctrine. It *had* to come. But, of course they chose the wrong time and the wrong issue. Militarism has no judgement. Don't let your conscience be worried. You did all that any mortal man could do. But nobody could have done anything effective. We've got to see to it that this system doesn't grow up again. That's all.'[1]

[1] The editors of *Die Grosse Politik* quote House's letter to Page as a proof that House blamed England for the failure of his mission. They do not mention Page's answer to House. (D.G.P. xxxix. 109–16.)

CHRONOLOGICAL SUMMARY OF EVENTS:
1896–1914

The events belonging to general political diplomatic history chosen for inclusion in this summary are those which have a particular bearing upon Anglo-German relations, with special reference to Anglo-German naval rivalry.

1896.

Jan. German Emperor sends a telegram of congratulation to President Kruger on the suppression of the Jameson raid.

1897.

June. Tirpitz appointed Secretary of the German Admiralty.
Nov. Publication of first German Navy Law.
German occupation of Kiao-Chau.

1898.

Feb. Anglo-German loan to China.
Mar. Russia demands the surrender of Chinese rights over Port Arthur and Ta-lien-wan, with a threat to occupy Manchuria.
British naval estimates reach a 'record' figure of £25,500,000.
German Navy Law passed by 212 to 139 votes after a debate of two days.
Mr. Chamberlain suggests to Germany an Anglo-German alliance. Offer refused by Bülow.
Apr. China leases Wei-hai-wei to Great Britain.
Battle of Atbara.
United States send an ultimatum to Spain.
May. Defeat of Spanish fleet off Manila—no casualties in U.S. ships.
Mr. Chamberlain in a speech at Birmingham suggests an Anglo-American alliance.
July. Major Marchand arrives at Fashoda.
Destruction of Spanish fleet at Santiago.
Aug. Signature of preliminaries of peace between Spain and U.S.A.
Sept. Battle of Omdurman.
German Emperor at Stettin describes Germany's future on the water.
British post established at Fashoda.
Oct. Anglo-German agreement concerning spheres of economic influence in China.
Crisis over Fashoda.

Formation of British flying squadron in the Channel.

Major Marchand leaves Fashoda.

Nov. U.S. Minister the only foreign diplomatic representative present at an official banquet to Lord Kitchener at the Mansion House.

1899.

Jan. Tirpitz informs Budget Committee of the Reichstag that the German Government does not intend to bring forward a new Navy Law.

Speech in London by Paul Cambon, newly appointed French Ambassador, on the need for mutual concessions between nations.

Feb. German Emperor, at a dinner of the Brandenburg provincial diet, announces that on the Mount of Olives he renewed his military oath of service to Heaven.

Mar. Signature of Anglo-French convention defining possessions and spheres of influence of the two Powers in Central Africa.

May. Opening of first Peace Conference at The Hague.

June. Naval and military sub-commission of the Peace Conference at The Hague reports that Russian proposals for disarmament are unacceptable.

Oct. Outbreak of the Boer war.

German Emperor, at the launch of a German battleship, speaks of 'Germany's bitter need of a strong fleet'.

Hamburg branch of the pan-German League passes a resolution recommending the German Emperor to abandon his proposed visit to England.

Nov. Boers invest Ladysmith.

British negotiations with United States and Germany about Samoan territories.

Speech by Mr. Chamberlain at Leicester referring to the possibility of an Anglo-Teutonic alliance.

Dec. British reverses at Magersfontein and the Tugela river.

Roberts and Kitchener appointed Commander-in-Chief and Chief of Staff in South Africa.

1900.

Jan. German steamer *Bundesrath* seized off Delagoa Bay on suspicion of carrying contraband.

Text of new German Navy Law published.

French committee on national defence proposes large expenditure on the navy and on coast and colonial defences.

Feb. Relief of Ladysmith.

Surrender of Cronje at Paardeburg.

Mar. Outbreak of Boxer rebellion in China.

May. Annexation of Orange Free State to the British Empire.

June. German Navy Law passed, with reduction in cruiser programme.

July. German force embarks for China.

Aug. Waldersee appointed Commander-in-Chief of combined forces in China.

Relief of Pekin Legations.

Sept. Annexation of the Transvaal to the British Empire.

Oct. Bülow succeeds Hohenlohe as German Chancellor.

Anglo-German agreement recognizing the principle of the 'open door' in China.

Nov. Enthusiastic reception of ex-President Kruger in Paris.

Dec. Debate in the German Reichstag on Anglo-German relations.

1901.

Jan. Death of Queen Victoria.

Bicentenary of Prussian monarchy. German Emperor issues an order to the navy on the 'resolute work' necessary to make the German navy as strong as the army.

Feb. Subsidy given by Russian Government to a steamship service in the Persian Gulf.

Mar. Bülow states that the Anglo-German agreement over China is not concerned with Manchuria.

Failure of peace negotiations in South Africa.

Apr. Visit of Italian fleet to Toulon.

Oct. Mr. Chamberlain defends action of British troops in South Africa, and compares their behaviour with that of German and other Continental armies.

1902.

Jan. Turkey grants Baghdad railway convention.

Bülow replies to Chamberlain's speech.

Feb. Announcement of Anglo-Japanese Alliance.

Franco-Russian note on the Dual Alliance and the Far East.

Apr. Manchurian convention signed by Russia and China.

June. Treaty of Vereeniging. End of Boer War.

Renewal of the Triple Alliance.

Colonial Conference in London decides on increased contributions to the Imperial Navy.

July. Resignation of Lord Salisbury. Balfour becomes Prime Minister.

Nov. Revolt in Morocco.

Dec. President Roosevelt advises Congress to vote large increases in U.S. navy and army.

Great Britain and Germany announce to U.S.A. punitive measures against Venezuela.

Criticism in U.S.A. of severity of German action against Venezuela.

1903.

Feb. Shah of Persia invested with the Order of the Garter.

Meeting in London, presided over by Haldane, to advise the formation of a British North Sea Squadron and the establishment of a naval base on the North Sea coast.

Mar. British refusal of German terms of partnership in the Baghdad railway.

Apr.–May. King Edward VII visits Lisbon, Rome, and Paris.

May. Statement by Lord Lansdowne on British interests in the Persian Gulf.

June. Murder of King Alexander and Queen Draga of Servia.

Elections to Reichstag. Great increase in Social Democratic vote.

July. Visit of President Loubet to London.

Oct. Signature of Anglo-French Treaty of arbitration.

Austro-Russian agreement at Mürzsteg on Macedonian reforms.

Dec. British Mission to Tibet.

1904.

Jan. Herero rebellion in German South-west Africa.

Feb. Outbreak of Russo-Japanese war.

Apr. Signature of Anglo-French agreement.

June. Sir John Fisher appointed First Sea Lord.

July. Russian interference with British and other neutral vessels in the Red Sea and Far Eastern waters.

Signature of Anglo-German Treaty of arbitration.

Aug. British expedition to Tibet enters Lhasa.

Russian Far Eastern fleet defeated.

Sept. Anglo-Tibetan treaty signed.

Occupation of Liao-yang by Japanese.

Oct. Russian Baltic fleet fires on British fishing vessels off the Dogger Bank.

Orders for co-operation sent to Home, Channel, and Mediterranean fleets.

Nov. Re-election of Roosevelt as President of U.S.A.

Introduction of large naval programme in U.S.A.

Dec. Redistribution of British fleet.
German rumours of possible war with England.
British Admiralty appoints Committee on Designs of Warships.

1905.

Jan. Surrender of Port Arthur.
Outbreak of revolution in Russia.
Resignation of Combes Cabinet in France. New ministry formed by Rouvier.
Feb. German press attacks speech by Mr. Lee on British navy.
Mar. Battle of Mukden.
German Emperor visits Tangier, and announces German intention of dealing directly with the Sultan of Morocco.
Lord Cawdor succeeds Lord Selborne as First Lord of the Admiralty.
May. Destruction of the Russian Baltic fleet at the battle of Tsushima.
June. Resignation of Declassé.
July. German Emperor and Tsar of Russia sign an agreement at Bjorkö.
Aug. Renewal of Anglo-Japanese alliance.
Sept. Treaty of Portsmouth (New Hampshire).
End of Russo-Japanese War.
Oct. Dreadnought laid down at Portsmouth.
Nov. Publication of German supplementary Naval Law authorizing 6 additional large cruisers, 144 instead of 96 torpedo boats, and £250,000 for submarines.
Dec. Speech of Bülow in the Reichstag on anti-German feeling in Great Britain.
German Admiralty issues a memorandum on the development of German maritime interests during the previous decade.
Resignation of the Conservative Cabinet in Great Britain. Liberal Ministry formed under Campbell-Bannerman.

1906.

Jan. Opening of Moroccan Conference at Algeciras.
Liberal victory at British general election.
Jan.–Feb. French Ambassador asks for statement of British attitude in the event of a Franco-German war over the Moroccan question.
Feb. Prime Minister sanctions informal naval and military conversations between Great Britain, France, and Belgium.
Launch of Dreadnought.

Apr.   Signature of Algeciras Convention.
       Resignation of Holstein.
       Russia invites the Powers to a second Peace Conference at
       The Hague.
July. British Government announces reduction in ship-building
       programme, with promise of further reduction in the event
       of a general agreement at The Hague Conference.
Oct.   Dreadnought leaves Portsmouth for sea trials.

1907.

Jan.–Feb. Reichstag elections. Social Democrats lose 36 seats but
       poll more votes in the constituencies.
Feb.   Russian Ministerial Council meets to decide Russian attitude
       towards Persia and the Baghdad railway.
Mar.   Destruction of French battleship *Jéna* by explosion in Toulon
       harbour.
       Campbell-Bannerman writes an article in *The Nation* on 'The
       Hague Conference and Disarmament'.
Apr.   Colonial Conference in London.
       Bülow states in the Reichstag that the German Government
       would regard a discussion of the limitation of armaments at
       The Hague Conference as dangerous and unpractical.
June. Opening of Second Peace Conference at The Hague.
July. Renewal of the Triple Alliance.
Aug.   Signature of Anglo-Russian agreement over Persia, Afghani-
       stan, and Tibet.
       British plenipotentiaries at The Hague propose a general
       motion that the Governments of the States represented at
       the conference should study the possibility of a limitation
       of armaments.
Nov.   New German naval proposals shortening the 'life' of battleships
       laid before the Reichstag.

1908.

Feb.   Letter of the German Emperor to Lord Tweedmouth on
       Great Britain and the German navy.
Apr.   Mr. Asquith succeeds Sir H. Campbell-Bannerman as Prime
       Minister, and Mr. McKenna succeeds Lord Tweedmouth
       as First Lord of the Admiralty.
       Great Britain, France, Germany, Denmark, Sweden, and the
       Netherlands sign North Sea agreement. Russia, Germany,
       Sweden, and Denmark sign Baltic agreement.
June. King Edward VII meets Tsar of Russia at Reval.
July. Revolution in Turkey.

Aug. King Edward VII meets German Emperor at Friedrichshöhe. German Emperor refuses to discuss limitation of German naval programme.

Sept. Franco-German dispute about deserters from the French Foreign Legion.

Oct. Annexation of Bosnia and Herzegovina by Austria-Hungary. Great Britain and France refuse Russian demand for the opening of the Straits to Russian warships. Publication in *Daily Telegraph* of an interview with the German Emperor.

1909.

Feb. Franco-German Agreement concerning economic interests in Morocco.

Mar. Germany asks Russia to give an unconditional and immediate recognition of the Austrian annexation of Bosnia and Herzegovina. Debate in the House of Commons on the rate of German shipbuilding. British naval programme of eight Dreadnoughts.

July. Retirement of Bülow. Appointment of Bethmann-Hollweg as German Chancellor.

Aug.–Nov. Bethmann-Hollweg opens negotiations with Great Britain for a political and naval agreement. British Government considers German offers inadequate.

1910.

Jan. Sir A. K. Wilson succeeds Lord Fisher as First Sea Lord.

Jan.–Feb. General Election in Great Britain.

May. Death of King Edward VII.

June. Kiderlen-Waechter succeeds Schön as Foreign Secretary.

Nov. Meeting of German Emperor and Tsar at Potsdam.

Dec. General election in Great Britain. Reorganization of British Home Fleet.

1911.

Feb. Fall of M. Briand's Ministry in France. M. Monis becomes Prime Minister.

Mar. Speech by Grey in the House of Commons on the growing burden of naval and military armaments.

Apr. Revolt against the Sultan of Morocco. French Government sends an expeditionary force to Fez.

June. Secret Franco-German discussions on Morocco and the Congo. Fall of M. Monis's Ministry in France. M. Caillaux becomes Prime Minister.

July. German Government sends the *Panther* to Agadir.

Speech by Mr. Lloyd George at the Mansion House causes indignation in Germany.

Aug. Russo-German agreement on the Baghdad railway and railways in the Russian sphere of influence in Turkey.

German Emperor asks for further naval increase in order that Germany may be sure of 'her rightful place in the sun'.

Sept. Outbreak of Italo-Turkish war.

Destruction of French battleship *Liberté* by explosion in Toulon Harbour.

Oct. Mr. Churchill succeeds Mr. McKenna as First Lord of the Admiralty.

Nov. Publication of secret articles concerning Morocco in Anglo-French agreement of 1904.

Italy annexes Tripolitania and Cyrenaica.

Captain Faber's speech on alleged naval and military preparations in Great Britain during September widely reported in Germany.

Statement by Grey in the House of Commons that Great Britain would not oppose German colonial expansion in Africa.

1912.

Jan. Elections to Reichstag. Social Democratic vote increases by 1 million, and represents $\frac{1}{3}$ of the German electorate.

Feb. Lord Haldane's visit to Berlin.

Feb.–Mar. Anglo-German discussions about a political agreement.

Mar. Sultan of Morocco accepts French protectorate.

Reorganization of British Fleet for home defence.

Mr. Churchill proposes a 'naval holiday'.

Apr. Irish Home Rule Bill introduced into the House of Commons.

New German supplementary Naval Law.

Formation of Balkan League.

May. Prime Minister, Mr. Churchill, and Lord Kitchener visit British naval and military stations in the Mediterranean.

Announcement of recall of Count Wolff-Metternich and appointment of Baron Marschall von Bieberstein as German Ambassador at London.

July. Debate in the House of Lords on the naval position in the Mediterranean.

British answer to new German supplementary law.

Aug. Death of Baron Marschall von Bieberstein.

Sept. French Government announces transfer of battleships from Brest to the Mediterranean.

Appointment of Prince Lichnowsky as German Ambassador at London.

Oct. Outbreak of first Balkan war between Servia, Montenegro Bulgaria, Greece, and Turkey.

British memorandum on Naval Defence requirements affecting Canada.

Nov. Anglo-French exchange of letters on naval and military conversations.

Federated Malay States offer a Dreadnought to the Imperial Government.

Dec. Armistice between Turkey and the Balkan States. Opening of Peace Conference in London.

Sir R. Borden proposes that Canada should provide three Dreadnoughts for Imperial Defence.

Death of Kiderlen-Waechter.

1913.

Jan. Break-down of negotiations between Balkan States and Turkey. War resumed.

Jagow appointed German Secretary of State for Foreign Affairs.

Poincaré elected President of the French Republic.

Mar. Further increase in peace strength of German Army.

Capital levy in Germany for defence purposes.

Mr. Churchill renews suggestion of a 'naval holiday'.

French Government decides to propose the reintroduction of a three years term of military service.

Apr. Large increase in German air, naval, and military programme.

May. Treaty between Balkan States and Turkey.

Canadian Senate rejects Navy Bill.

June. Bulgaria attacks her allies.

July. French Chamber of Deputies passes the three years service law.

July–Aug. Defeat of Bulgaria.

Opening of Peace Palace at The Hague.

Nov.–Dec. Incidents between garrison and civilians at Zabern (Alsace).

1914.

Jan. Meetings in Great Britain for the reduction of armaments.

May. Colonel House sails for Europe to discuss with Great Britain and Germany the possibility of a limitation of armaments.

June. Murder of Archduke Francis Ferdinand and his wife at Sarajevo.

July. Home Rule Conference ends in failure.

Aug. Outbreak of Great War.

TABLES SHOWING THE COMPARATIVE STRENGTH OF THE GREATER NAVAL POWERS IN VARIOUS CLASSES OF SHIPS BETWEEN 1898 AND 1914[1]

I. (a) *Battleships not more than fifteen years old from date of launch.*
(b) *Battleships under construction or projected.*

	(a)	(b)
(i) March 1898:		
Great Britain	29	12
France	17	8
Russia	11	6
Germany	13	5
Italy	7	2
United States	5	8
Japan	2	3
(ii) January 1901:		
Great Britain	28	16
France	17	5
Russia	14	10
Germany	14	10
Italy	3	6
United States	7	11
Japan	5	1
(iii) April 1902:		
Great Britain	33	15
France	13	8
Russia	15	8
Germany	17	9
Italy	5	7
United States	10	8
Japan	6	(no figures given in return)

II. (a) *First- and second-class battleships not more than fifteen years old from date of launch.*
(b) *First-class battleships under construction or projected.*

	(a)		(b)
(i) March 1903:			
	1st class	*2nd class*	
Great Britain . .	34	0	15
France . . .	11	4 (+ 1 building)	7

[1] Tables I–VI are based upon the annual returns, *Fleets of Great Britain and Foreign Countries*, laid before Parliament. Between 1898 and 1910 this statement was commonly referred to as the 'Dilke return'; from 1910 to 1914 it was referred to as the 'Dickinson return'.

G g

(i) March 1903:—*continued*

	1st class	2nd class	
Russia . . .	10	3	8
Germany . . .	12	0	8
Italy	4	0	6
United States . .	10	1	14
Japan	6	0	(no figures given in return)

(ii) March 1904:

	1st class	2nd class	
Great Britain . .	40	0	12
France . . .	12	5	6
Russia . . .	13	3	9
Germany . . .	14	0	8
Italy	5	0	6
United States . .	11	1	13
Japan	6	0	2

(iii) March 1905:

	1st class	2nd class	
Great Britain . .	44	0	9
France . . .	12	5	6
Russia . . .	11*	2	8
Germany . . .	16	0	8
Italy	6	0	4
United States . .	12	1	13
Japan	5	0	2

* Including one interned ship.

(iv) March 1906:

	1st class	2nd class	
Great Britain . .	47	0	6
France . . .	11	5	12
Russia . . .	5	1	4
Germany . . .	18	0	8
Italy	5	0	4
United States . .	14	1	13
Japan	9*	0	6

* Including five ships formerly belonging to Russia.

III. ⌐(a) *Battleships not more than fifteen years old from date of launch.*
(b) *Battleships under construction or projected.*
(c) *Battleships of Dreadnought type completed.*
(d) *Battleships of Dreadnought type under construction or projected.*
(e) *Armoured cruisers not more than fifteen years old from date of launch.*
(f) *Armoured cruisers under construction or projected.*
(g) *Armoured cruisers of Invincible type completed.*
(h) *Armoured cruisers of Invincible type under construction or projected.*

(i) March 1907:

	(a)	(b)	(c)	(d)	(e)	(f)	(g)	(h)
Great Britain . .	47	5	1	3	30	8	0	3
France . . .	17	10*	0	0	17	5	0	0

* Including six ships of Danton class (18,000 tons, but carrying only four 12-in. guns).

(i) March 1907:—*continued*

	(a)	(b)	(c)	(d)	(e)	(f)	(g)	(h)
Russia . . .	6	4	0	0	2	4	0	0
Germany . .	21	8	0	4	6	4	0	2*
Italy . . .	4	5	0	1	6	4	0	0
United States .	23	7	0	4†	11	3	0	0
Japan . . .	13	2‡	0	0	10	3	0	No figures given in return.

* Including *Blücher* (intermediate type).   † Including two ships of Michigan class.
‡ No details given of armament of two ships of Satsuma class (19,000 tons).

(ii) March 1908:

	(a)	(b)	(c)	(d)	(e)	(f)	(g)	(h)
Great Britain . .	40	8	1	6	34	4	0	3
France. . . .	16	7*	0	0	16	4	0	0
Russia	5	5	0	1	4	2	0	0
Germany . . .	21	9	0	7	8	3	0	3†
Italy	6	3	0	1	5	4	0	0
United States . .	24	5	0	4‡	12	2	0	0
Japan	13	4§	0	2	10	3	0	0

* Including six ships of Danton class.   † Including *Blücher*.
‡ Including two ships of Michigan class.   § Including two ships of Satsuma class.

(iii) March 1909:

	(a)	(b)	(c)	(d)	(e)	(f)	(g)	(h)
Great Britain . .	43	6	2	6	38	1	3	1
France. . . .	14	6*	0	0	17	2	0	0
Russia	4	8	0	4	4	2	0	0
Germany . . .	22	10	0	10	8	4	0	4†
Italy	8	1	0	1‡	6	3	0	0
United States . .	22	6	0	6§	14	–‖	0	0
Japan	13	4¶	0	2	11	2	0	0

* Including six ships of Danton class.   † Including *Blücher*.
‡ Probably.   § Including two ships of Michigan class.
‖ No figures given in return.   ¶ Including two ships of Satsuma class.

(iv) March 1910:

	(a)	(b)	(c)	(d)	(e)	(f)	(g)	(h)
Great Britain . .	45	9	5	9	38	3	3	3
France. . . .	13	6*	0	0	16	2	0	0
Russia	4	8	0	4	4	2	0	0
Germany . . .	23	8	2	8	9	3	1†	3
Italy	8	2	0	2	7	2	0	0
United States . .	26	4	4‡	4	14	–§	0	1
Japan	12‖	3‖	0	2	12	1	0	0

* Including six ships of Danton class.
† *Blücher*.   ‡ Including two ships of Michigan class.
§ No figures given in return.   ‖ Including one ship of Satsuma class.

(v) March 1911:

	(a)	(b)	(c)	(d)	(e)	(f)	(g)	(h)
Great Britain	43	10	8	10	38	5*	4	5*
France	11	8†	0	2	17	1	0	0
Russia	5	7	0	4	4	2	0	0
Germany	24	9	4	9	10	3	2	3
Italy	8	4	0	4	8	–	0	0
United States	26	6	4	6	13	–	0	–
Japan	13‡	2	0	2	13	1	0	1
Austria-Hungary§	9	5	0	4	2	–	0	0

* Including one ship for naval service of Dominion Governments.
† including six ships of Danton class.　　‡ Including two ships of Satsuma class.
§ Austria-Hungary is included in the return for the first time in this year.

IV. (a) *Battleships not more than fifteen years old from date of launch.*
(b) *Battleships of Dreadnought or improved Dreadnought type completed.*
(c) *Battleships under construction or projected (all of Dreadnought or improved Dreadnought type).*
(d) *Battle cruisers completed.*
(e) *Battle cruisers under construction or projected.*
(f) *Armoured cruisers not more than fifteen years old from date of launch.*
(g) *Light cruisers not more than fifteen years old from date of launch (for 1914 only).*

(i) March 1912:

	(a)	(b)	(c)	(d)	(e)	(f)
Great Britain	43	12	10	4	6*	34
France	13	6†	7	0	0	18
Russia	7	0	7	0	0	5
Germany	26	7	10	2	4	9
Italy	8	0	6	0	0	7
United States	27	6‡	6	0	0	13
Japan	12	3§	2	0	4	13
Austria-Hungary	9	0	4	0	0	2

* Including one ship for naval service of Dominion Governments.
† Six ships of Danton class.　　‡ Including two ships of Michigan class.
§ Including two ships of Satsuma class.

(ii) January 1913:

	(a)	(b)	(c)	(d)	(e)	(f)
Great Britain	45	15	11	7	3*	34
France	13	6†	7	0	0	18
Russia	7	0	7	0	4	5
Germany	28	10	7	3	3	8
Italy	7	1	5	0	0	7
United States	29	8‡	5	0	0	13
Japan	13	4§	1	0	4	13
Austria-Hungary	10	1	3	0	0	2

* Including one ship for naval service of Dominion Governments.
† Six ships of Danton class.　　‡ Including two ships of Michigan class.
§ Including two ships of Satsuma class.

(iii) January 1914 (first-class protected cruisers are included under (f)) :

	(a)	(b)	(c)	(d)	(e)	(f)	(g)
Great Britain . .	43	18	14	9*	1	34	36†
France	15	8‡	10	0	0	19	0
Russia	7	0	7	0	4	11	2
Germany . . .	31	13	6	4	3	8	30
Italy	7	1	5	0	0	7	4
United States . .	24	8§	6	0	0	13	10
Japan	11	4‖	2	1	3	13	8
Austria-Hungary . .	11	2	2	0	0	1	3

* Including one ship for naval service of Dominion Governments.
† Including four ships for naval service of Dominion Governments.
‡ Including six ships of Danton class.   § Including two ships of Michigan class.
‖ Including two ships of Satsuma class.

V. (a) *Torpedo-boat destroyers not more than fourteen years old from date of launch.*
(b) *Torpedo-boat destroyers under construction or projected.*

Year.	Great Britain. (a)	(b)	France. (a)	(b)	Russia. (a)	(b)	Germany. (a)	(b)	Italy. (a)	(b)	United States. (a)	(b)	Japan. (a)	(b)	Austria-Hungary. (a)	(b)
1907	143	8	34	31	85	12	47	26	17	*	20	5	56	*	Not included	
1908	137	13	42	23	93†	4	58	27	17	*	20	5	52	4	in returns	
1909	128	25	56	16	97†	*	73	24	17	*	20	15	53	3	until 1911.	
1910	111	37	60	17	97	*	85	12	21	2	25	15	55	2		
1911	126‡	29§	63	21	96	1	92	17	23	10	36	10	55	1	12	6
1912	131‖	30	68	16	94	10	109	24	22	10	40	14	55	2	12	6
1913	132‖	38	73	11	93	45	123	9	22	10	45	14	55	*	12	6
1914	143‖	36	77	7	86	45	127	12	28	16	47	14	44	2	15	3

* No figures given.
† Including one ship believed to be a total wreck.
‡ Including two ships for naval service of Dominion Governments.
§ Including one ship for naval service of Dominion Governments.
‖ Including three ships for naval service of Dominion Governments.

VI. (a) *Submarines not more than six years old from date of launch.*
(b) *Submarines under construction or projected.*

Year.	Great Britain. (a)	(b)	France. (a)	(b)	Russia. (a)	(b)	Germany. (a)	(b)	Italy. (a)	(b)	United States. (a)	(b)	Japan. (a)	(b)	Austria-Hungary. (a)	(b)
1907	37	11	36	59	20	8	1	2	3	2	7	4	7	*	Not included	
1908	41	17	33	52	24†	12	1	2	3	2	7	8	7	5	in returns	
1909	39	23	37	49	24	11	4	4	6	*	5	16	9	2	until 1911.	
1910	54	11	41	23	30	3	8	‡	6	*	10	10	9	3		
1911	56	12	29	23	18	*	8	‡	6	13	11	17	9	4	4	2
1912	49	14§	27	25	13	7	13	13‖	7	10	13	19	12	3	6	1
1913	39	22§	42	8	12	19	17	14‖	8	8	16	14	6	*	6	*
1914	37	29§	35	26	7	18	23	14‖	14	2	19	21	6	2	6	5

* No figures given in return.   † Figures doubtful.   ‡ Number uncertain.
§ Including two ships built for naval service of Dominion Governments.
‖ Plus an uncertain number.

VII. *Estimate (given in December 1912 in answer to a parliamentary question), of combined strength, in 1915, in battleships and battle cruisers of the Dreadnought, or 'improved' type, of the fleets (a) of Germany, Austria, and Italy, (b) Great Britain, France, and Russia.*

(*a*) Germany . . . 23
       Austria-Hungary . . 7 (Including Radetsky class.)
       Italy 6
                    Total 36

(*b*) Great Britain . . 37 (Including *Lord Nelson*, *Agamemnon*, and
                              New Zealand, but excluding *Australia*,
                              and projected Malayan and Canadian
                              ships.)
       France . . . 12 (Including Danton class.)
       Russia 4
                    Total 53

(Hansard, 5th Ser. xlv. 1088: 16 December 1912.)

PARLIAMENTARY HISTORY OF THE 'TWO-POWER' STANDARD

THE definition of the 'two-Power standard' as the measure of British naval requirements is generally attributed to Lord George Hamilton. It is true that, in a speech introducing the Naval Defence Act of 1889, Lord George Hamilton, as First Lord of the Admiralty, spoke of the 'leading idea . . . that our establishment should be on such a scale that it should at least be equal to the naval strength of any two other countries';[1] but already in December 1888 Mr. Forwood, Secretary to the Admiralty, had said in Parliament that the British navy should be 'of larger strength than that of any other two European countries'.[2] In any case Lord George Hamilton's words do not imply that he was laying down any new standard; he stated that his predecessors in office had accepted the view that the British fleet should be equal in strength 'to the combined naval forces of any two other countries'.

This view was held by Shelburne in 1782; a century later, however, there was a certain novelty about laying down a definite standard of measurement, since the Admiralty appeared to have no standard at all. A select Committee on the Naval Estimates reported in August 1888 that 'no complete scheme had ever been laid before the Admiralty, showing apart from the financial limits laid down by the Cabinet, what, in the opinion of naval experts, the strength of the fleet should be'.[3] The Second Sea-Lord, Vice-Admiral Sir A. H. Hoskins, told the Committee that we should 'establish a sufficient superiority to [sic] any two nations combined', but that it would be difficult, to give an exact interpretation to the term 'superiority'. Admiral Hoskins thought that a comparison of tonnage and numbers was 'very misleading'.[4] Admiral Sir A. W. A. Hood, the First Sea Lord, was also asked what he meant by the 'supremacy of the Navy'. He answered that the term was not easy to define. He did not mean 'supremacy over all navies'

---

[1] Hansard, 3rd Ser. cccxxxiii. 1171: 7 March 1889.
[2] Id. cccxxxii. 210: 13 December 1888.
[3] Select Committee on Naval Estimates (1888), 3rd Report, p. vi.
[4] Id. 3rd Report, pp. 66–7 (questions 903–9).

or 'superior to a combination of two Powers', but 'supremacy as compared with that of the next most powerful navy in the world'.[1]

The difficulty of taking numerical comparisons was explained in the debate on the Naval Defence Act. Captain Columb pointed out that 'superiority was the power necessary to keep the enemy's battleships in their harbours, and . . . all abstract comparisons were absolutely valueless. . . . Ships which were inside (harbours) did not consume coal, while the ships which were outside were consuming coal every hour and minute. There were other causes beside coaling that would necessitate their leaving their position, and therefore one could not base calculations of superiority merely on the abstract question of numbers.'[2] It was also said that the great diversity in type and armour and armament of ships made comparative estimates of naval strength far more difficult than in the earlier years of the nineteenth century.

Lord Charles Beresford, in the debate on the naval estimates in December 1888, also protested, almost in Admiral Hoskins's words that 'nothing could be more misleading, nothing more ridiculous, than comparing the numbers or tonnage of the fleets of England with those of France or of any other Power. What should be compared is the work the respective fleets have to do'—in other words, the classical task of the British fleet would be the protection of commerce and the blockade of the French naval ports; but Lord Charles agreed that the British Fleet 'should be more than a match for the combined Fleets of any two European Powers which are likely to be our foes—one of which must necessarily be France—and that finding itself under such a contingency its strength would be sufficient for defending our coasts and our trade and our commerce . . . and securing the delivery of our food supply'.[3]

On the whole, however, most speakers on naval questions accepted a rough numerical standard, if only because in public discussion any more exact methods of comparison were impracticable. On this basis of measurement it was assumed that the British navy should be at least as strong as the navies of 'any two nations combined'. It was also pointed out that a French committee had laid down in 1888 as a standard for the French

[1] Select Committee on Naval Estimates (1888), 4th Report, pp. 32-3 (questions 4308–12).   [2] Hansard, 3rd Ser. cccxxiii. 1329–30.
[3] Id. 3rd Ser. cccxxxii. 125–6.

navy 'equality in numbers with two principal Continental Navies of Europe combined, in the same way as England makes it a rule to have a Navy stronger than any two Continental Powers'.[1]

The Naval Defence Act of 1889 was the nearest approach made by Great Britain to a 'long-period' plan on the lines of the German Navy Laws. The Act provided for a building programme covering five years; the cost of this programme was £21,500,000; £10,000,000 were voted as a special charge on the Consolidated Fund. The purpose of the Act was to bring the navy up to the strength required by the increases in the navies of France and Russia. Lord George Hamilton's definition of the 'two-Power standard' as the measure of these requirements was taken for granted by the Liberal Administration which came into office in 1892. The Opposition thought that the Liberal party was not taking sufficient account of the naval needs of the country, and that, after 1894, when the last ships of the Naval Defence Act had been laid down, the position might become dangerous. A vote of censure was moved in the House of Commons on 19 December 1893.[2] During the debate the question of standards of strength was again discussed.[3] Lord George Hamilton, in opening the debate, assumed a two-Power standard. 'I will lay down one further proposition as self-evident . . . it is admitted to be a cardinal part of the policy of this country that the minimum standard of security which the country demands and expects is that our Fleet should be equal to the combination of the two next strongest Navies in Europe.' Sir Charles Dilke thought that there was considerable risk in accepting a measure of this kind. 'There is no scientific authority for the arrangement between the two Parties in the State that we should have a fleet just superior to those of France and Russia. All naval experts who have been consulted on the subject have always laid it down that for safety you must have a supremacy of five to three in battleships; that you require that supremacy for the purpose of blockade, and even for the alternative policy to blockade, of masking your enemy's fleet.' Admiral

[1] Hansard, 3rd Ser. cccxxxii. 210.

[2] This vote has an importance of its own in English history; Mr. Gladstone differed from the majority of his colleagues on the question of naval expenditure, and these differences played an important part in determining his resignation. Mr. Gladstone himself replied to the vote of censure. His speech is of particular interest; no reader of the pages of Hansard would imagine that the speaker had made his first speech in the House sixty years earlier.

[3] Hansard, 4th Ser. xix. 1771–886.

Field added that 'it would not do to re-echo the cuckoo cry that our Navy should equal the Navies of any two other Powers'. The British fleet was dispersed throughout the world; foreign fleets were concentrated. Mr. Chamberlain proposed as a 'better formula' than the two-Power standard, a policy of building five for 'any three battleships built by any naval combination against this country . . . and two for every cruiser built by the same combination'. On behalf of the Government the Secretary to the Admiralty agreed that equality in numerical strength was not enough, and that in cruisers Great Britain should 'rank even more strongly than any combination of Powers'. Four months later Mr. Goschen again raised the question. 'We might be involved, say, in a war with France and Russia, and at the same time contentions might arise with other Powers. In those circumstances we should be in extreme difficulty if we had to barter away some of our claims in order to deal with the situation which had thus suddenly arisen. Or suppose we were at war with America, and Russia and France were suddenly to raise the question of Egypt . . . if we were not ready to meet not only two Powers, but a larger combination of Powers, we might be in a position of great danger.'[1] With the return of the Conservatives to power, the two-Power standard continued to be the general measure of British naval strength, though the cruiser strength was based upon general needs. Mr. Goschen in March 1896 pointed out that the Admiralty programme of cruisers was 'based not upon a comparison of cruisers other nations have, because their conditions are entirely different from ours, but upon the question what we have to defend, what services will have to be performed, in what direction the food supply will have to be protected, and what resources we have'.[2]

In 1898, after the announcement of a large Russian naval programme, the British Government introduced supplementary naval estimates. Mr. Goschen explained that the British standard of naval strength was based on 'the two-Power policy—the principle that we must be superior in power and equal in numbers to the fleets of any other two countries. . . . The system . . . has been adopted by successive Governments. It has been attacked as being inadequate. . . . Those who attack its insuffi-

---

[1] Hansard, 4th Ser. xxiii. 240: 12 April 1894.
[2] Id. 4th Ser. xxxvii. 1520: 2 March 1896.

ciency omit, in my judgement, the immense advantages possessed by a single Power wielding a single fleet with one system of organization, with the same signals, and with the confidence inspired by constantly working together. . . . I stand by the principle —which we have followed and intend to follow—that we must be equal in number to the fleets of any two Powers.'[1] Sir Charles Dilke considered that a safe margin of strength against two Powers would give Great Britain 'a bare superiority against three . . . that is to say sufficient power to make three Powers pause before they combined against us'.[2]

Once again, in 1899, the Government made it clear that they were following a 'principle . . . which has been consistently acted upon by Admiralty administrators for many years past . . . we believe that the country expects the Admiralty to maintain our Navy on an equality with those of the two leading Naval Powers in Europe'.[3] Sir J. Colomb protested against the 'fallacy of a rule of thumb standard of abstract equality of one Fleet to two'. This standard was 'mainly political . . . it is not a scientific standard, and you cannot base comparisons of naval strength simply on the abstract number of ships. . . . You allow no margin for a combination against us of more than two Powers. And you allow no margin for the result of errors of judgement in a commander. . . . The conditions and requirements our Fleet has to fulfil must vary with the quarter from which war comes. The question is one of the geographical distribution of the enemy's ports. That is the main factor in the problem. The further these ports are from this island the greater will be our difficulties, and the greater must be the numerical preponderance which we require to produce equality.'[4]

In 1900 the German naval programme was mentioned for the first time in the speech introducing the naval estimates. Mr. Goschen referred to the 'appalling figure' laid down in the German programme, and pointed out that constant attention must be paid to the 'great development of naval power which is being made, not only in France and Russia and Germany, but also in the United States and Japan'.[5] During the next three years the main attacks upon the shipbuilding programme of the Government came from those who criticized the increase in the

[1] Hansard, 4th Ser. lxii. 860: 22 July 1898.
[2] *Id. ib.* 882–3: 22 July 1898.
[3] *Id.* 4th Ser. lxviii. 1068: 16 March 1899.   [4] *Id. ib.* 589–90.
[5] *Id.* 4th Ser. lxxix. 1126–7: 26 February 1900.

naval estimates. The Liberal party insisted that the Government was going beyond the two-Power standard, and the growth of the navies of Powers other than France and Russia made this standard unsatisfactory. In 1904 Mr. Pretyman, Secretary to the Admiralty, had to defend estimates of £37,000,000—an increase of £11,000,000 over the figures of 1900, and £22,000,000 over the estimates of 1890. He discussed at some length the question of standards. 'The country had decided to adopt what was known as the "two-Power standard" in its naval policy; and this, in the view of the Admiralty, meant that this country should be able to engage in a naval war with reasonable probability of emerging victorious from a contest with any other two naval Powers.[1] This principle must be broadly applied, not solely to particular units or particular ships. . . . The First Lord of the Admiralty (in a speech at Glasgow in April, 1903, had said) "The standard applies only to battleships, because in the matter of cruisers there can be no question of equality" . . . In considering the question of cruisers, the Admiralty were not governed solely by the two-Power standard. The duty of a cruiser was not to fight in line of battle, but to protect our trade, our commerce, and our mercantile marine; and therefore it would be seen that the standard of strength to which they had to build was not a comparative one; it was a question of proportion to be considered in relation to the magnitude of the interests to be protected.'[2] Mr. Balfour also discussed the question of standards. He pointed out that the number of important navies had increased, and that Great Britain was bound to take this fact into account. He mentioned, tactfully and indirectly, the 'risk theory' which was taking an important place in Ger-

[1] See above, p. 53, for the view stated in *The Times* of 25 November 1903, that the changed relations between Great Britain and France made it necessary to measure British naval requirements by a 'more scientific and elastic formula' than the two-Power standard.

[2] Hansard, 4th Ser. cxxx. 1259–61. Mr. Pretyman modified his statement later in the debate. He explained that he did not mean entirely to exclude cruisers, but that a comparison between the naval strength of Great Britain and other countries could not be limited to cruisers. In August 1904 Lord Selborne stated in the House of Lords that the two-Power standard had never been applied 'to cruisers and torpedo craft', and Mr. Pretyman in the House of Commons again distinguished between the measure of strength in battleships and in cruisers. 'Taking the two-Power standard as the standard to work both for battleships and cruisers . . . the numerical test was the proper test for battleships. . . . In regard to cruisers, although we might adhere to the two-Power standard, the test of equality was not numerical. Regard must be had to the character of the work they would have to do'. *Id.* 4th Ser. cxxxix. 1528 and 1060–1.

man naval propaganda. 'Supposing—I hardly like even to suggest so tragic a possibility—that we were involved in war with two great maritime Powers—supposing such a war could hardly end without immense losses, immense maritime losses, immense losses in ships and material, both on the part of our enemy and on the part of ourselves. In that case other navies would possibly remain intact, and a country which had not allowed itself to be drawn into the vortex of the war would then occupy a position which they do not occupy now, and that would necessarily put their Government, in a position, from the naval and maritime point of view, which they do not at present occupy.'[1]

The defeat of the Russian fleet and the conclusion of the Anglo-French Agreement affected the question of standards. The two-Power standard had been applied to the French and Russian fleets at a time when there appeared to be considerable chance of a naval war between Great Britain and the fleets of the Dual Alliance. The Russian fleet had now disappeared, and the French fleet was unlikely to be used against Great Britain. On the other hand, the German navy was now becoming more powerful, and German policy was as potentially dangerous to Great Britain as the policy of Russia a few years earlier.

Henceforward the two-Power standard was gradually abandoned, and the successive increases in German sea-power were taken as the measure of British requirements. The change was, however, slow, and was never complete. The two-Power standard had taken firm hold of popular imagination; statistics which showed that this standard was not being maintained were always disquieting. Moreover, if the situation was less obscure than in the five or six years before 1904 when the increase in the naval strength of Germany, Italy, the United States, and Japan, seemed to require from Great Britain at least a three-Power standard, there was still a good deal of uncertainty. Were the navies of Japan and the United States to be excluded? Was Italy to be counted on the side of the fleets of the Entente Powers? Was the Austrian navy to be added to the German navy? What was the measure of superiority required in cruisers, in ships of the most modern type? What margin was required in the Mediterranean, or in the Far East? How far could the existing diplomatic alinements of the Powers be regarded as

---

[1] Hansard, 4th Ser. cxxx. 1410-11: 1 March 1904.

permanent, or at all events unlikely to change within five or six years?

The confusion of public opinion may be seen in the first year of the Liberal Government. In 1905 there had been little discussion of the question of standards. The interest of the public was centred on the bold policy of the Admiralty in scrapping a large number of obsolete ships and concentrating to a greater extent upon a strong force ready for immediate action. Moreover, at the end of 1905, from the point of view of numerical comparison with the fleets of other Powers, the British navy was in an extremely strong position. The position was less satisfactory for those who looked three or four years ahead; but public opinion, as reflected in Parliament and the Press, was accustomed to take the years as they came.

In July 1906 the Government announced that they were reducing their shipbuilding programme for the current year from four to three large ships; that they would provide for two large ships in the estimates of 1907-8, but the third ship would be laid down only if the proposals in regard to the reduction of armaments laid before the Hague Conference proved to be abortive.[1] This announcement brought the question of a two-Power standard into the debate on the naval estimates. Mr. Balfour and Mr. Lee pointed out that the introduction of the Dreadnought made it necessary to secure a safe margin in this new class of ship. Henceforward the two-Power standard must be considered not merely in relation to battleships, but battleships 'of the newest and latest types'. Captain Hervey added that the two-Power standard implied also a 10 per cent. margin of superiority to cover battleships away on foreign service.

The Prime Minister, on the other hand, raised the point that the two-Power standard had not been adopted without reference to political conditions. 'When you talk of the two-Power standard, after all you cannot quite keep out of your mind who the two Powers are. When we have elaborate calculations made as to what France and Germany are building, is it really a very likely combination that France and Germany should be allied and should go to war with us? I do not object to the two-Power standard as a rough guide, but this is a two-Power standard of almost a preposterous kind.' This statement was criticized with-

[1] Hansard, 4th Ser. clxii. 67–119: 27 July 1906. For The Hague Conference and the British naval estimates, see above, pp. 121–40.

in a few days in the House of Lords. Earl Cawdor accused the Government of giving up the two-Power standard. 'There is no half way in this matter. Either the Navy is to be maintained strong enough to make us absolutely safe against any two Powers—I care not which they are—who might combine against us, or it is not. If you drop below the two-Power standard, what standard are you going to adopt?'[1]

The discussion was renewed in the debate upon the naval estimates in March 1907.[2] Mr. Robertson, Secretary to the Admiralty, claimed that the two-Power standard was being maintained, but added that this standard was 'not a standard in the abstract—a mere *chimaera bombinans in vacuo*—it was a concrete thing; but at the best it was only a rule of thumb—a rough-and-ready test. There may be conceivable circumstances in which a two-Power standard might be too much, and there may be imaginable circumstances in which a three-Power standard would be too little.' Mr. Lee asked for a clear definition of the view taken by the Government. The Prime Minister again gave an inconclusive answer. He accepted the two-Power standard, but deprecated 'a too slavish use of a useful phrase such as this. . . . Supposing we were at any time to be in close alliance with the two Powers with the largest navies—however close that alliance may be, however almost [*sic*] inconceivable it would be that we were to be on bad terms—should we still rigidly adhere to this two-Power standard (Opposition cries of 'Yes') or go on putting down ship for ship if one or other of these Powers went on building?' Mr. Balfour asked for a less ambiguous statement. There were two possible views. 'One is that this country should have, and always have, no matter what its foreign alliances and relations may be, at least a naval strength which will enable it to deal, with good hope of success, with the fleets of any two other nations which may be brought against it.' On the second view, 'the two-Power standard is a convenient phrase and may represent a good ordinary working hypothesis, nevertheless, if you feel you are on really good terms with one of the great naval Powers whose strength was to be taken into account in measuring the fleet we ought to build, then we may rightly and safely . . . fall below that two-Power standard'.

[1] Hansard, 4th Ser. clxii. 297–8: 30 July 1906.
[2] *Id.* 4th Ser. clxx. 654–716, 1005–56, and 1061–96: 5, 7, and 8 March 1907.

Mr. Balfour asked the House to accept the view that the country should be 'safe against any combination of any two Powers throughout the world'. There were cries of 'Agreed'. Mr. Balfour replied, 'Yes, agreed by everybody but the Prime Minister.' The Prime Minister answered: 'The worst of it is I shouted it too.' Mr. Balfour then said that at last he had been given an explicit statement by the Prime Minister, 'even by way of interjection'. The question was raised by other speakers. Mr. Wyndham held that there was great danger in giving to other Powers the impression that Great Britain did not intend to maintain the two-Power standard 'as it was commonly and easily understood'. On 18 March a question was asked whether the Admiralty proposed to abandon the two-Power standard. The answer was in the negative; but it was also said that the British programme of new construction would not be increased to a total equal to the combined figures of new construction in France and the United States.[1]

When the shipbuilding vote was under discussion in the House on 31 July 1907, Mr. Robertson explained that 'the two-Power standard was not applicable to the destroyer section of the British Navy.[2] The number of destroyers wanted depended on the use that was to be made of them, and not on the number which might be in the possession of other Powers.'

There was little reference to the subject between the summer of 1907 and the introduction of the naval estimates in March 1908. Meanwhile the failure of The Hague Conference to secure any general measure of disarmament made the problem of naval competition more severe, and the question of standards more difficult.

On the day before the opening of the debate on the naval estimates of 1908–9 Mr. J. M. Macdonald brought forward a motion in favour of further reductions in expenditure on armaments.[3] The supporters of the motion thought that, in view of the changed political circumstances, the two-Power standard was no longer a suitable measure of naval strength. Owing to the illness of the Prime Minister Mr. Asquith defended the policy of the Government. He used somewhat vague terms, but left no doubt that the Government accepted a two-Power standard.

---

[1] Hansard, 4th Ser. clxxi. 450. The question was discussed in both Houses on 17 April, but no new facts or statements of policy were brought forward. *Id.* 4th Ser. clxxii. 924–35 and 1066–99.   [2] *Id.* 4th Ser. clxxix. 981–1048.

[3] Hansard, 4th Ser. clxxxv. 355–468.

'We believe it to be our duty to maintain our standard of relative naval strength. . . . I do not think the historical origin of
the standard matters very much. The combinations of Powers
and the relations between Powers necessarily shift from time to
time. The standard which is necessary for this country—you
may express it by any formula you please, though I believe it
to be a convenient and practical formula—the standard which
we have to maintain is one which would give us complete and
absolute command of the sea against any reasonably possible
combination of Powers. I do not think it desirable, on the
contrary, I think it in the highest degree undesirable, in the
public interest to speculate as to what the possible groupings
may be; whether this Power or that may or may not become,
in the future, the enemy of this country. Of this I am perfectly
certain . . . there is none of the great Powers of the world . . .
which views with animosity, jealousy, or misgiving the Navy
of Great Britain being maintained at what we call the two-
Power standard.'

During the debate on the estimates the main subject of discussion was not the measure of naval strength, but the question
whether the shipbuilding programme of the year was sufficient
to meet the needs of the two-Power standard which had been
accepted by the Government. The discussion centred round
the comparative strength of the British and German navies.
The debate on the shipbuilding vote in July took a similar
course. Mr. Lee suggested a 'two to one standard' against our
chief rival. The two-Power standard was best translated as the
'twice one standard'.[1] On 12 November Mr. Lee put a question
to the Prime Minister: did the Government accept the two-
Power standard of naval strength as meaning a predominance
of 10 per cent. over the combined strengths, in capital ships,
of the two next strongest Powers; and, if not, what was the
definition of the two-Power standard accepted by the Government? Mr. Asquith replied: 'The answer to the first part of
the Question is in the affirmative.'[2] *The Times* commented that
this statement was very satisfactory. If Great Britain did not
define her policy, there was a chance that 'some other Power
might hope by persistent effort to tire us out in the race'.[3]

[1] One sentence in Mr. Lee's speech is of interest to the social historian. '*As the
motor cabs superseded the older class of vehicles* so no doubt the Dreadnought would
be superseded.'

[2] Hansard, 4th Ser. cxcvi. 560.   [3] *The Times*, 13 November 1908.

A few days later Mr. J. M. Macdonald asked the Prime Minister whether 'in accepting the definition of the two-Power standard as meaning a preponderance of 10 per cent. over the combined strengths, in capital ships, of the two next strongest Powers, he intended to extend the definition given by himself earlier in the year to the effect that the standard we have to maintain is one which would give us complete command of the sea against any reasonably possible combination of Powers'. Mr. Asquith answered that in his opinion, 'the two statements (were) under existing conditions identical in meaning and effect'. Mr. Lee then asked whether 'by the words "the two next strongest Powers" ' the Prime Minister meant 'the two next strongest Powers whatever they may be, and wherever they may be situated'. To this question Mr. Asquith replied: 'Under existing circumstances, and under all foreseeable circumstances, I think that is so.' Whereupon Mr. Macdonald once more raised the question 'whether, in taking into consideration the two Powers (the Prime Minister) has had regard to any reasonably possible combination among those Powers against us'. The Prime Minister answered: 'The dominating consideration with us is that we should maintain our superiority at sea. As has often been explained by those responsible on both sides of the House, we regard the two-Power standard as a workable formula to give effect to that.'[1]

Mr. Lee again raised the question on 17 December 1908. He called the attention of Mr. Asquith to the fact that the signatories of a memorial on the reduction of armaments claimed that he (Mr. Asquith) would shortly 'make a public announcement modifying the statements which he had recently made in (the) House on the subject of the two-Power standard'. The Prime Minister answered that the views of the Government were unchanged; they would 'continue to pursue a policy which has now been followed for a number of years'. On the other hand, he did not wish to discuss matters of such importance merely in answer to a question, when a Minister 'on the spur of the moment' might 'use language, which, however carefully chosen, may always be liable to a certain amount of misinterpretation'.[2]

During the debate on the naval estimates of 1909–10 the

[1] Hansard, 4th Ser. cxcvi. 1768–9: 23 November 1908.
[2] Id. 4th Ser. cxcviii. 2113–14: 17 December 1908.

question of German acceleration, and the British countermeasures, took up the main attention of the speakers. The
Conservatives attacked the Government for neglecting even to
maintain a 'one-Power' standard in ships of the Dreadnought
class. The Prime Minister insisted that the question of a 'two-
Power' standard was distinct from the special question of the
construction of Dreadnoughts. 'You must not take into account
merely . . . the number of your Dreadnoughts and Invincibles,
but you must take the total effective strength for defensive
purposes as compared with the combined effective strength of
any two other fleets for aggressive purposes.'[1] On 29 March
1909, the Opposition moved a vote of censure on the naval
policy of the Government. Before the debate Mr. McKenna
stated in answer to a question, that the 'standard of power'
taken by the Admiralty had been explained in the Prime
Minister's speech on 16 March. He refused to go beyond this
statement. The debate on the vote of censure was concerned
with the question of German acceleration. One member (Captain Kincaird-Smith) pointed out that 'a stranger listening to
(the) debate would have felt surprised at the utter absence of
all reference to the two-Power standard. We seem to have forgotten all about the two-Power standard. It is never mentioned
at all. . . . I have never thought myself that we are going to be
able to permanently maintain [*sic*] the two-Power standard if
other countries, and notably the United States, choose to build
up their navies.'[2]

The question of a two-Power standard was, however, soon
revived. Questions were asked on 27 April, 29 April, and
3 May 1909, about the definition of the two-Power standard,
with particular reference to the inclusion of the navy of the
United States in a calculation of the strength of foreign navies.
A full debate was held on the subject on 26 May.[3] Captain
Craig rose 'to call attention to the divergent and contradictory
opinions expressed by various members of His Majesty's Government on the subject of Naval Defence'. He moved 'That this
House would view with alarm any modification of the two-
Power standard as defined by the Prime Minister on the 12th
and 23rd November 1908, viz., a preponderance of 10 per cent.
over the combined strengths in capital ships of the two next

<hr/>

[1] Hansard, 5th Ser. ii. 956: 16 March 1909.
[2] *Id.* 5th Ser. iii. 110: 29 March 1909.   [3] *Id.* 5th Ser. v. 1278–1320.

strongest Powers, whatever these Powers may be and wherever they may be situated.' The opening speech for the motion was made by Mr. C. Craig. He reminded the House of the different pronouncements made by the Prime Minister, and asked for a clear statement whether the Government did or did not include the United States in their calculations. The Prime Minister's answer was neither clear nor consistent with his earlier declarations. He refused to consider the 'two-Power' standard as an immutable rule. 'It is spoken of sometimes as if it were like the law of gravitation or the precepts of the Decalogue—a sort of immutable truth dictated to us by Nature or Providence, which it is absolutely profane to criticize, and which under no circumstances can be questioned. . . . The two-Power standard is nothing more than an empirical generalization; it is a convenient working rule of thumb under existing conditions—conditions which have prevailed for a considerable number of years. We do not know how much longer they are going to prevail.' The navy must be strong enough to safeguard Great Britain from invasion, and to protect the British Empire and British commerce. 'I much prefer to state our purpose and our naval policy in terms of means, and I say you must adapt your means from time to time, having regard to the ever-shifting exigencies of the ship-building policies and ambitions of other countries. . . . We must take our total effective strength for defensive purposes, as compared with the combined effective strength of any other two fleets.' The Prime Minister then suggested three 'practical considerations' in the application of the rule. (1) Two hostile fleets were not as effective as one homogeneous fleet belonging to one nation, and under one command. (2) The two-Power standard applied only to battleships. (3) The question of distance was of importance in considering any probable combination of hostile Powers. 'As regards the United States they would not count under existing conditions as one of the two Powers which you have to take into account.'[1]

The Prime Minister's statements were wrapped in elaborate verbiage, but the discrepancy between his reservations and the

[1] As early as February 1904, Haldane had excluded the navy of the United States from any calculation of the two-Power standard. He said in the House of Commons that he had 'always maintained that the two-Power standard had nothing whatever to do with the United States. He refused to contemplate war with the United States as being within the range of practical politics.' Hansard, 4th Ser. cxxx. 1301.

plain statements which he had made in the previous November could not be concealed. Mr. Bellairs described the speech as a 'complete abandonment of the two-Power standard'; Mr. Balfour asked that the Government should state exactly what was their standard. Finally, Mr. McKenna repeated, in less elaborate phraseology, the statement of the Prime Minister, and the debate ended without any more explicit definition.

The debate on the shipbuilding vote in July 1909 again showed that the two-Power standard was no longer applicable to the requirements of the time, or rather, that this standard was being applied not to the two navies nearest in strength to the British navy but to the fleets of Germany and Austria. The Opposition accused the Government of building to a one-Power standard. The Prime Minister referred once more to his general reservations, but on neither side of the House was there any clear statement of the standard required. Mr. Ashley suggested that a new standard should be taken, and that Great Britain should 'build two ships to every one laid down by the next strongest Power'.[1] On the other hand, Dr. Macnamara complained that the two-Power standard, which had been applied only to capital ships, was now being used in a comparison of all classes of vessels.[2] It is curious that no member of the Opposition noticed that this interpretation was entirely new, and that, in earlier years, the limitation of the two-Power standard to battleships meant that the British margin of superiority in other classes of ships was higher.[3]

The large programme of eight capital ships in 1909–10 was followed by a programme of five ships in 1910–11. In his explanation of the naval estimates of 1910–11 to the House Mr. McKenna was able to state that 'the British Navy maintains, in the strict sense of the term, the two-Power standard laid down by . . . the Prime Minister'.[4] Mr. Lee denied that the standard was being maintained in its traditional form. Lord Charles Beresford attacked the Prime Minister's view that the

[1] Hansard, 5th Ser. viii. 1717: 3 August 1909.   [2] *Id. ib.* 1797.
[3] The point was raised in the following March by Mr. Leverton Harris. 'As a ship-owner . . . the two-Power standard never seems to me complete or entirely satisfactory. . . . The two-Power standard deals entirely with capital vessels. . . . It leaves out of account the number and size of our Mercantile Marine and the great length of the ocean routes which have to be protected and kept open in time of hostilities.' *Id.* 5th Ser. xv. 277.
[4] *Id. ib.* 38–147 (14 March 1910), 198–316 (15 March), 363–478 (16 March), 532–603 (17 March).

question of the geographical disposition of other strong navies affected the interpretation of a two-Power standard. British interests were world-wide; 'it would be more difficult for us if there were a large hostile fleet at the other end of the world than it would be if there were two hostile fleets in European waters, because we could then concentrate against them. . . . The fleet abroad will have to be stronger on account of reliefs, supplies, and keeping its units. But you must be prepared to have two fleets unless you observe the two-Power standard.' Mr. Gibson Bowles stated the case for the opposite view. 'The two-Power standard is a mere hollow formula. It is the kind of notion which a man desires who wishes to relieve himself from thought and action and to put his mind into a pigeon-hole and leave it there once and for ever. A two-Power standard at one time may be excessive, and at another time it may be deficient. . . . The standard of efficiency for our Navy . . . is this: You must first find out who all your probable enemies are going to be, and then provide such a Fleet, so manned and so handled, that you are sure to beat them. . . . To arm against the whole world, against your friends as well as against your enemies, is foolish and unnecessary.'

The references to the subject in the discussion of the ship-building vote were similar. The Prime Minister left no doubt that the Government intended to 'maintain an ample margin of security against all probable or even possible risks'; but he did not commit himself to any particular numerical standard.[1] In the following March Mr. McKenna stated in answer to a question that the Government accepted the definition of the two-Power standard given by the Prime Minister in 1909, and not the definition given in November 1908.[2] The question was asked immediately before a general debate on the reduction of armaments.[3] Mr. J. M. Macdonald, in opening this debate, opposed a two-Power standard on the ground that it imposed upon Great Britain 'the necessity of maintaining a standard of strength equal to the two next strongest Powers without any regard to the relations between them or to their relations with us'. The standard was justified at a time when Great Britain was not on good terms with France and Russia; 'it was forced upon us by the existence of a real danger, but the danger dis-

---

[1] Hansard, 5th Ser. xix. 639: 14 July 1910.
[2] *Id.* xxii. 1860: 13 March 1910.   [3] *Id. ib.* 1877–1996.

appeared in the face of a wise diplomacy'. Mr. Balfour agreed that the two-Power standard might not fit the conditions of the time, but asked for a definition of the standard which was to take the place of the two-Power rule. Grey repeated the Prime Minister's view that 'in dealing with the two-Power standard you must not take the United States into account in the same way that you must take European countries', and accepted Mr McKenna's definition of a 'fleet sufficient to hold the sea against any reasonably probable combination'.

The debate on the naval estimates of 1911–12 followed three days after the general discussion on the reduction of armaments.[1] Mr. Lee pointed out that the two-Power standard had now disappeared, and again asked for a 'two keels to one' standard in relation to the next strongest naval Power. He was supported on the Conservative side, though Mr. Balfour did not go beyond a criticism of the view that Great Britain need not consider naval Powers outside Europe. The answers of the Government were still evasive. The Prime Minister was asked to state plainly whether he had abandoned his definition of the two-Power standard as a preponderance of 10 per cent. over the combined strength of the two next strongest Powers, wherever these Powers were situated. His answer was merely a reference to his speech of 26 May 1909.[2] In a later stage of the debate on the estimates Mr. Lee appealed to the First Lord to explain the standard adopted by the Government. Mr. McKenna found it difficult to elude the contradiction between the two statements made by the Prime Minister. He pointed out that the numerical basis of the two-Power standard was properly applicable to ships in European waters, and could not be used in comparing fleets which were too far apart to act together against Great Britain.[3] Further discussion in the summer brought no plainer definition of the standard.

The whole question was treated with clearness and precision by Mr. Churchill in the spring of 1912. Mr. Churchill introduced his first naval estimates with a number of general remarks. He said that the Government was not prepared to recommend the immediate introduction of a 'two keels to one standard in new construction against Germany. The time may come when that will be necessary, but it is not necessary now. . . . Standards

---

[1] Hansard, 5th Ser. xxii. 2457–558: 16 March 1911.

[2] *Id.* 5th Ser. xxiii. 22–3: 20 March 1911.   [3] *Id.* 5th Ser. xxiii. 2542–3.

of naval strength must vary with circumstances and situations'.[1] The Admiralty proposed, while the pre-Dreadnought ships retained their fighting value, to adopt a standard of 60 per cent. superiority in Dreadnoughts; this standard would be higher in the case of other classes of ship, and would be increased to meet any further increase in the German programme.[2] Mr. Churchill finally dismissed the two-Power standard. 'When the next two strongest naval Powers were France and Russia, and when these two Powers were also what one might call the most probable adverse diplomatic combination, the two-Power standard was a convenient rule, based upon reality, for us to follow as a guide. The passage of time and the rise of a navy of a single Power to the first place upon the Continent has changed this. We have no longer to contemplate as our greatest potential danger, the alliance, junction, and co-operation of two naval Powers of approximately equal strength. On the facts of to-day, the Navy that we should require to secure us against the most probable adverse combination would not be very much greater than the Navy we should require to secure us against the next strongest naval Power.'

Mr. Churchill's statement put an end to the uncertainty about the standard to which the Government were building; his speech was well received by the Conservatives, and the question of a return to a two-Power standard was now settled. During the next two years there were further discussions about the strength of the navy, but these discussions dealt for the most part with the number of ships to be maintained in the Mediterranean. The Conservatives doubted whether Mr. Churchill was actually making provision for the preponderance in capital and other ships which he had described as necessary. These debates were not less heated and controversial than the earlier debates on the two-Power standard, but they took full account of the changed conditions.

The last discussion of importance took place on 17 March 1914. Mr. Churchill's words summarized the history of the two-Power standard from the time of Lord George Hamilton to the outbreak of the Great War: 'Formerly we have followed the two-Power standard—that is to say, 10 per cent. over the two next strongest Powers. Now that standard has become quite meaningless. The two next strongest Powers, if you take

---

[1] Hansard, 5th Ser. xxxv. 1554-5.   [2] See above, p. 369.

the whole world, would be Germany and the United States, and if you left out the United States, as common sense would dictate, the two next strongest Powers would be Germany and France, which is not a very helpful or reasonable standard to adopt. . . . The 60 per cent. standard was adopted by the Admiralty in 1908 or 1909, and it was announced publicly by me two years ago. That is a building standard of new construction only, and it refers to capital ships only. For cruisers we follow a 100 per cent. standard, and have been for many years. There are other standards for other classes.'[1]

[1] Hansard, 5th Ser. lix. 1926–7: 17 March 1914.

APPENDIX III
'CAPITAL' SHIPS

THE eighteenth-century term 'capital' ship was revived about 1907. The older terms used were 'ships of the line' or 'battleships'. A book on naval policy published in 1907 by Captain R. N. Custance under the pseudonym of 'Barfleur' brought back the adjective 'capital' into modern use. The term was of importance in view of the development of the large and powerful armoured cruisers of the 'Invincible' type. *The Times*, in a leading article on the subject on 28 December 1908, pointed out that if the British cruisers of the Invincible type were included in any calculation of 'capital' ships, the cruisers of foreign Powers should also be brought into the account. Mr. Lee used the term on 12 November 1908, in a question to the Prime Minister; the Prime Minister did not comment on the word 'capital' in his reply.[1] On the other hand, three weeks later (7 December 1908), Mr. McKenna was asked in the House of Commons to state the number of 'capital' ships in commission in the navies of Great Britain, France, Germany, and Russia. He answered: 'I am not aware what interpretation my hon. friend places upon the term "capital" ship.' He then gave a list of 'first-class battleships'.[2] Three months later Mr. McKenna was asked to define the term 'capital' ship. He answered that the Board of Admiralty had 'never sanctioned the official use of the term, and they do not deem it expedient to do so'.[3] In May 1909 Mr. Asquith mentioned the term. 'The phrase has recently crept in ... of "capital ships". I do not know what a "capital ship" is, or I do not think [*sic*] anybody else knows. . . . At any rate it was used in regard to ships to be put in the line of battle. In other words, it does not include the great bulk of your cruisers. . . . It applies to battleships who, as the lawyers would say, were ejusdem generis.'[4]

In March 1910 Mr. Lee gave a definition of the term:[5] 'The term "capital ships" is an old eighteenth-century term applying to a ship which is capable of lying in line of battle.' The term was used in this sense without question from 1910 onwards.

---

[1] Hansard, 4th Ser. cxcvi. 560.   [2] *Id.* 4th Ser. cxcviii. 40.
[3] *Id.* 5th Ser. i. 1110: 1 March 1909.
[4] *Id.* 5th Ser. v. 1294: 26 May 1909.   [5] *Id.* 5th Ser. xv. 267.

The difficulty of defining ships 'capable of lying in line of battle' had arisen since the development of a larger and more powerful type of cruiser. For some years the new cruisers of the Invincible type were known as large armoured cruisers, or even as 'fast battleships'. In 1911 these ships were officially described as 'battleship-cruisers' and in 1912 as battle-cruisers.

Note. The term 'super-Dreadnought', to denote later ships of the Dreadnought type, was used in *The Times* of 3 March 1911. *The Times* described the word as 'misleading'; the 'super-Dreadnought' was as much an advance on the Dreadnought type as this type of ship had been an advance upon earlier battleships. Moreover, some of the later ships classed as Dreadnoughts were not 'all-big gun ships', and if such ships were counted as Dreadnoughts, the *Lord Nelson* and *Agamemnon* should also be included.

BRITISH OFFER OF A REDUCTION IN SHIP-BUILDING PROGRAMME AT THE TIME OF THE FIRST HAGUE CONFERENCE

Mr. Goschen, in a speech explaining the naval estimates of 1899–1900, told the House of Commons that the great increase in the shipbuilding programmes of foreign Powers, particularly in the Russian programme, necessitated a corresponding increase in the British programme. At the same time he offered to reduce the British programme if a reduction were made by other Powers. 'An International Conference is to be assembled. Will the deliberations of that Conference—will the actions of other nations resulting from that Conference—make it possible for us to diminish or modify our programme for new construction, while, of course, maintaining our standard and not altering our relative position? We have been compelled to increase our expenditure as other nations have increased theirs, not taking the lead, not pressing on more than they. As they have increased, so we have increased. I have now to state on behalf of Her Majesty's Government that similarly, if the other great Naval Powers should be prepared to diminish their Programmes of shipbuilding, we should be prepared on our side to meet such a procedure by modifying ours. The difficulties of adjustment are no doubt immense, but our desire that the Conference should succeed in lightening the tremendous burdens which now weigh down all European nations is sincere.'[1]

It is interesting to notice that this offer was regarded by some of the supporters of the Government as dangerous, and that the arguments used against it were not unlike those used by Germany at the second Hague Conference. Sir J. Colomb said that 'an official intimation of readiness to determine the extent of our naval force by reference to the wishes of a selected number of European maritime nations is a regrettably new departure

---

[1] Hansard, 4th Ser. lxviii. 323–4. The closing words of Mr. Goschen's speech are of interest. 'If you think that war is simply an absurd impossibility, if you think you can have peace without power, if you believe in the sweet reasonableness of Europe in arms, then I admit that these estimates are a crime. If, on the other hand it is not so, then these Estimates are a necessity, and they are simply the embodiment of the will of a peace-loving but determined people.'

in British policy. I object to allowing our naval policy to be saddled with any conditions laid down at any conference, only representing certain maritime powers, and not all. My reason for that is that there is no parallel at all in the British position and in the position of any other nation in the world' . . . 'What about the United States and Japan? We cannot deal with this question of the relative strength of our Fleet, and of European Fleets, and be bound by a proposal for a reduction of our Fleet, if any portion of the great maritime Powers is left out of account.'[1] Mr. Macartney, the Secretary to the Admiralty, answered this speech in a curious way. He pointed out that Mr. Goschen had not committed himself to any 'reduction of the naval power of this country in the event of an agreement of the European Powers without regard to the responsibilities of the Empire at large. . . . My right honourable Friend said, "If Europe does not agree, the programme must stand".' Mr. Macartney denied that 'a converse should be deducted from (this) statement'. On behalf of the Opposition, Mr. E. Robertson pointed out the inconsistency between Mr. Goschen's and Mr. Macartney's statements. Mr. Macartney then explained that he was only protesting against the view that 'the naval expenditure of (the) country was (being) placed in the hands of the European Conference'. He had no wish to 'diminish' the statement that 'if the Peace Conference does carry out the object which we all believe His Majesty the Tsar sincerely has at heart, an opportunity will probably be afforded to all European Naval Powers of in important elements diminishing [sic] their programmes of naval construction'.[2]

The proposal was given little notice in the British or foreign press. No other announcement was made on the subject, and the public gave small attention to the matter. The Russian invitation to the Peace Conference came at a time when Russia was making a large increase in her navy, and Germany was about to extend the scope of the naval programme laid down in the law of 1898. No proposal for the reduction of armaments was likely to receive serious consideration, and the discussions ended in a simple vœu that the Governments represented at the Conference should examine the possibility of an agreement upon the limitation of their armed forces and their military and naval expenditure.

[1] Hansard, 4th Ser. lxviii. 587–91.   [2] Id. ib. 636–7.   [3] Id. ib. 1065–6

MR. LLOYD GEORGE ON THE POSSIBILITY OF ECONOMY IN ARMAMENTS, 23 JULY 1914

(This speech has a particular interest in view of the date upon which it was delivered.)

'I THINK . . . that next year there will be substantial economy without interfering in the slightest degree with the efficiency of the Navy. The expenditure of the last few years has been very largely for the purpose of meeting what is recognized to be a temporary emergency. . . . I think it is a very serious thing . . . to assume that this expenditure on armaments is going on, and that there is not likely to be a stop to it. I think there are symptoms, not merely here but in other lands, not merely that the industrial classes, but that the financial interests of the world are getting alarmed. I have always held that you cannot arrest armaments by mere political moves against them and by mere political criticism. I have always thought you could not arrest them by motives of humanity, and I regret that that is so. I am firmly of opinion that they will only be arrested when the great financial interests of the world begin to realize what a menace they are to capital, to property, to industry, to the prosperity of the world, and I think they are beginning to realize it. . . . It is very difficult for one nation to arrest this very terrible development. You cannot do it. You cannot when other nations are spending huge sums of money which are not merely weapons of defence, but are equally weapons of attack. I realize that, but the encouraging symptom which I observe is that the movement against it is a cosmopolitan one and an international one. Whether it will bear fruit this year or next year, that I am not sure of, but I am certain that it will come. I can see signs, distinct signs, of reaction throughout the world. Take a neighbour of ours. Our relations are very much better than they were a few years ago. There is none of that snarling which we used to see, more especially in the Press of those two great, I will not say rival nations, but two great Empires. The feeling is better altogether between them. They begin to realize they can co-operate for common ends, and that the points of cooperation are greater and more numerous and more important than the points of possible controversy.' Mr. Lloyd George then quoted a speech made by the Duke of Wellington in 1842 in defence of the income tax. The Duke of Wellington described the measures of the years immediately preceding 1842 as 'war measures'. He used the words: 'I believe we have been at something as like war, if it be not war, as anything could well be.' Mr. Lloyd George commented: 'That is exactly a description of the present situation, not merely in this country, but throughout the whole world. We have been engaged in something which is as like war as you could imagine. . . . Here in Europe we are spending £350,000,000 a year upon all this machinery of slaughter. . . . It would really make one despair of the common sense of nations to imagine that that state, not of armed peace, but of armament which is equivalent to war, could continue. It is true that it is warfare carried on by means of taxes and all sorts of scientific devices, but none the less it is war between the nations. I cannot help thinking that civilization, which is able to deal with disputes amongst individuals and small communities at home, and is able to regulate these by means of some sane and well-ordered arbitrament, should be able to extend its operations to the larger sphere of disputes amongst States.'[1]

Hansard, 5th Ser. lxv. 726–9.

APPENDIX VI

THE QUESTION OF GERMAN ACCELERATION

(*a*) The following is an extract from a report drawn up by
Colonel Surtees, British Military Attaché at Constantinople in
1908. The report described a conversation between Colonel Surtees and a representative in Constantinople of the German firm
of Erhardt, the most important rival of Krupp in the manufacture of armaments. The date of the report is 20 December 1908.
It therefore reached the Foreign Office some time after the
British Government had reason to believe, on other grounds,
that the German naval authorities had taken steps which would
make possible the acceleration of work on the large ships of the
1909–10 programme of construction.

'During recent years (as can be proved) enormous quantities
of heavy machinery have been purchased by Krupp's which
can be required for no other purpose than that of manufacturing
big guns and big naval mountings. This present machinery is
far in excess of any requirements for the existing naval programme of Germany. German naval mountings are simpler in
construction than English ones, and are designed particularly
with the object of being manufactured quickly. The date of
delivering a battleship depends upon the date when the big guns
and mountings can be delivered and erected. The ship can
(with pressure) be built in about half the time necessary for the
guns and mountings, if both were actually ordered at the same
date.... Krupp makes ship plates and structural iron work, also
armour plate and ammunition and could get all such material
ready secretly. From information received it seems safe to say
that it is, or was, the intention, of the Emperor to secretly
prepare all the mountings, ship's plates, ammunition, &c., at
Krupp's and then to suddenly commence the creation of a
number of battleships sufficient to, at least, equal the naval
strength of England. The programme has been already settled;
it would only mean manufacturing earlier than expected. The
financial reserve of Krupp's alone would get over the money
difficulty. Notwithstanding the reserve fund of Krupp's (estimated by Erhardt to amount to £20 millions) Messrs. Krupp
have, during the past few years, borrowed further capital of

several millions. The difficulty of suddenly providing the necessary number of trained seamen appears to have been also considered, by training the present rank and file to take over more important duties if required and by using their Naval Reserve. The comparative simplicity of German naval mountings, and the fact that each of the new ships would be duplicates of each other, would assist in this direction.

'Assuming for argument that such ships were to be built by Germany, as soon as it became known that they were being constructed, England might reply by laying down an equal or greater number, expecting that they would be constructed in our country as rapidly. However with such a start as indicated, it is conceivable that the new German fleet would be ready two years the earlier.

'It must however be remembered that the position has changed by the recent loss of power by the German Emperor and from conversation with Germans it would seem that such loss of power is far more real than might be credited from a perusal of the accounts which have appeared in the English press.'[1] (F.O. General: Correspondence respecting affairs of N. and W. Europe, pt. 20. Oct.–Dec. 1909.)

(b) *Mr. Mulliner and the Cabinet.*

During and after the debates in Parliament in 1909 upon the question of German acceleration a certain prominence was given to the action of Mr. H. H. Mulliner, of the Coventry Ordnance Works. Mr. Mulliner had been a partner in a Birmingham firm which manufactured scientific measuring instruments and tools for manufacturing complicated parts of ordnance. After the Boer War the firm moved to Coventry, and amalgamated with Cammell's of Sheffield. The Ordnance section of the firm became a separate company owned by Cammell Laird, the Fairfield Shipbuilding and Engineering Company, and John Brown & Co. Mr. Mulliner became managing director of the company.

While visiting continental centres in order to obtain information about the latest types of plant and machinery Mr. Mulliner found that German machine and machine tool makers were working at large orders for Messrs. Krupp. He came to

[1] The publication of the *Daily Telegraph* interview had taken place in October 1908.

the conclusion that this work implied an extension of Krupp's productive capacity which would give Germany greatly increased facilities for rapid construction of armour plate and guns. Mr. Mulliner wrote to the War Office on 11 May 1906:[1] 'These extensions will give them [Krupp's] a possibility of output far in excess of the whole capacity of Great Britain. The scheme must be either immense future requirements for their own country, or that they mean to obtain the whole armament trade of the world outside the few Great Powers who build for themselves. . . . Are you aware of the enormous expenditure now going on at Krupp's for the purpose of manufacturing very large naval guns and mountings quickly?' Mr. Mulliner gave full details of the orders placed by Krupp. The War Office passed his letter to the Admiralty on 13 May 1906. The Admiralty, according to Mr. Mulliner's statement, suspected him of giving tendencious information in the hope of getting orders for his firm. In November 1908 he spoke to 'one of our greatest generals'. The Admiralty continued to ignore his reports. He then wrote to other officials. In February 1909 he was asked to lay his information before the Committee of Imperial Defence. The Committee told him that his information corroborated evidence already obtained by them. A week later he was invited to Downing Street. Here he saw Sir John Fisher, Sir John Jellicoe, and members of the Cabinet.

There is no reason to doubt that Mr. Mulliner had approached the War Office and Admiralty for patriotic reasons. The enlargement of Krupp's works was undisputed; the Government had knowledge of the facts, they might or might not draw the inferences which had alarmed Mr. Mulliner. In any case the facts, though they were important in relation to the potentialities of German naval construction, had no direct bearing upon the question of the actual collection of material, giving of contracts, &c., for ships in advance of the published time-table and the votes of credits in the Reichstag.

Mr. Mulliner's information was therefore corroborative, but not in any sense decisive. The matter was discussed in the press, and Mr. Mulliner's name was subsequently associated with the whole question of acceleration because he insisted in

[1] Mr. Mulliner gave an account of his correspondence and interviews in letters to *The Times* on 2 and 6 August, 21 September, 17 December 1909, 1, 3, 6, 8, and 18 January 1910. A criticism of his statements was made by a naval correspondent in *The Times* of 5 January 1909.

public statements (i) that he had been the first person to call attention to the facts about Krupp, (ii) that his information had been ignored for over two years, at grave risk to the security of the country, (iii) that Mr. McKenna, in his speech on the naval estimates on 16 March 1909 concealed the fact that the Government were given in 1906 information about Krupp's increased facilities for the manufacture of guns and armour, and (iv) that as a result of the steps which he (Mr. Mulliner) had taken, his firm was being 'victimized' by the Admiralty. He wrote to the press in December 1909, that, after his interview at Downing Street in February 1909, the Admiralty had 'begun a campaign against him', and that Admiralty officials refused to see him to discuss work which was being undertaken by his firm. His company did not receive certain orders which they had expected, and at a board meeting several of his fellow directors told him that they had been approached, directly and indirectly, by Admiralty officials, 'with a strong hint that these orders would not come until he (Mr. Mulliner) left the firm'. Mr. Mulliner therefore left the board of directors. His place was taken by Admiral Bacon, who, as Captain Bacon, had been Director of Naval Ordnance. Shortly after Mr. Mulliner's retirement from the firm the expected order arrived. Mr. Mulliner also offered a reward of £100 for any statement from a responsible member of the Government giving the date upon which they first knew of the 'enormous acceleration for the production of armaments which commenced in Germany in the beginning of 1906'.

Mr. Mulliner's statements in *The Times* about the potential output of Krupp's works produced answers from Mr. J. Leyland.[1] Mr. Leyland thought that the enlargement of Krupp's works was generally known, and that the *Statistische Angaben* published by the firm were clear and explicit. According to these statistics, the increase in plant and in the number of employees did not take place until the year 1909, though there was a very considerable addition during this year.

Mr. Mulliner's charges against the Admiralty were mentioned in Parliament by Mr. Duke, Conservative member for Exeter, on 16 March 1910.[2] The facts were denied by Mr. McKenna. Mr. Duke did not press the matter to a division. There was no further discussion in the House, though the Conservative

---

[1] *The Times*, 3 September 1909, 4 January 1910.
[2] Hansard, 5th Ser. xv. 418, 420–8, 456.

Opposition was not satisfied with Mr. McKenna's treatment of the matter.

(c) *Possible technical reasons for the acceleration of the 'Oldenburg'* *(one of the ships of the 1909–10 programme).*

On the basis of the facts known to the Admiralty and admitted by Tirpitz, it was suggested in an article in *The Times* in 1910[1] that the acceleration of the *Oldenburg* might have been due to the fact that this ship was the fourth of a squadron of four ships of the same type. The other three ships of the squadron belonged to the 1908–9 programme, and the German Admiralty wished to complete the squadron as quickly as possible.

This explanation was not given by Tirpitz or suggested by the British naval attachés in Berlin. It has no bearing on the main problem which faced the British Government in 1909. This problem was set by the facts (i) that Germany possessed facilities for rapid construction of ships which might ensure their completion in advance of the published time-table, (ii) that these facilities were being used in 1908 and the early part of 1909, and therefore, (iii) that, if the German authorities wished to do so, they could complete the ships of the 1908–9 and 1909–10 programmes in advance of the dates publicly announced. The completion of these ships would have made possible a similar acceleration in the case of ships belonging to the 1910–11 programmes, since the contractors and manufacturers would have been free to begin work at an earlier date on these 1910–11 ships.

(d) *The following correspondence between Grey and Goschen is supplementary to the material published in B.D.D. vol. vi.*

(i) Grey *to* Goschen, 19 *March* 1908

Count Metternich supplemented his conversation of yesterday, by informing me to-day that the two ships for which contracts had been promised in advance of the financial year 1909–10, will be built in thirty-six months from the moment when the Reichstag votes the money for them. They will be ready for trial trips at the earliest in April 1912, and will not be ready for commission before October 1912.

I said that I wished to tell him, quite informally, what had

[1] *The Times*, 9 February. Cf. also a letter from Mr. J. Leyland in *The Times*, 3 November 1910.

been passing in my mind. A real scare was arising in this country. He said it was an artificial scare. I replied that no doubt some of the Opposition, for party purposes, would exaggerate this scare at elections; but, for wider reasons than this, I had been considering how the scare might be ended. I was sure it could not be stopped by simple repetition in Parliament of his assurance to me as to the thirteen ships, and what Admiral Tirpitz had said. We should at once be asked whether this was an undertaking on the part of the German Government, and I should have to answer, no.

Count Metternich said he thought it would be difficult for the German Government to put their assurance in the form of an undertaking.

Then we should be asked whether our Naval Attaché was allowed to see what was actually going on. Our answer to this would also have to be, no. This would give rise to a new cry that the Government were too easy-going, and were in danger of being taken in, for they could have no knowledge from one half-year to another of what was actually being done. If I were to repeat in the House of Commons what Count Metternich had told me as to the thirteen ships, and were to state that, acting upon that information, the Government did not propose to give orders for the four hypothetical ships which they had put into the Estimates this year, matters would only be made worse. Public opinion would concentrate on the point that the Government could not, and ought not to, trust the statement of the German Government so implicitly, at any rate with regard to the future. This would be the most undesirable form that agitation here could take.

We had a long conversation, in which I spoke most earnestly to Count Metternich as to the opportunity there was now for creating confidence. We knew the German programme, but we could not know the time it would take to carry it out. If our respective Admiralties put their cards on the table and let our respective Naval Attachés see from time to time the actual stage of construction of the capital ships, we should go before Parliament with a statement that the two Governments, knowing that their Navies were not intended for hostile operations against each other, had agreed to keep each other informed as to the work which was being done, in order to put an end to the suspicions which must arise in the minds of people so disposed if they insisted on concealing the facts of construction from each other.

We should then from time to time be able to state the facts, and thus dispose completely of such statements as those made by Mr. Balfour and Mr. Lee. We should be able to convince the House of Commons that they had not to face the contingency of seventeen German ships in 1912 to which we ourselves had referred. We should turn back the whole tide of public opinion, and create not only a *détente*, but a most favourable reaction.

Count Metternich said, as he had said before, that he was not authorized to say anything on this point.

I told him that I was not pressing him for a reply, I was simply discussing what could be done.

He remarked that he did not know whether Naval Attachés could be admitted to see ships without their noticing secrets which no Government would wish to disclose.

I said I should have thought that nowadays those secrets were of too special a kind to be revealed by a mere visit to a yard.

He also thought it would hardly be possible to allow a Naval Attaché to inspect every gun, and he reminded me that I had said the armament was a most important matter in the construction of a ship.

I said these were details. I could not say off-hand how much or how little would satisfy our Admiralty.

Finally, Count Metternich promised that, as far as he personally was concerned, he would do all he could in the matter to find some solution.

Though he said little, the impression he left upon my mind was that he personally was sympathetic to some arrangement, but he did not think that his Government would agree to anything of the kind, and that he therefore confined himself to stating such objections as occurred to him.

(ii) GOSCHEN *to* GREY, 21 *July* 1909

Herr von Schoen told me, at his official reception yesterday, that the Imperial Minister of Marine had called his attention to the Naval Debate in the House of Commons and had expressed some surprise that the First Lord of the Admiralty, in spite of the assurances which had been given, had again stated that the Imperial Government had anticipated their Programme by commencing last year one of the ships belonging to the current year. His Excellency asked me what I thought of the matter. I replied that of course I could only give him my personal views. As far as I understood the German point of view it was that there had been no anticipation of the 1909 Programme, in that no official authorization had been given, or Government money appropriated, for the construction of any ship belonging to that Programme before the time specified, namely the 1st of April, 1909. This was, from a departmental point of view a perfectly correct exposition of the facts, all the more that as far as I knew the keel of no 1909 ship had been laid before the specified time. On the other hand it could not be ignored that by promising and practically giving the contract for the construction of one of the 1909 ships to Herr Schichau of Danzig, as far back as October last, the Minister of Marine had placed the contractor in a position, of which as a man of business he was practically certain to have availed himself, to collect material and so generally get work on the ship in an advanced stage before the period specified for the laying of her keel. This was evidently a strong possibility, and in framing their Naval Policy His Majesty's Government had to reckon with possibilities as well as with facts. It was therefore my opinion that Mr. McKenna, without throwing any doubt upon the assurances of the Minister of Marine with regard to the intentions of his Government, could not, upon being pressed for an answer respecting German Ship-building, pass over in silence the possibility that Herr Schichau had taken advantage of the early contract and placed it in the power of the Imperial Government to have the ship completed before the specified time, should such an acceleration be for one reason or another considered necessary.

Herr von Schoen replied that he had always been of the opinion that it had been unwise to place the contract so early and that misunderstandings might arise in consequence. He had reminded the Minister of Marine of this when the latter spoke to him on the subject of Mr. McKenna's speech. Herr von Schoen said that the facts were more or less as I had stated, and that he was sure that there had been no intention on the part of Mr. McKenna to throw doubts on the assurances of the Imperial Government. But he was glad that the Naval Debate was over as the discussion of naval matters on either side always seemed to have an exciting effect on both sides, particularly in the Press. He added that, as regards the subject we had been discussing, even if there had been a sort of unpremeditated anticipation of the Programme, it had been of such a very slight and unimportant nature that it was scarcely worthy of notice. In any case I might rely upon the assurance which he had so frequently given to me that no ship would be completed before the time specified in the Programme.

The *Cologne Gazette* as reported in *The Times* states quite recently as an established fact, that the ship contracted for by the Schichau works and belonging to the 1909 programme was actually begun in 1908, so that Admiral Tirpitz has no reason to affect an attitude of injured innocence.   C. H.

I have been over all this in conversation with Count Metternich.   E. G.

(iii) GREY *to* GOSCHEN, 28 *July* 1909

Count Metternich spoke to me to-day about the naval debate which took place in the House of Commons on the 26th. Count Metternich seemed displeased because Mr. McKenna still spoke about the acceleration of the German programme. He said he would not refer to the views expressed by Mr. Balfour, as the latter had no official position. The general impression conveyed by Count Metternich's observations was that he thought Germany had not been fairly treated in the debate, the report of which, he informed me, had taken some hours to read.

I told him I had, so far, been too busy to read any report of the debate of the 26th. But I knew, of course, what it had been settled to say, and I assumed that Mr. McKenna had said it. When he spoke about acceleration, no doubt he meant that certain German firms had been put in a position, last autumn, to prepare in advance for the construction of certain ships; this would, naturally, accelerate the beginning of construction. I understood the German statement to be that, though the beginning might be accelerated, the ships would not in the long run be completed any sooner, and I thought Mr. McKenna was referring to the beginning. In any case, it had been arranged that Mr. McKenna should call attention to the proposed new Austrian ships, to the actual increase in the Italian naval estimates, and probably to the report that the French Naval Committee had urged an increase in the French naval expenditure. The general expenditure of Europe was a factor to be taken into account, and we did not wish to make Germany too prominent in connexion with our proposals. I gathered from Count Metternich that reference had been made to Austrian and Italian shipbuilding.

As to what Mr. Balfour might have said, I told Count Metternich that of course Mr. Balfour knew the statements which had been made in the previous naval debate, but there had not been any communication with him about the debate on the 26th. I had asked some one yesterday what the tendency of Mr. Balfour's speech had been, and had been told that it did not show satisfaction with the proposals of the Government; but that was all I knew about it.

(iv) GREY *to* GOSCHEN, 9 *August* 1909

[Count Metternich] again remarked that he had noticed statements as to German Acceleration in debates in Parliament. I once more pointed out to His Excellency that it was admitted that there had been acceleration in beginning the construction of one or two of the German ships. I had seen this admission in the German press. This initial acceleration would, naturally, make it possible for the ships to be completed earlier than the German Government had intended. It was quite possible the latter might change their mind and decide that circumstances rendered it undesirable that there should be any unnecessary delay in completing the ships. Those who criticized German Shipbuilding could always say that, even if the German Government were to inform us that they had altered their mind it would be too late when a change of this sort took place, for us to attempt to meet the new situation, unless we had made preparations in advance. This was what was really meant by the talk about acceleration.

(e) *Reports from Captain Heath, British naval attaché at Berlin, October 1908–June 1909*

(i) *Visits to Wilhelmshaven and Bremen, 20 October* 1908
(F. O. Germany. N. A. Report 46/08.)

The Nassau has all her armour plates in position with the exception of a few right forward, it is anticipated that she will be ready in ample time for her trials in October next.

A good deal of work has been prepared for the 'Ersatz Oldenburg' in the shops, but my guide explained that the official laying of the keel was delayed as long as possible 'in order to make a record'.

At the Weser Yard the Westphalen was alongside, her armour is not yet all in position, but it seems that she is well up to her date of Xmas/09. I could get no satisfactory information as to the disposition of the armament, but I rather think it may be somewhat similar to that of the Brazilian battleship building at Elswick.

I was shewn a quantity of work in preparation for the Ersatz Beowulf, the blocks are being prepared for laying the keel on the same slip from which the Westphalen was launched.

The works generally are well equipped and organized, but owing to lack of orders they are in a shaky financial condition.

(ii) *Letter of* 21 *October* 1908. (F. O. Germany. N. A. Report 47/08.)

The estimates for /09-/10 are not yet published, but there seems no doubt that the contracts for two of the battleships for that year's programme have already been placed. This is six months at least before the usual time, and before the money has actually been voted.

Krupp's works appear to be keeping well up to date with armour and guns, for I hear on good authority that the armour for Cruiser 'G' is almost complete, although the vessel herself is only just started.

(iii) *Letter of* 16 *November* 1908. (F. O. Germany. N. A. Report 48/08.)

The announcement in the press, that the contract for the three battleships belonging to the /09-/10 programme, had already been awarded to the firms, Vulkan of Stettin, and Schichau of Dantzig, has been partially confirmed by one of my confrères, who was specially invited to attend the launch of the 'George Washington' built for the Hamburg-America line at Stettin.

He states that he has reason to believe that the story is a true one, and that material is now being collected, and preparation being made to start building early in the new financial year.

Assuming that Schichau is acting likewise, and allowing thirty months for the completion of each vessel from April next, it is possible that Germany may have the following vessels ready for sea by October 1911.

10 Battleships of 'Dreadnought' type.

3 Battleship-Cruisers of 'Indomitable' type.

In answer to questions in Parliament, as to finding work for the unemployed, the Naval authorities have stated that they can find work in the Imperial Dockyards for over 2000 additional mechanics during the coming winter.

(iv) *Remarks on the German naval estimates for* 1909–1910. 9 *December,* 1908. (F. O. Germany. N. A. Report 52/08.)

By making an analysis of the sums already spent, and those voted for the forthcoming financial year, I arrive at the following conclusions as regards the probable rate of completion of battleships and battleship-cruisers.

'Nassau' and 'Westphalen' were laid down theoretically in July and August of 1907, but it is quite safe to assume that preparatory work on material was started by 1st April 1907.

By 1st April 1909 (viz. 24 months) these two ships will have each been advanced just over 17/22 as regards hull and machinery.

It is therefore probable that they will be advanced the remaining 5/22 and completed within 6 months of 1st April 1909.

'Rheinland' and 'Posen' were theoretically laid down at the same time as those above, but their construction has been delayed. It may be assumed that these two ships will be completed towards the end of 1910.

'Oldenburg', 'Siegfried', 'Beowulf'. The estimated cost of these ships (hull and machinery), is not yet stated, but it is probably something approaching 26,000,000 marks.

By 1st April 1909, these ships will be advanced 5.6/25ths.

By 1st April 1910, these ships will be advanced 16/25ths. They should therefore be completed by the end of 1910.

'Frithjof', 'Hildebrand', 'Heimdall'. I have assumed that these ships are to cost the same amount as the Oldenburg class. Supposing that they are to be built at the same rate as the 'Oldenburg' class, they will be advanced to 16/25ths by 1st April 1911, and will be completed by the end of that year.

As regards large cruisers, the Blücher is to be completed during 1909. Cruiser 'F' will be completed towards the end of 1910.

Cruiser 'G'. Estimated cost unknown but perhaps 30,000,000

marks is a safe estimate. She is to be advanced to 16/30ths by
1st April 1910, and it looks as if she would not be ready until the
early part of 1911.

Cruiser 'H'. It is not safe to prophesy much about this craft,
except that if she is to be similar to 'G', she will probably be built
a little quicker and will be ready by the end of 1911.

As regards gun armament, the total estimate for the first four
ships is identical, and the yearly sums allotted for the advance in
armament is in the same proportion as that allotted for hull and
machinery.

That is to say that 'Rheinland' and 'Posen' are some months
behind 'Nassau' and 'Westphalen'.

'Oldenburg', 'Siegfried', 'Beowulf'. The total estimate for
armament is not given, but the sum allowed for the first two years
is 50 per cent. more than for 'Nassau' class. This (is) an indication that these ships are to carry 12 in. guns. The rate at which the
armament is advanced is similar to that for hull and machinery.

'Frithjof', 'Hildebrand', 'Heimdall'. Nothing is yet known
as to the nature of armament, but the sum allotted in the first
year is similar to that allotted for first year of 'Oldenburg'
class.

As regards the armament of the large cruisers. The total
estimate for gun armament of cruiser 'F' is 10,000,000 marks.
The total for cruiser 'C' is not given but each year a sum of
1,000,000 more marks is allowed for 'G' than in the corresponding year for 'F', the sums required for armament are provided
in the same ratio as those required for hull and machinery.

(v) *Letter of 14 January* 1909. (F. O. Germany.
N. A. Report 3/09.)

From another source, also fairly reliable, I was informed 'as
a positive fact' that Messrs Schichau had commenced work on
one of the battleships of the '09–10 programme.

It has already been rumoured that Messrs Schichau had been
promised one of these ships, and it seems quite possible that
material is being collected. I may add that Messrs Schichau
'regretted that they were unable to shew me over their works'
last autumn at the time of my making a visit to the Imperial
Dockyard. My informant added that he thought Messrs Schichau
could easily borrow the necessary money until the commencement of the new financial year. My informant had himself

visited Schichau's yard, for the firm were anxious to get an order from his government.

(vi) *Letter of* 21 *January* 1909. (F. O. Germany.
N. A. Report 4/09.)

The report that Messrs Schichau have commenced collecting their material for a battleship of the '09–10 programme has reached me from a second source.

(vii) *Visits to dockyards*, 24 *May* 1909

In the early part of May I was informed verbally, that if I wished to visit any private dockyards, it would facilitate matters, if I made a formal application to the German Admiralty, who would then make arrangements with the Yard in question. This method was adopted for my recent visit to the Vulkan Yard, at Stettin, in which case the visit passed off smoothly and satisfactorily. Some ten days ago I made similar application for arrangements to be made for a visit to Schichau's Yard at Danzig. The Admiralty made formal reply, that on reconsidering the matter, the State Secretary had decided that the German Admiralty would not in future, take any part in arranging such visits and that I must make my own application to Schichau. This I have done, and have today received their answer that they are unable to permit me to visit their yard.

It is known that Schichau is building some five vessels for the Russian Volunteer Fleet and one Battleship for the Imperial German Navy, on which latter it was officially stated that not one penny would be expended before 1st April/09. It would have been interesting to see how far she had advanced in seven weeks.

(viii) *Ship-building*, 21 *June* 1909. (F. O. Germany.
N. A. Report 17/09.)

With reference to the reports recently published in the local press and reproduced in *The Times* as to the contracts for the last two ships of this year's programme having been awarded to Kiel Dockyard and to the Vulkan Company of Hamburg respectively, I believe the facts to be as follows. The authorities of Kiel Imperial Yard have reported that the Blücher is now practically completed, and have asked whether they may expect to build one of these battleships in order that arrangements may be made to avoid the otherwise necessary discharge of workmen. It is understood that Kiel Yard have been informed that in all probability, one of these ships will be built at Kiel, but that as the plans are not yet complete, very little preliminary work can be carried out. There seems to be delay in the preparation of the design of engine. The fact of the designs not being ready points to some new departure, as compared with the ship being built by Schichau. I think it is probable that a similar communication may have been made to Vulkan Company, but I cannot speak with any certainty.

(*f*) *Extract from a draft letter from Admiralty to Foreign Office, May 1909.* The letter was, however, for other reasons, not dispatched.

If the German Government desire to put His Majesty's Government in possession of full information as to their shipbuilding programme, there is no longer any necessity for them to place restrictions upon the visits of the British Naval Attaché to the German Shipbuilding Yards. As a matter of fact, however, every obstacle has been placed in Captain Heath's way in order to prevent his obtaining the least inkling as to what is happening in the Shipbuilding Yards. He has never been allowed inside Schichau's Yard at Danzig, where the order for one of the 1909–10 battleships is admitted to have been given and even in the Germania Yard at Kiel where the 'Posen' was launched only in December last, and where it is thought another of the 1909–10 battleships may be built, he was allowed to see no Government work at all. He was further directly advised not to apply to go into the Vulcan Yard at Stettin.

The denials received by the Naval Attaché at the German Admiralty until quite recently that any orders for the 1909–10 battleships had been given, in spite of references to such orders having been published in the press must necessarily cast doubt on any subsequent statements made by the same officials that cannot be checked by independent observations. Should these restrictions continue to be placed upon the visits of Captain Heath to German Shipbuilding Yards, etc., it will be matter for consideration whether the German Government should not be directly approached on the subject and informed that unless the attitude of the German Admiralty to the British Naval Attaché is changed, Their Lordships on their part will be obliged to exclude the German Naval Attaché from H.M. Shipyards and Establishments.

LIBERAL OPPOSITION TO THE NAVAL AND FOREIGN POLICY OF THE BRITISH GOVERNMENT, 1907–1914

REFERENCE has frequently been made in Chapters xi–xvi, to differences of view within the Liberal party on the question of naval policy and the dissatisfaction felt by Liberals at the failure of the British Government to come to an understanding with Germany on the subject of the limitation of naval armaments.

The following extracts from *The Economist* may be taken as typical of this opposition to the continual increase in the naval estimates. A number of extracts from *The Economist* in the years 1903 to 1906 have been included to show the change in the policy of the journal after 1907. The extracts are given in chronological order.

It should be pointed out that a chronological or analytical series of extracts of this kind from a newspaper tends to give the impression of a lack of sequence in the policy of the paper. This impression is not necessarily right. A daily or weekly journal is bound to deal with matters of current interest to its readers. The readers are not interested in the correction of earlier news or comments in the light of later events or more accurate information. Apart from the natural wish of an editor to call as little attention as possible to mistaken forecasts or errors of fact, writers and readers alike treat each successive number of a journal as complete in itself, and, if there is no sudden change in the general policy of the paper, neglect or overlook minor inconsistencies.

The policy of *The Economist* before 1907 was clear. The paper distrusted the methods, and to some extent, the aims of German foreign policy, supported the Anglo-French entente and the plan of an understanding with Russia, and accepted the British naval estimates as reasonable and necessary. A change appears at the end of 1907. From this time until 1914 the editorial notes and comments are directed, without exception, against the naval policy, and very often against the foreign policy, of the Government. Opposition to the naval estimates was based largely upon financial grounds and upon the traditional Liberal view of economy in armaments. The attacks were concentrated for the most part upon Mr. McKenna and Mr. Churchill. At times the attacks on British foreign policy were directed against Grey, but generally expressed the view that Grey was badly supported by the Foreign Office and diplomatic service.

It is possible, after collating the comments and news in *The Economist* with other sources of information, and particularly with the diplomatic material now available on the subject of Anglo-German negotiations to notice certain outstanding features of this strong advocacy of a limitation of naval armaments and an Anglo-German understanding.

(i) There was an exaggeration of the personal part played by the First Lord of the Admiralty in determining naval policy. The Cabinet as a whole was rarely taken to task for important decisions which were accepted at its meetings and supported in the House by Ministers and by a parliamentary majority known to be in full sympathy with the idea of a limitation of armaments. The comments of the paper therefore did not altogether face the issue that the successive increases in the naval estimates, however distasteful, were put forward by a Government convinced of the necessity of these estimates and fully aware of the discontent and financial difficulties caused by increasing naval expenditure.

(ii) Technical questions connected with naval construction or the disposition of the fleets were rarely discussed. *The Economist* objected to the Dreadnought policy, and regarded large battle-ships as wasteful; but the treatment of the subject from the technical side was superficial. Technical arguments in favour of the large 'all-big gun' ship were not stated, and supporters of these arguments were swept aside as parties interested in 'armour-plate'.

(iii) There was a marked tendency to assume that the British Admiralty carried the sole responsibility for the increasing competition in naval armaments, and that all measures taken in Great Britain to meet the steady increase in German sea-power were provocative. This tendency is shown very clearly in the treatment of the problem of German acceleration. On this question the journal accepted Tirpitz's statements rather than the statements of British Ministers. The fact that after the spring of 1909 there was no further acceleration of the German programme was regarded as proof that the 'Dreadnought scare' was a 'hoax' costing the British taxpayer many millions of pounds. No account was taken, for example, of the considerations (a) that the British Government acted on information subsequently admitted by Tirpitz to be essentially correct, (b) that the increased facilities for rapid construction in Germany made it necessary for Great Britain to consider 'possible' as well as 'actual' acceleration, (c) that the British programme of 1909–10 might have been one of the main reasons why there was no further acceleration of the German programmes.

(iv) There is also a tendency to assume, upon very little data, that, in Anglo-German or Franco-German differences, the faults lay mainly on the British or French side. The British Foreign Office is held responsible for the failure to reach an understanding with Germany. No account is taken of the possibility that this understanding could only be obtained in terms prejudicial to British interests. The provocative German action in sending a gunboat to Agadir during the Moroccan dispute of 1911, for example, was toned down. Germany was regarded as working for the 'open door' for all nations in Morocco. In 1912–13, and in the crisis of July 1914, greater attention was given to the Austrian case against Servia than to the Servian case against Austria. The increase in the German army in 1913 was attributed mainly to French chauvinism. As late as 1 August 1914 *The Economist* advocated neutrality in a continental war, and foresaw no danger to British interests from a defeat of France and Russia.

(v) There is also an exaggeration of the financial burden of armaments. This burden was irritating and excessive; but at all events in Great Britain the cost of armaments could not be described as 'crushing', without a considerable distortion of fact. It is interesting to notice the growth of the view that the profit-seeking interests of armament manufacturers were primarily responsible for the policy of increasing the size and cost of armies and navies.

(vi) Two other points suggest themselves for consideration: (a) The persistent advocacy of naval retrenchment and an Anglo-German understanding is evidence that large and influential sections of business and financial opinion in Great Britain did not believe in the 'inevitability' of an Anglo-German war for commercial purposes. (b) On the other hand, the volume and intensity of criticism of British policy, the condonation of many features of German or Austrian policy which were certainly not in harmony with Liberal principles, and the attacks upon the policy of France and Russia, may have encouraged influential sections of German opinion in the view that persistent effort would force Great Britain to surrender to German naval ambitions and that the tactics of shock diplomacy could be applied to France and Russia without much danger of British interference.

EXTRACTS FROM 'THE ECONOMIST': I. 1903–1906.
II. 1908–1914.

I. 1903.

14 March. (*Industrial aspects of the British naval programme.*) 'In round numbers the project will supply ten million pounds' worth of work to the . . . yards of this country' at a time of depression in the shipbuilding industry. The yards undertaking the work 'will remain the centres of attraction for the best of our skilled workmanship, and will afford large employment in a great variety of allied industries'.

1904.

26 March. (*Anglo-German relations.*) There is no 'general conspiracy against Germany'. If there were ever any thought of encircling Germany, the cause would be 'the amount of indulgence, if not of direct countenance, which from time to time has been given in Governmental quarters to the extravagant and—if it could be regarded as serious—generally menacing propagandism of the pan-German school'. Then follows an examination of the aims of the pan-Germans. 'The Imperial Government have not always been above profiting by the temper carefully fostered under pan-German influences, as, for example, in connexion with the expansion of the Navy.'

1905.

11 February. (*Mr. Lee's speech at Eastleigh.*) Unreasonable that Germany should complain that British Ministers refer in their speeches to the German navy. Even in its uncorrected form Mr. Lee's speech was not objectionable. British Government obviously has to take account of the growth of the German navy and also of concurrent 'manifestation of unfriendliness towards England on the part of large and

influential classes which was for a considerable time hardly realized (in England), but which, when it became realized, was recognized as making the hostility of Germany a possibility to be reckoned with.'

25 March. (*France, Germany, and Morocco.*) Mischief done by semi-official statements about Morocco in the German Press. 'It is inconceivable that Germany can consider herself entitled to prevent France from developing her influence over Morocco in the manner imperatively required by the vital interests of her North African colony. She has not the slightest reason to apprehend any such unfair treatment of her commerce or shipping as, for example, she is herself inflicting . . . upon Australian vessels trading to her Pacific islands.'

24 June. (*Pan-German Congress. Germany and Morocco.*) Co-operation with Germany difficult owing to the 'manners of the German Government' and 'the display of certain influences likely to be potent with it for some time to come'. Pan-German League 'expresses, in an extreme form, some of the present tendencies of the German Government'. The Emperor obviously not really interested in the 'open door' in Morocco, but trying to persuade France that Great Britain wants war with Germany for commercial reasons. Criticizes Schiemann's articles in the *Kreuz Zeitung*. British Press campaigns against Germany 'deplorable', but 'German writers bear the palm for ingenious invention and baseless malevolence'. 'Montrous fictions' spread abroad to the detriment of England. 'As a matter of business, we have not found co-operation with (Germany) altogether profitable in the past.'

23 September. (*Germany and Morocco.*) 'The truth is, of course, that the German Government has from the first interfered in Morocco not for the sake of German interests there, but for the sake of the reflex action of her interference on Europe.'

1906.

6 January. (*Morocco as a test of German policy.*) 'But for the excuse of an extraordinary degree of self-restraint on the part of France last summer a situation might very easily have been brought about in which honour, duty, and interest alike would have compelled this country to stand side by side with France in opposition to an intolerable assertion of German predominance in Europe.'

13 January. (*Disarmament.*) Great difficulty of discovering a fair standard of measurement.

8 September. (*British diplomacy and German enterprise.*) British experience of co-operation with Germany in China and Venezuela 'unfavourable'. What does Germany want? 'Everything would be cleared up if we were only sure that the aims of the German Government were not those of the Pan-German expansionists and colonial enthusiasts, with their eighteenth-century and Protectionist views of the functions of colonies and their desire to bring new territory under the German flag.'

II. 1908.

22 February. (*Protest against British naval estimates.*) Thinks German financial position will make the realization of the German naval programme 'extremely doubtful, in fact so improbable that it ought not to be regarded seriously'.

29 February. (*Large battleships.*) Doubts whether in case of war with Germany 'either·belligerent would dare to send a battleship that cost it from £1,500,000 to £2,000,000 into the North Sea. For the North Sea would be sown with floating mines and scoured by submarines.' Objects to Rosyth.

15 August. (*An understanding with Germany.*) 'The anti-German campaign conducted by an unholy alliance between *The Times* and the *Daily Mail* and the anti-English campaign conducted by the chauvinist press of Germany, have at last produced a healthy reaction. . . . Is it likely, or reasonable, that two Governments like the British and German Governments of to-day . . . will go on deliberately building warships of unexampled cost, at an unexampled rate, in order to prepare for a collision' which would do immense harm to each side? 'The authorities in Berlin might as well recognize that whatever they do we are bound to keep well ahead of them, and that our financial resources are very much greater than theirs.' German opinion recognizing this fact.

22 August. (*An Anglo-German agreement.*) Confidence in the prospect of an Anglo-German naval agreement, and in the favourable outcome of the Cronberg interview between the German Emperor and Sir Charles Hardinge. 'It is tolerably certain that the inclination of the German Government to come to an agreement' is based on financial reasons.

5 September. Hopes of a naval agreement sensibly 'strengthened by an article in the *Kölnische Volkszeitung*.'

31 October. (*The* 'Daily Telegraph' *interview*.) Fear prevalent 'among sane Englishmen is not that the Kaiser is insincere in his profession of friendship . . . but that at some great crisis he may be carried away by the influence' of those 'large numbers of self-styled German patriots' who want 'their Government . . . to act as supreme arbiter in Europe . . . and believe that war, and preparations for war are an indispensable means of advancing national trade. . . . Meanwhile German diplomacy will be as purely self-regarding and as punctilious as it has been in the case of the Baghdad railway, the interests of the Powers in the Yangtse valley, or Venezuela. . . . What is wanted is an abatement not only of German Anglophobia, but of the German belief in the "mailed fist" as an instrument of commerce.'

1909.

20 March. (*The question of German acceleration*.) 'The most amazing thing of all is the prompt denial' of the assertions of the Prime Minister and the British Admiralty by Tirpitz, and also the denial that Great Britain has offered to come to an understanding about shipbuilding. 'If we are to believe (Tirpitz's figures), and surely the German Admiralty's statement on this point must be accepted in preference to the information collected by our own Admiralty from its spies in Germany', the Government should reconsider the position. If Mr. McKenna's information is correct, 'his Dreadnought programme is, in our view, justified', but new cruisers are unnecessary.

27 March. (*Dilke return*.) 'Our general opinion has been, and still is, that British expenditure on armaments since the Boer War has been on an altogether excessive scale, a scale provocative towards others and perilous in regard to our national finances.'

17 April. (*Dreadnoughts*.) Article attacking the adoption of the Dreadnought type.

5 June. (*Naval estimates*.) Quotes a speech by Mr. Lambert with the comment that the naval estimates were 'floated . . . on a tide of fictions and false hypotheses', which has resulted in fleecing the taxpayers.

24 July. (*Shipbuilding vote*.) Additional expenditure of £3,000,000 unjustifiable. Vote 'provocative in character . . .

connected with an anti-German policy' and 'with the refusal of the Government to consider international proposals for the protection of peaceful, non-contraband merchandise and shipping in time of war'.

31 July. (*Shipbuilding programme.*) 'We fully admit that, in spite of our enormous preponderance in battleships, the British Admiralty was bound to take steps to meet any sudden or provocative move on the part of Germany; even though that move is the direct result of our own frantic act in constructing and advertising the first Dreadnought.'

2 October. (*Shipbuilding programme.*) Clear that the Government need not have yielded to the 'foolish agitation' of last spring. The Austrian programme had now 'disappeared'. 'Public opinion in Germany among all classes is rapidly setting against the big Navy movement.' No acceleration of German programme.

1910.

12 March. (*Naval estimates.*) 'The natural result of the ferocious newspaper war between England and Germany, of the attempt made for party purposes to inflame this costly antipathy, and of the absolute abandonment of economy by His Majesty's Opposition.'

19 March. (*Naval estimates.*) An Anglo-German understanding impossible while the British naval estimates continue to show such great increases.

2 July. (*British naval manœuvres.*) Large concentration of ships for manœuvres unwise owing to provocation given to Germany.

16 July. (*Mr. Asquith's speech on armaments.*) British naval margin too great. Mr. Asquith's 'direct invitation to the German Government, the German Reichstag and the German people. If it fails the next step should be to invite the Powers to a Conference.'

23 July. (*Anglo-German agreement.*) German reception of Mr. Asquith's speech gives reason for hope that before the autumn session 'some arrangement will have been arrived at'.

30 July. (*Anglo-German agreement.*) Krupp's newspaper (*Neueste Nachrichten*) suggests that an Anglo-German agreement should be postponed until the German 14-in. guns are ready.

3 September. (*Anglo-German agreement.*) Martial speech by the German Emperor at Königsberg unfortunate when the

most important issue is an Anglo-German agreement for the limitation of armaments.

19 November. (*Supplement on the growth of expenditure and the call for economy.*) History of naval expenditure. Prospect of retrenchment in 1906, but 'the craven spirit of the Jingoes and panic-mongers rose' with the expansion of the navy. 'The naval contractors clamoured for more.' The German fleet was used as a pretext. 'The German fleet which has struck such panic is largely imaginary, and the supposed danger is entirely due to the fact that our Admiralty invented the Dreadnought and fostered the impression that this type of ship had superseded all others . . . Number, be it remembered, counts, quite apart from the type or size of the ships, for torpedoes are no respecters of patterns . . . every serviceable ship that carried a good gun may fire a decisive shot. . . . The time seems to be at hand when naval opinion will pronounce against the monster battleship. . . . Nevertheless, spurred on by the contractors, who love these huge jobs in ironmongery, the Admiralty goes on enlarging the size of the battleships.'

17 December. (*German naval estimates.*) The German reply to 'enormous' British increase is 'a comparatively trifling increase. . . . Tested by expenditure, the rivalry is non-existent.'

1911.

7 January. (*Naval estimates.*) 'If (Mr. Lloyd George) again submits to the Admiralty after what has taken place in Germany, he cannot expect his speeches and declarations to be taken seriously by those who really object to public waste.'

21 January. (*Mr. McKenna.*) Attack on Mr. McKenna for his estimate of German construction. Reprint of article in *The Economist* on panic in 1848.

4 February. i. (*Mr. McKenna and the Admiralty.*) 'The Board of Admiralty which we venture to call the Naval Cabinet' are asking for a further increase in the estimates. Mr. McKenna's increases are a 'record for a Minister who based an alarmist demand for five and a half millions sterling upon a misstatement of naval construction in Germany'.

ii. (*Large battleships.*) Speech by Mr. Arnold Hills, Manager of the Thames Ironworks and Shipbuilding Company, at the launch of the *Thunderer*, attacking the type of large battleship, advocating his own plans for smaller ships, and protesting against the monopolizing of contracts by firms in the north of England.

11 February. (*Naval extravagance.*) Mr. McKenna's 'exploded statistics about German Dreadnoughts'.

18 February. (*Mr. McKenna.*) Agrees with article in *The Nation* that Mr. McKenna 'must realize that his personal position is a serious one'. His facts must have been supplied by the Admiralty Intelligence Department. This department in the last financial year cost £16,185. The director of the department was Rear-Admiral the Hon. A. E. Bethell. 'On his own showing . . . Mr. McKenna has built eight Dreadnoughts in excess. . . . This outrage upon public confidence and upon the good faith of a friendly Power.' The announcement of another 'unprovoked increase after a period of comparative economy in Germany will give a fresh stimulus to naval shipbuilding all over the world'. Growth of Socialism due to the belief that Liberals are sacrificing social reform 'to enlarge the already excessive profits of the contractors'. Quotes Mr. Hill's speech. Naval opinion turning against the 'worship of mere size'.

25 February. (*Mr. McKenna's statement.*) 'It would seem that Mr. McKenna hopes to escape from his difficulty about German dates, not by sheltering himself in the Naval Intelligence Bureau, but by a subtle distinction between facts and inferences.'

11 March. Mr. McKenna 'exaggerated and misrepresented the German programme. . . . Our naval and military scares . . . largely engineered from the dockyard and armament constituencies.'

18 March. (*Means of escape from the burden of armaments.*) 'German panics sedulously promoted by the Press and cleverly engineered by Mr. McKenna and Mr. Balfour, by means of chronological forecasts . . . have come to an end; but while the statistical basis has collapsed the superstructure of bloated Estimates remains.' Refers to Grey's speech about the possibility of an Anglo-American treaty of peace. 'We shall be more pleased than surprised if the mere mooting of the project does not pave the way to substantial arrangements for a mutual reduction of naval expenditure between London and Berlin. . . the ratio should be fixed for a term of years, and the expenditures reduced.' Italy and Austria should be included. Reference to 'the striking diplomatic failures of (Grey's) ambassadors in Berlin and Vienna and Constantinople'.

8 April. i. (*Grey and armaments.*) Grey's 'dawning consciousness of the paradox that, while the relations of the Great Powers
are rapidly improving, their armaments are rapidly increasing.
. . . If the recent additions, which have raised our naval expenditure from 32 to 44 millions, had not been made, there need have
been no increase in the death duties, and no super-tax, and no
land tax; or again, the whole of the duties on tea, coffee, and
cocoa might have been swept away and substantial reductions
made in the income tax; or, again, the money might have been
used for destroying the slums.'

ii. (*The German answer to Grey's speech.*) 'The German Chancellor has done himself a great deal of harm by misrepresenting
the aims of England, and by exaggerating the difficulties of an
international agreement.' Great Britain does not want a fleet
superior to any 'possible' combination of Powers. The word
'probable' was used by British Ministers, and the United States
were excluded. 'That the British navy should be strong enough
to defend our islands from the attack of any probable Continental
combination is surely a proposition which a reasonable statesman on the Continent might be willing to admit as part of a
general understanding for the relief of taxpayers and the promotion of civilization.' Bethmann-Hollweg 'almost as unfriendly
to the idea of excluding war by arbitration as to proposals for
limiting armaments by agreement. . . . There is an undisguised
brutality of tone in this whole utterance, which has given
civilized nations throughout the world a very unpleasant idea
of Prussian sentiment and Prussian civilization;' but the German
Chancellor has agreed to an exchange of information, and the
Reichstag has disapproved of his speech by adopting a resolution asking the Chancellor 'to declare his readiness and willingness to enter into joint negotiations with other Great Powers as
soon as proposals for the simultaneous and proportionate reduction of armaments are made by one Great Power'.

iii. *Large battleships.* Quotes criticisms of the Dreadnought
type by naval and civilian experts.

29 July. (*Morocco.*) Thinks Mr. Lloyd George's speech unfortunate. 'French commercial policy is more exclusive and hostile
to British merchants than is the commercial policy of Germany.
. . . Even the naval experts at the Admiralty see no possible
danger in the Germans establishing a naval base at Agadir.'

19 August. (*Germany and a Moroccan port.*) It would be 'the

height of wisdom and common sense . . . to give Germany every facility for coaling stations in return for a definite, mutual, and substantial reduction of armaments, and a definite joint limitation of shipbuilding programmes'. Franco-German quarrel over Morocco due for the most part 'to the exclusive and aggressive policy of France'.

2 September. (*Franco-German negotiations.*) 'The attempt of Germany to prevent France from closing Morocco against foreign trade is an attempt which Great Britain, in her own interests, should have warmly seconded.' The situation has been badly handled, and has led the German Emperor to ask for a further increase in the German navy. It is not very probable that the Germans will 'respond' to the suggestion.

23 September. (*Morocco. British support of France.*) 'We have been deliberately siding with the Power which has not only exceeded her treaty rights, but has exceeded them for the purpose of making a new tract of territory a preserve for French manufacturers. It is to these absurdities and inconveniences that we are being pushed by stubborn adherence to a mistaken policy.'

30 September. (*Modern battleships.*) Suggests that a modern battleship could place itself *hors de combat* in an action through the effect of its own gunfire. Megalomania of naval constructors 'unabated'.

14 October. (*Anglo-German naval agreement.*) Suggests that Great Britain and Germany should agree to return to their 1909–10 expenditure.

4 November. (*British foreign policy.*) Agrees with Mr. Massingham that Grey has not sufficiently explained his policy to the country. Our ententes and agreements 'certainly have procured some advantages, and the question whether those advantages outweigh the disadvantages is a matter of opinion on which critics may reasonably differ'. If Germany had not interfered, there was 'every reason to suppose that a high preferential tariff would soon have excluded British goods from Morocco. . . . The quarrels of our diplomatists with the diplomatists of Germany' have been the cause of the increase in British naval expenditure.

11 November. (*British foreign policy.*) Reaction of opinion against the efforts of the war Press and the 'diplomatic reluctance of those who control foreign policy to pursue a rational

course as the trustees' of British national interests. Supports a 'business understanding with Germany'.

18 November. (*Germany and Morocco.*) 'Something . . . has been gained by manufacturing countries through the maintenance of the open door in Morocco, and we hope that this achievement of German Diplomacy may serve as a precedent.' The German and British Governments are ready to 'open up a better chapter' in Anglo-German relations.

25 November. (*British foreign policy.*) Grey not a linguist, has not travelled, and is too cautious and isolated. 'We are, in fact, paying twelve millions a year for Sir Edward Grey.' The Foreign Office 'has evidently been working under French influence for French ends, without any proper regard for British interests. . . . The open door policy of German diplomacy is no small matter, and a hearty co-operation between Berlin and London on these lines might achieve very fruitful results. . . . Both nations have come to the end of their financial tether.'

2 December. (*Morocco. Grey's speech in the House of Commons.*) Admits that Grey was able to show that Germany did for a time try to bargain exclusively with France, and to disregard the attempts of the British Foreign Office to 'edge its way into the negotiations', but Grey was wrong to have 'deputed his functions to Mr. Lloyd George'. The War Office should have been called severely to account for losing its head during the crisis.

23 December. (*Limitation of armaments.*) 'If Sir Edward Grey has the will, he can certainly find the way to arrest the growth of armaments. . . . If, on the other hand, he keeps up the friction (between Great Britain and Germany) until after the new Reichstag has met, he may easily provoke a new navy bill.'

1912.

6 January. (*Armaments 'ring'.*) Suggestion by Mr. Hills, of the Thames Ironworks Company (in liquidation), alleging that the northern combine undercut the T.I. Company in Shipbuilding contracts in order to fleece the public in armour and gun contracts. This charge not answered by the Admiralty. A further allegation (also unanswered) that at least one firm in the 'ring' charges foreign Governments at a lower rate than its charges to the British Government.

20 January. (*German elections and an Anglo-German agreement.*)

'From the standpoint of those who wish for an Anglo-German understanding—and we believe that the Cabinet will soon be in accord on this head—it is at least comforting to know that Sir Edward Grey's policy . . . has only succeeded as yet in irritating a section of the German people. . . . If it turn out to be true that antipathy to Germany is confined to a few unenlightened diplomats, who find their account in playing up to Sir Edward Grey's Balance of Power notions, whereas an overwhelming body of opinion in this country would like to shake hands, and come to a friendly settlement, then surely the situation is promising. We are, indeed, far more hopeful than we should be if the Foreign Office desired peace with Germany, and the people of Great Britain desired war.'

27 January. (*German armaments.*) German armament policy 'grossly and shamefully exaggerated by the armour-plate interests at home and abroad. . . . The talk of a new Navy Bill is quite premature, and will depend mainly on the competence of Sir Edward Grey. . . . We are not altogether without hopes that our Foreign Office will at length see the light, and try to conform itself to the intelligent wishes of public opinion.'

3 February. (*Spies and the naval position in 1909.*) 'We believe this . . . plague (of spies) dates from days when the Intelligence Department of the Admiralty was employed in preparing certain notorious statements and forecasts of German shipbuilding for the benefit of the House of Commons. . . . If spies were employed, the false information they supplied involved this country in a needless expenditure of many millions of pounds on the unnecessary construction of four additional Dreadnoughts and wantonly inflated hostile passion against a friendly Power.'

10 February. (*Anglo-German agreement.*) 'It is evident that if Sir Edward Grey plays his cards tolerably, an understanding with Germany can be achieved on the basis of a mutual reduction of naval armaments, which would bring immense relief to the taxpayers of both countries. . . . The Kaiser evidently will not play up to (the) longing for another naval scare.'

17 February. (*Naval estimates.*) Thinks it would be safe and prudent to suspend construction of armoured cruisers and destroyers for several years. 'Enormous costly monstrosities of the "Lion" type have already been found . . . a mistake.'

16 March. (*Naval estimates.*) Quotes previous statements by

Mr. Churchill on retrenchment. Germany has laid down 12 Dreadnoughts in three years to 18 laid down by Great Britain, but British figures should count as 22, because Great Britain builds more rapidly. Similarly the 4 ships in the present estimates should count as 5½. British total programme of construction 'superfluous and provocative'. Points out the 'chief rules or dodges' for increasing naval expenditure. (1) Instead of multiplying ships, increase their size and speed. This also means increasing dock accommodation. (2) Insist on expensive machinery which gives a very small additional speed for a large amount of coal consumption, and therefore increases cost of upkeep. (3) Resist all proposals for economy. (4) Compare programmes instead of ships, and ships building instead of ships built. 'This kind of deception' was 'most effective' in the case of Mr. McKenna's 'false forecasts . . . and panic programme'. (5) Build faster than your rivals, and on 'some peculiarly futile work, such as R—, [Rosyth], pay a bonus to contractors'. (6) Keep a good press.

23 March. i. (*Danger of war.*) According to 'competent observers', the military wish for war is especially strong in France.

ii. (*Anglo-German negotiations.*) 'If the opinion of (Great Britain) were fairly represented by H. M.'s representatives abroad and by leading officials of the Foreign Office, the course of (Anglo-German) negotiations would run more smoothly.'

iii. (*Mr. Churchill.*) Mr. Churchill no longer an economist, but a 'promoter of naval extravagance'.

30 March. (*German supplementary law.*) 'Small additions . . . due to the fact that the German fleet is inadequately manned, and so more men are required.'

20 April. i. (*Haldane mission.*) If the Haldane mission has failed, 'we should not be too ready to blame either Lord Haldane or the German Emperor or the German Chancellor. If the military and naval professions in Germany, backed by armament firms, have prevailed, their success must be attributed very largely to the policy of our Foreign Office, and especially to the blunders committed by it, and by our Ambassadors abroad during the Morocco crisis of last autumn.' Tirpitz and Churchill responsible for the new supplementary law. Mr. Churchill's 'foolish and incomprehensible proposal to build two to one on any additions made by Germany to her capital ships'.

ii. (*Germany and Africa*.) Explains Delbrück's plan for a consolidation of German possessions in Africa. 'England would seem to have little, Germany everything to gain', but at least the German wishes are known.

18 May. (*Mr. Churchill*.) 'Mr. Churchill's luncheon and dinner speeches since his unfortunate promotion to the Board of Admiralty have been admirably calculated to promote naval rivalry and naval expansion.' British supplementary estimates unnecessary.

25 May. (*Anglo-French entente*.) Great Britain has fulfilled her share of the bargain as regards Morocco. 'We have paid more than 20*s*. in the £, and we are now able to take another leap forward in armaments as a result of this affair.'

8 June. (*Naval estimates 1909*.) 'An annual panic, supported every three or four years by a big supplementary panic, has of late become an element of success in the armaments trade.' Refers to '1909 panic'. 'The profits which flowed into private pockets from that amazing output of imaginative journalism and false information will never be known.' Mr. McKenna's figures denied at the time by Tirpitz.

13 July. i. (*Naval review*.) 'So many miles of armour plate.' 'Common ground to every serious citizen . . . that the taxpayers of the United Kingdom must be ready and willing to keep a fleet . . . indubitably stronger than that of any other European Power.'

ii. (*Foreign policy*.) 'We wish we could think better of the Foreign Office and its policy during the last few years. But we are afraid that there can be no doubt that it has gone out of its way quite unnecessarily to entangle us in European rivalries, jealousies, and complications.'

iii. (*Limitation of armaments*.) Supports Mr. Ponsonby's suggestion that Great Britain should call a conference of Powers to discuss the subject.

28 September. (*Foreign policy*.) Attacks Russian aims in Persia and Scandinavia. British foreign policy 'appears to have been developed without regard to the natural friendships and real interests of this country. . . . Undefined connexions with France and Russia, which have so far brought us few advantages but many dangers and much mischief.'

16 November. (*Balkan War*.) 'We fear that the Embassies of the Great Powers, co-operating with the diplomats who travel

for armour-plate, are to blame for luring Young Turkey along the path of disaster.'

7 December. i. (*Balkan War.*) 'The armament industries worked the Embassies with great skill, and soon the bones of Young Turkey were picked bare.'

ii. (*German navy.*) 'The increase of the German navy is tolerated by the German taxpayer mainly because successive British Governments, ill-inspired by their naval experts, have clung to the so-called Right of Capture.'

14 December. (*British navy and Mr. Churchill.*) 'Mr. Churchill's passion for armour-plate has been increasing.' Canadian offer very disadvantageous to Great Britain. Malayan offer will affect British tin and rubber companies. In any case these offers are not being used to relieve the British taxpayer.

21 December. (*Southern Slav question.*) 'If Vienna had the foresight and magnanimity to adopt a really generous policy of commercial concessions' to Servia in the direction of Gravosa and Spalato, the question would have been settled. 'The real danger to European peace lies perhaps even more in Budapest than in Vienna or in Belgrade. The policy of Magyarisation of Hungary and of Magyar dominion in Croatia prevents the solution of the Southern Slav question and poisons the relations of the Monarchy with her southern neighbours.'

1913.

11 January. i. (*Austro-Russian relations.*) 'We could have wished that our representatives in Vienna and St. Petersburg had been able to bring about a better feeling between these two Great Powers; for it is in crises like this that a good ambassador should be able to make his influence felt . . . we fear . . . that the seriousness of the situation is not fully appreciated in London.'

ii. (*Armament firms.*) An inquiry needed into armour-plate ring and the 'too close association' between Admiralty officials and armament firms.

15 February. (*Anglo-German relations.*) Tirpitz's acceptance of a 1·6:1 or 8:5 ratio satisfactory. 'Fair prospect has at last opened out for . . . (a) friendly business understanding' on the question of armaments.

22 February. (*Dreadnought type.*) 'Many and possibly . . . most of the intelligent men in the Navy' think that Dreadnoughts and

super-Dreadnoughts 'do not give good value for their cost. . . . Every enlargement of battleships makes it more certain that these monsters will be torpedoed. . . . All these criticisms are so obvious, that the armour-plate business, aided by the popular passion for size and the gullibility or worse of the Press, is the only explanation which can possibly account satisfactorily for the Dreadnought and super-Dreadnought era.'

1 March. i. (*Anglo-German relations.*) Tirpitz's acceptance of the British Government's proposed ratio. 'All that is required now is an honourable performance of the compact by Mr. Churchill.'

ii. (*Increase in German army.*) 'The threatening attitude of the French and Russian Governments (stimulated originally by hopes of British assistance) has led to proposals for strengthening the German Army, to which the French Ministry is endeavouring to reply.'

8 March. i. (*Increase in German army.*) 'Defensive military preparations against Russia and France.' 'Menacing tone of the French Press ever since it was led to hope for English assistance.'

ii. (*Limitation of armaments.*) 'Why should not Mr. Asquith and Sir Edward Grey give a lead to Europe by proposing a Conference for the limitation of armies and navies?'

15 March. i. (*Anglo-French relations.*) 'A great service has been done to peace by Mr. Asquith's timely repudiation of the oft-repeated myth that Great Britain is under an obligation to give military assistance to France in time of war.' Absurdity of 'the idea that French chauvinists should be encouraged into a suicidal war of revenge by suggestions that the British Army and Navy would co-operate'.

ii. (*German and French military proposals.*) Germany might give up her new levy, since 'it is quite possible—indeed probable— that a great majority of Frenchmen will oppose and eventually overthrow' the new French proposals.

22 March. (*British naval estimates.*) Exclusion of the Malayan Dreadnought from Mr. Churchill's ratio would be 'a subterfuge unworthy of a great nation and an honourable Government'. Light cruisers 'intended, presumably, for privateering or cruising for prize money'.

29 March. i. (*Foreign policy.*) 'Matter, tone, and temper of Sir Edward Grey's speech (on the Balkan settlement) leave

nothing to be desired. . . . . Great satisfaction in England and Germany.' Prime Minister's statement that Great Britain has no 'unpublished obligations which could lead Parliament and Government into a war' equally satisfactory.

ii. (*Mr. Churchill's speech on naval estimates.*) Naval programme 'utterly unworthy of a great country like ours'. Hopes that Mr. Asquith and Sir E. Grey will see the 'blot' removed. Naval holiday proposal all to the good 'if he (Mr. Churchill) can make foreign countries believe that he would carry out his own proposals'.

5 April. (*Russo-German relations.*) Quotes from Schiemann's articles in the *Kreuz Zeitung* to show that Russian revolutionaries are using anti-German feeling in Russia to bring about a war which would mean the destruction of the Tsarist régime.

19 April. (*Airships.*) Opposes campaign for airships. 'Pressure by contractors'. Ten out of sixteen German Zeppelins 'have perished miserably'.

26 April. (*German armament scandals.*) Krupp and Waffen- und Munitionsfabrik cases reported at length.

3 May. (*Russia, Austria-Hungary, and Servia.*) 'The Czar's Government naturally wishes the whole Slav race to look for protection and guidance to St. Petersburg, and this wish might be nearer to realization, if Austria-Hungary could be represented as the oppressor, or would-be oppressor, of the Servian race.' 'Patience and moderation' of the Austrian Government in the crisis.

7 June. (*Canadian Dreadnoughts.*) No immediate danger to Imperial interests or 'pressing need for protection' outside European waters. If Great Britain adds the Canadian Dreadnoughts to her programme, 'Germany will not unreasonably assume that we are throwing overboard our mutual understanding, and intend to establish a more than 60 per cent. superiority in 1916'. 'Preposterous view' that Great Britain must maintain Dreadnoughts to meet single-handed 'hypothetical and ill-defined dangers in each of the seven seas'.

14 June. (*Anglo-German relations.*) 'The British Government varies its naval schemes in such a way as to break its understanding with Germany.'

29 November. (*National Liberal Federation and limitation of armaments.*) Speeches against Mr. Churchill's programme drew 'rounds of cheers'. Resolution passed by Federation 'a severe

vote of censure on Mr. Churchill'. 'For the first time since he became Prime Minister, Mr. Asquith seemed to be aware that the moral support of the party had been withdrawn from the policy which he inaugurated in 1909 under the influence of false statistics concerning the German programme.' Hopes of a naval agreement in 1917. 'That large concessions would have to be made on the English side is obvious.'

6 December. i. (*Zabern incident.*) Behaviour of military censured by Reichstag; 'Chancellor's defence extremely weak'. Expected that he will offer to resign, though his resignation may not be accepted.

ii. (*Three Years Service law.*) 'In France the anti-German feeling so skilfully aroused by the armaments Press, and maintained ever since the Morocco crisis, was just sufficient to carry the Three Years Service Bill.' Thinks Krupp and Creusot Press and bankers engineered for trade purposes 'the outbreak of ill-feeling between France and Germany, which came to a head during the Morocco crisis'.

iii. (*British armament firms and Turkey.*) 'Semi-official operations of the British Armament Trust which has now established itself, not only throughout the British Empire, but in Russia, Turkey, Japan, and Italy.'

13 December. (*Limitation of armaments.*) Blames Prime Minister for ignoring the suggestion that Great Britain should take the initiative in a European conference on armaments. Reference to the 'shameful hoax' of 1909.

20 December. (*Mr. Churchill.*) 'Profligate extravagance and wasteful administration.'

1914.

10 January. (*Mr. Churchill.*) Mr. Churchill convicted of the 'grossest bad faith' in breaking his 16 : 10 agreement. His 'extravagance on the Admiralty yacht, and use of a good battleship for target practice'. Similar attacks on 17 and 24 January. ('The Board of Admiralty and the Day of reckoning.')

31 January. (*Mr. Churchill.*) 'The Prime Minister must be well aware that in shielding Mr. Churchill and encouraging the Admiralty to go on, he will be courting political disaster, and bringing his own career as Prime Minister to an inglorious close.'

7 February. (*German naval expenditure.*) Berlin correspondent compares figures given by Grey with those of Tirpitz. 'It must

be confessed that the period has been chosen (by Tirpitz) some-what arbitrarily to the advantage of Germany.' 'To expect a modification of the German Law, unless some more cogent reasons are produced than have been brought forward up to now, or unless a more satisfactory scheme is evolved than the naval holiday, is to shut one's eyes to the facts.'

7 March. (*Overspending at the Admiralty.*) 'It is quite clear now that Mr. Churchill is the head and front of the offending. It is for his slackness in administration and carelessness and contempt for parliamentary procedure that the country is paying the piper.'

14 March. i. (*Armaments.*) The Russian panic in the German and Austrian Press is being engineered under the influence of armament firms. 'Does the (British) Foreign Office encourage armaments abroad?' Points to the naval missions to Turkey and Greece.

ii. (*Naval estimates.*) Nine objections to Mr. Churchill and his policy. (1) 'Foolish rhetoric' which has apparently lost the contributions to the Imperial navy from Canada and New Zealand. (2) Oil muddle. (3) Neglect of the real business of the Admiralty for aerial flights and sham visits of inspection in the Admiralty yacht. (4) The maintenance, if not the exten-sion, of secrecy in regard to business prices and contracts. (5) The adaptation of shipbuilding expenditure to the demands of contractors. (6) The reckless increase in numbers of officers and men, which contrast [*sic*] strangely and absurdly with the loan of picked officers to Greece and Turkey. (7) Wasteful amusements, such as target practice against a serviceable battle-ship. (8) The cost of making things pleasant all round in the Admiralty Office. (9) The arming of passenger vessels as 'defensive' privateers, in violation of the Treaty of Paris.

21 March. (*Mr. Churchill.*) 'Not a word about a naval holi-day' in his speech on the estimates.

9 May. (*Italian armaments.*) Ruinous race in armaments an 'opportunity of splendid dividends to the naval contractors, who form together a strict international compact, and sedul-ously excite, by means of a sadly debased Press, national pre-judices and hatreds in the different countries'. Connexion of Italian armament firms with British and French firms. 'In this manner the hardly earned money of the people is diverted from the general welfare and pocketed by a small group of capitalists.'

30 May. (*Admiralty and Persian oil.*) The real object of the measure 'we take it, may be to conceal from Parliament the absurd cost of oil fuel for naval purposes'.

6 June. (*Dreadnoughts.*) Quotes Sir Percy Scott's view of the effect of aeroplanes and submarines upon battleships.

13 June. (*Anglo-Russian naval convention. Grey's statement in the House of Commons.*) 'This is not a plain answer to a plain question, but so far as it goes, it is satisfactory.'

18 July. (*Austro-Servian crisis.*) Long extract from a semi-official Austrian communiqué appearing in the *Daily Telegraph*. 'Happily for the peace of Europe, the excitement is cooling down.... Some of the Viennese journals are also to blame for exaggerated reports of the proceedings of the Pan-Servian league. But it is clear that Austria is entitled to expect that the Servian Government, which has quite enough to do in settling and pacifying its new possessions in Macedonia and Albania, should keep its fingers out of the Austro-Hungarian pie.'

ii. (*Third Hague Conference.*) 'It is to be hoped that before long (Sir Edward Grey) will be able to give more attention to the problem (of armaments), and to develop a more hopeful and honest policy than that which has found expression in the naval missions to Athens and Constantinople, and in the co-operation of diplomacy with armaments.'

25 July. (*Austro-Servian crisis.*) Long letter from Professor Redlich stating the Austrian case. Editorial comment on the Austrian Note. 'The fear that Servia may be deliberately provoked by the Dual Monarchy in order to lay the spectre of Pan-Servianism has been revived by the tenor of the Austrian note, though the German Government promises that it will endeavour to work for peace.'

1 August. (*General crisis.*) A second long letter from Professor Redlich stating the Austrian case. Editorial comment on the situation: 'It is clear to the impartial observer that there have been faults on both sides'—Austria intolerably provoked, 'after the fair and moderate part which (she) played (in) Servia's successful war'. What would Great Britain have done, if the Afghan Government had raised a rebellion on the N.W. frontier of India, and Afghan assassins had murdered a Prince and Princess of Wales? ...'It is only after saying this that we feel justified in stating that the terms of the Austrian Note, and the action of the Austrian Government, when most of these terms have been

conceded, appear too stiff, too rigid, too relentless. There should have been more solicitude for the peace of Europe. . . . All the same . . . city men sympathize with Austria . . . the provocation begun by Servia has been continued by Russia. If a great war begins, Russian mobilization will be the proximate cause. And we fear the poisonous articles of *The Times* have encouraged the Czar's Government to hope for British support. . . . In maintaining strict neutrality Mr. Asquith and Sir Edward Grey can count upon the support of the Cabinet, the House of Commons, and the nation. . . . So far Great Britain has taken the lead in Europe on behalf of peace.' (Praise of Grey's policy in the Balkan wars.) Great efforts made in England and in Germany 'during the last two or three years to re-establish the old friendship which ought never to have been disturbed. It is very noticeable that there were many cries of "Hoch England" as the crowds which demonstrated in Berlin on Sunday passed by the British Embassy. . . . It is deplorable that at such a moment Mr. Churchill should have given sensational orders to the Fleet. . . . Every British interest points irresistibly to the maintenance of strict neutrality. And of course, by so doing we shall be in a far better position later on—if the worst comes to the worst— to mediate effectively between exhausted combatants.'

INDEX